Fathers, Mothers and Others

By the same authors

Leisure and the Family Life Cycle (Routledge & Kegan Paul, 1975)

Dual Career Families Re-examined (London, Martin Robertson; New York, Harper & Row, 1976)

Fathers, Mothers and Others

Towards New Alliances

Rhona Rapoport and Robert N. Rapoport and Ziona Strelitz
with Stephen Kew
Institute of Family and Environmental Research

Routledge & Kegan Paul
London and Henley

First published in 1977
by Routledge & Kegan Paul Ltd
39 Store Street,
London WC1E 7DD and
Broadway House,
Newtown Road,
Henley-on-Thames,
Oxon RG9 1EN
Reprinted and first published as
a paperback in 1978
Set in 10 on 11 Imprint 101 by
Kelly & Wright, Bradford-on-Avon, Wiltshire
and printed in Great Britain by
Lowe & Brydone Printers Ltd, Thetford, Norfolk
© Institute of Family and Environmental Research 1977

British Library Cataloguing in Publication Data

Rapoport, Rhona

Fathers, mothers and others: towards new alliances.

1. Parent and child—History
I. Title   II. Rapoport, Robert Norman
III. Strelitz, Ziona
301.42'7   HQ755.8

ISBN 0-7100-8577-X (c)
ISBN 0-7100-0048-0 (p)

Contents

Preface

Disclaimers are no substitute for actions, but they may help to avoid misunderstandings.

First, we recognize, as we shall elaborate in the text, that a survey of the literature covering a very broad spectrum of fields is at risk from falling between (or amongst) the various stools – being thought too superficial for experts, too technical for the layman. We accept the risk, but disclaim the inevitability of the judgment that breadth means superficiality. Of course we cannot go as deeply as might have been considered appropriate by specialists into any one area; but by taking the broader perspective we have tried to go deeply in another sense, to strike at the heart, so to speak, of an overarching scientific paradigm within which depth of specialist work takes on a different meaning and perspective.

Second, in establishing the need for a new framework for under-standing parenthood in modern society we have been critical of many ideas at the core of the previous model. This involves, amongst others, the work of psychoanalysts such as Bowlby and Winnicott, of socio-logists like Talcott Parsons, and of others who worked within the cultural and institutional context of their times. We disclaim any implication of disrespect that may derive from this criticism. Their work was an important and essential part of the development of the field; our criticism does not diminish its significance, and we would hope that our own work may serve as useful a function in the process of generating new and improved models of thinking about parenthood as did theirs.

Third, our emphasis on rationality, communication and planning ahead may reflect middle-class values, but we believe that they are also means for attaining healthy and enjoyable lives. We do not propose them as universally applicable panaceas. However, one challenge is how effective they really are and how much they can be usefully extended to other groups.

Finally, we recognize that our own work has strengths in certain

areas and weaknesses in others, aside from the overall limitation of
scanning the research literature of so many fields: it is stronger
in its understandings of middle-class than of working-class sub-
cultures and situations; it is firmer in its social-psychological than
in its macrosocial formulations. There is no disclaimer really possible
here, other than to hope that this may be a fruitful 'heel of Achilles' to
which improved future formulations may be applied.

Acknowledgments

The review of the literature, which serves as the basis for this book, was commissioned in the United Kingdom by the Department of Health and Social Security. From beginning to end, the Department has shown us the most acceptable face of bureaucracy—supportive, reasonable, uncoercive. We thank those members of the Department who have enabled the report to emerge, with no pressures or strings attached and with a maximum of good will despite many aspects of the work which they might personally or professionally have wished were otherwise. Geoffrey Otton, Joan Cooper, Michael Rodda, Joan Court, Peter Lewis and especially Suzanne Reeve were particularly helpful.

Many colleagues have become transiently involved, either through their work with us at the Institute or through our visits to other places. Amongst these, Mary Rowe, Ann Oakley, Michael Strelitz, Joseph Pleck, Charles Spaulding and members of his graduate seminar at the University of California Santa Barbara deserve special mention.

All of our colleagues at the Institute of Family and Environmental Research have been supportive throughout, and we thank them. For competent, patient and good-natured secretarial assistance we thank Marian Harrison and Mary Tayleur.

The authors and publishers would like to thank the following for permission to quote from the works cited: Charles Scribner's Sons for *Joys and Sorrows of Parenthood* by the Group for the Advancement of Psychiatry, reprinted by permission, Copyright © Group for the Advancement of Psychiatry; Victor Gollancz Ltd for *Giving Birth* by Sheila Kitzinger; The Bodley Head for *Bringing Up Children in a Difficult Time* by Dr Benjamin Spock; Michael Fogarty and the Bedford Square Press for *40 to 60: How we waste the Mildde Aged* by Michael Fogarty; the Hogarth Press for 'Hate in the Countertransference', in *Collected Papers* by D. W. Winnicott; Tavistock Publications Ltd for *The Child and the Family* and *The Child and the Outside World* by D. W. Winnicott; Allen & Unwin for *Infant Care in an Urban Community* and *Four Years Old in an Urban Community* by John and Elizabeth Hewson.

Parents are people too

Perspectives and concepts

This book is based on a selective review of the state of knowledge of the needs of parents. The fact that parents as such are not the focus of study in any scientific or professional field is indicative of a state of affairs which makes the study both necessary and difficult at this time. We have had to draw on fragmentary information from a wide range of fields concerned with family living, with human development and with personal care and services.

Because of the diversity of information available in these fields, as well as the nature of the topic, we became involved immediately in the issue of what is acceptable data, what constitutes valid knowledge and what should regulate our selection and presentation of materials. Are the views of Dr Spock and Dr Winnicott to weigh equally (based as they are on clinical observation) with the views of Dr Skinner (based as they are on experiments)? How are these to be related to the views of Dr Mia Kellmer Pringle, based as they are on a blend of research and social action? When Spock presents a new view, are we to take it that this reflects social changes that have come under the lens of his continuing systematic scrutiny, or are we to view this as the re-evaluation of a personal stance brought about through maturation, and perhaps the experience of grandparenthood? Or both? And, how are we to assess the reliability of the accounts of anthropologists back from other societies, who describe situations unseen by others; or of historians reconstructing interpretive accounts of times past? Are the findings of a social survey of comparable status to those of a laboratory experiment? Are data on family economics any less sensitive and subject to distortion than data on sex roles or sexuality? These are some of the issues that beset us from the outset.

We decided to cast a very wide net, to interpret broadly what constitutes data *but*, in so doing, to make our own biases (which inevitably inform the process of evaluation and selection) as explicit as possible. This review differs in style, then, from other reviews which have performed useful functions in relation to specific subject matter in related fields. The Maccoby and Jacklin review on sex differences, for example, confines itself to experimental psychological research; in that context a standardized format was developed for presenting abstracts of research data for the review (Maccoby and Jacklin, 1974). Hoffman and Nye's review (1974) of research on the effects of married women's employment, the British Department of Health and Social Security's review (1974) of research on *Dimensions of Parenthood*, and Talbot's review (1976) of research on child-rearing all used another format. They compiled collections of papers by specialists in the various areas covered so that the criteria for including and for assessing available information in specific fields was treated appropriately by specialists in those areas. This allowed the editors to base their integrative statements on data presented by selected experts.

In our approach we seek to integrate materials from the range of fields bearing on our topic, accepting Joan Cooper's conclusion to the Department of Health and Social Security symposium that a contemporary requirement is to 'build bridges across the contributions from several disciplines, to provide an organized basis for knowledge and understanding . . . to apply the knowledge and research we already possess' (Cooper, 1974, p. 12).

To do this, it is necessary not only to be diligent and insightful, but to be creative. In this, the values of the researcher assume critical dimensions. It is increasingly recognized in all branches of science that the philosophy of the investigator plays a powerful role. Even in the most objective and structured forms of experimental or quasi-experimental research, investigator bias affects the selection and formulation of a research problem, the choice of methods for data gathering and therefore the screening of data available for analysis, and the actual analytic procedures and interpretations of findings. Philosophers of science like Popper (1963) and Polanyi (1967) have illustrated how these biases govern developments in the natural and physical sciences; Anatol Rapoport (1971) and T. S. Kuhn (1962) have indicated how similar considerations govern, perhaps *a fortiori* the social and behavioural sciences. Liam Hudson, in his semi-lampooning treatise on 'the cult of the fact' (1972, pp. 157–72) suggests a new root paradigm for psychology – one that is based on the metaphor of acquaintance and places a paramount value on fostering the psychologist's acquaintance with people and their concerns rather than with research methods and tangible data. This plea is similar to that of Geoffrey Vickers (1965) for the cultivation of the art of judgment through striving for an *appreciation* of the multidimensional, highly complex and textured facets of modern life.

We approach the task, making explicit our own position, with three statements: first, a statement of the contexts in which we set the task;

second, a more extended statement of our assumptions and values in assessing data available for accomplishing the task; and finally a statement of our plan for presentation, which of course is itself a source as well as a reflection of bias.

Contexts of the study

The task which we undertake should be appreciated in several contexts – historical, academic, professional and social.

We approach the task with a strong sense of being involved in a historical process. Our thinking is informed by the fact that we are at a particular point in time at which the issue of parents' needs has become salient for many professionals and rising generations of parents. It seems to us that this occurs in the course of a process of shifts in orientation, in which the patriarchal tradition of family life in early industrial society (as epitomized in the Victorian and Edwardian middle classes) has been followed by a child-focused, mother-oriented, expert-guided society (from the dicta presented by Truby King to those distilled in the writings of Drs Spock, Bowlby and Winnicott). It has come to be assumed that:

> only the biological mother is capable of providing the emotional satisfaction and stimulation that is necessary for personality and intellectual development . . . [and] that dire consequences must follow from any separation of the child from its mother, even if only for part of the day (Wortis, 1974, p. 360).

As Rutter has put it, a 'myth' has come into being in our culture that 'parenting means mothering' (Rutter, 1974, p. 21).

The permissive ideology, which emerged in the psychoanalytically oriented response to perceived repressive patterns of parenting has produced its own reaction, in which both confused youth and their despairing parents seek a new direction. If an ethos of child-focus produces many disturbed rather than fulfilled young adults, perhaps other orientations for parenting are required. If the idea or practice of total commitment are to some extent counterproductive, a new balance may be desirable for parents and children. The new pressure towards parents being able to lead lives of their own requires that children be cared for sensitively as well. It requires an answer to the questions: how can parents do the best they can for their children without feeling that this requires their total dedication and that they are responsible for the totality of their children's fate? This is no more appropriate than is the notion that parents have no influence at all – their efforts being overridden by larger forces of social contradictions and social change in modern society. A new paradigm is required to understand and come to terms with the factors at work at different levels – familial, social network and societal. New balances are being sought, and this contemporary widespread search is one of the contexts of our work.

Another context is that of the evolution – biological and cultural – of the human being and the human family as a universal social institution. When professionals discuss the predicaments of contemporary families, they use different time spans and time units for analysing current issues. Some base their analyses on what they see as common factors in all animal life. Others use cultural bases with varying time spans from pre-literate human societies (hunters, gatherers, nomads, early agriculturists and pastoralists) to agrarian societies and early civilizations, through civilizations of antiquity, feudal and peasant societies, and various stages of our own civilization, such as the Reformation, the Industrial Revolution, and so on. Many other categories are also used, for example, the different centuries, the World Wars, the Depression and various social and political revolutions. The time span used in some analyses also extends into the future of the 'post-industrial society'.

Despite the diversity in historical orientations to contemporary families, it is useful to understand them as contexts within which present-day experts formulate their opinions. The next chapter deals with this in detail, but here we note that the writings and viewpoints of experts are partly based on a paradigm of family life that has become part of our culture, our assumptions about what is normal, what is desirable, what is right and proper. There is, of course, controversy over the relationship between these cultural ideas about family life and 'scientific' formulations. By giving some idea of the historical background of the contemporary situation, as we see it, the position that we take on these issues is made more intelligible.

Ethologists, archaeologists, anthropologists and historians of the family interpret the data of their disciplines in different time perspectives. Cross-cutting the different disciplines there are different interpretive philosophies. It is generally recognized that the purely biological evolution of the human species has slowed to an irrelevant pace, with the emergence of 'homo sapiens' over a million years ago. From then onward there has continued to be a slow process of biological change, but of far greater consequence for the character of human life are the changes in ecological conditions, in population dynamics of reproduction, morbidity and mortality and in the socio-cultural structure governing the life of any social group. Even so, if one views the issues of family life against the backdrop of human history as a whole it is clearly appropriate to consider longer time spans than events since the Second World War, or since the Industrial Revolution. As Blurton-Jones (1974, p. 58) points out, for biologists (who also view the Industrial Revolution as an important event in that it changed the nature of the ecological niche in which the species seeks survival) it is only a brief flash of time in an evolutionary perspective. It seems inappropriate for people to 'contrast nowadays with 50–100 years ago, taking the Victorian family as an ultimate yardstick'.

There is little doubt that there have been a number of 'great transformations' in the social evolution leading up to modern times. The changes from folk-type societies to modern urban societies, from societies based on kinship and religious ties to societies based on rational-legal institutions, from societies based on personal forms of association to those based on impersonal ones, from societies in which marriage was regulated by custom and social group to ones where it is regulated more by personal choice, from societies based on feudal economies to those based on capitalist economies, and eventually to those based on socialist or mixed economies of one kind or another, and from societies with little human control over energy to those with a relatively great control. All these changes have been documented by technologists, anthropologists, sociologists and political philosophers from Durkheim (1893/1960), Marx (1867/79, 1925/26), Tönnies (1883/1963) and Weber (1922/57) to Polanyi (1944), Redfield (1953), Emery and Trist (1973) and Bell (1975).

As relevant as the appreciation that changes have occurred is how they should be interpreted. The social Darwinists of the last century tended to view the diversity of human cultures as reflecting an evolutionary process that led in an orderly fashion – for each social institution – from simple origins to complex higher orders. This was demonstrated for a range of social institutions – legal, governmental, religious, and familial as well as material and economic. This viewpoint is still prominent in Marxist theory, with its emphasis on the inevitability and ultimate triumph of superior forms of social integration, growing at each stage out of resolutions to the internal contradictions and deficiencies of the preceding stage.

This approach has been weakened by the exposure of many flaws in the data, methodology and conceptualization underlying it. A recent emphasis has been on deterioration, degeneration and decline of many social institutions, including the family. The argument that we are living in a runaway world (Leach, 1967) that may have passed out of human control and is losing valuable elements of the past has been widespread in modern writings. 'Doomwatchers' of family life exist, as they do for the environment, the educational system, and the moral order generally (Cooper, 1970; Maddox, 1972). This orientation may be a nostalgic one for the 'world we have lost' (Laslett, 1972), for the integration and certainty of folk cultures (Redfield, 1941), or the vitality of human relationships historically documented in European societies (Aries, 1962).

A more complex view is now emerging. Elements of earlier societies may be seen as valuable or useful for us today; but there are also elements which are antithetical – the goldfish bowl existence in folk societies, their irrationalities and vulnerabilities, their sheer lack of the benefits of civilization such as medical health care (Lewis, 1960). An example of the more complex approach to historical data and interpretation can be seen in relation to the issue of whether or not the nuclear family living separately is a new product, or casualty, of industrialization. Laslett has shown that it is not as new as has generally been supposed. In Britain it has been the predominant form for as far back as there are records. However, generally, it is found to be more prevalent among specific types of society. In one study of 500 societies about which household data is available, a curvilinear relationship between societal complexity and the family structure is reported (Blumberg and Winch, 1972). In the simplest societies on the one side and the most complex societies on the other, the nuclear family predominates.

Perhaps more important is the question of what difference it makes in relation to the more important issues of the type of human relationships enjoyed or frustrated in such a household situation. To some writers the observed correlation makes sense in these terms because at both ends of the scale of societal complexity there is a 'relatively low need for family labour and [a relatively high need] for physical mobility. The hunter is mobile because he pursues the game, the industrial worker, the job' (Nimkoff and Middleton, 1960, p. 225). This conception lies at the heart of the 'man as ape' analogy that has attracted much popular attention. It implies that the basic attributes of muscle power, speed and aggressiveness are so programmed into males (and conversely that domesticity is so programmed into females) that – with the exception of a period of agrarian life in between which was anyway patriarchal – the basic relations between men and women have been constant and reflect inbuilt biological characteristics.

But is this kind of analysis useful in assessing the predicament of parents in modern society? Some would argue against the utility of this analogy, based on a very limited similarity of functions. Wilensky (1968) for example, asks what relevance the presumed physical prowess of the hunter has for making management decisions in an automated factory. And Donald Michael, analysing the capacities required for management planning in large modern organizations (for which women are stereotypically considered unsuited), mentions 'expressiveness', a trait stereotypically seen in women in our society (Michael, 1973). Is the prolongation of childhood noted by Arensberg and Kimball (1968, p. 48) for the Irish countryman who remains a 'boy' until the death or retirement of his father, comparable in its effects to the prolongation of youth in today's society with its inordinately prolonged education (Keniston, 1971)? In what way is the sharing of work in the agrarian farm household comparable to that of the modern dual-worker couple, as Turner (1971, p. 537) has suggested? What can be learned from the similarities and differences in the two patterns, the first conducted under a patriarchal régime but required for survival, the second practised under an egalitarian régime but usually not so crucial for economic survival?

How relevant are the practices of the Mbuti pygmies for modern family life? The Mbuti have few formal rules for the division of labour by sex; men and women may hunt together without ridicule or social disapproval; the roles of father and mother are not sharply differentiated and women are not alone or chiefly responsible for child-care. Children of either sex may accompany parents on the hunt or be left alone with youths or elders of either sex. They may be picked up and fondled by anyone (Oakley, 1974a, p. 12).

Among the Zhun Twa Bushmen there is no age-layering of residential patterning as in our society, where young couples replace families with children in town flats while the latter move to the suburbs, and old people retire to places out of touch with either. Does the 'free access' across age groups, which contrasts so sharply with the modern isolation of mothers and their young children in separate dwellings allow for any implications to be drawn for modern parents (Blurton-Jones, 1974, p. 71)?

It seems that historical and cross-cultural study can serve at least two useful purposes, other than the more general goal of increasing knowledge:

1 It puts our own contemporary practices and the rationales associated with them into perspective. Beliefs and practices which may have a dogmatic certainty about them may be seen as myths of our time, variables open to study and possibly also change.
2 It places at our disposal an inventory of human patterns of behaviour which, while perhaps suggesting limits to human potential for change, is not necessarily definitive.

An example of the first is seen in Barbara Laslett's (1973) demonstration that the idea of privacy of the family household is a genuinely modern conception (*like* the idea of childhood, *unlike* the idea of the conjugal family living separately). What are we to make of this in relation to our present problems of family life? Is the privatization of the family a significant factor in the contemporary malaises and discontents? One set of studies argues and attempts to document the ways in which it is. The heightened dependence of family members on one another in the intense intimate environment of the home is felt by

many to contribute to the sense of loneliness (Gavron, 1966), and confusion (Flacks, 1973) when so many different kinds of signals must come
through so few channels. Mishler and Waxler (1968) review many of
these studies and test their validity experimentally. Less amenable to
such systematic assessment are the views that family process reflects
the sense of alienation and confusion generated in the parents by a
society full of contradictions (Laing and Esterson, 1970) particularly
when fathers are so frequently absent (both symbolically and physically) (Mitscherlich, 1969). On the other side, there is the argument
that there are advantages to be gained through privatization of the
household that go beyond its flexibility of response to economic
imperatives. These include the increase in freedom of choice and the
development of more effective alliances between morality and science
than was possible in the past (Shorter, 1975). Hemming (1969) argues,
for example, that the insulation that individuals now have from the
social constraints and pressures formerly regulating moral behaviour
allows them to develop a stronger moral conscience than previously.
This contributes ultimately, he argues, to a stronger democracy. Lasch,
summing up the issue for historians over controversies of this kind,
asks:

> To what extent do families contribute to (contemporary psychic)
> devastation and to what extent does it originate in dehumanizing
> influences outside the family? When did the family cease to provide
> emotional refuge from these influences, if it ever did? Was there a
> clearly demarcated point in history when the classic bourgeois family
> based on privacy and the need to train autonomy in the young,
> gave way to the demoralized family of today? Or did these two
> tendencies in the modern family – the one promoting autonomy and
> the other undermining it – coexist from the beginning? (Lasch, 1975,
> part 3).

The question of what has been part of the human way of life from
the beginning and what is new is not only of academic interest. It is of
concern in taking a position in relation to such issues as how much one
can alter the traditional roles of father and mother without running
counter to biologically essential conditions of life. But there is no
unanimity on this issue, and the lines of argument are not drawn
between the disciplines but within them. Within anthropology, for
example, there is the position of Margaret Mead (1949) emphasizing
great plasticity in the human capacity to develop and sustain different
patternings of sex roles; and on the other side there are anthropologists
like Tiger and Fox, who argue that anything as universal as the
sex-linked division of labour must represent a genetically established
order which it would be most unnatural to try to alter (Tiger and Fox,

1972). The medical legitimation for this kind of position, is provided in statements like those of Gadpaille:

> one cannot repudiate the whole gamut of innate masculine–feminine traits without a different kind of potential danger to the species. To enforce shifts in sexual identity and characteristics that run contrary to those that both biology and evolution have bred into the species risks disintegration of the individual, disorientation of task performance, and maladaptive influences on children.
>
> (Gadpaille, 1976, p. 157).

He argues that maternalism is 'instinctual to females, not only in this species but in mammals generally' and sounds the warning that anyone advocating 'male mothering' may bring about harm to all concerned – themselves, the sexual relationship between the spouses, and to the children who will be deprived of their 'need for exposure to the mutual complementarity of the uniquely masculine and feminine qualities of both parents, both sexes'.

Dr Gadpaille's view, and those of others who infer from the history of the human being as a biological species that it is important to maintain contrasting sex-role definitions, is that one is at risk if one advocates changes. He presents a good deal of data on hormones, genes, animal behaviour, clinical syndromes and the like to support that side of the argument. The contrary side, based on similarly firm but differently selected data, is seen in a range of studies which conclude either that the case for the biological basis for the division of labour is inconclusive, or a 'myth' (Oakley, 1974a), or that the possibilities for change and variation are strong, and subject to a complex of social, cultural and ecological conditions.

The analyses by Beatrice and John Whiting exemplify this (1975). Their statements are based on the systematic selection, study and analysis of a small but wide-ranging sample of world societies. Beatrice Whiting also demonstrates the second 'use' of this type of research in comparing data from the North Indian village that was part of the same cross-cultural study in which comparable data was collected from a New England village. She notes that children, boys as well as girls, were more nurturant in the Indian village, more concerned with the welfare of the family, less egoistic in their demands:

> At . . . age between three and eight when children are eager to play the role of adults they are permitted to do so and are made to feel that they are important contributors. It is true their parents exert more pressure toward obedience and are more punitive when they fail to perform their tasks responsibly, but this is not surprising when one considers that 5–7 year olds are being entrusted with human

lives and valuable livestock . . . These young children have a self-
assurance and task orientedness which seems truly remarkable to a
middle-class American observer. There is no indication that the
children are cowed or intimidated (Whiting, 1972, p. 7).

She traces this not to some genetic anomaly, but to the cultural and
economic conditions in which they live and the child-rearing practices
by which they are reared.

In this context, our contemporary emphasis on child development
can be seen as over-stated, demanding more of parents than ever before.
But we also gain knowledge of variables which could affect the situation.
We first take another look at ourselves, asking anew whether we *are*
such a child-centred society as we think. If the answer to that question
is as qualified as it seems to be, we may be more open to the search for
improved practices.

It is increasingly apparent that the idea that we, *as a society*, are
child-centred is a contemporary myth. It is based on an element of
truth, and a wished-for value. But there are many senses, increasingly
crucial ones, in which it is not true.

Parents are expected to give all to child-rearing – and in so doing to
fulfil both their own and society's goals and values. But not all parents
do so; and even for those who do, there are often problems in aligning
personal fulfilment, optimal child development and social conformity
or responsibility. The fact that these different goals may become
disengaged from one another is one explanation of why specialists in
child-care from Bowlby to Kellmer Pringle and Talbot have felt it
necessary to reassert the dictum that the interests of the child come first.
In many families the contradictions and strains experienced by the
family produce casualties in the weakest members – the children.
Talbot and his colleagues, though engaged in a similar search for new
balances to our own, conclude with this note of warning:

We believe that the great majority of . . . family defaults can be
avoided by means of a universal, benevolent family screening and
support system. . . . However, for such a system to succeed there is
a fundamental need for society to take a stand that when it is a
question of deciding between the rights, wishes and welfare of parents
and those of children the well-being of the child must be the decisive
factor (Talbot, 1974, p. 492).

They observe that though our self-conception as a society is that we
are child-centred, the actual centring of attention on young children is
confined for the most part to the family.

Other institutions have also evolved on the basis of an assumption
that the support and nurturance required to sustain high standards of

child-care will be provided by families. But many, perhaps most families, are unable to attain these idealized values. The strains entailed for them in trying to attain high standards with few social supports are very great. The success of experts whose advice has provided modern substitutes or supplements to traditional child-rearing advice of kin and neighbours attests to the search of the past few generations of parents for support of this kind. However, many parents have not sought this support. While there are clearly many causes of individual and family breakdown, it seems justified to argue on the basis of available data that a common element shared by families who take too great a burden on themselves and those that take too little is the relative absence of social supports for parents and children in recognizing that *both* have needs; families often need assistance in establishing and sustaining the right balance.

The child-centred, mother-focused paradigm for parenting is the one that has prevailed recently in our society, and it is sorely in need of revision. The conditions which made the paradigm acceptable in the past are changing. But the issue now is how a more balanced formulation is to be developed. We begin by considering current conceptions of the needs of children. The lists set forth by Kellmer Pringle and by Talbot provide a useful set of contemporary formulations:

Talbot's premises

(Talbot, 1976, p. 171)

1 that children must have such obvious material supplies as food, clothing, shelter, medical care and other services designed to promote their bodily well-being;

2 that they must also have certain psychosocial supplies that nourish and nurture their minds and their spirits:
   (a) being needed and wanted;
   (b) being attended to, cared for, and protected;
   (c) being valued, accepted and given a sense of belonging;
   (d) being educated and guided toward social capability;
   (e) being given opportunities for life satisfaction through useful work and creativity.

Kellmer Pringle's formulation

(Kellmer Pringle, 1974, 33, pp. 148–51)

1 Children have a basic need for survival (e.g. food and shelter).

2 Children also have psychological needs:
   (a) need for love and security;
   (b) need for new experiences;
   (c) need for praise and recognition;
   (d) need for responsibility.

One thing that is immediately apparent is that these lists, based on Maslow's 'hierarchy of needs' concept, could be applied equally to adults (Maslow, 1954). The fact that adults are responsible for children, who could perish without their care, does not obliterate the fact that the adults themselves have needs – both for themselves, and for the maintenance of family life, wherein both their children's needs and to some extent their own are satisfied.

The prerequisites for the existence and functioning of families, like other social groups, include such factors as recruitment (or reproduction), socialization, communication, social control, formation of values and norms which are acceptable to members, and the capacity to resolve internal conflicts and sustain external relations. In the Department of Health and Social Security symposium, Cooper (1974) sums up the specifically *family* functions in terms of a similar fundamental dichotomy between the survival functions (shelter, space, food, income, physical care, safety and health) and the more social-psychological functions (socialization of children – encouraging, guiding, supporting and rewarding them – and creation of a group life that is supportive of the parents as well as the children, and which is co-operative with external social institutions).

But families functioning well may act counter to simple system-maintenance requirements. For example, parents may provide support for their adolescent members' attempts to break away and achieve personal independence though these individual growth requirements may run counter to the maintenance of the family group's established equilibrium. Functions and needs are not the same, for individuals or for families.

Concepts
The concept of 'need'

When one considers more deeply the issue of what is meant by the term 'need', one encounters complexity. 'Need' sometimes refers to psychological motivation. Henry Murray, the Harvard psychologist, described several dozen of them. Some, like the need for achievement, have been systematically studied in great depth, and are fairly thoroughly understood in terms of expressions of basic drives (Murray, 1938; McClelland, 1951).

But the term is also sometimes used to indicate a lack. People 'need' to be able to relax, to escape from the pressures of work (if their work is of that sort), or to obtain stimulation if their work is dull, not because of a drive they have, seeking outlets, but because the conditions of their lives set up feelings of privation. Or, a 'need' may be seen as resulting from the experience of deprivation created partly by what a person was used to before. Needs are sometimes formulated by experts and prescribed for people. Some needs are couched in moralistic terms, others in medical or public health terms. Individuals who are supposed to 'need' whatever it is, may or may not themselves feel the need according to this conception.

A perceived or conscious need that exists in an individual's awareness is sometimes referred to as a 'felt need'. In this sense, no other person – psychologist, priest, parent or doctor – can say what a person needs; only the individual.

Some needs are conceptualized as 'latent' – ready to come into awareness with appropriate 'consciousness raising'; others are considered to be 'potential', perhaps a step further away from the conscious mind, and still others are thought as implanted from outside, produced by suggestion, 'brain-washing', advertising, etc., and therefore represent 'false consciousness', pseudo-needs.

As the term 'need' is used in so many different ways, it becomes relatively useless as a framework either for increasing our scientific understanding, or guiding social policies. A more rigorous set of definitions is required. We suggest that a beginning be made by using three different terms to distinguish three different meanings often assigned to the term need:

(a) *Preoccupations* – which are the concerns that people have which are intrinsic in the developing organism and which change with different stages of the life cycle. Adolescents are preoccupied with achieving a sense of identity in their lives as a whole. This, and the other preoccupations that go with specific life-cycle stages, are felt to some extent throughout life but they become salient at given stages, and in so doing they provide the impetus for the development of interests which give meaning to people's lives (Rapoport and Rapoport, 1975). People may or may not be aware of these preoccupations.

(b) *Needs* – which we use to refer to the ideas and feelings that people themselves have about what they need in given situations. In this sense, an adolescent may be preoccupied with the search for identity, but may not feel that he/she 'needs' to be told who or what he/she is. This distinction is one that well-intentioned parents have often experienced when they seek to meet the preoccupations of a young person by providing help when it may not be perceived to be a need by the adolescent.

(c) *Requirements* – are the formulations and assessments of people's 'needs' by 'experts' or authorities. In this sense when Kellmer Pringle, Maslow and others have written about people's basic needs, they prescribe people's requirements, whether or not the individuals feel them as needs (Kellmer Pringle, 1974; Maslow, 1954; Talbot *et al.*, 1974).

In the chapters that follow, we indicate how people's preoccupations change in emphasis as they move through the life cycle, and how they may become aware of different sorts of needs according to the situation in which they find themselves.

In a given set of relationships – between parents and children, between husbands and wives – it is important to appreciate one another's preoccupations and felt needs as far as possible. This appreciation eases the work of reconciling the different ways in which each perceives his or her needs. It is not that compatibility cannot be arrived at intuitively or through a minimum of explicit discussion. Nor does making things explicit guarantee the harmonization of needs. It can have the reverse effect.

What is required is an approach that clarifies the nature of the fit between parents' and children's lives. Children first, last and always is no longer a tenable maxim for family life, on anyone's account. In earlier times, when children were often treated as little people who should be seen and not heard, the authoritarian régime laid the groundwork for a reaction which eventually contributed to the exceedingly permissive child-focused values of family life we have recently experienced. The new resolution that seems to be required is not a return to parent-centred authority, but a new conception based on an appreciation of how parents' preoccupations, needs and requirements can be reconciled with those of children. There has been no scientific research on this issue of intergenerational meshing of lives comparable, for example, to the study of 'need complementarity' in the field of mate selection and marital adjustment (Winch, 1958).

In the area of child development, parents have been assumed to be there, ready to do what is defined as necessary for the children, not so much because the researchers and clinicians involved have been callous to the needs of parents, but because they have worked within relatively closed-system conceptual frameworks. A similar blinker effect has been seen in the adult world, where the organization of the workplace implies the presence of families in the background backing up male workers. In effect, work has been organized as though families and their requirements did not exist, not so much because industrialists did not care about families, but because the paradigms of social organization allowed them to be taken for granted. These and other closed-system formulations which treat families as though they are self-contained are in need of revision.

Our biases

We use a more open-systems approach which emphasizes the linkages between families and other institutions; *parents* as well as children have needs in family living; children's *strengths* as well as their

vulnerabilities should receive attention (as should parents' vulnerabilities as well as their strengths); and family and society require new
forms of integration. We try now to make the values and assumptions
which have governed this review as explicit as possible.

It is not only the presence of biases that leads to distortions in
scientific enterprises (there are always biases); but when the biases are
implicit, unrecognized and inaccessible to critical evaluation, that is a
more insidious impediment. This does not mean that if one analyses
and makes explicit one's biases scientific progress will automatically
ensue. It is one step in the process of nurturing the scientific venture,
the quest for valid knowledge. Our own orientations are set forth in a
series of propositions, which underly our selection, analysis and
discussion of materials in the field. We feel that they reflect important
trends at the leading edge of social changes in family life. Our use of
these propositions as premises is meant to reflect what we see as in a
state of becoming – not as personal inventions but as integrations of
the work of many scholars, researchers and health professionals. Our
propositions based on our reading of the available data, are as follows.

1 *Parents are people*

Both parents and children are people. As people they have certain
generic requirements – basic material requirements for shelter and
subsistence, and the psycho-social requirements for support, security,
recognition and approval. Over and above these, more specific 'parents'
needs' arise at different times in the family cycle and with change in
situation or life style. But, as parents are people, it is not enough to
assume that intellectual understanding and competence at skills of
parentcraft are sufficient to make for a satisfactory family environment.
Emotional responses also require understanding (Rutter, 1974, p. 23).
These go beyond a sense of duty and responsibility, and include the
whole gamut of human 'joys and sorrows' as indicated by the Committee of the Group for the Advancement of Psychiatry (GAP) that
recently reviewed the situation of contemporary parenthood:

> Parenthood is a stage in the life cycle of the individual during
> which emotional growth and development continue. Though not
> often emphasized, this is probably the most enduring joy of parent-
> hood. It is an active joy, derived from doing and becoming as
> opposed to the passive joy of receiving. The successful completion
> of this stage of life leads to increased ease in functioning . . . (GAP,
> 1973, p. 15).

The Committee also recognize the implicit contradictions of parenthood as a period of personal development when they say that:

Ideally, the needs of the child, of the parents, and of the mate mutually reinforce one another. Practically, however, these needs are to varying degrees in opposition, imposing frustrations and sorrows and forcing mutual adaptation. Often the literature appears to assume that the child, encountering his parents' attitudes as he grows and changes, interacts with a fixed quantity – the adult. Yet parenthood itself is a developmental process. Not only do inner and societal forces effect changes in the parent; the child too has an influence on the adaptation and personality development of the parents.

Parenting involves reliving one's own childhood experiences during each stage through which the child passes. Parents and children develop together and interact with each other. To be able to feel what the child feels enlarges the parents' capacity for empathy in other interpersonal relationships (GAP, 1973, p. 16).

Obviously there are conditions militating *against* this ideal. For example, when there is extreme poverty both children's and parents' needs are likely to be interfered with by the oppressive environment of the home and neighbourhood. This view is documented by Robert Holman (1973a). Harriet Wilson discusses the issue as follows:

The complex process of 'ghettoization', which involves a high population turnover and aggregations of large low-income families in housing scheduled for clearance, also attracts homeless and rootless people and hastens the departure of families who have the initiative to get out. Ghettoization is a process over which individuals who are caught in it have no control.

In that sense, Holman's contention that it is futile to expect changes in parental behaviour in an unchanged social situation is correct. Middle-class child-centred behaviour is not operable in conditions of the slum . . . preparation for parenthood or education of parents may be more appropriately focussed on families who have scope for a change in style of living. . . . The families in the slums need help urgently if their children are to live more abundantly, but the help they need is not retraining. They need large-scale fiscal measures to speed up slum-clearance and housing schemes, to improve local amenities, to boost family income . . . to improve the job market . . . (Wilson, 1974, p. 253).

Or, as Harris puts it: Deficiencies in parenting may be traced either to deficiencies in environments and resources available to parents; or to their own incapacities (Harris, 1974).

As we have learned from many studies ranging from the early Bethnal Green studies of Young and Willmott (1957) to the more recent studies of Boston's slum-clearance and redevelopment by Marc Fried (1973), and the London dock area by Peter Marris (1974), the establishment of a good material base (or conversely the abolition of a poor material base) does not automatically assure the fulfilment of people's needs. If the criteria of poor housing standards are mechanistically applied, people may be moved unheedingly into new situations in which they suffer a 'loss of community'. Frustration and alienation may develop in the new impersonal housing estates or suburbs, despite their affluence. This has its own psychological hazards which, though less tangible than the material deprivations, may be as damaging. In suburban life and environments many women are vulnerable to stress symptoms, comfortable though it may be materially. Their husbands may be more immune, particularly if they enjoy their work. And the children may or may not derive satisfactions from school and recreation in such environments, depending on the situation. According to the specific configurations of home, work and school, parents' needs and children's needs may be met and harmonized, or unequally satisfied and set at odds with one another (Young and Willmott, 1957; Fried, 1973; Marris, 1974).

2 *The place of parenthood in people's lives is being re-evaluated: there should be a balance of fulfilment within families and between family and other involvements*

The quest for balance is crucial in modern family life. People have obligations as parents. They also have other involvements as people. Parenthood is neither considered as universally effective nor as universally essential for the achievement of self-fulfilment as it was previously. As the GAP Committee point out, it is important to recognize that the

> experience of parenthood is not essential for the successful growth and development of an individual to maturity. The experience of parenthood in itself, does not achieve the goal of emotional maturity. The opportunity may not be utilised positively and may even be a deterrent to self-development in some individuals (GAP, 1973, p. 130).

The present generation of parents was reared in an ethos which pressed it to devote much of its resources to their young. 'It has been the guardian of the twentieth-century concept that the rearing of healthy children is a creative act' (GAP, 1973, p. 129). The result is that many people still feel guilty if they wish to pursue their self-development in other ways – either by not having children or by sharing the care of the children in communal groups, child-minding or play-groups, or with paid help.

If a person feels that other channels for gratification and self-development are abnormal, unmasculine or unfeminine, self-conceptions may be fundamentally impaired. This may also be the case if there is a feeling that once having embarked on parenthood anything less than full commitment may be damaging to the child.

Conceptions of how parenting can be put into perspective are a health issue as well as an issue of understanding processes of social values and social change. The GAP Committee describes the situation thus:

> Parents are not only vehicles for the care of their children. They were persons before the child arrived; are persons while they are parents; and will be after the children leave. . . . They were once told to listen to their parents. They are now told to listen to their children. Both directives are valuable. They must, in addition, listen to themselves. If parents do this, things may not turn out as well as desired, but their fulfilment will be solidly based on their own growth and development (GAP, 1973, pp. 131–2).

This calls for a conception of balance. The Committee writes further that:

> When individuals marry and have children, they are either oblivious to the dangers of parenthood or under the general impression that for them the joys will predominate and they will be relatively free of the sorrows. The joys are experienced when a state of harmony exists among such diverse and powerful forces as the biological and emotional needs of children, the responses and expectations of parents, and the requisites and demands of society. The sorrows occur when these forces are antagonistic and efforts to regain harmony are difficult or even futile (GAP, 1973, p. 79).

This formulation is oversimplified as some of the joys come in the struggles of living, even if the forces do not reach a harmonious state of balance. And harmony itself can entail risks. Many people who achieve harmony become bored with it after a time and may seek outlets for stimulation and adventure which may be disruptive for themselves or their families. Nevertheless, there is a continuous set of challenges that confront parents and that centre on the question of how much of themselves to give to parenting and how much to other interests – friendships, community involvements, leisure interests and work. This involves another kind of balancing, one that individuals confront as members of a family and as persons with other involvements as well. These include:

1 Occupational demands in the specific situation through which the family livelihood is earned.

2 The position of the parent(s) in relation to who should be responsible for earning the family livelihood – the mother or father only, the father *and* the mother, either according to the opportunities available, and so on.

3 The pattern of values and behaviour of the parent(s) about the sharing of household responsibilities and those of child-rearing.

4 The environmental conditions of the family – their local neighbourhood and community, their network of friends and associations, the availability and character of enjoyment opportunities.

Every family lives with a degree of imbalance, of unresolved conflict and discord over these and other issues. The tasks confronting parents today are less centred on 'fitting in' to the traditional pattern of their forebears, than on working out new patterns that will suit them and their situation. This involves the ability to resolve conflicts and disagreements repeatedly, and to continue to seek enjoyment even though there are residues of unresolved issues – for example, in relation to how permissive or disciplinarian to be with the children, how egalitarian or traditional to be in relation to the domestic division of labour between the parents.

A major contemporary change is in ideas about the balance of men's and women's behaviour in the family. Anti-discriminatory legislation has, to date, concentrated on the paid workplace. While many issues still need to be resolved to create equality of opportunity and of conditions of occupation for men and women, the trends toward equalization are there. In the home, by contrast, the task of equalization has only begun. Resistance to this process seems to centre on three linked issues: how domestic and child-care work is to be accomplished; how to deal with the external occupational demands in relation to family requirements and values; and how to co-ordinate and resolve the apparent conflicts arising from these two sets of demands. The first of these issues presents few organizational problems in the technical sense, but many emotional problems stemming from quite primitive levels of sex-role conceptualizations. The second issue centres more on the workplace. In the recent past, the workplace outside the home has been organized for men, more or less without reference to the needs of women or children. A set of assumptions has developed as will be documented in the next chapter – that this, together with women caring for house and children, is a natural and correct form of organization. These assumptions are no longer tenable. Many more women are in fact earning, and a high proportion of them (one third in the USA) are the

principal family breadwinners. Though it is mainly women who have
changed, there are some men who see advantages in new patterns for
themselves, and conversely, many women who wish to retain conventional patterns. The balance between what each member gives to
parenting and what each gives to other relationships is variable. For
some people being a 'good parent' coincides with being a 'good person'
because their lives are so concentrated on parenting. For others there is
considerable conflict and difficulty because they may not feel that
they are good at parenting, or they may not wish to make it such a
prominent part of their lives. For some family life will continue along
the conventional pattern, with the wife doing most of the parenting
and the husband involved only peripherally. Others will share more of
the domestic responsibility and the economic provision of the family;
for still others there may be a reversal of the conventional pattern, with
the wife being the principal breadwinner while the husband centres
his activities on the home and takes the main responsibility for
parenting.

The balances achieved are dynamic in the sense that they may be
revised as circumstances change through the life cycle. In later chapters
we look at these variations and dynamic processes at different stages of
the life cycle and describe the preoccupations, needs and requirements
of parents.

3 *Parents' needs and children's needs are not always coterminous*

This is true no matter what the family structure is, what definition of
needs is used, and what cultural expectations exist. It is the potential
disjunction between parents' and children's needs that makes the
separate concern for the needs of parents an issue at all.

As was forcefully documented in the Talbot symposium as well
as in the British Department of Health and Social Security symposium,
there is lip-service to our society being child-focused, while families
are left to carry out these responsibilities for society as well as for
themselves. Where families fail to provide effective care society pays
a very high price – possibly in disordered lives, criminality and
delinquency.

Children's needs and parents' needs sometimes coincide; sometimes
they are irreconcilable and sometimes accommodations are possible
which allow for mutual satisfaction. In most families, arrangements
have to be worked out to arrive at a tolerable mixture so that neither
of the parties concerned will suffer unduly, and these arrangements are
subject to change as the individuals develop and the family structure
changes.

For the developing infant, it is not only necessary but desirable to come to terms with the idea that the world is not organized to gratify him/her alone. For the parent, no matter how devoted to the joys of parenthood, it is desirable – for the child's sake as well as the parent's – to avoid martyrdom. Arriving at compromises, exchanges and settlements for families to achieve a tolerable degree of harmony is a major part of the work of parenting.

4 *Families vary in structure and culture*

Not only are there differences in family size and composition, in the presence or absence of non-family members and of handicapped individuals – all of which affect the conditions under which parenting occurs – but there are a number of other variable conditions which affect parents' needs and requirements. Aside from the demographic and health variables mentioned, perhaps most attention has been given to material conditions – particularly in the economic and housing areas. These have been recognized as foundation elements of life which if unattended to create such an overpowering set of needs themselves as to make it pointless to consider others. On the other hand, we assume that the solution of these survival requirements is not enough. Once the survival requirements are minimally attended to, an understanding of variations becomes more important. Parenting functions may be arranged differently according to whether there are one or two parents, whether one parent goes out to work or both – and it is essential to recognize this rather than assuming that all families are organized with the mother at home most of the time. As families become more diverse in the patterns of relationships they contain – including 'boyfriend', 'girlfriend', stepparent, stepsibling and other combinations stemming from the increased tendency for divorce and remarriage, and more living together without marriage – it is important to recognize that different patterns of parenting may evolve and be legitimate in different contexts without necessarily being irresponsible or deviant.

Within different kinds of families, different goals and values are developed, and needs will vary according to these as well as according to different theories of child-rearing that parents hold, and different ideas they have about the sort of adults they wish to be and the sorts of adults they wish to rear. Within a family, values may differ in the parental and child generations and such differences themselves give rise to varying needs. Single parents who opt to live without marital partners are likely to have different needs from those who unwillingly find themselves in such a position. Similarly, the environment – physical and social – in which different families are embedded will affect the satisfaction of needs.

But in accepting that families differ in their values and goals, in their consciousness about them, and in the strategies they use for achieving them, we also note that there are limits to the toleration that is acceptable in our society. Opening up the parenting process to larger social participation provides some safeguard against abuses of parenting and support for families requiring a broader basis for sharing their obligations.

5 *Parenting consists of many elements*

Activities, interests and qualities may be distributed in various ways. Because mothers have 'always' played the major part in looking after very young children, we do not assume that this is inevitable or universally and perpetually desirable.

The needs of parents and children may be better served by a redistribution of parental activities and responsibilities, for example with fathers taking a more active part. 'Mothering' can be performed not only by biological mothers and other women, but also by fathers and other men. Robert Fein sensitively described how two fathers take on activities usually associated with mothers.

Mack is a truck driver and father of a four-year-old son, Brian, who goes to nursery school because his mother feels that 'Brian needs to have a chance to play with kids his own age, rather than hang around all day with me and the baby'. At school, Brian loves to play with trucks, especially those he says are like 'my Daddy's truck'. As part of the nursery school's program to encourage fathers to share their lives with children in the school, a male teacher visited Brian and his family at home. After suggesting that there might be a relation between Brian's love of trucks and the fact that Mack was a truck driver ('Naw', said Mack, pleased despite himself, 'he doesn't like me, he likes trucks') the teacher invited Mack to come to school to play with the children. Mack, a bit taken aback and gruffly shy, muttered that 'he wouldn't want me to come to school. School's for kids. Wouldya, Brian?' Brian, playing with a truck in the corner, obediently said no.

Several days later, Mack called the teacher and said that he had been able to find a morning when he would come to school. 'But what'll I do there?' he worried to the teacher. 'They're just kids.' 'Let's play with the truck', said the teacher.

On the appointed day, Mack showed up nervously at school, a library book about trucks tucked under his arm. 'What are they going to do today?' he whispered anxiously. Brian, who had been glowing for four days with the news that his daddy was coming to school, played quietly on the other side of the room, ignoring his father. While a female teacher showed Mack the toys and equipment in the room, the male teacher began building a road out of blocks and moving around some trucks and cars. Several children started playing with the toys and soon Mack came over, first to watch, then to 'drive' a truck. After half an hour of make-believe engine 'brrmms' and car 'beep-beeps' and driving trucks and autos around and through the block city they had built, Mack read his truck book to eleven captivated boys and girls who sat circled up on the rug.

Mack emerged from the classroom at the end of the hour slightly dazed. 'Thanks', he mumbled to the teacher, 'that was . . . uh . . . really great.' Then going down the steps, the young father turned with a puzzled, almost anguished look. 'What'll I tell the guys at work about this?' (Fein, 1974a, p. 39).

A rising lawyer, forced to spend several weeks at home recuperating from an operation, found himself playing each day with his four-year-old son. 'Billy really took good care of me', he mused to a friend. 'He knew when I felt sad, and when I wanted to be alone. And I learned a little of what the world looks like through his eyes. It's a different world than mine, and it's pretty nice. You know, I had no idea what's on the underside of a parking meter. And I'm not used to watching people's faces the way he is. I really like my work but I'm considering trying to change my schedule so I can spend more weekday hours with my son.' (Fein, 1974a, p. 61).

Our assumption is that both men and women are able to undertake most tasks that have been considered as only possible for women. It is still often assumed that males who undertake baby-minding are either socially incapacitated (for example, failures at work, unemployed, deviants), or somehow psychobiological 'queers'. A father who enjoys playing with his baby, bathing it and changing its nappies need not be seen as 'funny' either by little children or other adults; a mother who does not like doing these things is not necessarily 'unnatural' or irresponsible.

If parents are skilful in defining their range of tasks, their available resources for meeting them, and their inclinations to achieve an equitable division of labour and responsibility, their needs as parents will be better met as well as the needs of the children, than if they try willy-nilly to fit into the conventional moulds.

6 *Biological parents are not the only people who are involved in parenting functions – nor should they be*

In most human societies, people other than the biological parents have been involved in parenting. In primitive tribes and in pre-industrial societies, members of extended families, joint families, and other kin groups are closely involved in many elements of socializing children to adult roles (Goody, 1974; Blurton-Jones, 1974; Whiting, 1975). It is less often recognized that even in our own society with its emphasis on the autonomy of the nuclear family, there are a range of caring figures who are involved in parental or quasi-parental roles. These figures may exert important influences on children and they are not necessarily less reliable for being kith rather than kin. Doctors, social workers, teachers, neighbours, friends and others may become involved in 'care-giving' on a more than casual and intermittent basis. They may form the nuclei for caring groups of support and co-operation, as studies in Oregon and elsewhere have shown (Emlen, 1970). We assume that this can be a positive element in a child's life.

> The Day Care Neighbor Service is a different kind of day care service. It does not directly provide day care, it does not supervise day care, and it does not even require the day care consumer to make contact with an agency. The service makes it possible to intervene at the neighborhood level where families privately and without benefit of a social agency make day care arrangements with neighborhood 'sitters' or caregivers. The approach is indirect and makes use of informal relationships to provide a service that is decentralized to the level of the neighborhood. The purpose of the service is to strengthen existing child care arrangements, recruit new day care givers, and facilitate the information and referral processes by which new arrangements are made.
>
> The method of intervention involves a creative use of consultation by social workers who avoid working directly with mothers or sitters; instead they provide consultation to 'day care neighbors' who, in turn, help the potential users and givers of care to find each other and to make mutually satisfactory arrangements (Emlen, 1970).

Conventional wisdom holds that while natural parents may sometimes be defective and even dangerous (as among those who batter their babies) generally they are better than non-biological care-givers. Blood, so the saying goes, is thicker than water. Having a baby that is your own 'flesh and blood' is expected to bring out nurturant feelings, to humanize a person, and a baby is considered the best catalyst for giving direction and meaning to parents' lives as well as vice versa.

But even if most biological parents have a greater constructive involvement in their children than do other people, this is not universally or necessarily true. Any particular parent may feel differently; and, even where there is high nurturance it is apparent that hazards exist when there is too much. The exclusive involvement of parents in their children may not be the best arrangement for either. The private, unobservable, intense and isolated involvement of biological parents (mainly mother at present) is in fact a new feature of society. It is both unusual and potentially harmful. Parents who expect all of their satisfactions from their children, and hope that their needs will be fulfilled by them, are likely to be disappointed. At worst, there may be serious disturbance. There may be an attempt to manipulate the child to do what the parent needs. Conversely, if parents' interests are all channelled into the relationship with the child, their own involvements and interests may be stunted, and there may be a difficult period of readjustment later in life.

7 As parents are people, parenting ordinarily constitutes one set of interests among others

Parents, like their children, grow as they move through their own cycle of life, and accordingly experience different preoccupations. The preoccupations with 'productivity', characteristic of people in their mid-twenties and thirties, may be expressed in child-bearing and rearing. But even in this period of life, parents are unlikely to find complete fulfilment for their preoccupations via their children, particularly if the parent has a wide range of interests. If the parent is very young, preoccupations with personal identity issues may be prominent, and parenting may conflict rather more with the felt need to have a range of stimulating self-discovery experiences than in an older parent. If the parent is in a later life-cycle phase, there may be other conflicts of interest because children's demands may be incompatible with those of established commitments, and the preoccupation with consummation of earlier life investments may be fairly intensive. Older parents tend to be less tolerant of the noise and physical activity of young children than are younger parents, and parents who have had other children or who have been married before and are stepparenting or parenting in a second or third round of families confront different situations; their preoccupations and interests as people may create felt needs which are even more incompatible with the requirements of parenting when conceived of as a total commitment.

Parents who function under different conditions of housing and economic well-being or poverty, parents who function with different occupational situations (for one or both spouses) confront and must deal with different sorts of life requirements. Work (at home or outside), the marital relationship, and leisure or community interests engage parents' attention and involvement as well as their children. If any of the interests overrides the others, there may be suffering for parents and for children. On the other hand, when the expectation is that the needs of children constitute the be-all and end-all of parenting to the exclusion of other interests, there is likely to be trouble of another sort – reflected in marital discord, psychological stress and depression. We assume that it is possible to work out patterns that allow for a reconciliation of parents' preoccupations, interests and requirements and those of their children.

If parents are drawn into the expectation that nothing is enough, nothing is too good, nothing is too great a sacrifice for their children – they are not only likely to surrender their own satisfactions to the altar of child-centred family life, but to damage the child as well. This does not contradict the opposite danger – that child-neglect is harmful. We assume that parents who are more satisfied people, are better influences on their children. The mother who does not give up completely her outside interests – in sport, drama, music or whatever – when her children arrive is less likely to press them into doing what she had to renounce; less likely to resent (even if unconsciously) the sacrifice she has had to make on their behalf; less likely to arouse their guilt at the sacrifices she has had to make for them and so on. This implies the necessity for other potential child-care in the environment.

Eventually, parents' 'other interests' may become positive options for their children. If available to children, these wider interests and involvements may become part of the child's early extensions of experience outside the home, enriching life and providing potentials for development.

8 *There are many ways of being a 'good parent': there is no single 'right' kind of parenting*

Parents, as people, have different capabilities; they cannot all be fit into a single mould of 'correct' behaviour; nor do their children all require a standardized response. Furthermore, it would be inhibiting to assume that any parent, however competent and self sacrificing, could control the total course of events governing their child's development:

> The parent may be the best kind of person he can be, but the final product is not entirely within his control, no matter how much of his life he devotes to the children. This might be called the 'True Dilemma Theory of Parenthood'. There is such a thing as a true dilemma – a situation that has no solution, in which, whatever choice is made among those available, the end result may be less than desired. Should the result turn out to be better than the parent wishes, a fortunate turn of events, something beyond parental control may have been the decisive factor giving it the final direction. There are no simple formulas on how to rear an individual child to

reach the parents' expectations. There is no how-to-do-it recipe book. Many factors are involved in rearing children, some outside the parents' control. Even at a single point in time, with a small problem that appears to be simple, there may be no 'right' or 'good' answer – merely a choice. Choices are made with no certainty that good consequences will outweigh bad ones. Parents care terribly whether the consequences are good or bad, but the intensity of their wishes does not influence the outcome (GAP, 1973, pp. 33-4).

There are many considerations in assessing parenting – including quantity, content, quality and timing. What is 'right' for one child or parent may be 'wrong' for another; and what works in one situation may be counter-productive in another. Yet, *we know much more about what can go wrong in parenting than the different ways of being 'right'*; more about what produces guilt and dissatisfaction than what is likely to produce satisfaction. One of the major fallacies of parental pre-scriptions is that the opposite of harmful is what is 'right'. It is said to be harmful to remove children from loving, concerned care of parental figures and to expose young children to impersonal, unstable influences. This does not mean, as it has sometimes been taken to mean, that the biological mother (and no other) must be there (always and exclusively). This is neither true logically nor psychologically; not for the child, and not for the parent.

Healthy and happy children grow up in a variety of parental family situations. In some it is the father who is around a good deal of the time and provides caring nurturance for the child while the mother is out and about – trading, looking after animals, visiting. In other societies, the reverse is true. In some families, where there are large numbers of people in the household, it is necessary to find ways of getting along together so the control of aggression is a major task. In other, smaller families such as are characteristic of our own society, this is not a major concern, but there may be a problem of providing sufficient stimulation and a varied range of personal relationships. Also, where people must be so much to one another there may be mixed feelings which can hamper relationships.

However aware parents are of the 'best' principles for child-rearing, the application of such principles must be modified to take into account both their own temperaments and those of their children. And both may vary; one child in the same family may require a different approach from another; and the parents at one stage of the life cycle may be much more involved or tolerant than at another stage. The same parent who was permissive of noisy behaviour in the first-born child may be hard on subsequent children showing this behaviour.

9 *Some components of parenting, like other skills, can be learned*

Some elements of ideal parenting activities, such as 'warmth', may be less amenable to learning than others. However, we assume that 'caring' behaviour – or at least a great deal of it – can be learned. The conventional assumption has been that every mother, if not father, 'naturally' knows how to care for and nurture children. This capacity is considered to be inborn, 'naturally' developing so as to respond to the unique needs of particular children in specific family situations. But we assume that many, if not all, parents have mixed attitudes and feelings about parenting. Mothers, for instance, do not always have immediate 'maternal' feelings towards their newborn infants. In some instances these may grow in time, and in others they may not emerge strongly at all. In the meantime, parents need to know how to look after their infants. Even those with strong 'maternal' or 'paternal' feelings may have negative, angry, resentful feelings as well. While these are frequently regarded as antithetical to loving parental feelings, we assume that they are widely prevalent and should therefore be made explicit as part of what parents may have to learn to cope with. While people cannot be commanded to love, they can be taught how to care for a child and to some extent how to deflect feelings of guilt or anger so as not to overwhelm their knowledge of caring behaviour. Disowning these feelings may lead indirectly to consequences which are deleterious for child and/or parent. Parents may vary in relation to what age or sex child they find it 'naturally' easier to care for. Some may easily take to parenting infants while others experience a real arousal of parental interest only with older children. Learning to carry out the tasks of parenting that arise at different stages of the life cycle may be eased by remembering that both children and parents are people moving along from one to another stage in their respective lives.

10 *Parents learn about themselves through the experience of parenting*

Parenting is neither undiluted joy nor an unqualified burden. It stimulates new experiences of all kinds. Parents learn, through parenting, something about what kinds of persons they are. Many of their reactions and feelings in this new situation, tell them something about themselves and their attitudes and values to life as well as about their capacities in the specific role of parent. They see themselves exposed to experiences such as the handling of stresses and discomforts that may be new to them, and what they see may require a reappraisal of themselves as people. They see themselves being frustrated and losing sleep and perhaps behaving in a new way under stress. They see themselves attempting to influence another person, the child. If they are irritable or selfish, their self-conception as calm or generous persons may be called into question. They see themselves negotiating, communicating, reacting and compromising under new circumstances and they may revise their conceptions of themselves and/or their spouses according to what they see.

This need not be a discouraging or depressing experience. In the course of these new experiences, particularly when coupled with reflection, discussion and communication, people may grow as individuals. They may realize new facets of their personalities which enhance their self-esteem. They may feel themselves to be more human, more complete, as they recognize and accept their negative or ambivalent feelings as well as their nurturing, caring and loving ones.

The marital relationship also may grow and consolidate through the shared experience of parenting as well as suffering from the new strains placed on it. The relationship with one's own parents may improve through experiencing parenthood and perhaps gaining in empathy for what they had earlier experienced in child-rearing. The experience of parenting may also help to replace the sense of psychic loss that occurs in everyone in growing up. In a sense, one regains the child one once was in one's own child, and one regains the parents that one has lost in becoming a parent oneself. We assume that a positive balance in the field of stressful forces can be achieved by an awareness of the different potentials in the experience, negative as well as positive.

11 *Parenting creates as well as interferes with life opportunities*

There is no doubt that parenting entails 'sacrifices', of time, money, interests and energy. But many people obtain great joy from being a parent, interacting with their child and seeing it smile, play and grow. Doing something for another person, at first helpless and dependent on one, and later reflecting one's self, may be a uniquely satisfying experience.

As we move into an era that recognizes the value to children as well as to their parents of making a contribution to the domestic economy, children may become a resource in the home. A new kind of intergenerational partnership may evolve, beneficial to both.

When the children become mobile and go out of the home, meet others, parents may, through the school and community, meet others too and form new friends. Children develop new interests, and at first parents may learn themselves in helping their children – for example with their literature, geography, history, crafts or games.

Later, when children confront tasks and challenges that may go beyond the range of the parents' earlier experiences, parents may develop new skills and interests, either with their children as companions or independently. Woodworking, sports, camping, music and other activities may emerge as the child expresses an interest and the parent is stimulated also to take an interest. There is the risk, particularly at adolescence, that the parent who uses these interests to hang onto the child, and to deny the parent's own ageing, may not be as helpful as possible in facilitating the necessary loosening of bonds. But sensitively shared excursions into new experience can be pleasurable and beneficial to both parent and child if these hazards are recognized.

Parents continuously learn to relate to their children in new ways as they grow. The work of parenting and its associated mourning-like feelings is an essential element of the family cycle, but one can learn to give up some things without giving up everything. It is often the parent who gives up a close parental tie gracefully who gains a young friend, and a new kind of tie.

12 *Reciprocity is of key importance in family relations*

This is a corollary of the proposition that parents are people. Parents influence and give to their children, but so do children influence and give back to their parents. Both sides of the interaction should be recognized.

It is important to bring 'human relations' principles back to the home. Other organizations have recognized and developed these principles: of exchange, communication, participation and planning. Many families have lost sight of them, though they may be crucial in regaining feelings of harmony and equity. Though parents may be willing to sacrifice a great deal for their children, even life itself, a satisfactory family life is more likely to emerge if there is a sense of proportion in the sacrifices being made and the rewards received. If the wife feels that her husband is too concerned with his own career to be interested in the family and to derive at least some of his pleasures from it, she may feel lonely or oppressed. If she feels that he is enjoying it while she works without respite, resentment may mount to rage. Conversely, if the husband feels that his wife is too involved in her own concerns, or in the children, so that he is being neglected or the home is being neglected, he may feel resentful and take what he feels to be corrective action. What action each spouse takes will depend on a number of factors in the situation, but the options include attempts at coercion, flight from the marriage, or redistribution of domestic responsibilities.

Reciprocity as a principle of family life is a dynamic aspect of maintaining some kind of balance and harmony. Achieving balance and harmony requires communication, a learning orientation, and a readiness to work out some kind of fair balance in the pattern of exchanges – who is getting and giving what in the family life. As this increasingly includes children helping parents (and not only when they are old and infirm), opportunities for implementing a true sense of reciprocity should be on the increase.

In summary, we see parenting as a dynamic process, in which there are potentials for individual development and for stress and distress. We see it as subject to learning – from experience, from information and from interaction. It is an experience which, though not essential for a rich life, can enrich life when it is constructively managed.

While parenting can, and indeed must, be cultivated as a continuous change process once it is entered, it is not a seamless web of experience. There are critical points for learning. At these points, orientations are set up that may have a powerful effect and be difficult to reverse. Good management of these critical transitions (such as the birth of a child, a child's going to school, the child's leaving home, etc.) is therefore particularly important. To the extent that they are capable of assessing what the points are, what their hazards and potentials are, parents may make best use of opportunities as they arise. They can avoid pitfalls and make the most constructive possible resolutions of dilemmas they confront, providing the kind of living environment that will most benefit themselves and their children.

Plan for presentation

In Chapters 2 and 3 we shall present first the bases in available literature for our argument that the prevailing level of recognition of parents' needs is unsatisfactory, and requires reformulation. We shall then present in a set of five chapters (Chapters 4–8) an account of the issues surrounding the meshing of parents' and children's preoccupations, needs and requirements at different stages in the family life cycle. Finally, in Chapter 9, we shall present a restatement of the current predicament of parents, and suggest implications, both scientific and for policy.

Before embarking on this venture, we would like to re-state important points to bear in mind.

1 This is the kind of review which seeks a creative integration of materials in various fields bearing on parents' needs. It cannot be either as systematic or as encyclopedic as reviews in more circumscribed fields. But, while selective, it seeks to present a judicious and balanced account which is geared to a perception of social trends and an explicit set of values.

2 We approach our analysis with a sensitivity to human evolution and history, but without the assumption that our recent pattern of family life and parenting is 'right' because of elements that reflect

human universals, or is 'wrong' because of elements which represent
losses or distortions of what existed and was enjoyed in the past. It is a
particular form, it has advantages and strains, it is in difficulties and
probably needs new kinds of support.

3 While there are many questionable conceptions – 'myths' – which
have bolstered the contemporary tendency to relegate child-care
entirely to the family, and within the family to the mother – iconoclastic
approaches are not enough. New paradigms are required for achieving
a balance in family life and in the relations between family and society
which is neither unduly child-centred nor unduly parent-centred to
the point of lowering standards and abandoning human responsibilities.
The new integrations are likely to be multiple, depending on circumstances of family, work, government policy, and individual preference –
rather than monolithic and narrowly prescriptive.

2

Social expectations of parenting
The impact of experts

When a person becomes a parent, all sorts of influences – inner and outer – come to bear on the process of adaptation to the new role. Whatever 'natural' instincts there may be to care for and nurture a tiny dependent baby, these are shaped and moulded, sometimes transformed by the expectations that come from social experience in the culture and contemporary expectations expressed through friends, relatives, experts and authorities of various kinds and the mass media. In times past, and in societies still orientated today to the norms provided by sacred prescriptions, the expectations are symbolically expressed in myth and ritual. Rites of pregnancy, birth, parenthood, child-stages and so on, express these expectations. Van Gennep (1909/1960, p. 51) described how when a boy baby was born amongst the Hopi Indians of Arizona, for example, his umbilical cord was cut with an arrow, as in the Punjab it was with a knife. When it was a girl baby, the cord was cut with a stick used for piling grain in jars, as in the Punjab it was severed with a spindle. These rites express from the outset the different kinds of expectations that are placed on boys and girls. Naming rites, rites purifying the household, rites governing the father's behaviour (e.g. the couvade), all express the kinds of relationships that men are expected to have with women, parents are expected to have with children, and families are expected to have with their society – e.g. their tribal groups, their lineages, their in-laws.

In our own society, where lineages are reckoned rather shallowly, except for 'status symbol' purposes, and where the symbolic associations with myths and rituals are diluted by secularism different sorts of influences, not necessarily less powerful in their emotional impact, are at work. Leaving aside the issue of the validity of the beliefs and practices with which we are concerned, it seems that in our own society there are many strong and pervasive influences governing the expectations of people as they enter parenthood. Rather than being conveyed through the channels of priestly practice and public ceremonial, these beliefs and practices may be communicated by doctors, lawyers, teachers, social workers and journalists, as well as by relatives and clergymen. Even though these specialists are set apart from one another in different social institutions, so vast and differentiated is our society, they share a common culture of our times. This culture is an amalgam of scientifically based knowledge, folk belief, plausible inference and extrapolation, and sheer wish. Together they create expectations of parenthood, with variations for this or that social class, ethnic group or region.

Within the diverse and often conflicting bodies of expert opinion, there has emerged over the past few decades a set of prevailing expectations about parenthood which have been mutually re-enforced amongst the different fields and disciplines, and widely influential in their impact. They have reflected a set of cultural beliefs and orientations which arose under somewhat different social conditions than the present. We have a 'cultural lag' phenomenon, although expert authorities on parenthood have now begun to revise their opinions and expectations in the face of new social realities which make them obsolete.

The debates carried on among scholars do not touch upon the lives of families and influence their conceptions of parenthood in the same way as do articles and booklets handed out in general practitioners' waiting rooms, the lectures and discussions by public figures, the advice of teachers and social workers. Nevertheless, the issues that are discussed seem to centre on the same themes; these analyses appear to be sophisticated expressions of many folk issues of the day. It is not only sociologists and social historians who are engaged in controversy about whether the family as a social institution is gaining or losing ground, has a constructive or deleterious effect, and mirrors or counteracts social pressures – it is also the man and woman on the street. An issue such as that raised by Mitscherlich on the effects of the loss of the father (in religion as well as in the contemporary family, segregated geographically from the workplace) is discussed from pulpits and in personnel departments of industry, as well as in academic conferences. The sense of isolation and personal wastage that is experienced by many housewives in the presence of material well-being is also discussed, not only by feminists and specialists in psychological medicine, but by planners and architects, and by families with options as to where they want to live and how they want to organize their lives.

The issue of whether an explicit 'exchange' emphasis should be incorporated into marriage, with contracts explicating responsibilities and constraints is not only one for lawyers and their clients, but one which enters into the ethos of our times. Along with scholarly treatises on marriage contracts in legal journals (Weitzman, 1974) there are descriptive evaluations for the general consumer published in journals like *Which?* (Moorsom, 1975). There is, indeed, a kind of circular flow of ideas and information: from the people to the social scientists and educators, from the expert authorities in these fields to the journalists, from the journalists in the media to the people.

We are part of this cycle. We seek, however, to take an overview that puts people and experts, journalists and other disseminators, into a single perspective – one that views the issues as multiple: biological, social structural, cultural – all in an historical context of conflict and change. Nevertheless, we must be selective. No overview, however eclectic and impartial, can cover all. It would require something too encyclopedic to be either feasible or useful. So we choose; and in so doing, suggest that the issues we highlight are based on an appreciation of historical salience.

In our review of the relevant literature of the past few decades, we suggest that the following conceptions relating to parenthood have been dominant. Some are still current, but our analysis suggests that some are changing – in detail and in configuration.

Conception 1   Children are society's most valuable resource, peoples' most precious 'possessions' – therefore, children's needs are paramount, and always take precedence over those of adults.

Conception 2   The care of children involves not only feeding, sheltering and looking after them physically; but also giving them the kind of experience that will form the basis for healthy personality development. In this, the first few years of life are believed to be critical for all subsequent experience and parents are responsible for this.

Conception 3   While others are involved in a secondary and peripheral way, the single crucial element in providing this essential kernel of constructive early experience is mothering. Parenting means mothering. 'Good' mothering leads to healthy personality development in children and their capacity to take constructive social roles; its absence leads to the reverse. And 'good' mothering requires the constant presence of the mother.

Conception 4   The mother–child bond is biologically determined, and is the best basis for sustaining the long-term trials and tribulations of parenthood.

Conception 5   Mothers' needs and infants' needs are complementary.

Conception 6   The foundations, other than biological, for parental experience are in one's own childhood experiences. Parents who had good parenting themselves know how to be good parents. Parents who did not, do not.

Conception 7   The father is not directly important, only indirectly as protector and provider of the mother–child couplet.

Conception 8   Being a good parent comes naturally. Special techniques and information (e.g. baby books) are easily applied by parents, who readily 'learn on the job'.

Conception 9   Parenting involves sacrifice, but the rewards balance the sacrifices, and anyway no sacrifice is too great when it comes to children, for having children brings its own rewards; people who do not accept this should not parent.

Conception 10   No compromises are possible with the totality of dedication that is required to be a good parent – because children's requirements are total and their neglect brings irreversible damage.

We proceed to indicate how these views have been expressed by influential people in a number of fields; this forms cumulatively a kind of expert set of culturally patterned expectations on parents. We then go on to indicate how we think these conceptions may be altering, even though many of them still prevail.

Expectations deriving from psychoanalytic writings in the 1950s and 1960s

First we consider the expectations about parenting that have arisen from the psychoanalytic writings of the 1950s and 1960s and the assumptions contained in those writings about the requirements of mothers, fathers and children in relation to one another. We use Bowlby and Winnicott to represent this arena, as they have been highly influential in the general population. The use of their work does not constitute a review of more modern psychoanalytic theory on this topic.

Bowlby worked essentially with fellow professionals and care-givers rather than with parents themselves; whereas Winnicott based his work on direct clinical experience and directed his later work in particular to ordinary parents. Bowlby's work focused on the consequences of extreme deprivation and the situations he wrote about do not relate directly to ordinary family life. He himself indicated that he would one day produce a book which would deal with issues of partial deprivation more closely related to the processes of everyday life, but his work was taken up in the meanwhile, became very popular and was generally applied to ordinary life as well as to special situations. Winnicott's work, however, specifically excluded special situations, and disturbed cases, and was addressed to the processes in ordinary family relationships. Nevertheless, the basic position of both writers is very similar, and their influence has been in the same general direction.

Both writers emphasized the crucial importance of mothering. Major works which were widely influential were Bowlby's *Child Care and the Growth of Love* (1972 edn, based on a report for the World Health Organization in 1951 and first published by Penguin in 1953); and Winnicott's *The Child, the Family and the Outside World* (1973 edn, based on two volumes published by Tavistock Publications in 1957 and first published by Penguin in 1964).

It is important to note that in presenting an abbreviated statement of complex and important works, an element of caricature inevitably occurs. We feel, however, that we present a fairly accurate picture of what has filtered through to general public awareness and to care-givers' conceptions of these writers' views; these in turn affect the expectations parents have of themselves as a consequence of the work of these writers. Along with others like Salter Ainsworth (1972) and Rutter (1974a), who have clarified some of the original issues by further research, Bowlby refined and developed his contribution in his later work (Bowlby, 1969/1971, 1973) but these have not yet had the wide-spread and historical impact of the earlier work that we present here. It is the more historic writing, rather than the contemporary state of knowledge, that we believe still has a considerable influence on parents.

Neither Winnicott nor Bowlby dealt much with parenting as a joint enterprise; they saw it in terms of fairly rigid sex-role conceptions, in which the mother was intimately and continuously involved in child-care – a response which came naturally – and the father was seen to have a secondary and supportive role. This orientation relates in part to their heavy focus on child-care in the early stages, a focus consistent with the psychoanalytic emphasis on the primacy of a child's early experience for his or her later development. It follows from this perspective of infants' early needs as paramount, that parents are required to give their infants' needs top priority. The negative outcome of irreversible damage to children's development became a widely feared alternative.

Both Bowlby and Winnicott saw 'good' parenting as best undertaken by children's biological parents and in the family setting. This is the context which they saw as facilitating continuous relationships, and conducive to 'intensity of feelings and richness of experience' (Winnicott, 1973 edn, p. 175). Both called for support to ordinary families as a starting point to improved standards of child-raising.

Within this family context the mother–infant relationship was dis-tinguished from the parent–child relationship – and from the parent–parent relationship, and given special prominence. Winnicott wrote in his introduction to his book: 'It is about mothers and babies, and about parents and children, and in the end it is about children at school and in the wider world' (Winnicott, 1973 edn, p. 9).

The mother–child relationship, was portrayed as having intimate, loving, dedicated, and similar characteristics. Bowlby visualized it like this:

What is believed to be essential for mental health is that an infant and young child should experience a warm, intimate, and continuous relationship with his mother (or permanent mother-substitute – one person who steadily 'mothers' him) in which both find satisfaction and enjoyment. It is in this complex, rich and rewarding relationship with the mother in early years, varied in countless ways by relations with the father and with the brothers and sisters, that child psychiatrists and others now believe to underlie the development of character and mental health (Bowlby, 1972 edn, p. 13).

A child needs to feel he is an object of pleasure and pride to his mother; a mother needs to feel an expansion of her own personality in the personality of her child; each needs to feel closely identified with the other. The mothering of a child is not something which can be arranged by rota; it is a live human relationship which alters the character of both partners. The provision of a proper diet calls for more than calories and vitamins; we need to enjoy our food if it is to do us good. In the same way, the provison of mothering cannot be considered in terms of hours per day, but only in terms of the enjoyment of each other's company which mother and child obtain (Bowlby, 1972 edn, p. 97).

Winnicott sensitively conveyed the feelings involved in this conception of the mother–infant relationship and gave prominence to his view of the *naturalness* of the mother's response as follows:

you found yourself concerned with the management of the baby's body, and you liked it to be so. You knew just how to pick the baby up, how to put the baby down, and how to leave well alone, letting the cot act for you; and you had learnt how to manage the clothes for comfort and for preserving the baby's natural warmth. Indeed, you knew all this when you were a little girl and played with dolls. And then there were special times when you did definite things, feeding, bathing, changing napkins, and cuddling. Sometimes the urine trickled down your apron or went right through and soaked you as if you yourself had let slip, and you didn't mind. In fact by these things you could have known that you were a woman, and an ordinary devoted mother.

I am saying all this because I want you to know that this man, nicely detached from real life, free from the noise and smell and responsibility of child care, does know that the mother of a baby is tasting real things, and that she would not miss the experience for worlds. . . .

If a child can play with a doll, you can be an ordinary devoted mother, and I believe you are just this most of the time (Winnicott, 1973 edn, p. 16).

We shall return to the way in which ordinary mothers were thus told just how good and devoted they are – or should be. Meanwhile, what was the psychoanalytic conception of the 1950s about fathers? Even in his chapter 'What About Father?' Winnicott did not deal with the meaning of the parenting experience to fathers, or the possible feelings it invokes. Though he ordinarily wrote far more about feelings than about roles, the element that he dwelt on was the *supportive role* that he saw the father playing in relation to the mother and baby.

> I am trying to draw attention to the immense contribution to the individual and society which the ordinary good mother with her *husband in support* makes at the beginning, and which she does simply through being devoted to her infant (Winnicott, 1973 edn, p. 10; italics ours).

Describing the mother's need for freedom to grow in her parenting job, and in the richness she finds in her minute-to-minute contact with her baby, Winnicott amplified:

> This is where the father can help. He can provide a space in which the mother has elbow-room. Properly protected by her man, the mother is saved from having to turn outwards to deal with her surroundings at the time when she is wanting so much to turn inwards, when she is longing to be concerned with the inside of her circle which she can make with her arms, in the centre of which is the baby. This period of time in which the mother is naturally preoccupied with the one infant does not last long. The mother's bond with the baby is very powerful at the beginning, and we must do all we can to enable her to be preoccupied with her baby at this, the natural time (Winnicott, 1973 edn, pp. 25–6).

And he encouraged mothers: 'Enjoy the way in which your man feels responsible for the welfare of you and your baby' (Winnicott, 1973 edn, p. 26).

This perspective on fathering was shared by Bowlby. His explanation for not considering the father–child relationship in any detail is now widely quoted:

> The reason for this is that almost all the evidence concerns the child's relationship with his mother, which is without doubt in ordinary circumstances by far his most important relationship during these years. It is she who feeds and cleans him, keeps him warm and comforts him. It is also to his mother that he turns when in distress. In the young child's eyes the father plays second fiddle and his value increases only as the child becomes more able to stand alone. Nevertheless, as the illegitimate child knows, fathers have their uses even in infancy. Not only do they provide for their wives to enable them to devote themselves unrestrictedly to the care of the infant and toddler. but, by providing love and companionship, they support the

mother emotionally and help her maintain that harmonious contented mood in the atmosphere of which her infant thrives. In what follows, therefore, while continual reference will be made to the mother–child relation, little will be said of the father–child relation; his value as the economic and emotional support of the mother will be assumed (Bowlby, 1972 edn, pp. 15–16).

The child's early needs were seen as paramount, but they were also seen to change as the child developed. By implication, the requirements of parents were also seen to change, with demands on parents believed to be most intense in the early years, tailing off after several years until adolescence.

Bowlby identified developmental phases in terms of the child's vulnerability in his capacity to develop human relationships. He accordingly defined the phases in terms of the supposed requirements of the child for the mother's presence.

a) The phase during which the infant is in the course of establishing a relationship with a clearly identified person – his mother; this is normally achieved by five or six months of age.
b) The phase during which he needs her as an ever-present companion; this usually continues until about his third birthday.
c) The phase during which he is becoming able to maintain a relationship with her in her absence. During the fourth and fifth years such a relationship can only be maintained in favourable circumstances and for a few days or weeks at a time; after seven or eight, the relationship can be maintained, though not without strain, for periods of a year or more (Bowlby, 1972 edn, p. 61).

Intrinsic to this definition is the view that the mother's constant presence is critical to her child's satisfactory development, and hence the expectation that she must observe this if she is to succeed as a mother. But the *goals of parenting* were not discussed explicitly. Winnicott came closer to making explicit the rationale for constant personal mothering:

The mother takes trouble because she feels (and I find she is correct in this feeling) that if the human baby is to develop well and to *develop richly* there should be personal mothering from the start, if possible by the very person who has conceived and carried that baby, the one who has a very deeply rooted interest in allowing for that baby's point of view, and who loves to let herself be the baby's whole world (Winnicott, 1973 edn, p. 88; italics ours).

He, too, saw the intense interaction tailing off with the life-cycle:

Tremendous forces are at work in the small child, yet all you need to do is to keep the home together, and to expect anything. Relief will come through the operation of time. When the child is five or six, things will sober down a lot, and will stay sobered down till puberty, so you will have an easier few years, during which you can hand part of the responsibility and part of the task over to the schools, and to the trained teachers (Winnicott, 1973 edn, p. 102).

Both Bowlby and Winnicott dramatized the importance of the early years of mother–child relationship in sharp contrast to later periods, even though they differed in their views on the degree to which early experiences are irreversible and the inevitability of atypical experiences catastrophic.

This created an enormous onus on parents in the children's early years, an expectation often specially difficult to live up to, because the writers concerned did not always concretize what constituted or con- travened adequate parental response. Bowlby, for example, posed the question 'Can I then never leave my child?', but his answer – 'better safe than sorry' – is equivocal in relation to concrete situations.

Bowlby strongly held the view that lasting emotional ill-effects followed early negative experiences, a process he likened to the lasting biological harm in infants that followed early physical damage. The fact that the critical factors he isolated in this process related to extreme situations unlikely to occur in most families, seems not to have lessened the application of his views by others. In part this may have related to his emphasis to care-givers of the importance of the early years. An example was his recommendation that in the provision of child guidance and counselling services on a large scale, priority should go to those with young children, because it is very difficult to reverse a bad early start (Bowlby, 1972 edn, pp. 105–9).

The underlying ideas became well known in Bowlby's familiar cycle of deprivation thesis, that the impoverished child becomes a socially incapable adult and depriving parent.

Thus it is seen how children who suffer deprivation grow up to become parents lacking the capacity to care for their children, and how adults lacking this capacity are commonly those who suffered deprivation in childhood. This vicious circle is the most serious aspect of the problem and one to which this book will constantly revert (Bowlby, 1972 edn, p. 79).

He also wrote of a positive cycle, which confirmed for him 'that deprived and unhappy children grow up to make bad parents' (Bowlby, 1972 edn, p. 96). Whilst the kind of evidence used would not be considered scientifically acceptable now (e.g. Bowlby, 1972 edn, p. 118), it seems to have been powerfully persuasive in relation to parental expectations.

Winnicott was less consistent about the absolute primacy of early experience. Sometimes he asserted that the child's experiences in early years were not inevitably decisive:

> It should not be concluded that every baby who is sensitively fed and managed by a devoted mother is necessarily bound to develop complete mental health. Even when the early experiences are good, everything gained has to be consolidated in the course of time. Nor should it be concluded that every baby who is brought up in an institution, or by a mother who is unimaginative or too frightened to trust her own judgment is destined for the mental hospital or Borstal. Things are not as simple as this. I have deliberately simplified the problem for the sake of clarity (Winnicott, 1973 edn, p. 106).

Yet it is the simple rather than the complex form of the message that is remembered, especially when addressed to other care-givers and parents, rather than fellow professionals. This explains the discrepancy between what is credited to people like Winnicott and what they may actually believe. And whilst Winnicott did suggest that the influence of early experiences was limited, he also emphasized their overriding importance. In *The Child, the Family and the Outside World*, he said: 'the foundation of the health of the human being is laid by you in the baby's first weeks and months' (Winnicott, 1973 edn, p. 16).

There are other examples of Winnicott's writing, sometimes telling mothers both that they are not totally responsible for their child's development, and sometimes suggesting that they are.

> Mothers reading what I have written must not be too upset if they have failed in their first contact with one of their children. There are so many reasons why there must be failures, and much can be done at a later date to make up for what has gone wrong, or has been missed. But the risk of making some mothers unhappy must be taken if one is to try to give support to those mothers who can succeed, and who are succeeding, in this the most important of all mothers' tasks. At any rate, I must risk hurting some who are in difficulties if I am to try to convey my opinion that if a mother is managing her relation to her baby on her own, she is doing the best that she can do for her child, for herself, and for society in general.
>
> In other words, the only true basis for a relation of a child to mother and father, to other children, and eventually to society is the first successful relationship between the mother and baby, between two people, with not even a regular feeding-rule coming between them, nor even a rule that baby must be breast-fed. In human affairs, the more complex can only develop out of the more simple (Winnicott, 1973 edn, p. 34).

Further on, he wrote:

It is not my intention to say that the baby's whole life is wrecked if there has been a failure actually at the breast. Of course a baby can thrive physically on the bottle given with reasonable skill, and a mother whose breast milk fails can do almost all that is needed in the course of bottle-feeding. Nevertheless, the principle holds that a baby's emotional development at the start is only to be built well on a relationship with one person, who should ideally be the mother. Who else will both feel and supply what is needed? (Winnicott, 1973 edn, pp. 91–2).

For many people this kind of writing promotes the tendency to think of parents as either 'good' or 'bad'. Bowlby's book, for example, was structured in terms of this polarity. Because he considered only 'complete deprivation', and not 'partial deprivation', as he called the situation where children lived with their parents who have some negative feelings towards them, he implicitly overlooked anything less than complete loving or complete deprivation. The idea that parents also have mixed feelings, or ambivalence, towards their children was integrated in his work. This lack of attention to feelings of ambivalence was a curious inconsistency for Freudian psychologists, and one which we believe was taken over widely by care-givers. This contributed to setting up idealized expectations for parents who may find them impossible to attain. (Bowlby recognized a range of feelings and motivations in relation to parents of illegitimate and adopted children but did not apply them to 'ordinary' parents.)

Winnicott's writings also suggested that ordinary mothers should express only positive feeling for their children. Whilst he wrote elsewhere on the topic of ambivalence (Winnicott, 1958), and his own conception of mother's love did allow for some negative elements, the latter loomed very small in his writing to parents.

A mother's love is a pretty crude affair. There's possessiveness in it, appetite, even a 'drat that kid' element; there's generosity in it, and power, as well as humility. But sentimentality is outside it altogether, and is repugnant to mothers (Winnicott, 1973 edn, p. 17).

Winnicott was concerned above all with the things a devoted mother does just by being herself:

It is surely tremendously important for a mother to have the experience of doing what she feels like doing, which enables her to discover the fullness of the motherliness in herself . . . (Winnicott, 1973 edn, p. 25).

The expectation arose here, however, that the ordinary good mother, in being herself, would be all loving. The exceptions are few and special. For example, he wrote of women who had not yet begun to want their babies, and whom he saw as possibly having feelings of resentment at the babies' interference in their own lives, though the 'yet' implied that they would eventually come around to wanting them. And whilst Winnicott recognized that child-care did not always entail joy for the mother:

> What cannot be taken for granted is the mother's pleasure that goes with the clothing and bathing of her own baby. If you are there enjoying it all, it is like the sun coming out for the baby. The mother's pleasure has to be there or else the whole procedure is dead, useless and mechanical (Winnicott, 1973 edn, p. 27).

He explained away this observation: 'This enjoyment, which comes naturally in the ordinary way, can of course be interfered with by your worries, and worry depends a great deal on ignorance' (Winnicott, 1973 edn, p. 27). So, the argument came across, natural good will prevail unless disturbed:

> The stomach . . . is a muscle, rather a complicated one, with a wonderful capacity for doing just what mothers do to their babies; that is, it adapts to new conditions. It does this automatically unless disturbed by excitement, fear, or anxiety, just as mothers are naturally good mothers unless they are tense and anxious (Winnicott, 1973 edn, p. 36).

Accordingly, when the ordinary good mother does have any negative feelings, they do not involve her child, and are not expressed to him or her:

> The mother does not involve her baby in all her personal experiences and feelings. Sometimes her baby yells and yells until she feels like murder, yet she lifts the baby up with just the same care, without revenge – or not very much. She avoids making the baby the victim of her own impulsiveness. Infant care, like doctoring, is a test of personal reliability. Today may be one of those days when everything goes wrong. The laundryman calls before the list is ready; the front door bell rings, and someone else comes to the back door. But a mother waits till she has recovered her poise before she takes up her baby, which she does with the usual gentle technique that the baby comes to know as an important part of her. Her technique is highly personal, and is looked for and recognised, like her mouth, and her eyes, her colouring and her smell. Over and over again a mother deals with her own moods, anxieties, and excitements in her own private life, reserving for her baby what belongs to the baby. This gives a foundation on which the human infant can start to build

an understanding of the extremely complex things that is a relationship between two human beings (Winnicott, 1973 edn, p. 87).

The major tenets portrayed here have two underlying values: that the conventional division of labour in parenting (mother the primary care-giver and father providing secondary support for the mother–child couplet) is the natural and preferred one; and that the ideal patterns of child-raising be geared to the facilitation of the child's psychological as well as physical developmental needs. The latter has led to the expectation that families should provide maximally favourable conditions for child development.

As we emphasize throughout this review of influential psychoanalytic writings, there has been considerable clarification of the research content of this work. Michael Rutter's *Maternal Deprivation Reassessed* (1974a) offers a thorough review of the experimental research relevant to the 'maternal deprivation' umbrella in purely research terms. His main conclusions, as they pertain here, are that: 'the very existence of a single term "maternal deprivation" has had the most unfortunate consequence of implying one specific syndrome of unitary causation' (Rutter, 1974a, p. 122).

The concept of 'maternal deprivation' has undoubtedly been useful in focussing attention on the sometimes grave consequences of deficient or disturbed care in early life. However, it is now evident that the experiences included under the term 'maternal deprivation' are too heterogeneous and the effects too varied for it to continue to have any usefulness. It has served its purpose and should now be abandoned. That 'bad' care of children in early life can have 'bad' effects, both short-term and long-term, can be accepted as proven. What is now needed is a more precise delineation of the different aspects of 'badness' together with an analysis of their separate effects and of the reasons why children differ in their responses (Rutter, 1974a, p. 128).

There is also discernible amongst psychologists and psychiatrists like Rutter (1974b) and others (e.g. Hoffman, 1974 and Maccoby and Jacklin, 1974) a shift of professional attitude reflecting changing values. The 'unproven' elements of the case for the maternal deprivation hypothesis are now taken by many to open the way for new experimentation in parenting, rather than – as previously – to close the door to it. Some of these more recent attitudes and 'experimentations' will be looked at in later chapters of this book. While we note in passing the impermanence of the value content of the most influential psychoanalytic writings of the 1950s, our intention here is not to trace dimensions of change in professional thinking, but rather to explore the prevalent influences on recent and current expectations of parents. The earlier work of Bowlby and Winnicott in this respect embodies many assumptions and values which are still widely held by parents today, even though the 'leading edge' of professional thought, has been moving on.

Expectations of parenting in medical care-givers' advice

The past two or three decades have also seen change in the pattern of expectations stemming from medical care-givers – doctors, health educators, etc. Here, too, the focus has been on the mother–infant relationship, and an almost exclusive emphasis on being responsive to the expressed needs of the child. We shall illustrate this by examining *infant care manuals* for the period.

Infant care manuals express professional opinion; some are published by official bodies like the British Medical Association, others by agencies or firms drawing on expert professional consultation. These manuals are addressed to parents, and there is a strong likelihood that at some point prior to having a baby (particularly a first one), a parent (particularly the mother) will be given at least one. The many child-care manuals available are put out in the same currents of professional thought, and their contents tend to be similar. The most famous of these, perhaps in Britain as well as the USA, is Dr Spock's *Baby and Child Care*, first published in 1946. Over 20 million copies have been sold worldwide and parts of this were serialized in *The Observer* (London) in 1958. Successive editions of this popular book reflect the changes in prevailing professional opinion. Martha Wolfenstein examined the pattern of change systematically as reflected in the content of the journal *Infant Care* (published by the United States Department of Labor's Children's Bureau) over a forty-year period (Wolfenstein, 1955, 1972). Though her review relates to the period 1914 to 1951, it provides a perspective for trends also manifest in Britain in the 1950s and 1960s, because American trends in theories of child-care have tended to filter through to Britain after a time-lag. In Britain, the Newsons surveyed patterns of infant care amongst 709 mothers of one-year-olds in the late 1950s (with subsequent studies of parents of four-year-olds and of seven-year-old children). This provides a complementary type of study. While the Newsons did not analyse the medical care-givers' advice directly, they provided data on how the expectations of these care-givers were perceived and applied by the parents to whom they were directed (Newson and Newson, 1963/1972).

Wolfenstein was uncertain whether the child-care manuals which she studied influenced parents effectively, though she suspected they did. The Newsons indicated that it was primarily the middle-class parents amongst their Nottingham respondents who read the baby books. Whilst the Newsons felt that such books did not reflect what actually happens in the home, their work suggests that care-givers do convey expectations to parents, so that there is an indirect as well as a direct influence from the books. This was suggested in their finding that respondents who were interviewed by academic interviewers gave different replies from those who were interviewed by lay health visitors. This suggests that the expectations of care-givers in the health fields make themselves felt by parents, who respond in terms of these expectations when confronted with health visitors.

The literature in child-care manuals relates, in the main, to events around a first birth. People are likely to read most about child-care at this time, in preparation for parenthood; because of their inexperience and uncertainty, they may be especially receptive to direction from 'experts', and susceptible to their expectations. It is also a period in parents' lives in which attitudes and patterns once evolved are likely to become established and to persist for some time.

The child-care manuals of recent decades have reflected the cultural biases already noted. They have not generally distinguished parenting from mothering. The baby books, focusing on aspects of the parent–child relationship, have assumed it is the mother who is the parent primarily involved. Where father was mentioned in the baby books, it was usually in a separate section on father's part. This was true for Spock's *Baby and Child Care* (he takes a markedly different line in his most recent book, *Bringing Up Children in a Difficult Time*, published in 1974), and a variety of other baby books of the period. The role portrayed for father has invariably been very secondary, and when he came into the picture it was from his wife's point of view, rarely from his child's and, until very recently, almost never in terms of his own experience. The key points made about fathers were couched in terms of the mother's task: mothers were admonished to ensure that fathers were not made to feel too jealous of the baby. She was advised, for example, to do this by her letting him assist her with little jobs if he wished to. Fathers were told that they should be sympathetic, understanding and supportive of the mother's self-involvement in pregnancy and her involvement with the child in the post-natal period. The Newsons confirm this interpretation:

> Articles addressed to mothers-to-be invariably include a section on the importance of remembering that fathers are parents too, and often it is stressed that they must be encouraged to do things for the new baby so that they do not feel excluded and become jealous (Newson and Newson, 1972, p. 134).

In the more recent period the father's contact with the child has not been seen in quite the same limited and cautionary way as in the articles that Wolfenstein quotes *Infant Care* to have advocated in 1914:

> It is a great pleasure to hear the baby laugh and crow in apparent delight, but often the means used to produce the laughter, such as tickling, punching or tossing, makes him irritable and restless. It is a regrettable fact that the few minutes' play that the father has when he gets home at night . . . may result in nervous disturbance of the baby and upset his regular habits (Wolfenstein, 1955, p. 172).

Nevertheless, possible points of contact between a working father and a child tend to be overlooked or assumed to be minimal. One example relates to bathing the child. In discussing whether a mother should bath the child in the morning or evening, a factor which was rarely, if ever, considered was the time which would be convenient for the father to participate in this 'event'. A similar point related to feeding method. The more recent baby books make *the choice* to bottle feed rather than breast feed an infant more open. Although it is suggested that the mother would have the advantage of leaving the bottle-fed child to others to feed, it is rarely explicitly suggested that this facilitates a potential active involvement for the father in the feeding experience. These 'omissions' illustrate the extent to which the writers have assumed that parenting equals mothering.

Many of the advice manuals are produced by baby product manufacturers, collaborating with professional care-givers in formulating and disseminating the advice to parents. The advertisements also reflect the same themes. In line with the traditional assumptions that parenting means mothering, pictures of mother and baby together have been ubiquitous. Pictures of mother, father and baby together have, by comparison, been rare. Rarer still have been references to father and baby alone. One recent advertisement appearing in a British Medical Association 'Family Doctor' publication for 1972, shows a young father feeding his infant a bottle of fruit cordial. But even in this attempt to get with the times in de-stereotyping the parental sex-roles the caption ensures that too effeminate an ideal is not portrayed. It reads: 'The best thing a chap can give another chap'. It then describes the special characteristics of the product and says: 'What better for your baby? Start him drinking today.' It is the male market not the male parent that is in focus.

The manuals have tended to focus on the details of child care, as these relate to behavioural tasks such as feeding, changing, responding to crying. Some infant care manuals discuss childbirth, and may include sections on: pregnancy and the changes it brings in women; the development of the foetus; do's and don'ts for the pregnant mother;

available maternity benefits and services; baby's layette and recommended equipment; the processes of the confinement; the post-natal experience, including the establishment of feeding, followed by various aspects of baby care, which may be discussed in a 'returning home' section. Typical here is the advice on feeding – breast or bottle, weaning, then mixed; bathing and changing and laundry; how to deal with crying, spoiling; toilet training; and relations with the health visitor.

What assumptions have been made about the parents? One has been that new mothers frequently find themselves in a state of disorganization following the birth of a first child and are unfamiliar with methods of coping. The baby books suggest routines to mother to cope with this problem. In the main these are proposed as guidelines; some consist of a 'framework of minima', related to feeding, changing and sleeping, leaving open how the remainder of the time is filled in. One such example comes from *The Baby Book*, edited by Professor Norman Morris:

On Waking:
Change baby, feed him and bring up his wind. Change him again if necessary and put him back to sleep.
Around 9.30 a.m.
If you bath him in the mornings, have everything prepared so that he can have his bath as soon as he wakes for the second time (some babies get lively after a bath, and therefore should have it in the morning. Others get sleepy and do best with an evening bath). Let him kick on your lap for a few minutes after his bath. Then feed him, bring up his wind, change his nappy and put on his day clothes. Then put him to sleep in the pram, outside if the weather is suitable, or inside near a window.
When baby wakes up
Change him, feed him, bring up his wind, then let him kick a little on your lap and talk to him while you change his nappy again (if need be). Put him back in the pram, and take him shopping if you need to go at this time.
About 5.30 p.m.
Top-and-tail him (this means washing his face, hands and bottom), and put him into his night clothes. Feed him, bring up his wind, change him again, if necessary, and then put him in his cot to sleep.
About 10.00 p.m.
Feed him, bring up his wind, change him again, and settle him down for the night.
The Daily Routine
A steady daily routine gives your baby a sense of security and thus

makes things easier for you too. But such a routine should never clash with baby's natural inclinations, and nor should it be followed slavishly. By all means have fairly set hours for such things as waking and going to sleep, but if baby sometimes wakes up hungry a little earlier than usual, try to feed him right away rather than leaving him to cry.

Although your baby won't be able to talk to you, do take every opportunity of talking and singing to him. Flexibility within a regular framework is the thing to aim at. The following notes are meant only as a rough guide . . . (Morris, 1973, p. 55).

Some suggested routines tend to be more prescriptive, however, and are couched in terms suggesting ideals, rather than suggestions. The following, from *The Bounty Baby Book*, is a good example:

6 am   (or when the baby wakes). Change baby's nappy, feed, put him down for rest. Do baby's washing, make breakfast for rest of family, wash up, make beds, start house cleaning.

10 am   Change baby's nappy, wash top and tail, feed, put in pram in garden (if possible). More housework.

11.15   Mother's coffee break and rest. Lift baby, change nappy and give Vitamin C drink, take baby out shopping in pram (or do this in the afternoon, finishing housework in the morning).

12.15   Mother's lunch and rest until 2 o'clock feed.

2 pm   Change baby's nappy, feed, put out in pram in garden (or take shopping if necessary). Finish housework.

4.30   (or when baby wakes). Bring indoors, change nappy, allow to play and kick with a few clothes on rug or floor. Give multi-vitamin drops. Bath.

6 pm   Playtime with father, feed, put baby to bed.

10 pm   (or when baby wakes; if it's later, so much the better because there's a chance of his sleeping through). Feed, change and put back to bed.

2 am   (if necessary). Feed, change nappy.

As the baby grows older, you will naturally adapt the routine to include more playtimes and fewer feeds. By six months, the baby will be well on the way to three meals a day. Playtimes with toys and plenty to watch will be very important, and it will be really necessary to let him tire himself with activity before he's put to bed at night. Some people find it more convenient to bath their babies in the morning before the 10 am feed, but once the baby is 'out and about', even before the crawling stage, he can get surprisingly dirty by the end of the day. Also a bath helps to relax baby and make him sleepy. However, you will soon find which fits in most conveniently with your own routine (James, 1973, pp. 45–7).

Even relatively non-prescriptive remarks like the following from Spock can set up expectations of the mother, perhaps making some feel guilty about not doing the best by their babies if they do not comply: 'It's good for a baby (like anyone else) to get outdoors for 2 or 3 hours a day, particularly during the season when the house is heated' (Spock, 1973, p. 153).

Many baby books assume that the mother's role corresponds with that of the housewife; the question of working mothers is rarely dealt with in the period under examination. Later editions of Spock's *Baby and Child Care* are exceptions, but even here he places strong pressures on mothers of young children not to work, unless they absolutely *have* to, either 'to make a living', in which case he thinks: 'It would save money in the end if the government paid a comfortable allowance to all mothers of young children who would otherwise be compelled to work' (Spock, 1973, p. 500). Alternatively, work outside the home may be understandable if a mother feels *very unhappy* not working. This is considered to be an unusual situation which requires a special dispensation:

> A few mothers, particularly those with professional training, feel that they must work because they wouldn't be happy otherwise. I wouldn't disagree if a mother felt strongly about it, provided she had an ideal arrangement for her children's care. After all, an unhappy mother can't bring up very happy children. What about the mothers who don't absolutely have to work but would prefer to, either to supplement the family income or because they think they will be more satisfied and therefore get along better at home? That's harder to answer (Spock, 1973, pp. 500–1).

It should be pointed out that in *Baby and Child Care* Spock envisaged ideal substitute child-care arrangements as individual care arrangements. Several of the booklets for expectant parents do discuss the issue of working during pregnancy, but not after birth.

The Wolfenstein studies of American expert opinion as expressed in *Infant Care* over the past half century indicated clear trends not only in relation to how infant and child behaviour is to be interpreted and responded to, but in relation to parents' own involvements. In her earlier more famous paper on 'fun morality' (1955) she contrasted the issues highlighted in 1914 with those in the 1940s in America. In the early period, the child was seen as embodying a set of needs which make themselves pretty directly felt as 'wants', e.g. through crying. If the baby's crying expresses a legitimate need, such as being ill, hungry, thirsty or in pain, the parent should pick it up and deal with the needs. If, however, the crying represents an 'illegitimate' striving for the pleasure of being picked up and coddled, this should not be tolerated.

After the baby's legitimate needs have been checked, the parent is advised to put it down and allow it to cry lest the baby learn that crying will bring it what it wants, 'one of the worst habits he can learn' (Wolfenstein, 1955, p. 171).

In contrast, in the 1940s, the baby's needs are seen as less egocentric and less bent at manipulation of the parents. The baby is depicted as intent on exploring his world, and it is regarded as entirely legitimate if he puts a thumb in his mouth for pleasure, touches his genitals and so on. She cited an article as stating: 'A baby sometimes cries because he wants a little extra attention under some circumstances, just as he sometimes needs a little extra food and water. Babies want attention. They probably need plenty of it' (Wolfenstein, 1955, p. 171). She observed that the baby's pleasure wants become as legitimate a demand as what he needs for physical well-being, and an assumption in the later period is that there will be an inversion of the old maxim, 'give the devil a little finger and he'll take the whole hand'. The suggestion is that pleasure can be legitimated by focusing on the baby's play activities rather than its instinctual urges. Diverting the baby from the potential danger of seeking libidinal pleasure as an end in itself is accomplished by getting involved together in play, which serves to channel developmental learning as well. Also, the mother, in becoming involved in the play (obligatorily, according to this new 'fun morality') is expected to derive enjoyment herself, rather than being dominated by the sense of 'duty':

> In the most recent period parenthood becomes a major source of enjoyment for both parents (the father having come much more into the picture than he was earlier). The parents are promised that having children will keep them young, and give them fun and happiness. As we have seen, enjoyment, fun and play now permeate all activities with the child. 'Babies – and usually their mothers – enjoy breast feeding'; nursing brings 'joy and happiness' to the mother. At bathtime the baby 'delights' his parents and so on. The characterization of parenthood in terms of fun and enjoyment may be intended as an inducement to parents in whose scheme of values these are presumed to be priorities. But also it may express a new imperative: You ought to enjoy your child. When a mother is told that most mothers enjoy nursing, she may wonder what is wrong with her in case she does not. Her self-evaluation can no longer be based entirely on whether she is doing the right and necessary things but becomes involved with nuances of feeling which are not under voluntary control. Fun has become not only permissible but required, and this requirement has a special quality different from the obligations of the older morality (Wolfenstein, 1955, pp. 173–4).

In her later paper, summarizing the trends in severity of parental response thought to be appropriate for such behavioural problems as thumb-sucking, masturbation, toilet training, etc., Wolfenstein observed a general relaxation of attitudes toward these instinctual processes, expressing psycho-biological needs:

> In the last decade (up till the sixties) they [the authors of the *Infant Care* bulletins] have been telling mothers to behave with great tolerance toward the child's auto-erotic impulses, his urge to suck, his soiling and wetting. But what has become of the feelings which not so long ago were being expressed with a clear conscience in strenuous struggle against these same impulses in the child? These feelings have certainly not been worked through or transformed, but seem much more to be suppressed or repressed. . . . But the mother who feels uncomfortable (e.g. when she observes the child touch its genitals when on the toilet) and so must distract her baby (e.g. by giving it a toy) may convey, albeit covertly and indecisively, considerable disapproval. And so with other things; changes in behaviour too quickly superimposed on less quickly alterable feelings may fail to obtain the hoped-for results. The problem remains of how to help people to face the realities of human nature and yet to treat it gently (Wolfenstein, 1967, p. 483).

But, she observes, while parents are expected to take an increasingly sensitive and lenient attitude toward their children's feelings and impulses, there is little to indicate how they are to deal with their own.

The trends have been similar in Britain, a decade or two in arrears, and the pointer is in the same direction at the present time. The Glaxo baby book notes in 1960 (though it was still circulating in the 1970s):

> Even very small babies want to be picked up and loved by their mothers and probably babies who cry while lying in their prams or during the night for no ascertainable reason just want to be loved. Not so long ago, baby books insisted that babies must not be picked up when they cried: it would be spoiling them to take them up between feeds – they must be left to 'cry it out'. Fortunately for us, it is not now considered at all desirable to leave a baby crying for long; it is recognised as the natural and right thing for a mother to go to a baby if he is distressed and try to soothe him. It does baby no harm but, on the contrary, all the good in the world to be constantly assured of his mother's love for him. Children who have always been treated with loving attention grow up, not spoiled and demanding, but happy and confident human beings (*The Glaxo Mother and Baby Book*, 1960, pp. 56–8).

Another example is as follows:

> If you really can't find anything wrong, pick the baby up and make
> a fuss of him. This is what you will feel like doing, and you should
> follow your instinct. Do not believe people who tell you that you
> will 'spoil' the baby if you pick him up when he cries; it will have a
> far worse emotional effect on him when he's older if you always
> leave him to 'cry it out' (James, 1973, p. 42).

And, the Newsons, analysing the trends in Britain from their data
on parents in Nottingham, show that there has been an appreciation
of the impact of these changes amongst mothers, comparing as they do
advice that they received earlier from their own mothers, with advice
being received more recently. In Britain the social class phenomenon
was an impressive factor during this perid, and the Newsons note that
the discontinuities are less sharply experienced by middle-class parents:

> A. S. Neill, Bertrand and Dora Russell, Susan Isaacs and the psycho-
> analysts were writing thirty years ago, and being read by forward-
> looking young middle-class professional people; since that time,
> there has been a steady percolation of educational ideas through the
> social class structure. Thus middle-class mothers, expecially among
> the upper professional group, were more inclined than working-class
> ones to say that they were using much the same methods as their
> own mothers, though the change towards greater permissiveness and
> especially frankness, was noted by some (Newson and Newson, 1972,
> pp. 251–2).

They note that other aspects of the social situation affect parental
reactions to these shifts in authoritative philosophy of child-care –
among them the lack of availability of servants, the increased attractiveness of occupational work and leisure interests outside the home,
etc. Also, it is probably true to say that the place of expert advice in
the home has been less overpowering in Britain than in America, while
the rate at which technological aids have replaced servants has been
greater in America. But in Britain, as in America, we enter the current
decade with an ethos of being child-focused. The Newsons cite a
typical respondent as saying: 'People nowadays think more about what's
good for the children, from the children's point of view . . .' (Newson
and Newson, 1972, pp. 257–8).

Aside from the movement toward greater sensitivity to children's
needs – not yet being matched with an awareness of the parents' – the
other trend that is observable both in the USA and Britain is the recognition of diversity in parental situations. The Newsons note that many
parents have been confused by the shifts in authoritative advice given
over such issues as crying, breast feeding, etc. They note that parents

may feel conflict or guilt over such issues as whether to let a child cry or not. They also chide the medical establishment for presenting an air of authoritative certainty in these issues, which manifestly are subject to revision and modification in specific situations (Newson and Newson, 1972, pp. 94–5).

In the newer baby books there seems to be a growing trend, in *parallel* with fine delineation of children's needs, towards a more sensitive approach towards parents. This is not easy to substantiate but the following is a suggestive example:

> Settling in with a new baby is rather like fitting together the pieces of a jig-saw puzzle. At first it all seems a jumble, then gradually you build up the outline, then a picture emerges.
>
> It's impossible to set down a time-table. You will work out your own routine around the baby and household. Somewhere in this 24-hour round of feeds, nappy changing, washing, cleaning, cooking and caring there is one person you must not lose sight of – yourself. Rest is all-important. Take as many cat-naps as you can fit in during the day while the baby sleeps. You're going to need them in the first few weeks.
>
> Some days may go like a dream. Others may seem hellish. You're cross with your husband. You can't stand his mother's advice. You're overtired. You hate the baby. It seems to cry non-stop. You're overwhelmed and feel you can't cope. If things really get on top of you for any length of time, don't hesitate to look for help (Health Visitors Association, 1973, pp. 35–6).

The newer orientation is illustrated by Jolly, in his role as Paediatrician of the London *Times:*

> It is now becoming more accepted that not all mothers feel instant love for their newborn babies. 'It may take time for you to fall in love with your baby' could well be displayed as a sign in labour wards (Jolly, 1975a).

The mother is not being told to look after her baby less well, but she is being told that if she has quite strong negative feelings, she is not failing. This represents an important change. Similarly, the changes in nuances in whether to breast or bottle feed show increasing sensitivity to the mother. There is fairly general feeling amongst medical caregivers at present that babies benefit from breast feeding, all things being equal, but more traditional baby books assume that all mothers will *want* to breast feed their children.

Increasingly, baby books seem to acknowledge that not all mothers prefer to breast feed and that some even have strong negative feelings about it, or that others merely find it inconvenient. It is now often presented as a choice to mothers to bottle feed if they wish, even if this is marginally less beneficial to the child. The mother is advised not to feel guilty about the choice she makes. The following conveys the ethos of the newer approach:

> There is no doubt that breast feeding will give your baby a wonderful start in life if you really want to undertake it and are able to do so. Your milk will provide all the nourishment he needs. The close contact with you is very good for his emotional development – and very good for your own relationship with him. And breast feeding is simple, convenient and safe.
>
> But if you have decided for one or other reason that you do not want to breast feed, or if you cannot do so for medical reasons, there is no reason to reproach yourself. Baby will not be deprived of anything vital, and provided you handle the bottle feeding in the right way, a very warm and close relationship between you will still develop (Morris, 1973, p. 58).

It is easy enough to feed a baby once you have got the knack of it, and once you are well started. But breast feeding your first baby isn't as easy as all that. It does not come by instinct. It has to be learnt.

It is no good deciding to breast feed your baby if you do not really want to. A mother who feels like that will soon be put off and it is better that she should start with the bottle from the very beginning. Other girls long to feed their own baby, but they have not been told that there are snags, that it can be uncomfortable, and it is not always easy (Weston, 1972, p. 7).

Look at it from the mother's viewpoint first. What's good for the baby is not necessarily always good for her. Some want very much to breast feed. Others feel they have breasts only to hang sweaters on. Somewhere in the middle is the mother who will try – and succeed – because she is encouraged and supported by those around her. Whichever way you look at it, it should be the mother's decision (Health Visitors Association, 1973, p. 41).

The cultural redefinition of mothers' and fathers' roles goes on in the new baby books, magazine articles, mass media talks and consultations – as well as in research and its dissemination. An advertisement in a Canadian journal, *Chatelaine*, states:

> The era of the hands-off father is ending and it's high time. . . . forget all those stereotypes of the fumbling father trying to look after the baby. Father knows more than he thinks he does! . . . [and] letting that relationship thrive and grow in a warm and loving environment can only enhance it. There's ample opportunity. That early morning feeding, for example, when Mom's really feeling tired. The times

when baby is fretful, and it's Dad who goes in to turn him over and rub his back, or pick him up, and rock him. In short, there's nothing 'he-man' about leaving the baby alone until he's a 'person'. He's a person from Day One. Nor is there anything soft about the man who cuddles and feeds the tiny baby (*Chatelaine*, November 1974, p. 18).

The Health Visitors Association takes an explicit (if non-militant) line on the importance of viewing parenting as a joint enterprise:

Some hospitals are happy to have fathers present at the confinement. Others are not at all keen. Check this point in good time if it matters a lot to both of you. It is possible for the closest family bond to develop right from the start if couples take on parenthood together (Health Visitors Association, 1973, p. 11).

What about all the other people living with you and this pregnancy? There's the man who gave you this baby. It would be so easy – and so wrong – to shut him out. He's lived with you and your mood swings, your aches and pains, your morning sickness, your tiredness. Parenthood starts in pregnancy. It can be a unique and wonderful time for closeness. The 'expectant' father needs to feel equally close to you and his baby before it arrives (Health Visitors Association, 1973, p. 22).

While even this says nothing about which partner should perform given tasks in child-care, it reflects a changing orientation to parenting which sets up changing expectations.

While writings in the USA seem to be more articulate and voluble in recognizing variations in parenting situations than those in Britain, representations of the following viewpoints are now apparent on both sides of the Atlantic. Spock, in his newest book on *Bringing Up Children in a Difficult Time* (1974), now argues that fathers should be involved in the nitty-gritty of parenting chores, whether or not the mother goes out to work. He states that 'the father should take on a fair share of the household chores' as well as playing with the baby in the evening and weekends. According to his new conception, shopping, cooking, cleaning and washing clothes come under the purview of the parenting role, to be accomplished in each family according to preferences and possibilities rather than stereotyped patterns of task allocation.

De Frain, an American sociologist, concludes from an analysis of trends in American child-care journals that the newer orientation is based on the following assumptions that seem to be gaining acceptance:

a) The burdens of child-rearing are too great to place on the shoulders of mothers alone.

b) The benefits of child-rearing are too great to be the sole possession of mothers, and

   c) Children are not a mother's responsibility, nor a father's. They
   are parents' responsibility.

He urges an emphasis on the similarities between men and women and
their family roles (De Frain, 1974, p. 14).

Our analysis of the themes and issues involved is only partial, but
it indicates the trends in changing orientations. There is a movement
away from idealization of parenthood to a more balanced appreciation
of the joys *and* sorrows of becoming parents; there is a movement away
from the assumption of *total sacrifice* to one of limited, or balanced
sacrifice; and a movement from the assumption of *unitary parenting*
toward shared parenting; and a movement within the health-care
professions toward a more social and preventive approach to the issues.

Expectations of parenting in the social sciences

Tracing the expectations of parents that emanate from the work of
social scientists is extremely complex – with many fields and 'schools'
of thought involved, and many ways of presenting viewpoints, opinions
and findings to the public. Some social scientists act as consultants or
research collaborators to care-givers, and others write books or articles
that reach very wide audiences. Margaret Mead and Claude Lévi-Strauss
would be examples of the latter, and in England Richard Titmuss,
Barbara Wootton and Michael Young. Many, like Talcott Parsons, are
influential through the work of their students and other professional
intermediaries. Social scientists have suffered from speaking with a
babel of tongues and we do not claim to encompass a complete picture
of what they have all had to say in a brief review.

Nevertheless, there are a number of points about parenting that
seem to have been widely accepted within the social sciences during the
past two or three decades, and which at the same time have been
influential among care-givers and the public at large. Some of the
concerns are now 'dated' in that they were salient in an earlier era but
are no longer relevant in the same way. Viewing the more pervasive
emphases we list and briefly describe four that are highly important
for their implications for parenting.

1 *The biological emphasis*

*Parental behaviour, like other behaviour, is biologically rooted. Human
beings are higher forms of animals, and their biological roots provide one
set of expectations particularly in familial relationships.* The work of
ethologists and physical anthropologists has been, and still is, influential
in this area.

There has always been a facet of the social sciences which has taken a special interest in animal behaviour and in the 'animal in man'. This has been particularly true in some branches of psychology and in anthropology. For a time, in the last century, and extending into the present in some areas, the concept of human nature – 'ascent or fall' – was a matter that gripped the public consciousness, with debates over Darwinian theory and over the teaching of evolution in the schools extending into many households. Then the issues of 'nature *vs* nurture' more or less retreated into academic backwaters and byways, with a general acceptance that there are biological facets to human nature and human life, that these manifest themselves in specific ways – such as the basic needs for food, warmth and shelter, certain modes of instinctual expression, and in reproduction. While animal metaphors are abundant in our culture, as in others, in relation to 'mating', 'nesting', and so on, there has not been much to link popular parlance with authoritative works of specialists in physical anthropology, zoology and eugenics.

Recently, with the growth of ethology as a field – combining naturalistic observation with psychological interpretations – there has been a resurgence of interest in man-as-animal, and accordingly a new emphasis on the degree to which patterns of social behaviour may be based on biological imperatives. The popular works of Desmond Morris, Robert Ardrey, Lionel Tiger and Robin Fox draw on generations of groundwork by zoologists and physical anthropologists to arouse new interest in the animal basis for human behaviour. They concentrate on certain drives – such as sexuality, aggressiveness, and territoriality; and on certain proclivities that humans and animals have in common – e.g. 'bonding'.

In the family setting, people who become parents have been seen as engaging in a form of mating behaviour in which pair-bonding of the couple is followed by reproductive behaviour and the formation of bonds with the infant offspring.

Blurton-Jones (1974, p. 61), reviewing the immense body of animal parental behaviour concludes:

> A common biological tool of parenthood is to provide an environment in which it is safe for the young to explore and teach themselves and in which to varying extents the stimuli necessary for learning are present.

Ethologists differentiate human animals from other animals, but the language used makes it seem that whatever humans do that has links with the animal world is 'natural' and if they wish to do something different it is not. Hence the notion of a 'biological tool'.

Tiger and Fox (1972, p. 148) argue that the basic biological patterns of human life were laid down genetically at the time humans split off from their ape-like ancestors, descending from the trees and taking up a life of hunting on the ground. They write:

> One of the few general rules about human cultures . . . is that in all known societies a distinction is made between 'women's work' and 'men's work' . . . this goes back to the evolution of the hunting animal, where male and female were assigned radically different tasks. . . .

And Fox (1970, p. 2) puts together the biological emphasis on how the meshing of adults and children occurs in families in the following way:

> It is a basic ground-rule for the primate species that, if we want healthy and effective adults, we have to associate mother and child safely and securely through the critical period of birth at least to the point where the children become independently mobile. In humans, with their extremely long dependency period, this is even more important, so that in a very real sense the mother–child tie is the basic bond in our system of social relationships and one that is really taken over from nature.

These views have clear implications for expectations of parents. However, they are heavily criticized by many other social scientists for the direct analogy with animals: these range from those sympathetic to the feminist cause (Oakley, 1974b) to those simply demanding more rigorous logic and evidence (Leach, 1973).

A more tempered view is that of Martin Richards (1974, p. 1), who summarizes the way many psychologists view children in a biological context:

> Though in many respects we may regard an infant as a presocial being he is not fully social as he is not yet a competent member of a social community. Rather, he is a biological organism with biological propensities and organization who becomes social through his encounters with social adults.

The ethological view has been widely influential and fits closely with the views of Bowlby and others who emphasize the importance of the mother–child bond. The view implies that:

1 Mothers are the primary nurturing parents.
2 Fathers are peripheral, and while they are expected to 'protect and provision' the mother–child couplet, substitutes of various kinds are more acceptable for them than for the mothers.
3 The domestic division of labour that reflects the above is the most natural and appropriate one.

While the ethological perspective has come into prominence more recently than in the 1950s and 1960s, it has served to underpin and perpetuate that particular authoritative stance. However, it is important to note that though this serves as the basis for modern writers to arrive at conventional conclusions (cf. Hutt, below), it also stimulates new revisionist approaches within ethology.

Exemplifying the first, Hutt (1972, p. 138) concludes from her analysis of biological indications of innate sex differences that: 'It would be a pity indeed if women sought to make this less a man's world by repudiating their femininity and by striving for masculine goals.' Her research emphasized the conventional expectations about parenting. A much greater body of literature is now accumulating, however, which allows for variation within the gender groups, and for a sorting of ways in which biological differences may be relevant in certain contexts and not in others. The studies based on Harlow's famous experiments with rhesus monkeys, for example, show that mothering and its absence is not the only basis for the development of character in adult life, and indeed, that it may not even be the strongest. As Gadpaille notes (1976, p. 136) behavioural scientists have been surprised at the evidence that peer-group social and sexual play was more important than mothering in relation to eventual sexuality. Lack of peer-group experience left ineradicable incapacities, whereas deficient mothering has been shown to be capable of being overcome by peer experience, particularly for females. This has led to the impression, supported by other animal research as well, that male sexuality is more susceptible to dysfunction than is female sexuality.

This last finding has been used both as a basis for the backlash response against sexual equality, and as a basis for reconsidering the kinds of relationships that we should value and try to encourage between the sexes. Gadpaille, accepting the innate biological differences as established, argues that they should not be used to perpetuate 'irrational inequities'; and that men will have to learn means other than devaluing women to achieve and maintain their separate masculine identity. He comes down, nevertheless, against any attempt to 'learn out' what he considers to be innate characteristics of the two sexes:

Maternalism is instinctual to females, not only in this species but in mammals generally. Children need exposure to the mutual complementarity of the uniquely masculine and feminine qualities of both parents, both sexes. . . . The interaction between the sexes can be usefully understood only if one accepts the inevitabilities inherent in the fact that the two sexes, from conception to death, grow up in different bodies (Gadpaille, 1976, pp. 157–8).

But Hinde (1974) and others have noted that neither the dictates of the body nor the conceptions of what constitutes masculinity or femininity are as uniformly standardized in animals, even the higher primates, as is to be assumed from statements of this kind. Male animals may also be involved with their young, particularly in relation to protective behaviour and play. And, this too may form part of the nurturance that is necessary for them to develop satisfactory adult behaviour patterns. If such views are propounded they may come to be influential in altering the cultural ethos surrounding expectations of parents' behaviour.

2 *The systems emphasis*

The family is a social system in which the actions of one member affect those of the other members. Most family sociology – indeed, most social analysis of family and kin relationships in sociology and social anthropology – has used some sort of systems approach. The family has been viewed as a micro-system, mirroring social structures adapting responsively to social values. In earlier societies, where integration between the different social levels was closer and social change was less rapid, the assumptions underlying this 'structural-functional' model were perhaps more tenable than they are today.

The most influential sociological analysis of the western family in systems terms has been that of Talcott Parsons. Parsons, in a series of books and papers beginning in the 1940s set out his position, which argued that the contemporary, relatively isolated nuclear family with its conventional sex-linked division of labour, 'fit' its environment and was 'functional' for both society and individual family members (Parsons, 1942, 1949). Our contemporary urban industrial society, he argued, requires labour mobility, stability of income and reliability of personal relationships (particularly for growing infants).

In his work with Bales, Parsons outlined some important mechanisms. Bales (1950) had already demonstrated that in small task-oriented groups (and the family is one such group), there tend to emerge two kinds of leaders; an instrumental leader (who deals largely with external adaptation) and an expressive leader (who deals primarily with the harmonization of roles within the group, the reduction of tensions and the increase of commitment to the group). Within the family, Parsons argued that a similar process occurs along two axes – the power axis (on which the parents retain a superior position through their age and maturity) and the task axis (in which the sex differences are fundamental – with males more 'instrumental' in orientation and females more 'expressive').

In the idealized family with a father, a mother, a son and a daughter, the four roles indicated by these two axes are seen as efficiently filled.

Boys learn instrumental leadership by identifying with their fathers, and girls learn expressive leadership by identifying with their mothers. The concentration of fathers in economic-provider roles, and mothers in home-maker roles was seen not only as serving society's requirements for flexibility of labour response, but also for individuals' requirements for stability of socializing environments. The division of labour on the basis of a clear biological criterion reduces the parents' competitiveness with one another. This, in turn, makes for an optimum internal environment for healthy socialization of the children. The expectations on parents are that family living involves the management of four fairly well defined sets of role relationships (husband–wife; mother–child; father–child; sibling–sibling).

The husband/father is the 'instrumental leader' and as such is expected to earn the family living, to work in a sustained and productive way to assure economic support. He is expected to behave in a way that places the family appropriately in the social setting – in relation to housing, schooling, politics and the law. In return, his home is made a haven of comfort and recreation by his spouse.

The wife/mother is the 'expressive leader' and as such is expected to be at home, to provide unconditional love for her children without interfering with her providing an affectionate haven for her toiling husband. In return for this she receives from him not only economic security but social status. If she wishes to participate in community life outside the home, she may cultivate a number of activities and interests, which are expected, however, to remain subordinate to her primary role. She may engage in community welfare projects, hobbies or even occupational work, but her central task is to remain a 'good mother' for her children and a 'good companion' for her husband.

Children are expected to identify with their parental role models and internalize a set of values which, when they grow up, will motivate them to take appropriate adult social roles.

If these conditions are met, the cycle is complete and all systems are attuned one to another. Zelditch provided partial cross-cultural support for this model and also argued for its face validity in logical terms:

> to be a stable focus of integration, the integrative-expressive leader can't be off on adoptive-instrumental errands all the time . . . and . . . if you are inhibiting emotions in order to perform instrumental tasks, you cannot at the same time release them in integrative-expressive behavior (Zelditch, 1955, p. 312).

The whole conception of the 'Parsonian family' model has been under increasing criticism recently – theoretically, ideologically and in terms of actual research findings of various kinds. Nevertheless it expresses in conceptual form the most prevalent appreciation of what the nature of the modern family was. It was the best available explanation of how the family survived under threats of various kinds in the process of industrialization and the growth of individualism. The task now is to understand how family members are adapting to new social conditions, new ideas of sex and gender roles, and new conceptions of parenting. It is around this focus that a new sub-group of sociological studies is emerging, as we shall indicate below.

3 *The cultural emphasis*

The family is the universal social institution for reproduction and socialization of infants, but its structure and norms for parental behaviour vary according to cultural context. The family reflects, in its culture, the culture of the society of which it is a part. Family socialization practices help to mould the central core of a child's personality, and according to the beliefs and values laid down in the family context the child will grow up and take on a set of expectations about parenting which derive to a large extent from this experience. These beliefs and values vary according to culture, and any specific element of attitude or behaviour – e.g. the exchange of economic goods at marriage – should be interpreted in its cultural context.

Cultural analysis, and its emphasis on the relativity of the meaning of any trait, has tended to highlight the variability rather than the common features of parental roles. Parental norms and expectations vary according to culture; cultures vary greatly and are probably capable of still further variation. The most widely known and influential of this school of 'cultural relativists' has been Margaret Mead (1939). Though her work was used amongst *avant-garde* reformers during the early post Second World War period, it is only more recently that her views have come to be more widely accepted.

In New Guinea, an area known for its diversity, Mead studied a set of tribal cultures which provided evidence for another paradigm, as neat and logical as the Parsonian one, but arguing a contrary case for men's and women's roles (see Figure 1).

		Males	
		Assertive	Gentle
Females	Assertive	Mundugumur	Tchambuli
	Gentle	USA	Arapesh

Figure 1 *Tribal cultures illustrating sex-role variability*

This paradigm indicates that while in American society men are expected to be aggressive and women passive (fitting the Parsonian model), amongst the Tchambuli the expectations are the reverse; and among the Mundugumur both are expected to be assertive, and amongst the Arapesh, both docile and nurturant. It is these characteristics, argued Mead, rather than who thatches the roof or tills the soil, that provide the meaningful definitions for sex-roles and parenting.

The link between general cultural norms such as the ones described by Margaret Mead and specific family role structures and different patterns of parenting is, however, complex. It is a continuing topic of multi-disciplinary study (cf., for example, Inkeles and Levinson, 1954; Leichter, 1974; LeVine, 1973; Whiting and Whiting, 1975).

In a society such as our own, which is complex rather than simple, and changing rather than static, what part can cultural norms be said to play for the society as a whole? Is there any cultural concept which has as powerful an influence on parents' expectation as the structural one of the conjugal family with its pattern of sex-role differentiation described above?

Some recent work has emphasized the importance of the idea of equality. Gorer (1973) and Young and Willmott (1973) speak of the development of a new conception of complementarity in marriage, one that emphasizes *symmetry*. Both husbands and wives expect increasingly to take on two meaningful roles, one inside the family and one out externally in the world of work (also see Fogarty *et al.*, 1971; Rapoport and Rapoport, 1971; 1976).

Robert LeVine's formulation seeks to reconcile cultural analyses with the emphases of biologically-oriented family authorities:

> Psychobiological investigators (e.g. Bowlby) argue that . . . humans are innately programmed for attachment . . . and they can vary culturally only within limits established in the distant evolutionary past without inflicting developmental damage on the child . . . [but] cultural evolution within human populations also produces standardized strategies of survival for infants and children, strategies reflecting environmental pressures from a more recent past encoded in customs rather than in genes and transmitted socially rather than biologically . . . culture no less than biology contributes to the presumptive task of rearing children, [and] that these ways are rational in that they contain information about environmental contingencies previously experienced by the population and assimilated into its cultural tradition . . . (LeVine, 1974, pp. 53–4).

Another group of studies attempting to apply the cross-cultural perspective to the conditions of modern living has been emerging around the concept of *modernization* (Inkeles and Smith, 1974; Smelser, 1966).

One example of the way in which cross-cultural analysis can be used without a necessary linkage between complexity and progress is seen in the work of Bronfenbrenner (1971). He has argued that many of the family's contemporary difficulties in the USA are associated with modern conditions – protection of children, lengthy schooling, changing roles of women, the growth of child-care experts, television and so on. He notes that in America this has given rise to a strong peer-oriented youth, who spend their time with one another less as a matter of preference than out of feeling 'dropped' by their parents, accompanied by a corresponding growth of anger and aggression. In both America and England there has also emerged a pattern of relatively little overt demonstration (particularly by fathers) of affection to children.

In the USSR, a society no less complex or modern than the USA, he finds different cultural norms for parents, which have a powerful impact on family life and the development of national character. Parents recognize their own importance as models for their children; and they also recognize the importance of groups, and of goals to which individuals and groups can commit themselves.

While the Western middle classes may be better off economically than their Soviet counterparts, Western societies have a greater discrepancy between the privileged and under-privileged parts of the society which he considers to be indicators not only of the system's success or failure, but of its special vulnerabilities.

Just as a chain breaks first in its weakest link, so the problems of a society become most pressing and visible in the social strata that are under greatest stress. Thus it is not surprising that we should first recognize the disruption of the process of socialization in American society among the families of the poor (Bronfenbrenner, 1971, p. 158).

Western countermeasures (e.g. the 'headstart programme' or Educational Priority Areas) aim to compensate for the demonstrated deficits of the system. The ideas of many professionals and the expectations these imply for parenting are often used for developing policies for action.

Bronfenbrenner's work, while subject to many of the criticisms that have been levelled at studies relying on the culture concept to depict complex situations such as those prevailing in the USSR and the USA, is nevertheless useful in making a diagnosis of a complex social situation and process. It is also important in the context of this chapter as a type of influence by social scientists. It illustrates the *use of social science for social policy* in the area of parenting. Bronfenbrenner proposes the development of policies in which:

1 Parents are expected to *learn* to become involved.
2 They are expected to learn *tactics* for dealing with problems of children.
3 They are expected to learn how to *enhance*, rather than lower the self-esteem of the child.
4 They are expected to learn to be *constructive models* for their children in their own behaviour, and to appreciate the importance of this.

The more competent and fortunate parents are expected to help those who are less so; to help them to learn, and to provide role models for them in such a way as to enhance rather than lower the self-esteem of the learner parents. Bronfenbrenner implies, therefore, that a sense of community is essential, and, though this is more implicit, that it should be based on a middle-class value model.

Bronfenbrenner, throughout his work, is more concerned with facilitating family *involvement* in child-rearing – e.g. by communication, modelling, conflict resolving, and so on – than to specify which parent does what. He emphasizes father-absence as much as mother absence. In his own research he found that:

Children who reported that their parents were away from home for long periods of time rated significantly lower on such characteristics as responsibility and leadership. Perhaps because it was more pronounced, absence of the father was more critical than that of the mother, particularly in its effect on boys (Bronfenbrenner, 1971, p. 104).

Drawing on these newer approaches by social scientists, we conclude that the newly emerging expectations of parents, in influential social science writing, include the ideas that:

1 They should be involved and committed to their tasks as parents.
2 They should recognize that parenting involves the need to learn.
3 They should share with others the problems as well as the pleasures of the experience, and
4 They should adopt a 'teacher' or 'learner' attitude as appropriate, without pride or prejudice, and apply this flexibly through life.

The cultural emphasis suggests that parental practices vary not only with such gross determining variables such as income, size of family and housing conditions – but with the beliefs and values of people who share a culture. This may cut across the other differences to some extent, the resulting pattern being a product of multiple determination. The importance of the cultural approach, as implied in the discussion of Bronfenbrenner's work, is two-fold. First, the idea that parenting practices can be deliberately regulated is a cultural idea, and it is a product of the socialist values of a planned society on the one side, and the capitalist values of manipulation and control of one's personal situation on the other. In both cases, described by Bronfenbrenner in terms of Russian and American cultures, the emphasis on taking into account a *cultural dimension* is crucial. As well as altering material conditions, institutional provisions, etc., it is essential, in this framework, to attempt to alter beliefs and values.

The developmental emphasis, which follows in the next section, is presented as one of the emphases within the social sciences within which a focus on intervention and the influencing of patterns of individuals and familes has been given explicit attention. The potentials of this approach are only now coming to be recognized as crucial supplements to the more static analytic approaches.

4 *The developmental emphasis*

Social expectations of parenting are affected by what stage of the life cycle the parents are at. New parents face tasks which differ from those confronting parents of adolescents. Parents face different tasks for their second, third or fourth children than they do for their first. Parents whose children are themselves parents confront new expectations as grandparents.

The work of 'developmental' social scientists has highlighted the contrasts in task confronting parents at different stages in the life cycle (Duvall and Hill, 1948). Early studies, like those of Reuben Hill, highlighted the importance of life events such as moves of home, loss of job, death of loved ones, in affecting the developmental course of a family's life career. The application of some of this early work with 'crisis theory' to the normal events of the family life cycle only came later.

'Normal' transitions from one social status and role to another sometimes have the properties of 'crisis'. They may upset people's ways of doing things, disturb routine patterns and expectations, stimulate anxieties about whether the new challenges can be handled creating emotional tensions. Major transitions, like that of becoming a parent, tend to have this 'critical' character (Rapoport, 1963).

But each major status transition has specific challenges. Each developmental stage has key tasks which become salient for family development. Hill and Duvall have outlined some of them, as perceived in the 1950s (Duvall, 1957; Hill and Rodgers, 1964). The following is an abridged summary:

Family stages	Family goals
Establishment of the family	Adjusting to living as a married pair
Childbearing	Reorganization around needs of infants

School age   Reorganization to fit into expanding
                                  world of school-agers

Young adult launching   Reorganization into egalitarian unit
                                  and releasing of members

Middle years   Reorganization around marriage pair
                                  Strategy of disengagement

Aging years   Disengagement

Many of these goals and tasks as originally formulated now seem somewhat dated, but they are important in defining the expectations of parents that were enunciated then and are still somewhat prevalent. Parents were expected to do what was necessary to meet the family goals.

In a recent study, *Family Development in Three Generations*, Hill and his colleagues (1970) report similar trends to those indicated by Young and Willmott, toward more sharing of work inside the family and the greater likelihood that both husband and wife will have an occupational role for a major part of the cycle; both of these tendencies accompany a loosening of inter-generational ties (Young and Willmott, 1973).

The implications of the developmental approach for expectations on parenting are:

1 Each stage presents its own challenges and goals.
2 Parents, like their children, develop.
3 Each stage differs in its goal not only from preceding stages, but from the way the same stage was experienced by one's own parents.
4 The expectation then, is that parents be open to change and resourceful in meeting transitions.

But, as recent workers have emphasized, the family presents individuals with inter-contingent development potentials for several different kinds of careers – sexual, marital relations, parent–child relations (Feldman and Feldman, 1975); and rather than a single cycle trajectory, it should be thought of in 'game-tree' terms subject not only to multi-variate influences, but to multiple processes of decision, power, exchange and alternative pathway choices (Broderick, 1971).

By implication, the fixity of patterns assumed in earlier models, emphasizing socio-cultural as well as biologically determined elements, is open to review.

Expectations of parenting in social work literature

Social work is concerned with family life and parenting primarily at points of difficulty in which there is either a felt need for help on the part of one or more members of the family or a statutory obligation for the state to intervene, or both. The main duties and responsibilities of the local authority social worker in Britain *vis-à-vis* parents have been summarized from Younghusband (1966) as follows:

1 To investigate the need for children to be received into care and to recommend their reception in suitable cases; to accept responsibility for the supervision of children committed to care or placed under statutory supervision.

2 To offer a casework service to families with children at risk of coming into care, or appearing before a Juvenile Court.

3 To offer a casework service to unsupported mothers and single parent families.

4 To investigate cases of alleged neglect or ill-treatment of children and to make enquiries into the need to bring care proceedings in respect of any child or young person.

5 To supervise children who are boarded out, privately fostered, or placed in residential accommodation provided by a statutory, voluntary, or private body.

6 To recommend the placement of a child for adoption, and to supervise all children pending adoption under the Adoption Act.

7 To ensure the regular review of children in care as required by the Children and Young Persons Act.

8 To represent the Council in Court in respect of proceedings concerning a child, young person, or person in need of care and attention, and to prepare reports in this connection.

The values and assumptions about parenting, implicit in many of these responsibilities have undergone changes in the past two or three decades, just as they have in the other fields we examine. In attempting to describe the type of expectations that have been applied by social workers in recent decades, certain observable patterns emerge which correspond to the others described. As with the law, social work moved from a still earlier position of a more moralistic kind – (the classical era of the 'do-gooder', the 'lady bountiful', and of *noblesse-oblige*), to the contemporary era emphasizing professionalization of care. By the period under examination, the decades post Second World War, the balance in social work had shifted from the amateur philanthropic basis to the more professional one – though contributions from both sources continued to be important. Within the professional approach, different models were evolved – from medicine initially (Wilensky and Lebeaux, 1955), and in psychiatric social work (particularly in America) from psychoanalysis. The notion of 'maturity' was prominent, and a healthy family was seen as one approximating this ideal.

Examining the kinds of expectations of parenting that were prevalent in this earlier professional period, one finds this tendency toward depicting an idealized type of family and parent. Gardner Murphy sums up the position as follows, in a volume of papers assessing 'social casework in the fifties':

> Our discussions of the family have often implied an ideal, a standard or norm, for the mother. She is expected to be warm, strong, direct, to enjoy her femininity and her motherhood, to give affection and support, to protect her children, to be firm but not overbearing, tender but not mawkish; to provide stimulus and support for the child's growth and his ultimate achievement of independence (Murphy, 1962, p. 100).

Father, too, was expected to be strong and reliable, aggressively coping with the family's struggle to survive in a dangerous world. His role was seen as complementary to that of the mother. Josselyn wrote in the same summary volume:

> The family unit provides the child with rich and broad sources of security. The experience of being part of this unit not only gives the child a feeling of safety in the world beyond his relationship with his mother, but also encourages him to relinquish his dependence on her in favour of the more mature dependence on the family (Josselyn, 1962, p. 111).

According to this conception of the family as a *safe* environment, the child has been seen as able, within it, to broaden its base of relationships from the mother to others – father and siblings. Provided the family is not *too overprotective*, the family has been seen as facilitating the child in developing his or her base of relationships to others outside the family in a way that will allow for *realistic*, rather than unrealistic expectations of people.

The maturity model, borrowed from psychoanalysis, like many other social work concepts, was very widely applied in family case work, though many other theoretical and practical approaches have also been developed (Roberts and Nee, 1970). This model emphasized being 'realistic', and much of the work of organizations like the Family Welfare Association, has aimed at co-operating with parents to get them to confront reality and cope with the problems presented more adequately (Family Welfare Association, 1961; Younghusband, 1966). But what is 'realistic' and what is 'immature'?

Stiber (1954), an American social worker writing in the context of a family health-maintenance experiment much like the English Peckham experiment of the pre-war years (Pearse and Crocker, 1943), makes the following observations about characteristic strains in family life at that time. She noted that though most husbands and most wives accepted the conventional occupational role models of breadwinner and homemaker, in fact many wives took employment outside the home and many husbands helped in the home. However, those wives who remained at home, doing their homemaking jobs, did so with little interest or enjoyment; and, conversely, those husbands who accepted their wives employment outside, did so with little enthusiasm. Mostly these patterns were seen as undesirable evils that had to be put up with. People were seen to drift into such patterns with mounting discontent. However, the social work analysis retained the maturity model:

> The overall picture of relationship between husband and wife reveals much confusion, dissatisfaction and resignation. Few of the adults appeared to be mature enough to support the demands of such a relationship. Men were on the whole passive, immature, undepend-able in an emotional sense. Women were more aggressive, immature, unable to accept the feminine role of wife and mother. Disappoint-ment in their expectations of the possibilities of the relationship was common. The resignation comes, I believe, from some awareness which they have that some of the difficulty rests with themselves and that another or different partner would not bring about a different relationship (Stiber, 1954, p. 56).

The implication of this was that mature men were not passive, and that mature women were not aggressive. 'Reality' involved conforming to the cultural expectations; other patterns made for difficulties. This view has never been as widely used in Britain as in American social work but it is represented in one thread of thinking that has been very influential. The programme developed at the Tavistock Institute under the Family Discussion Bureau in the 1950s reflected this approach. The FDB argued for the need for the psychoanalytic perspective after a study of the background characteristics of their case load which deter-mined that there were no sociologically distinctive characteristics ('no unusual feature'). They concluded that this was of interest, though a negative finding, because 'of the popular tendency to attribute marriage breakdown to one or more relatively simple external factors, and the inadequacy of any study based solely or mainly on these external factors . . .' (FDB, 1955, p. 183). Marriage difficulties (and this could be extended to other parental difficulties) are seen as determined there-fore by the personalities of the individuals, crucially affecting the way they handle the challenges confronted. The social worker's role definition was based on the model of parental roles. Elizabeth Irvine, for example, wrote:

> The worker has most chance of success if he plays the part of a warm, permissive and supportive parent, thus supplying the basic

experiences of the early stage of socialisation, which for some reason the client seems to have missed (Irvine, 1954, p. 27).

In summary, the kinds of expectations toward parenting that have been prominent until recently implied that:

1 Mothers are the main figures involved in parenting, and fathers are peripheral.
2 Families function as whole units, and parents ought to be able to generate a healthy internal environment in which to raise children.
3 If parents do not do this, it is because they are immature as individuals.
4 Immaturity is characterized by unrealistic attitudes, or deficiencies in performing in roles as defined in our society. According to this conception, a mature mother accepts her 'feminine role' and her 'maternal' responsibilities whole-heartedly and warmly; and a mature father accepts his role as protector and provider and concentrates on being aggressive outside the family.
5 As a haven for the father, the family ought to provide rest and relaxation, enjoyment and recreation – not additional strains.
6 In order to achieve this, parents have to recognize their personal problems and come to grips with them in a prescribed way, reflecting conventional models of mothering and fathering in our society.

Contemporary social work approaches retain some elements of the earlier ones, but in a different perspective. The family still tends to be seen as a *whole functioning unit*, though one which needs, and has, a right to social supports. It is seen as capable of change; but there are elements in the situation which may be beyond the resources both of parents and of social case workers. There are, in short, societal issues which need separate attention.

Take the issue of the father's role. Timms notes that social workers who have dealt with the mother as though she were the only person involved, for example in planning the child's future, have tacitly failed to involve the father and thereby exacerbated one of the sources of the family's difficulties; i.e. father's non-involvement. But this may reflect more than personal immaturity. It relates to cultural norms, occupational constraints, etc. as well (Timms, 1962).

Take the issue of idealization of the 'normal family'. Goldberg points out that this is a kind of professional myth, comparable to the myth of the 'mature personality' with which psychoanalysts have worked, and the concept of 'the family' as a social system in equilibrium, as many sociologists have conceived of it. This relates to cultural norms and values which require change at a societal level (Goldberg, 1959).

Take the issue of the capacity of the mature mother to manage everything on her own. Holman has observed that the supportive social services for families are increasingly geared to the notion that women cannot, and perhaps should not, be expected to be capable of handling the demands they face in the modern family setting with social services being provided only when they break down. Five thousand British children were received into care in a single year because of their mothers' desertion. The provision of services for the families prior to this sort of occurrence – play facilities and day nurseries for the children, for example, might reduce the strains contributing to mothers feeling trapped. This assumes not that the parents are necessarily immature but that their circumstances are unmanageable and require supports (Holman, 1970b).

Take the issue of 'reality confrontation' that comes with diagnosis. Sainsbury notes that this is increasingly couched in social as well as psychological terms, and in relation to events throughout the life cycle rather than at stages presenting symptomatic difficulties. Family case-work is conducted in a framework which attempts to help individuals to cope with the practical material problems, for example, but without assuming that social-psychological problems within the family will necessarily disappear and not recur. Relating psychological capacities to social expectations through time is called for: '[diagnosis] is based on scientific understanding of likely relationships between certain events or experiences in the client's life; and between his social back-ground, developmental history and present behaviour and needs' (Sainsbury, 1970, p. 33). And Hammond writes: 'the process of helping involves a study and diagnosis of the problems (involving as far as possible all the people concerned) and an awareness of the implications that changes may have on others concerned' (Hammond, 1973, p. 43). The assessment of strengths and weaknesses may include material resources, environmental conditions, interpersonal patterns of relation-ship, and social service agencies – but not one or another as an exclusive channel.

The newer conception, in social work as well as in theoretical social science, is one that emphasizes various possibilities for families, each with its own psychosocial climate and its own characteristic problems of communication, conflict resolution and management of social ties.

This formulation is in advance of general usages in the profession, as in the general public. The new approach under way contrasts with the established approach, according to which, as Jordan observes:

Families are judged in accordance with a single inflexible standard, designed to judge their performance as an isolated unit, which fails to take account of their total social situation, and the environmental context of their lives. The help they are offered is often as a result inappropriate to their needs (Jordan, 1972, p. 45).

Timms adds that a better conception of the family than the one emphasizing the importance of the 'family as a whole', is one that views the whole family but analytically in terms of the ways in which the various individuals 'fit' together in their pattern of relationships (Timms, 1962; Rapoport and Rosow, 1957). There is room here both for the appreciation of variation in family roles, and of the linkages between family and social environment that affect family functioning. Modern social workers are confronted with a new range of issues as to how to deploy their efforts in a way that combines attention to here and now individual and family problems on the one side and to the social and community environment within which family problems are bred and may be resolved.

The legal system

We now turn to the prevailing influences and expectations of parenting implied in the legal system. As in other fields, our concentration is on the past few decades, but here above all – where a rigidification of thought and practice is an intrinsic part of the system of common law – it is important to have some deeper historical perspective. Many ideas and practices no longer congruent with modern conceptions are still present and inevitably affect expectations (Zander, 1974).

Within the legal system, expectations of parenting are highly differentiated by sex. This stems from the earlier position according to which families were organized along hierarchical and patriarchal lines, where it was assumed that the father's views would prevail automatically. In the past few decades the law has continued to base its expectations generally on a division of labour between husband and wife, father and mother, which is fairly traditional.

The language of the law is couched in such notions as rights and obligations, responsibilities and duties, blame and punishment of one or another of the parents for omissions or commissions of specific kinds. The expectations in the law are backed up by specific sanctions; actions enforced by social workers, the courts and the police. They affect not only feelings but tangible assets – cash flow, property, rights in relation to children and the like. While these matters tend to be the cause of legal actions only when difficulties arise, the rationales behind them, the interpretations made in applying them, the public statements and advice of counsel and of police authorities, influence people's expectations generally. They serve as incentives and constraints, expectations and aspirations. The points at which representatives of the law take action indicate not only the limits of society's tolerance for *unacceptable* parental behaviour but by implication they re-enforce social values about the norms of 'good' parenting. By making it explicit what the boundaries of 'normal' behaviour are, and what the reasons are for enforcing these boundaries, the law defines qualitatively what is 'good' as well as what is 'bad' in relation to parenting.

The legal situation can best be understood in historical context. In law, the family of the last century was one of patriarchal authority, with the husband/father having extensive powers over the persons and property of his wife and children. On marriage, the wife became part of the social and legal entity that was defined by her husband, and all her chattels became the absolute property of the husband. Graveson has written: 'Subject to the institution by the Court of Chancery of what was known as the wife's separate estate in equity, the married woman, both physically and economically, was very much in the position of a chattel of her husband' (Graveson and Crane, 1957). And O. R. McGregor dramatized the pervasiveness of the patriarchal pattern thus:

> Outside the family, married women had the same legal status as children and lunatics; within it they were their husband's inferiors. By marriage they moved from dependence on fathers or male relatives to dependence on husbands. To the Pauline conclusion that they two shall be one flesh, the Victorians added the explanation: 'and I am he' (McGregor, 1955).

While the laws have changed and are changing still, residues of this heritage remain in attitudes and practices both in the legal system and in associated public and private services based on the statutes. Patriarchal authority in the law has diminished but there persists as a dominant feature of the law over the past few decades the assumption that the male contribution to society and to the family is intrinsically different from the female one; and that this is and should be recognized in the rights, duties and expectations embodied in the laws.

Traditionally, the father has been recognized as the 'natural guardian' of his child and protector of his wife. Both took his name, and it was assumed that his views would prevail in all important life decisions – the choice and standard of the matrimonial home, the policies and specific decisions about child-rearing – for example, choice of school, choice of religion, and all the decisions embodied in the notion of maintenance. A wife did not have (and still has no legal right) to know about or have any particular proportion of the husband's earnings, and therefore funds available for housekeeping, clothing and feeding the children came from whatever allowance the 'lord and master' of the household saw fit to provide.

A parent or guardian – and here the expectation has been that it was the father – was free to punish his child within reasonable boundaries, beyond which it became a criminal offence. The loss of parents' rights over the care and control of their children could occur only in extreme cases, in which a 'fit person order' is made by the court, and the child is forcibly placed in care other than that of his natural parents.

Though many elements of patriarchal tradition have given way to a more even-handed consideration of parenting as the responsibility of both parents, the stereotyped conceptions of sex-role differences have persisted and are only now being revised. Though there was little residue in the post-war period of earlier double standards of punitiveness in relation to adultery (prior to 1923 adultery on the part of the woman was much more likely to lead to the judgment that she was unsuitable to be given care and custody of the child following divorce proceedings than the same behaviour on the part of the man) there are still a host of expectations which are sex-linked in the practice if not in the theory of the law.

Considering modern divorce practice in the light of the more recent laws, as embodied, for example, in the basic principle that the law should act in the best interests of the child, the court must be satisfied in any divorce proceedings that appropriate arrangements are made for the child. Where the arrangements are not satisfactory, or are in dispute between the couple, the court will delay granting the *decree nisi* until the matter is dealt with – by hearing evidence in private, by seeking the views of experts such as child psychiatrists or social workers and, where the child is old enough, to ask the opinion of the child. While a wider range of conduct is taken into account and adultery as such is no longer a major concern, the financial arrangements are, and the wife's capacity to earn her own living is one of the elements in the situation that increasingly is likely to be taken into account. Technically there is a distinction between *care and control* (the day-to-day management of the child's upbringing) and *custody* (the power to decide major questions such as education, religion, etc.). These distinctions conform to the traditional sex-based division of labour in the family, but it is rare that the court will nowadays segregate the two as they were in the past. However, the assumption that modern parents will work out mutually acceptable patterns of joint participation in the two sets of responsibilities is not always upheld, even in the most enlightened and resourceful families. Organizations like 'Families Need Fathers' express the dissatisfaction of many fathers at the way in which the practice of care and custody may deviate from the theory following a divorce proceeding. The theory is that a solution will be evolved which is in the best interests of the child. The different interpretations of what is in the child's best interest, and the changes that may occur following the dissolution of a marriage, may become a bone of heated contention in a way that is not in the best interest of the child (Goldstein *et al.*, 1973).

Although biological parents still have the law on their side, there is a noticeable trend in opinion toward the protection of the rights of the child, and to this end, to institute a system of children's representation through advocates, guardians or some form of ombudsperson.

A recent case in which the principle of the paramountcy of the child's welfare was expressed was that of J *vs* C (House of Lords 1969) when a child was kept in the care of fosterparents in England and not returned to his natural parents in Spain. Although both sets of parents were considered suitable, and although the natural parents were anxious to take back their child, it was felt that the child's welfare was best served by him remaining in this country with his fosterparents and in the environment to which he had become accustomed.

In terms of the expectations of parenting, the law seems to say that it will provide mechanisms for sorting out the various issues – maintenance, custody and care, and other elements of support – in such a way as to do what seems to be in the best interests of the child. In actual practice, the difficulties that are often in the way of achieving this ideal in many families are so great that it becomes apparent that improved legal mechanisms are required and that improved parental competence to manage divorce or separations constructively are also called for. This is a matter for parent education, and, as in other fields, is becoming more clearly a matter that is in the interests of the parents as well as of the children.

Notwithstanding the exceptions, the notion of natural parenthood is still forceful. Enshrined in all sorts of aphorisms such as 'blood is thicker than water', this is manifest in a range of laws and practices, among them the idea of legitimacy itself. Though strictly speaking this simply means duly registered according to law, and includes adopted as well as biologically-bred children, it tends to be associated with natural parenthood, with all the rights, privileges and social esteem that is associated with legitimacy. The stigma of illegitimacy attaches not only to the child but to the parent, and the law re-enforces this in making available to legal wives many benefits that are not available to common-law wives – for example, widow's allowances, pension rights and property rights.

Examples of how blood relationships have been given precedence are seen in the situation where a child is taken into care. Technically the natural parents are no longer responsible, except to keep the local authority informed of their whereabouts. They continue, however, to have rights. At their request they can, in the normal course, have their children returned to them. This practice has been increasingly questioned by social workers and child psychologists, and in Britain recent tragedies connected with child-neglect or injury have supported those who do not assume that the blood tie will necessarily entail a more caring set of attitudes and practices in the best interests of the child.

Recent tendencies have included giving less weight to the sexual morality of mother or father and also less weight to the assumption that the blood tie will suffice as a motivation to make parents care. In the case of unmarried mothers, for example, maintenance orders can be made for the children to be supported by the putative father, but it has been the responsibility of the mother to collect this. This responsibility, should the recommendation of the Finer Commission on Single Parent Families be adopted, will be transferred to the state (DHSS, Finer, 1974). The effect will be to diminish the residue of double standards of parenting deriving from earlier conceptions. George and Wilding (1972, p. 45), in their study of 'motherless families' have documented the pervasiveness of these split attitudes and practices. Whereas there is considerable ambivalence about unmarried mothers, it is accepted, by and large, that they stay at home and care for their children if they wish to. Unmarried fathers, on the other hand, are expected to hire a housekeeper and to go out to work – and to stop 'living off the community'.

Another indication of the power of the idea of non-interference with the natural workings of the 'normal family' is that no order for custody or maintenance can be enforced if the parents of the child cohabit. This means that the principle of the best interests of the child is subordinated to that of the natural rights of guardianship of the child's parents unless something goes seriously wrong; for example, if the child is excessively punished, or if the marriage breaks down and there are problems of maintenance, care, custody or welfare. The tendency is to do all possible to preserve the family and, conversely, to be reluctant to ease its dissolution. Measured financially as well as in terms of social control – both elements of concern to the law – the state benefits by the work that parents do as a matter of their familial role obligations. Family allowances provide financial support where this element is a threat to the family. Older ideas of guilt and reparation which stemmed from ecclesiastical courts are still present in many magistrates' courts, there the law of condonation (whereby a spouse may be penalized if he or she attempts but fails to effect a reconciliation) is still practised.

There has been a notable lag in the law's willingness to make divorce easier. Prior to 1923 there was a double standard in divorce law, particularly stigmatizing the wife for adultery. This stemmed from earlier and even more punitively couched legislation of the ecclesiastical courts, which affected not only divorce proceedings but judgments as to suitability for parenting. In the period following the Matrimonial

Causes Act of 1937, the number of decrees granted rose sharply, as it did when the law still further broadened the bases for divorce in the Divorce Reform Act of 1969 and the Matrimonial Proceedings Act of 1970 when the idea of guilt and the punitive elements of court proceedings were theoretically eliminated in law.

While the *de jure* provision that the needs of the child have always been provided for in the law, the provisions of the Children Act 1975 for child representation and for increased speed of court proceedings in making determinations, reflects the new views that family circumstances are more complicated generally than can be encompassed with simple rules of thumb such as that emphasizing the rights of natural parents. On the other hand, a broader conception of what may constitute a satisfactory family life is emerging. While there are still disadvantages, financial and social, to declining to marry, for example, the courts as well as society generally are more ready to acknowledge the possibility that a child may enjoy a healthy environment in various familial settings, including that of the single-parent family and that of the foster family.

Expectations of parenting in educational institutions

A convenient point of reference for exploring assumptions about parenting during the past two or three decades in the British educational situation is the Education Act of 1944. While this was primarily concerned with the establishment and demarcation of different types of schools and the definition of the duties and rights of different personnel associated with them, it also indicated – albeit obliquely – some expectations of parents. The minimal duties of parents are spelt out in section 36:

> It shall be the duty of the parent of every child of compulsory school age to cause him to receive efficient full-time education suitable to his age, ability and aptitude, either by regular attendance at school or otherwise (Education Act, 1944, Section 36, p. 29).

The education officer in any given area is obliged to serve notice on parents who do not comply with this provision and is empowered to serve a 'school attendance order'. The parent should, under the Act, have an opportunity to select the school to be named in the order. If the local education authorities feel that an inappropriate selection is made by a parent, they may appeal to the Minister, who has the right to direct as he sees fit. Ultimately, if the parents fail to comply, they may be brought to the courts. Parents are also responsible for the regular attendance of registered pupils.

The 1944 Education Act reflects the prevailing situation in the home–

school relationship, received from the past and characteristic of the period under discussion. According to this, the home and the school are two social institutions legally charged with socializing the young; the home entirely in charge up to school age (5 years), then the school compulsorily taking over 'in loco parentis' for school hours and school days. The Act is careful to detail the limits of expectations that may be placed on school personnel. This limitation is particularly relevant to the point that the functions of the school and the family are considered to be different – and it is in the area of 'ancillary services' (medical, nutritional, transport, etc.) that overlaps are experienced that make it necessary to draw lines. For example, in section 49 of the Act (which has since been revised in respect of the provision of milk), it was stated:

> [local education authorites shall have] the duty of providing milk, meals and other refreshment for pupils in attendance at schools . . . [but the provision of such services] shall not impose upon teachers . . . duties upon days on which the school or college is not open for instruction. . . .

Schools are considered to be concerned primarily with formal instruction, with ancillary services only secondary; and the family is seen as concerned with the provision of care and services. The sharp age-grading in schools, as many writers have now pointed out, is a recent innovation in our society, since industrialization. It has been accentuated partly as a protection of children against the inequities of child labour. But primarily the evolution of schooling reflects the requirements of education imposed by an increasingly complex society with ever expanding specialist demand for skills and capacities which lie outside the competence of most families (Aries, 1962).

The expectations of parents expressed by the educational institutions during this period were that parents should prepare children for school, see that they attend regularly, and not intrude too much, even if they considered their intervention to be in the child's interest – for example, with 'homework' – because there may be a conflict between the parents' approach and that of the authorities at school.

The past few decades have been famous for boundary-drawing that saw signs on the school grounds along the lines of the 'No parents admitted without appointment with Head' variety. This exclusion was not confined to the uneducated parents, toward whom teachers often felt exasperation at having to cope with the symptoms and byproducts of deprivation – but included the eager and supportive parents as well. Michael Young quotes Leonard Woolf's *Sowing*, in which he recounts his mother's experience in an interview with the highmaster at St Paul's, where instead of being embraced as the splendid mother of

such a clever scholarship boy, she was made to feel that she had perpe-
trated near-crimes by having produced a child so deficient in the
rudiments of Latin and Greek (Young, 1965).

Young and McGeeney conducted some action research in 1967 which
focused on the link between parents and school in one particular
school in an Educational Priority Area in London. Although the project
was aimed at discovering the nature of the optimum link in terms of
enhancing the child's school performance, it nevertheless succeeded
in identifying many of the felt needs of the parents in relation to the
school and highlighted the discrepancy between these and the school's
expectations of the parents. The parents' contacts with the school
prior to the research were first assessed. The major contact occurred
on the child's first day of school when two-thirds of the mothers
accompanied their children. The rest of the children went with older
siblings or other relatives. The proceedings were described as being
similar to other confrontations of working-class people with authority:

> when conscripted into the Services, put on the register at the
> 'Labour', or when applying for a job at the factory, it was much the
> same as when a child was being put to school. They had to supply
> 'the particulars' that bureaucracy requires (Young and McGeeney,
> 1968, pp. 13–14).

For most of the parents the question of choosing schools for their
children had not arisen – even for those who had asked for official
advice, it was just a matter of going to the nearest one. The same finding
in relation to working-class parents was reported by Dennis Marsden
(1967, p. 54). Furthermore, 'none of the mothers was given the
opportunity to talk about the organisation of the school or about the
curriculum' (Young and McGeeney, 1968, p. 14). However, judging
by their comments, many parents would have welcomed the chance
to discuss such matters. Contact between parents and school had not
been encouraged by staff except on a few formal occasions such as
Open Day and the school play. A notice over the teachers' entrance
said 'Private. Trespassers will be prosecuted', and only if one finally
reached the headmaster's door could one read the notice that said 'The
headmaster may be seen by appointment'. Not surprisingly only 22
per cent of the parents had spoken to teachers on occasions other than
the child's first day at the school, and even then 'such special visits as
were made were usually when there has been "trouble"' (Young and
McGeeney, 1968, p. 15). Such 'trouble' could consist in the child's
illness, or an incident in which the child's behaviour had led to dis-
ciplinary measures being taken by the school or police, or some specific
difficulty of the child at school such as scape-goating by a teacher,
bullying by other children or a work problem of some sort.

Sixty-five per cent of mothers and 45 per cent of fathers, prior to the action research, attended the school on Open Day. But many of them found the contact unsatisfactory as there was no real chance to discuss their children with staff in private. Indeed, in this case staff and governors had their tea in a special room, visible but not accessible to parents.

The overall 'feel' of this research project was expressed by Lady Plowden in the foreword to the publication:

> What comes out so strongly in this book is the passionate but impotent interest of so many of these parents. They wanted their child to do well, they wanted to help but they felt ignorant and did not know how to do so. They welcomed particularly the opportunity for private talks about their child with his teacher (Young and McGeeney, 1968, p. 8).

The school's expectation of parents was that they should not interfere in the educational *process* though they might wish to be informed about educational *theory and methods*. Thus, in writing about PTA meetings elsewhere, McGeeney observes that:

> In all three of the meetings the teachers came along with blocks of information that were conceived in terms of what the staff thought to be essential and not what the parents might want to know (McGeeney, 1969, p. 134).

> When asked what problems they wished to discuss, invariably from time to time some parent would stand up to ask specifically a question related to his own child's difficulties in reading or arithmetic, only to be disappointed on being told that was not the particular purpose of their being invited (McGeeney, 1969, p. 136).

Another feature of schools in relation to parenting expectations has been the assumption of a division of interests and abilities along stereotyped sex lines. Girls for the humanities and boys for the sciences in the academic schools; boys for the trades and girls for the 'female' jobs of nurse, teacher, secretary, clerical worker – and only temporarily while waiting for marriage. These norms were not always explicit, and often took the form of assuming that the girls would prefer the costume museum while the boys would prefer the visits to the engineering exhibits; or that girls are better at certain subjects like art and biology, but inept in others, like mathematics, science and engineering. Although this sort of sex role division is arguably of minimal importance in respect of the school's expectations of the children's parents, as a preparation for parenthood for the children themselves it is an important factor.

So, the school's expectations and assumptions *vis-à-vis* parents have been:

1 That education is a matter for professionals; it involves different skills and is orientated to different objectives than the kind of work that parents do; often it has to compensate for deficiencies in parenting or to protect children from parental interference while the school does its work 'in loco parentis' during school hours, days, weeks, and years – all prescribed in law.

2 That the differences between males and females are fundamental – both educationally and in terms of ultimate social roles for which the individuals are being prepared. While boys and girls should receive an equally good education according to the same curricula, it is to be expected that they will have different interests and objectives in the educational process.

In education as in other fields these assumptions are being questioned and revised. The Department of Education and Science, for example, backed the recommendations of the Plowden Committee and the Gittens Committee for closer home–school interaction by a series of Reports on Education, outlining different parental factors which can produce unfavourable background conditions: broken homes, illegitimacy, prison records, lack of parental interest, cultural impoverishment, poor communications, poor health and sanitation. Each of these was supported by research (Douglas, 1964, 1968; Kellmer Pringle *et al.*, 1966; Wiseman, 1964; Bernstein, 1965).

Other assumptions die hard – thus the recommendations of the Department of Education and Science, while making for major alterations in home–school interaction (especially at the primary school level) continued to assume traditional sex-role stereotypes. For example, fathers were visualized as becoming involved in the school and its work by helping to construct buildings, play areas or pools, or, if professionals, to give consultations to children on project work. Even among leaders in research and theory the assumption persisted that parents would keep to conventional roles. Michael Young, for example, wrote as late as 1965:

How can [working people] bring this asset [their pride in work they can do with their hands] to the service of the school [so that they can feel more part of it]? Most obviously by adding to its physical equipment. This has already been done by fathers who have with their own hands built swimming pools and sports pavilions, and the same kind of effort could be called upon for the construction of other buildings. . . .

As for mothers, their part could be inside the school. The

shortage of teachers will become intolerable unless other people, not fully trained, are brought in as assistants . . . in dining halls, playgrounds and swimming baths, typing, clearing up classrooms, preparing for lessons and generally just being around. . . . Such jobs can be as well done (often better done) by mothers of the children in a particular school as by anyone else . . . (Young, 1965, pp. 76–7).

It is clear that the contemporary movement toward equality between men and women has major implications for the expectations of parenting inculcated in schools. Ann Oakley, for example, in her analysis of conventional housewife role, highlights how the restricted occupational distinction of women (described elsewhere by Fogarty *et al.*, 1971) is assumed in the informal if not the formal educational system (Oakley, 1974b). Changing social values amongst both parents and teachers in this respect, however, are bringing increasing pressure to bear on schools to revise their traditional approach to sex-role expectations.

The school's assumptions about parenting have also moved recently from the expectation that parents could and should do everything to facilitate the development of children up until the age of six and then stay out of it, to a newer set of assumptions that parents should not be seen as responsible for the total environment at any stage, and commencing from school age they should work in partnership with educators and others, sharing responsibility. A good deal of the social research in education during this era was directed toward analysing the factors contributing to (or impeding) an improved quality of home environment in relation to educational goals (Douglas, 1964; Douglas *et al.*, 1968; Kellmer Pringle *et al.*, 1966; Bernstein, 1963, 1971; Jackson and Marsden, 1962; Musgrove, 1964; Pines, 1969; Beck, 1968; Halsey *et al.*, 1962).

In the USA, as in England, recognition of the complexity of factors interacting with the influences exerted by the educational system has also played a part in thinking about what is expected of families and of parents. Moynihan, Coleman, and others have documented how gross environmental conditions of the north and south, urban and rural, black and white communities affects the patterns of achievement of children in schools, and therefore in society (Moynihan, 1969; Coleman, 1966). Both in the USA and in Britain, compensatory education programmes, positive discrimination, educational priority programmes, etc., have approached the issue of what is expected of parents in different ways: ranging from ignoring parents as necessary evils for which schools must work overhard to compensate, to attempting to see the educational process as a family process and working with people in their diverse social settings to facilitate the development of each child.

In education the 'deschooling' movement also had implications for parents and parenthood as well as for schools, their teachers and pupils. Illich's challenge that schools are failing to fulfil their original intention because of their large size, and rigidities of bureaucratization was an important contribution which has given rise to a reformist social movement (Illich, 1971; Lister, 1974). Coleman's paper 'The Children have Outgrown the Schools' (1972) has added another important impetus to the idea that more and bigger of the same will not be the solution. There are implications for parents of the notion that we live in an 'information rich' society. Because of mass media and the rising levels of general education, schools are seen as boring and irrelevant to many adolescents but they are also engaged in work that is out of the grasp of most parents, even well-educated ones. This is not only a problem for working-class youth who must look forward to manual jobs and therefore cannot see the relevance of parsing verbs, but to middle-class youth as well. In a series of studies, Mary Engel and her colleagues have produced data that argues that children are put into a prolonged state of uselessness – both at home and at school – because of outmoded ideas and ideals. Conforming may produce demoralization and alienation, whereas work, particularly work of a socially useful kind, may not only provide community service, but also contribute to the personal development of the child (Coleman, 1972; Engel *et al.*, 1967, 1968, 1971).

What are the implications of all this for parents?

First, the contemporary movement toward equality of education between men and women is to some extent being related by educators to changes in expectations of parenting. Boys and girls are both being prepared for occupational as well as familial roles.

Second, there is a growing movement to make education a life-long process, allowing for changing expectations of parenting. Parents, like their children, are increasingly able to benefit from a society that is flexible in the promotion of 'permanent' and recurrent education, not necessarily confined to formal institutions. The newer movement acknowledges the many forces involved in educating – such as the media, the neighbourhood, the schools, the workplace, friends and helpers – rather than restricting all efforts in this direction to one or two arenas or to specialists only. Parents are also involved in the educational process as educators (Leichter, 1974) and as learners. In this context, parents are expected to participate in the process of their children's development, but not to be the exclusive arbiters of their child's fate. This gives them more leeway to examine and respond to yearnings of their own, without feeling selfish or irresponsible.

Summary and discussion

In this chapter we have tried to indicate how a widely prevalent set of authoritative opinions emerged in recent decades across various fields and disciplines. The choice of materials was selective with no claim to be presenting a comprehensive analysis of the fields, but rather to present work of authorities known to be influential in the lives of ordinary people in forming their expectations about parenthood. While there is no 'hard' evidence that the authorities described were more influential than some of the less academically 'respectable' media writers, e.g. in the advice columns of newspapers and magazines and in the paperback presses, we suggest that they were very widely influential *indirectly* as well as directly, a suggestion that obviously merits further investigation.

By and large, the picture that has emerged is one in which there was an authoritative set of formulations in the period following the Second World War that idealized a conception of the nuclear conjugal family, with relatively standardized composition, division of labour and life-cycle timetable. This conception, with its expectation that 'normal', 'mature' men will be economic providers, 'normal', 'mature' women will be housewives and mothers – has been bolstered by clinical psychiatry (as in the work of Bowlby and Winnicott), medicine (as in the early work of Spock), sociology (as in the work of Parsons) and by professionals in law, education and social work. The conception has been rationalized as 'natural' in the sense of biologically determined, universal amongst human societies and therefore reflecting a human imperative, adapted to our own society and therefore 'functional'.

In the current decade this model of family life has been increasingly questioned within each of the disciplines. The contemporary predicament of the family – for parents as well as the authorities who seek to guide them – involves searching for new models. The issues that are important today are important because of what has gone before. They require highlighting as issues both for seeking new knowledge through research and for suggesting ways of looking at existing (controversial, continually changing) authoritative information. The issues are: How to acknowledge variation and diversity without chaos and confusion? How to emphasize development through the life cycle and a continuous requirement to adapt, change and create without placing excessive burdens on families? How to handle the problems of sex-role definition? And how to define the optimal relationships between domestic life and work and the life of the occupational world outside the home?

3

Diversity of modern parental situations

It is often assumed in both professional and academic arenas that there exists a normal, average or model sort of family. This norm is usually held to consist of a 'nuclear' family unit comprising the two natural parents and their respective legitimate child or children living together in their own home. Not only is this image of the family held to be normal in a statistical sense, but also in terms of its social and cultural desirability.

The Skolnicks (1974) summarize the main assumptions underlying the prevailing idealized model of the nuclear family:

1) The nuclear family – a man, a woman, and their children – is universally found in every human society, past, present and future.
2) The nuclear family is the foundation of society, the key institution guaranteeing the survival and stability of the whole society.
3) The nuclear family is the building block, or elementary unit of society. Larger units – the extended family, the clan, the society – are combinations of nuclear families.
4) The nuclear family is based on a clear-cut, biologically structured division of labour between men and women with the man playing the 'instrumental' role of breadwinner, provider and protector, and the woman playing the 'expressive' role of housekeeper and emotional mainstay.
5) A major 'function' of the family is to socialize children, that is to tame their impulses and instil values, skills, and desires necessary to run the society. Without the nuclear family, the adequate socialization of human beings is impossible.
6) Other family structures, such as mother and children, or the experimental commune, are regarded as deviant by the participants, as well as the rest of society, and are fundamentally unstable and unworkable (Skolnick and Skolnick, 1974, pp. 7–8).

The Skolnicks suggest that 'The problem with the nuclear family model is intellectual: it influences thinking in certain directions or,

more precisely, it impedes us from considering alternative interpretations'. Advocates of this model promote not merely a view of how
families *are* organized but also a more or less rigid set of attitudes
about what the function and role of parents *should* be.

Cogswell notes another problem, closer to our focal concern in this
book:

> Although all cultures and societies hold idealistic models and cultural
> beliefs which misrepresent daily life, . . . this myth [of the idealized
> nuclear family which serves as a standard] leads professionals such
> as marriage counsellors, social workers, family physicians, clergy
> and teachers, who are sanctioned by society to manipulate the lives
> of individuals, to direct their clients, patients, and students toward
> unreality or toward passive acceptance of their failures in familial
> relationships (Cogswell, 1975, p. 393).

Dennis Marsden (1969) describes a situation which illustrates this
point. Discussing the difficulties encountered by one-parent families,
he notes that:

> There have always been covert or overt fears that to provide adequate
> financial support for women to live apart from their husbands, or to
> maintain illegitimate children, would effectively condone im-
> morality or blameworthy behaviour in marriage, and so erode
> marriage as an institution (Marsden, 1969, p. 311).

He points out that as a result of this fear, one-parent families have
been classified by both the law and the social services strictly according
to their marital status – that is as widowed, separated, divorced or
unmarried. Benefits have then been accorded to these families not on
the grounds of their social and personal needs, but in terms of the
degree to which their particular marital status accords with the socially
approved norms of parenthood and marriage. Widowhood is the most
acceptable because it is most consistent with the norm, for as Marsden
says:

> Widowhood cannot be seen as constituting a threat to the institution
> of marriage, and while widows may be pitied or even shunned, it is
> patently to the encouragement of child-bearing in wedlock that the
> financial risks of widowed mothers should be reduced (Marsden,
> 1969, p. 312).

For similar reasons unmarried mothers have been at the bottom of
the scale in terms of entitlement to benefits. To have placed them
anywhere else might have been seen as encouraging a situation which
runs counter to the norms that Western societies have tried to maintain. From this perspective any motherless or fatherless family is

'incomplete' by definition, and any working mother with a small child may be regarded with suspicion and disapproval since she is not fulfilling the role that a 'good' mother should fulfil. Characteristically she has been seen as 'selfish', 'non-maternal' or neurotic.

As with other aspects of the conventional paradigm of family life, there is an element of truth in the notion that deviation from the norm is associated with pathologies of one kind or another. For example, statistically speaking single-parent families tend to be poor families, and poor families tend to suffer the ills of deprivation and to generate social problem behaviour.

But this is a statistical tendency and is not adequate in considering particular cases. There are recognizable sub-groups: some mothers may choose to live without a partner and be able to derive satisfactions and provide a suitable environment for the child's development without marrying; others have 'unplanned' babies which are resented, dis-cordant relations with the other parent, and economic deprivation. In addition, it is important to recognize that statistical tendencies change. While there have always been a proportion of marriages in our society which have occurred after conception, recent reports from most of the advanced industrial societies indicate that this proportion is now very high, and probably increasing. Recent Swedish data indicate that about 10 per cent of heads of household are couples living together without the formality of marriage, and Linner (1967) estimated that one third to one half of Swedish brides are pregnant on their wedding day.

There are many other indications that there are changes under way that make the gap between the myth of the idealized nuclear family and the reality even more apparent. It is difficult to present an accurate picture of the actual percentage distribution of various family types when many of the statistics available are estimates and when so many categories used in reporting population characteristics overlap. Despite such difficulties, Cogswell and Sussman have estimated of the per-centage distribution of the United States population living in various family structures. Their estimate is based on a review of United States census data for 1970 on work-force participation, divorce, marriage, remarriage and separation. They arrive at the picture shown in Table 1 (Cogswell and Sussman, 1972, p. 139). This means that only 44 per cent of families in the USA correspond to the model of the nuclear unit with children which has been widely regarded as normal. Fifty-six per cent of families come under other classifications. More-over, we assume that the figure of 44 per cent includes the families of children who are adopted and fostered; arguably they also are a variant situation. If one supposes that many unmarried couples describe themselves as married in response to census questionnaires, the 44 per cent may be still further inflated at the expense of the totals in

Table 1 *Family types, USA, 1970*

Family type	% distribution
Nuclear family (with children)	
single work	30
dual work	14
Nuclear dyad (without children)	
single work	4
dual work	11
Single parent	13
Reconstituted (remarried nuclear)	15
Other traditional	
e.g. three generational, bilateral or extended kin	5
'Experimental' marriages and families	
(including unmarried couple and child)	8

the 'experimental' category. Also to be considered are families with handicapped and exceptional children, and families with mentally ill or retarded parents, two of the many sub-groups of which this table makes no mention.

Judging by the statistics so far presented from the British censuses, the number of variant families in Britain is smaller than that calculated by Sussman for the USA. Nevertheless, it is unquestionably large enough to challenge the validity of traditional assumptions about family organization and structure. What is more, there is strong evidence to suggest that variations of the sort described are becoming increasingly common in Britain. We can document the trend toward diversity by examining some of the component processes that have produced the contemporary pattern. We shall indicate some of the ways in which the trends observed are similar in Britain to those documented for the USA, and, indeed, for the more developed industrial nations generally. This has produced a situation described by Cogswell as a *hiatus* in social change, where 'the nuclear family myth is untenable for many, yet new myths have not developed to the point where they can serve as definitive guidelines' (Cogswell, 1975, p. 406).

Divorce

Divorce is a good example of what we are talking about. Until recently the law has required that guilt be apportioned to the marital partner most responsible for the breaking up of the marriage so that social entitlements be accorded to the 'injured' partner and withheld from the 'guilty' one. This exemplified the tendency for behaviour which threatened the institution of marriage to be punished, and the intact nuclear unit to be reinforced as *the* socially approved family structure. Nevertheless, the divorce rate in the years between 1960 and 1972 rose as shown in Table 2. As we noted above the laws governing the mechan-

Table 2 *Divorce rates per 1,000 married population, England and Wales, 1960–72.*

Year	Divorce rate
1960	2·0
1961	2·1
1962	2·4
1963	2·7
1964	2·9
1965	3·1
1966	3·2
1967	3·5
1968	3·7
1969	4·1
1970	4·7
1971	6·0
1972	9·5

Source: Registrar General's statistics.

isms and definitions associated with divorce have followed the facts. American statistics show a similar, if amplified trend over the same period, with a rise in the rate per 1,000 married women in 1963 of 9·6 to one of 18·2 in 1972–3 (United States National Center for Health Statistics, 1973).

In both countries, the incidence of remarriage has increased correspondingly, indicating that marriage and family life are less in question than the idealized assumption of life-long monogamy. Glick and Norton (1973) have documented this for the USA; they raise the question of whether the re-marriage phenomenon is linked to a particular cohort of individuals who were born in the disturbed years of the Second World War, or reflects a more fundamental trend.

In the United Kingdom there has also been an increase in the proportion of dissolved marriages with children – from 68·3 per cent in 1961 to 74·1 per cent in 1972 (*Social Trends*, No. 5, 1974). Plateris (1967) documents the same trend in the USA.

According to the United Nations Demographic Yearbook (1968 and 1971), the USA is classed among the highest group of countries for divorce rates (along with the USSR, Hungary, Egypt and Denmark). Britain is classed with the second group, along with East Germany, Czechoslovakia, Sweden and Austria. Countries with the lowest rates are Portugal, Venezuela, Canada and Mexico.

Extrapolating from this trend, it may indeed be 'realistic' to think in the terms suggested by Margaret Mead:

> If we could rephrase divorce as a necessary component of relationships between the sexes in a society as complex, as heterogeneous and as rapidly changing and with as long-lived a population as ours, we could then consider how to have good and appropriate divorces. As things are, we insist that the most flimsy, ill-conceived, and unsuitable mating be treated as a sanctified, life-long choice. At the same time, we insist that every divorce, however much it is dictated by every consideration of the welfare of the children and parents, be regarded as a failure and be listed as an index of social disorder – along with suicide, homicide, narcotic addiction, alcoholism and crime (Mead, 1971, p. 124).

Divorce statistics underscore another point. Divorce does not occur randomly throughout the life spans of the families affected, but is more prevalent in the early stages of family life:

> The official statistics contain three types of information bearing on the family life cycle, and these relate to age at divorce, legal duration of marriage and fertility (used here in the English demographic meaning of reproduction performance rather than reproductive potential). All three . . . concur in the indication they give, which is that in England divorce is more strongly associated with the earlier rather than the later stages of the family life cycle (Chester, 1973, p. 14).

Chester distinguishes between *de facto* and *de jure* duration of marriages, the latter being reflected in official statistics and lagging an average of 4·6 years behind the former. Official statistics therefore tend to distort the picture of family break-up in relation to family life cycle:

> De facto duration thus places divorcing couples much more strikingly in these earlier stages of the cycle, and indeed, detailed inspection shows the peak of breaking up in the third year of marriage, with the most hazardous years running from the first to the fourth wedding anniversaries (Chester, 1973, p. 12).

The concentration of marital break-up in the early stages of the family cycle, suggests that the reconstituted family type and the particular issues of stepparenting will predominate in mid-life. Similar findings relate to other changes in marital and parental status. The figures on single parents and on widows, for example, indicate that other structural situations also tend to occur at specific life cycle stages.

Nevertheless, it is likely that the characteristic issues associated with divorce will differ according to life-cycle stage. Also, there is greater sub-cultural heterogeneity than implied in Margaret Mead's statement, which derives part of its power from a caricature quality. As Dominian (1969) has shown, marital dissolution is a process that has different forms and meanings according to a person's situation. Chester has noted, citing Goode, that marriage breakdown is a wider concept than dissolution. Two forms of breakdown are conspicuous:

> (a) 'Empty shell' marriages, where cohabitation persists but with little meaning for the partners and with minimal or negative mutual affective support. Marriages, that is, which are socially and legally existent but so marked by disharmony or indifference that they must be counted as broken down.
> (b) Willed terminations, either mutual or through unilateral volition, via divorce, annulment, separation or desertion. Marriages, that is, which have broken up as well as broken down, whether or not the social nexus is intact (Quoted by Chester, 1972, p. 1).

Therefore: 'Divorce is but one course of action open to those whose marriages fail, and it is not known how far divorce statistics may serve as an index of marital disruption' (Chester, 1972, p. 1). Chester also notes that there is a significant difference between the number of *de facto* separations and the number of *de jure* separations, though it is unclear what the implications of this are for the quality of family life. But it is clear that available figures on divorce represent the tip of the iceberg in terms of the overall amount of breakdown, and of disruption in marriage. Similarly, the available statistics on household composition probably represent the tip of the iceberg in terms of the overall amount of variation in intimate living relationships.

Infertile and childless marriages

Another variation on the conventional nuclear family model consists in those families who are either voluntarily or involuntarily childless. There appear to be no reliable statistics on the number of marriages which are infertile because the couple are unable to produce children as opposed to those who are unwilling to do so. The statistics produced by the Office of Population Censuses and Surveys do not distinguish between the two. Robert Newill, a physician who specializes in artificial insemination, claims that: 'It is difficult to decide on the exact number of marriages which are involuntarily childless, because nobody has ever followed up a large number of marriages to see how many fail to

produce a child when wanted' (Newill, 1974, p. 13). He estimates, however, that about 40,000 new cases of infertility occur in Britain each year,
and goes on to point out that:

> It is generally accepted in medical circles that in Western Europe
> at the present time, about 10 per cent of all married couples are
> unable to start their family. The percentage is higher if we include
> cases of secondary infertility, i.e. couples who have one child but
> cannot conceive a second (Newill, 1974, p. 13).

Table 3 shows infertility amongst all women married once only,
regardless of their potential for child-bearing, for England and Wales.

Table 3 *Infertility amongst women married once only, England and Wales*

		3	5	10	20
		Duration of marriage (Percentage of first marriages childless, women under 45) Number of years married			
	1951	38	26	16	13
Calendar	1956	34	22	12	—
year of	1961	31	19	11	—
marriage	1966	33	20	—	—
	1969	39	—	—	—

Based on *Social Trends*, 1974

This table shows that there has been a relatively small range of variation
in proportions of childless marriages within the first three years of
marriage. From 38 per cent in 1951, the proportions dipped to a low
of 31 per cent in 1961, rising again to a comparable proportion of 39 per
cent in 1969. In so far as we have statistics on marriages of longer
duration, it seems that the proportions childless after five years of
marriage have dropped; and this tendency is even more marked for
marriages lasting ten or more years. But this does not necessarily mean
that more women have decided to have children. It may reflect advances
in medical treatment of infertility and in the wider availability of such
treatment. Also it may be affected by the trend towards marrying at
a younger age. The average marrying age for spinsters decreased by
two years between 1951 and 1961 and this would account for some
increase in fertility potential amongst married women.

Some people profess a desire for a child and seem to have no physical
obstacles to their reproductive potential, but remain inexplicably

infertile to the puzzlement of their doctors. The GAP Committee suggest that psychological factors may be at play:

> When all the medical procedures and examinations are futile, still another self-doubt may be raised. Could the fact of non-fertility have a psychological basis? Does one really want children? A physician might raise this question out of his own frustration and despair because his efforts have failed to result in pregnancy or to provide a definite answer on the cause of infertility. The question is not an idle one. For everyone, natural and adoptive parents alike, must face the ambivalent feelings inherent in becoming a parent (GAP, 1973, p. 82).

Whether or not psychological factors are involved for some, others make a clear-cut decision, and consciously and deliberately opt against having children. This is the stated aim of the National Organisation of Non-Parents (NON), which was started in the USA by Ellen Peck. In *The Baby Trap*, Peck (1975) attacks the assumption that a married couple must inevitably want to produce children unless there is something wrong with them. Instead, she argues, childbirth is a choice representing one amongst a number of potentially conflicting values in an adult's life. She makes out a case for not having children on the grounds that greater personal happiness and fulfilment are possible for the voluntarily childless couple than for the couple whose lives are 'restricted' and 'impoverished' by the obligations and expectations demanded of them as parents. In recent years there has been an increasing acceptance of this point of view as legitimate. Issues people face in whether to parent or not are taken up again in Chapter 4.

One-parent families

Another contribution to the trend toward diversity of family household types is the increase in the number and magnitude of forces making for single parenting in our society. Though statistics here, as in the other cases, are not always as illuminating as might be desired, it is possible to develop a picture based on them. The Finer Committee indicated some of the problems.

> Census methodology is unsatisfactory for identifying unmarried mothers living with their children. Where such a mother is head of a household the census procedure correctly identifies a family headed by a single woman. But if an unmarried mother lives in a household headed by her own parent(s) both she and her child(ren) will be treated as children in a family headed by her father or mother. Both the 1966 and 1971 census analyses understate the probable

number of unmarried mothers; the figure is clearly too low as it is exceeded in both years by the number of unmarried mothers in receipt of supplementary benefit (Finer Report, 1974, vol. 2, p. 79).

Administrative procedures of this sort tend to cause error in other statistics too; the number of widows with dependent children, for example, tends to be misleadingly high because it is the more socially acceptable category amongst one-parent families. The 1971 census produced a figure of 49,000 single mothers with dependent children, whereas no less than 61,000 such mothers were receiving supplementary benefit at the end of 1971. Because of such errors the Finer Committee made an estimate of the number of one-parent families with dependent children based on the 1971 census but adjusted in the light of supplementary benefit and national insurance statistics and in the light of data derived from the General Household Survey. The result is perhaps the most accurate figure available at present, and the complete table is reproduced here (Table 4).

Table 4 *Estimate of number of one-parent families with dependent children resulting from illegitimacy, factual separation, death and divorce: Great Britain 1971*

Parent	Number of families	Number of children
Female		
single	90,000	120,000
married (separated)	190,000	360,000
widowed	120,000	200,000
divorced	120,000	240,000
Sub-total	520,000	920,000
Male	100,000	160,000
Total	620,000	1,080,000

Source: Finer Report, 1974, vol. 2, p. 82.

Finer points out that nearly one tenth of all families with dependent children have only one parent, i.e. some 620,000 families affecting just over a million children. Of these, some 400,000 lone mothers are immediately responsible for 720,000 children whose fathers are alive but not living with the family. Some 100,000 families (i.e. 16 per cent of all single-parent families) are estimated to be male-headed. The US census material for 1970 has been analysed by Pleck to show a similar

proportion of male-headed single parent families (US 1970 Census of
Population, vol. 1, pt 1, Table 206, pp. 1–658). Out of a total of 3,690
single-parent families, 579,000 (i.e. 16 per cent) were estimated to be
male-headed. Analysing single parent families from the sample of
the British Child Development Study, Ferri (1976) points out that the
proportion of fatherless and motherless families varies according to the
age of the child: 'Fatherless children outnumbered those who had lost
their mother by approximately six to one at the age of seven, and four
and a half to one at eleven years' (Ferri, 1976, p. 38).

Single parents are less likely to have large families than are other
parents. According to the General Household Survey in Britain (1973,
p. 72) most married couples have more than one child, whereas most
lone parents have only one. It is helpful not to think of single parenthood in static terms, for many of these parents remarry at a later date,
and many families enumerated as intact have members who may have
been at some stage in single-parent families. This fact is substantiated
by comparing the overall divorce rates and the overall illegitimacy rates
with the respective categories of divorced and single one-parent
families. The Office of Population Census's figures on illegitimacy, for
example (Abstract of Statistics, 1973), show that in the year 1971,
8·2 per cent of all births in the United Kingdom, or 74,000 children,
were illegitimate, and in the same period the Civil Judicial Statistics
(1972) report that there were 110,895 petitions for divorce of which
some 80,000 came from families in which there was one child or more
(though it should be remembered that this is slightly higher than the
number of divorces granted). Both of these annual figures, however,
represent over one third of the total number of families in the equivalent
category of one-parent families, and this indicates that a significant
proportion of single parents change their marital status within a
relatively short time. Indeed the annual abstract of statistics (1973)
shows that about two thirds of all divorced persons marry again, the
proportion of women being slightly lower than men (Table 5). (The

Table 5 *Divorced persons who entered a second marriage in the decade
1962–71, England and Wales*

	Number	%
Divorced men remarrying	283,397	64
Divorced women remarrying	267,990	60
All divorced persons remarrying	551,387	62

Source: Finer Report, DHSS, 1974, p. 52.

number of divorces doubled between 1968 and 1971 as a result of the Divorce Reform Act 1969 which enabled a huge 'backlog' of divorces to be effected. This table therefore understates the proportion of divorced persons who will enter a second marriage because a disproportionately large number of divorces occurred in 1971.)

In line with this, Finer concluded that 'a significant proportion' of children who are born illegitimate eventually become members of a two-parent family, those who remain dependent on their unmarried mothers being a 'small proportion of the total, even though this total at any one time will in absolute numbers be high'.

Official figures on one-parent families do not take into account those families where the job of one of the parents requires a long absence from the family. The demands of such jobs on family members, however, impose structural arrangements and rearrangements which are in many ways similar to those imposed by the death or divorce of a parent. Seamen, entertainers, members of the forces and businessmen may all be required to undertake prolonged periods of travel, leaving their wives or husbands in the position of single parents while they are away. The GAP Committee list this as one of the three major causes of separation in a family, along with death and divorce (GAP, 1973, p. 106).

Whatever the reason for separation, single-parent families are in a structurally different situation from that of two-parent families, and this difference is itself a modifying influence on both the needs and obligations of the parent. One of the most important requirements of many single parents, according to the GAP Committee, is for the parent to achieve a separation on a psychological plane as well as the purely physical one. The authors point out that:

The fact that parents are separated by divorce or death does not necessarily mean that they have psychologically separated. Feelings of anger, remorse, guilt, retaliation, sorrow for oneself, and mixtures of both hatred and love can keep an emotional relationship going for long periods after the parents have ceased to live with each other. Feelings of being hurt or wanting to hurt the other may unconsciously persist. Inability to get the other person out of one's thoughts is also evidence that psychological separation has not yet taken place (GAP, 1973, p. 106).

The GAP Committee believe that the single parent is in need of achieving this psychological separation by experiencing grief or mourning or by otherwise resolving and facing his/her true feelings about himself. Single parents, almost by definition, are less able to share the burdensome tasks of child-rearing and housekeeping with somebody else in the way that is open to two-parent families. The burden of this task can lead to feelings of helplessness and distress. The sheer practical difficulty of coping with the child single-handed, coupled with the possibility of persistent and unresolved feelings about the absent father or mother, lies at the root of social isolation and loneliness which the GAP Committee indicate as another major problem for many single parents.

In an analysis of data from the National Child Development Study in respect of single-parent families, Elsa Ferri (1976) confirmed what Finer and others had found: that single-parent families are on the whole at a distinct disadvantage in terms of material well-being and living standard. She found, moreover, that the sex of the absent parent is 'of crucial importance . . . in assessing the extent of material disadvantage suffered by children in one parent families' (Ferri, 1976, p. 146). The results of her analysis showed that 'overall, children in one-parent families had a lower level of attainment in school and were less well adjusted than their peers from unbroken homes.' She goes on to point out, however, that:

> Wherever adverse effects were found to be associated with the absence of a parent the actual differences between the children concerned and those in two-parent families were quite small. In fact the influence of the family situation itself was much weaker than that of other factors such as low social class, large family size, and limited parental aspirations (Ferri, 1976, p. 148).

Ferri's analysis showed few adverse effects on fatherless children due to their family situation as such. The absence of a mother, regardless of the reason for her absence, was shown to have a more marked adverse effect on the children's development. However, Ferri points out that:

> It would be rash perhaps to interpret this as conclusive evidence of the relative unimportance of the mother-child relationship, particularly in a social context in which fathers, whether lone parents or not, are increasingly taking on aspects of a role which was formerly confined to the mother. While the role itself may well be crucial to the child's welfare and development, it is perhaps also true that the mother is not necessarily the only person who can adequately fulfil it (Ferri, 1976, pp. 147–8).

In an American study at Harvard's Laboratory of Community Psychiatry, Glick, Weiss and Parkes (1974) contribute some further insights to our understanding of the process underlying the production of single-parent families *vs* remarriages following bereavement. Earlier studies had indicated that bereaved individuals were less likely to remarry than divorced ones, but more likely to remarry than never-married individuals. Landis (1950) demonstrated that in the 1940s in America, a divorcee's chances of remarriage were better than 50 per cent until she was 45, whereas for widows the turning-point was 33, and for spinsters, 20. In both Britain and the USA, it was demonstrated by Glick (1957) that male chances of remarrying were greater during the first few years after divorce than females'. Some of the factors contributing to remarriage were described by Goode (1956), and against remarriage, by Bernard (1956). These were largely on the level of cultural norms and social pressures of various kinds. Glick, Weiss and Parkes also found that by approaching bereavement as a critical transition they were able to make sense of another major source of differentiation in their sample – namely, the difference between those who lost their spouses unexpectedly and who were therefore unable to prepare themselves for a transition in advance, and those who had some advance warning. The latter sub-group were found on follow-up to be much more likely to be planning remarriage.

These studies highlight the complexity and internal differentiation associated with parenting situations even within a variant pattern such as that of single-parent families. Similar complexities are revealed in considering other categories associated with family diversity.

Adoption and fostering

Another 'variant' parenting situation occurs when a child is adopted by, or fostered out to, 'parents' who are not the child's 'own' biological parents. Research on adoption in the USA, Canada and Great Britain between 1948 and 1965 has been reviewed by Kellmer Pringle (1966). There appear to be very inadequate statistics in the field of adoption and fostering generally; however, we know that the number of illegitimate children adopted into two-parent families in Great Britain in 1971 was 16,372 (Finer Report, 1974, vol. 1, p. 41), a rate of one in every 4·4 illegitimate children. Clearly not all adopted children are illegitimate and the overall number of adopted children would therefore be higher than this.

It is reasonable to ask why adoption should be seen as a structural variation in a family when the 'essential components' of two parents and a child or children are all present in the adoptive family. The answer, as in certain other variant situations, relates to the quality of parental experience rather than the formal components of the family, and in fact the essential difference between adoptive parents and other parents may be said to lie in the need of the former to reconcile the difference between the biological and social parentage of their child.

People adopt for a variety of reasons and their experience of parenthood will vary depending on the reason involved. Sometimes fertile couples adopt children, and some couples only succeed in conceiving *after* they have adopted a child. Many adoptions – about one half of all adoptions in Britain and the USA – are adoptions by stepparents and other relatives (Maddox, 1975, pp. 13–17). Stepparenting is itself a major form of structural variation: at the end of this chapter it will be examined in some depth as one of the two extended examples of variant parenting situations.

According to the GAP Committee, infertility in one or both of the parents is another major reason for adopting (GAP, 1973, p. 81). The adoptive parents in this situation will already have gone through many distressing experiences and the decision to adopt will usually involve a fundamental change of expectations in their approach to parenthood. Giving birth to any child involves a revision of expectations in the event of circumstances which cannot be foreseen. We shall see in the review of families with a handicapped child later in this chapter that under certain circumstances the discrepancy between expectation and reality can be distressingly large. The same is true, though in a different way, for couples who find they are infertile. Becoming a parent by adoption under such circumstances involves feelings which are more than usually ambivalent. The very act involves changing one's image of oneself from a person who is fertile to one who is not – a process which can be extremely painful and which can, as the GAP Committee point out, lead to a lowering of one's self-esteem.

Many variant parenting situations involve an intensification of feelings and difficulties which occur to some extent in all families. This is true for adoption, according to the GAP Committee, in respect of the desire to be an adequate parent. The intensified desire to be a successful parent can lead the adoptive parent to a false feeling of failure if the child continues to keep alive his image of the natural parents. But they point out that most children who are adopted over the age of two will do this anyway, and one of the major tasks of the adoptive parents is to help the child to accept the fact that he has had another set of parents. The problem varies, they write, 'depending on the age at which children are adopted and the age at which children are told' (GAP, 1973, p. 85). The generic problem, for both the parent and the child, is to reconcile the discrepancy between the biological and the social parentage of their child.

Communes and experimental living

Another form of family structure which affects parenting is to be found in communes, group marriages and other experimental forms of living. In general communal living is a pattern with great historical depth and current communal living arrangements are in many cases rooted in the past (Kanter, 1973). They may have religious ideologies, such as the Amish and other nineteenth-century sects; or political ideologies, as with the kibbutz movement or the Chinese collectives; or, they may be based on a theory of social psychological development and self-actualization as in the Walden Two experiments. They may be urban or rural (Berger *et al.*, 1972), and there may be a range of attitudes about division of labour, sexuality and sex-roles, children and child-rearing philosophies and about conditions governing inclusion or exclusion of non-members.

Cogswell and Sussman (1972) estimate that communal living arrangements accounted for 6 per cent of all family types in the USA in 1970. Comparable figures for Britain are not available. It is known that shared facilities or arrangements where two or more couples share a house or services are very common. Pawley (1971) holds that, 'In most of the urban centres of the West, shared dwellings *are the norm* – whether housing authorities like to admit it or not.' And indeed, between the 1961 and 1966 censuses, 19 of the 31 London boroughs showed an *increase* greater than 20 per cent in the number of households sharing kitchens or bathrooms. In, for instance, the London Borough of Islington in 1966, 57 per cent of households shared such facilities. But little is known about the prevalence of more intimate arrangements such as group marriages described by Ramey (1972) or Constantine and Constantine (1976) where three or more people each regard themselves as married to at least two or more others, children as well as possessions being shared by the whole group.

Involuntarily shared facilities may or may not give rise to an enduring structural variation in family life, but there can be no doubt that interest in communal living as a preferred life-style has increased rapidly in the past decade. In Britain the Commune Movement, for example, had a membership of over 300 groups in 1971 and the journal *Communes* had a bi-monthly subscription of just under 3,000 (Gorman, 1972). Many communes tend to be independent and self-sufficient in nature, therefore the numbers involved in organized 'movements' of this sort are probably a considerable understatement of the numbers involved overall.

Rigby (1974), a sociologist who made a study of British communes, describes the British Commune Movement as an attempt to create a federal society of communes in which people are free to do as they wish providing they do not transgress the freedom of others. He distinguishes between different sorts of intention underlying the formation and running of various communes, and describes six main types of commune operating in Britain, although communes do not always fit neatly into any one type: self-actualizing communes in which members attempt to discover themselves and develop their creative powers; communes for mutual support in which a sense of brotherhood is highly valued;

activist communes which are viewed by members as a base for involvement in social and political action; practical communes which are
defined by members in terms of economic and practical material
advantage; therapeutic communes which have the prime purpose of
therapy or preparing members for a more rewarding life; religious
communes which are viewed as fulfilling some purpose in accord with
the religious beliefs of members.

Rigby's approach was to 'put himself in the place of the actor', to
try to understand the communard by defining the world as seen and
defined by communards themselves. From this perspective he described
the members of communes as being commonly in search of an 'alternate
life-style' based on 'counter-definitions of reality' from those generally
prevailing in the culture. He identifies feelings of alienation, disillusion
and dissatisfaction with the prevailing social structure amongst many
communards, and argues that:

> What has rendered increasing numbers of middle-class youth
> available for recruitment to the commune movement has been their
> experience of what Klipp has termed the problem of personal
> identity, 'an inability to define oneself successfully, a milieu of
> inadequate symbolism': a situation experienced by the people as a
> consequence of such forces as the high rate of technologically
> induced social change and the loss of traditional sources of personal
> identity and self affirmation that has accompanied the development
> of large-scale, hierarchically organised institutions of economic,
> political and social life (Rigby, 1974, pp. 5–6).

One feature of contemporary society that many communards reject is
the nuclear family. Roberts (1971), in his book on American communes,
highlights the communards' search for a greater sense of fulfilment than
the traditional two-parent family affords. The communal family, like
the family of the voluntarily childless couple and that of the adoptive
parent (though for very different reasons and in very different ways)
is often a deliberately chosen variation on the traditional nuclear
model; the choice may express dissatisfaction with the overall social
structure as well as conventional family life. 'Young people in America
are attempting to create an alternative society', says Roberts. Their
aim is akin to Thoreau's advice: 'simplify, simplify':

> To simplify human relations, to make them more satisfying, great
> numbers of the young have rejected technological solutions to their
> problems. They have almost casually rejected the eternal optimism
> of liberalism along with the sterile conformism of current day
> conservatism. In a word many of the young wish to be 'retribalized'.
> They wish to be rid of the neurotic attention given to economics
> and property in modern America (Roberts, 1971, p. 1).

In attempting to achieve such goals the communard creates a new type of family which provides a very different setting for the tasks of parenthood from that of the two-parent family. 'The nuclear family cannot in many cases bear the brunt of the emotional demands of its members', writes Roberts. And members of the Reba Place commune declare that:

> The individual family was never meant to carry the load it is now trying to carry. The small family of mother, father, and children needs a larger supportive context. It thrives best in the give and take of a closely knit community of families (Roberts, 1971, p. 68).

Many communards share such a perspective and some experiment with new forms of family structure such as the group marriage in an attempt to find more satisfying relationships within the family group. Rigby argues that:

> whether group marriage is favoured or not there is fairly common agreement among many commune members that the nuclear family system is not the only natural way of organising social life, and that in its present enclosed and isolated form such a system only serves to separate people from each other rather than promote caring relationships between them (Rigby, 1974, p. 269).

One commune member is quoted as follows:

> The nuclear family is a repressive and horrible institution. It makes you realise how cruel two people can be to each other . . . where there are only two people, then misunderstandings can arise, you only get a restricted view of each other – in a commune there are others there to give an 'objective' account of their perceptions, clear the air, and so enable you to become more fully aware of each other as humans, clear up the misconceptions that develop through distorted perceptions (Rigby, 1974, pp. 266–7).

Others, however, remain sceptical of the potential of communes to solve the problems manifested by the conventional family unit. Abrams and McCulloch's study of 64 British communes for example, contrasts strongly with Rigby's in its appraisal of communal life in this respect:

> where Rigby tends to be humanistic and hopeful about communes and sees them as having a serious revolutionary potential, our view is plainly more sceptical; we would tend to see them . . . as alternative *unrealities*. And in this respect it is particularly noteworthy that Rigby does not deal directly or in much substance with the issue of gender relationships in communes (Abrams and McCulloch, 1976, p. 151).

Like other researchers in this field Abrams and McCulloch report that,

'The most often recurring and most precisely expressed single aspect of the whole broad pattern of estrangement which we encountered was "disillusionment with the nuclear family", the "farce of the semi-detached existence" ' (Abrams and McCulloch, 1976, p. 124). But the authors found in the communes they visited that the ideal of creating a new sort of family structure was not generally realized in respect of gender roles and parent–child relationships:

> If domestic tasks are not to be attached to types of people, it is not enough to free domestic relationships from the external–internal division of labour and the sweeping dominance of outside work-relations: in addition, domestic skills and a belief in their intrinsic validity (for the self) must be dispersed. The crucial difficulty in this respect, and not just for communes, appears to be that of dispersing mothering (Abrams and McCulloch, 1976, pp. 135–6).

> [in the communes] motherhood remains an all-demanding and totally female role. The notion that communal relationships are intentional and sustained only on the condition that both parties find the necessary relationship gratifying, breaks down in the face of child rearing (Abrams and McCulloch, 1976, p. 144).

Although generally more optimistic about the potential of communes to create genuinely alternative modes of family relationship, Roberts (1971) also describes problems associated with communal living. He points out that although the commune may provide a wider range of emotional supports for parents and children alike, the sexual jealousies, lack of stability and impermanence of many of the American communes threaten to offset the advantages with a type of insecurity and tension that the more traditional family, for all its shortcomings, is largely able to avoid. Other sources of couple strain and problems of parenting are described by Kanter et al. (Kanter et al., 1975; Jaffe and Kanter, 1976). In a study of American communards Kanter identifies three major sources of couple strain in relation to parenting: diminished sovereignty over the household, the presence of an audience in parent–child interactions, and strong pressures for individuation and autonomy for both parents and children to an extent rarely found in the nuclear family (Kanter et al., 1975). Communards are likely to accept such difficulties, however, not as a sign of a failed utopia but as the inevitable price of an evolving, experimental approach to the development of a family life style which is better suited to meet their needs (Speck, 1972).

Dual-worker families

Another widespread assumption that masks diversity in family patterns is that husbands are the breadwinners and wives the helpmeets –

child-rearers, housekeepers and emotional mainstays of 'normal' families. Available data counters this assumption.

In Britain, the employment rates for married women rose from 21·7 per cent in 1951 to 42·2 per cent in 1971, as compared with a drop for married males over the same period from 87·6 per cent to 81·4 per cent. Amongst the married women, the most rapidly increasing sub-group were mothers of young children (Tizard *et al.*, 1976, p. 126). This is the sub-group for which working outside the home has, in the recent past, been most strongly proscribed. While there have always been some women who have had to work, and others who because of high qualifications and privileged position have been enabled to do so if they wished (Fogarty *et al.*, 1971), the range of women working outside the home is now so great that it is being normalized.

When wives and mothers work outside the home to any extent, there are bound to be repercussions in relation to family structure. Working wives control a greater proportion of the family's resources, they have demands made on their time outside the home which are comparable to those of their husbands; this affects both their own self-concepts and the character of their relationships within the family. Studies of different facets of this situation are now accumulating, and are adding to our information on variant family forms (Rapoport and Rapoport, 1971/76). The situation in which the wife is earning more than her husband is of interest in assessing the plasticity of conventional role definitions. Here, too, the pattern has historic roots. Hilary Land (1975) notes that early precursors of the pattern are seen not among the rich but among the poor. In the 1890s Booth (1902) noted that the wages of the wife and children frequently amounted to more than those of the head of the family. But these are vague and not strictly comparable situations. Nor is the situation of the female movie star who earned more than most ordinary male breadwinners could hope to do. Similarly, wartime experiences were anomalous. And, as Land points out, in the post-war era it was in the interests of reconstituting the decimated population that women's roles should be defined as primarily re-productive, so that Beveridge (1944) treated women as a *dependent* class for social security, making them rely on their husband's work record, a system which persists to the present.

Recently a question was raised in the British House of Commons about the proportions of families in Britain in which the wife in fact, and despite all these constraints, earns more than her husband. The Department of Employment has estimated this figure at 5 per cent. In the USA the proportions are still higher. Carter and Glick (1976) report that the proportion of wives in intact husband–wife families earning more than their husbands rose from 5·7 per cent in 1960 to 7·4 per cent in 1970.

In examining some of the major variations on the idealized family, we have looked briefly at one-parent families, families broken up by separation and divorce, childless families, adoptive families, foster families, experimental and communal family groups, and dual-worker families. There are other variations besides these.

Although the *extended family network*, for example, is often assumed to be defunct in modern industrial society, such kin relationships exist and may be very important even though people do not necessarily live under the same roof. Extended kin relations are particularly important in certain sections of the community. It is undoubtedly the prevalent form of family organization for the Asian and West Indian population in Britain, for example, and still provides the context in which parenting takes place for large sectors of the non-immigrant community.

In America, there have been a number of studies which have documented the continuing importance of the extended family in modern life, though it is variable both in degree of importance and in the way it functions as a familial resource (Litwak, 1960; Sussman and Burchinal, 1962).

In Britain a number of studies show a similar prevalence of extended family relationships, even in middle-class urban settings (Firth *et al.*, 1969). In more traditional and village settings, this has been still more heavily documented (Young and Willmott, 1957; Stacey, 1960; Frankenberg, 1957, 1966). There is no way of estimating the number of multi-generational households from current census material, but this too cannot be discounted as a significant structural form.

Returning to Sussman's estimates of the distribution of family types, we find that only about 30 per cent of all US families fall within the traditional model outlined at the beginning of this chapter, that is the model of the nuclear family unit with a child or children supported by one parent at work. Even within this category many variables affect the structure of any given family. The quality of life, the style of parenthood, the experience of childhood must be vastly different, for example, for the 350,000 families in England and Wales who own more than one home (Downing and Dower, 1972) than for the 32,000 families who are officially recorded as applying for temporary accommodation as a result of homelessness (*Social Trends*, No. 5, 1974). It must be different again for families with, say, six or more children as opposed to those with only one child, and also for families in which the parents married after, say, the age of 35 as opposed to those in which the parents married before the age of 20. In the latter case, for example, the occurrence of key events in the life cycle of the individual, such as the menopause or retirement, would coincide with a different stage of the family life cycle than they would for parents who married at a much earlier age.

The picture that emerges from this review of family structure in contemporary Britain is one of great diversity. There is a sense in which variation, either by chance or by choice, is now the norm. Attempts to isolate any single 'normal' or even 'mainstream' type of family are thwarted by a host of variables which cut across every apparent 'type'. Moreover, even if we subdivide each type in accordance with the cross-cutting variables, we end up with a distorted view. Many families undergo radical changes in structure in the course of their life cycle and do not fit neatly into the static categories we devise. If, for example, we construct an unlikely but not impossible hypothetical case of a mother with an illegitimate child who, for the sake of argument, lived alone for a while, then cohabited with a man, then married and formed a nuclear unit, then divorced and remarried a man who himself had children, we would confront a family which had passed through many different structural forms and many different parenting situations. At any particular time we could classify the structure of the family in which the mother and child were living, but a single structural classification would fail to take into account the overall history of change which had taken place.

Some of the implications for parents of changes such as these have already been touched on in this chapter, though necessarily only briefly. We now examine two important situations by way of an extended illustration of some of the issues we have dealt with. The two situations – stepfamilies and families with a handicapped child – will both be examined in some detail with the aim of identifying the constraints that are imposed on parents by the particular structural arrangements that the respective situations compel. Aside from identifying the specific issues posed for parents in these situations we use these 'case studies' to enhance our general appreciation of parents' needs.

Illustration A: Stepfamilies

The numbers of people involved in a stepparenting relationship is growing rapidly every year in line with increasing divorce rates, and this must now be regarded as a major structural variation for families in the Western world. According to the Finer report (vol. 1, p. 50), the proportion of married men in England and Wales aged 65 who currently have been married more than once is 12 per cent. In the USA in 1967 nearly a quarter of white brides and grooms had been married before. A large percentage of these second and subsequent marriages involve children from a previous marriage and in these cases one or both of the marital pair will fall into the ill-defined category of stepparent.

The stepparent relationship is ill-defined for a number of reasons. One of these, as Brenda Maddox (1975) points out, is that very little professional attention has been paid to it even though it has 'fascinated story-tellers, gossips and dramatists since antiquity'. The usual perspective on the stepparent has been through the eyes of the child and this has prompted a set of stereotyped ideas which have gone largely unchallenged until recently.

> No one identifies with the stepparent. The relationship is so stereotyped that even stepparents themselves are unsure what their real feelings are. They fumble along with mixed emotions of guilt, irritation, duty, affection, and sometimes love (Maddox, 1975, p. 1).

Maddox identifies two reasons why the stepparent has been relatively ignored by the law, psychiatry and social etiquette, all of which 'virtually pretend that there is no such thing'. The first reason is that stepparents are not easily identified and are not easily accessible in the way, for example, that adoptive parents or divorcees are accessible. When a home is 'broken', or when a couple want to adopt, the family is automatically opened to the intervention and intrusion of social agencies and the law. Stepfamilies on the other hand are the opposite of broken; they are re-made: 'A break has been healed, the doors are shut, and the world and the stepfamily itself want to believe that it is just another nuclear family out of the pages of Talcott Parsons or the *Ladies' Home Journal*' (Maddox, 1975, p. 3). The second reason why the stepparent has been ignored is that the stepparent–child relationship stirs up a great deal of pain. Maddox quotes a psychoanalyst as saying:

> People go into second marriages with enormous hopes. They have failed once, or they have had their marriages broken by death, and they want everything to go right the next time. They idealize the new partner and then they find that they have the partner's children to deal with as well and the idealization does not extend to the children. Far from it. The hostility aroused by the children jeopardizes the marriage so they bury it. The feelings aroused by stepchildren, for many people, simply do not bear looking at (Maddox, 1975, p. 3).

Although the stepparent has been ignored as a subject of serious study, the stereotype of the stepparent as a cruel figure is one that is deeply rooted in many cultures. Helen Thompson cites many examples of the cruel stepmother in the folklore of countries as far apart as India, Hawaii, Chile, Indonesia and Iceland (Thompson, 1966, p. 37). Stories about Cinderella and her stepfather occur in various guises throughout the world. Shakespeare put a cruel stepmother in *Cymbeline* and a villainous stepfather in *Hamlet*. In *Anna Karenina*, Lvov says admonishingly to his wife, 'Anyone would think you were a stepmother, not a true mother.' The Fox Indians have a folktale about a cruel stepmother who was pushed into a fire by the ghost of the mother whose children she neglected. For centuries stepmothers in China were not allowed to punish their stepchildren.

Both Thompson and Maddox trace the image of the cruel stepparent to the peculiar ambiguity of the situation in which the stepparent is willingly or unavoidably placed. The two situations which most commonly lead to the formation of a stepfamily are the death of a parent followed by the remarriage of the spouse, or the divorce of two parents followed by the remarriage of one of the spouses. Although the specific stresses are likely to differ in these two situations, the basic problem for the stepparent of being a replacement and playing second fiddle to the 'real' or natural parent (who is either living elsewhere or has died) is the same in both. The ambiguity of this situation arises in part from a lack of consensus about exactly what function the stepparent *should* fulfil *vis-à-vis* the child, and in part from limitations in the extent to which a stepparent *can* play the part of a natural parent, no matter how much he or she may want or expect to do so. The problem is expressed by Maddox:

> In one sense the stepparent is a stranger. There is no blood tie between the stepparent and stepchild, and there is not even that sense of family that binds together uncles, aunts and cousins whether they like each other or not. The stepparent does not acquire any of a parent's legal rights over a stepchild. Yet on the other hand the stepmother or stepfather has become the person closest to the closest relative a child can have. He or she is right in the centre of the inner family circle with all that implies in physical and emotional proximity to a child . . . stepparents have acquired a status ridden with powerful myths and contradictory expectations and with no clear obligations at all (Maddox, 1975, p. 20).

The lack of clarity about the obligations of a stepparent is, again, reflected in the law. The term 'stepparent' is never used in ecclesiastical or civil law, both of which refer instead to the 'mother's husband' or 'father's wife'. In this way the parenting issue in the stepfamily is carefully bypassed; there is no suggestion that the mother's husband is in any sense a father to the mother's children or that the father's wife is in any sense a mother, even though in reality children are likely to *feel* related to their parent's spouse, and stepparents themselves quite frequently expect and are expected by others to play the role of a natural parent to their stepchild.

The problem for both stepchild and stepparent is to find an identity which is appropriate to the steprelationship and this may entail the ability of all the family members to match up their various expectations of stepparenthood and also to resolve any conflicts they may have concerning the replaced or displaced natural parent.

The stepparent, for example, may be eager to 'succeed' where the natural parent has 'failed' or appeared to fail. Brenda Maddox describes her own feeling of wanting to glide in like a Mary Poppins and sweep up the disaster of her stepchildren's lives after their own mother had committed suicide. And she describes a number of other stepparents who had similar hopes and expectations when they first entered a steprelationship. Maddox points out however that these 'sweeping-up' fantasies are often rudely shattered when the children reject the authority of the new stepparent, resist the imposition of a new régime, or continue to feel disturbed about the absence of 'replacement' of the natural mother or father.

The identity issue is brought to a head in a number of practical ways. For example, how much should the stepparent be responsible for disciplining the child? How much financial support should he or she be expected to give? How much of a say should he or she have in the educational planning for the children, or in the religious affiliation of the child, particularly if his own affiliation differs from that of the 'absent' parent? Some of the issues may be resolved easily depending on the age of the stepchild and the past experience of the family. Others may be a source of lasting conflict, particularly if the stepparent brings children of his or her own to the new marriage; this might clearly result in a different set of demands and expectations for each set of children which is unlikely to be conducive to good relations within the stepfamily as a whole.

The underlying difficulty in all of these issues is that the stepparent is in the position of having to share his parenting role not only with his spouse but with his spouse's previous partner – the parent who is missing from the original family. According to the GAP Committee this sharing must take place:

> In such parental functions as educational planning for the children, financial support, and co-ordination of vacation plans and holiday visits if the natural parent is living; in setting up ideals, in moral training, and in religious affiliation if the natural parent is dead. The reality of the natural parent's presence, be he or she dead or alive, is important to the stepchildren's development of their own identity but complicates the role of stepparent (GAP, 1973, p. 90).

It is not surprising that the role of stepparent is ill-defined, therefore, for no matter how many hopes and intentions the stepparent may have and no matter how many expectations are placed upon him by friends, grandparents and other relatives, the stepparent's power to fulfil them will always be modified by the influence of a shadowy, ambivalent, but ever present third person.

All writers in this field point to the fears and fantasies which this situation can arouse both for the stepparent and for the absent natural parent. Both are likely to feel they are being compared by the child and perhaps also by the spouse who has been married to them both. Helen Thompson describes families in which jealousies of this sort give rise to more or less overt hostility between the absent parent and the stepparent, both of whom vie for the attention and 'love' of the child (Thompson, 1966). She points out that the absent parent who sees his or her children only on 'special' occasions such as weekends or holidays has an advantage which is often used underhandedly. Such parents are able to avoid the mundane obligations of discipline and feeding and clothing the child and are able to ply him or her instead with treats, or try through the child to undermine the new relationship of the other parent.

The GAP Committee, however, make it clear that this does not always work out in the way it is intended. The authors point out that:

> At times children feel guilty about liking a stepparent better than their absent natural parent. This situation frequently arises when the absent natural parent has made attempts to undermine the relationship between the stepparent and the child ... sometimes nothing can be done to influence the hostile, destructive natural parent to stop trying to make the child a 'go-between' of the two families. A child generally handles this dilemma by 'tuning out' the offending parent, and by withdrawing in part from the relationship as he develops a growing awareness of his parent's behaviour (GAP, 1973, p. 93).

For reasons which are implicit in this, the situation is often no easier for a stepparent when the absent natural parent is deceased. As far as the child is concerned there is no harsh reality against which to measure feelings for the parent. The deceased parent is therefore easily idealized by the child and the stepparent shows up poorly by comparison. Maddox points out that the idealization of the deceased natural parent by the child can be accompanied by the fantasy that the stepparent has actually killed the parent he has replaced. And to some children the 'replacement' of the deceased parent by a stepparent may seem like a disloyalty on the part of the other parent. Thus Claudius, the smiling villain, killed Hamlet's father and married his mother and Hamlet observes that 'the funeral baked meats did coldly furnish forth the marriage table'.

There are a number of other common difficulties facing the stepparent. As with the handicapped family, the stepfamily may be

characterized by a conflict of values in so far as the stepchild's needs
and the stepparent's needs are inevitably opposed to a certain extent.
For most people, marrying a widow or a divorcee with children is
motivated primarily by a love of that person and a desire to establish a
deeper relationship with him or her. The fact that a marriage of this
sort puts one in the position of being a stepparent is often a secondary
consideration, something that has to be accepted more or less as a
condition of marriage. It is not at all the same as the decision of a
man and woman to have children together after they are married,
although the conflict of values between parent and child is present
to a lesser extent for the natural parent as well. Also, there are some
stepparents who want stepchildren because they cannot have children
of their own. This is not discussed much in the literature.

In the stepfamily the conflict is magnified right from the start,
even where the stepparenting goes well. The couple in a first marriage
are normally able to enjoy a prolonged honeymoon period during
which they can indulge their marital relationship and satisfy their
personal needs without having to weigh them against the conflicting
demands and needs of their children. Children do not come suddenly
but 'grow' into the family during a period of pregnancy which enables
the parents to grow accustomed to the idea of parenthood and prepare
themselves for the changes and sacrifices that they as a couple will have
to make. The stepparent, on the other hand, becomes a parent at the
moment of marriage. There is no 'honeymoon period' in which the
marriage itself can be consolidated and developed from the stresses
imposed by children. There is not even a period of gestation in which
the couple can adjust together to the changing family régime. For the
stepparent, marriage and parenthood come together, though the needs
of one and the demands of the other may not go hand in hand.

The GAP Committee point to a number of ways in which the marital
relationship can suffer as a result of the demands of the children:

The stepchildren themselves, in ways they are not fully aware of,
can interfere with the relationship between stepparent and spouse. . . .
When a natural parent remarries, the children are called upon to share
the parent on whom they are most dependent with another adult who
also makes emotional demands on their parent. This is experienced
by the children as a psychological separation from their parent
and is very often an upsetting experience. A child, especially if young,
may feel terror that he will be abandoned by the parent he needs so
much and consider the stepparent an unwanted intruder. On the
other hand, a child may be so hungry for a significant relationship
with a new parent that he literally wishes to have him or her all to
himself and may resent the time the newlyweds have to have to

themselves. Some children are very confused about having two fathers or two mothers; until they sort out in their own minds the new roles this natural parent and stepparent assume, they are irritable, fearful and angry (GAP, 1973, p. 92).

The relationship between the stepparent and spouse may be threatened in other ways too:

Unresolved relationships between natural parents can interfere with the full development of the relationship between stepparent and spouse. The stepparent may feel that there is still a relationship between the natural parents which often cannot be fully shared. The children may be a reminder that one's spouse was previously married and that a significant tie to that old relationship remains. Jealousy may arise, and fears (GAP, 1973, p. 92).

Clearly, then, the stepchild can be a disruptive force in the fulfilment of the stepparent's needs in a way which does not occur for a natural parent. Brenda Maddox describes one teenage stepchild who had not stayed with her mother for two years but who 'turned up' a week after her remarriage and expected to stay for several months. She quotes one stepparent as saying, 'It was destroying me, trying to be motherly to them and I was expected to *enjoy* it.' A stepfather said, 'The whole thing was a shock to my system. All the stages of children's development which other people go through gradually, for me were telescoped.' And another, 'What is really hard on the marriage, I think, is the lack of privacy in the mind. The children are always present. The marriage never has a chance to exist as a concept of just two people' (Maddox, 1975).

Despite all these difficulties the stepparent is frequently expected not merely to look after the child but actually to love it as well, to treat it exactly as if it was his/her own. Some of the stepparents interviewed by Maddox expressed doubts as to whether this was possible, but because the expectation was there they felt unable to express the negative side of their feelings toward their stepchild. A parent who shouted at her own child and sent him out of the house might readily be excused, but a stepparent, they felt, would immediately be vilified and branded as 'cruel'. A stepfather describes his desire to hide his negative feelings and the guilt he suffered on account of not doing as well as he might:

I was a very bad stepfather. . . . I should have tried harder to love him. No, I don't think I would have succeeded. You can't feign love. I feel guilty because I did not love him. Of course I feel guilty about my own daughter too. Because I'm the kind of chap I am, she's had a hard life. But the guilt for my daughter is more

inevitable. Nothing could have changed the way she is because of the
way her father is. But with my stepson, I feel that by trying harder I
could have done it better. It is a more complicated guilt. Stepparenthood is an accidental relationship. One has a great moral sense
of responsibility. One feels that one must do these things for a
stepchild (Maddox, 1975, p. 89).

The expectation on a stepparent to love the stepchild has an uneasily
defined limit when the child is a teenager of the opposite sex. Sexual
attraction between stepparents and stepchildren, and the complication
it creates, has been another favourite theme in world literature. We find
it in Euripides' *Hippolytus*, Verdi's *Don Carlos*, Eugene O'Neill's *Desire
Under the Elms* and the somewhat notorious *Lolita* of Nabokov. Clearly,
since there is no consanguineous relationship between stepparent and
child, the incest taboo that normally operates in a family between
parents and children is considerably weakened in the stepfamily.
'More than ordinary families', says Maddox, 'they are plagued with
flirtations, jealousies, fantasies and arguments, as well as the physical
revulsion that some stepparents complain about' (p. 71). The GAP
Committee make a similar point about stepfamilies:

> the ordinary intimacy that usually exists among members of a family
> may at times become highly sexualized in meaning. Fondling,
> kissing, and hugging take on meaning beyond the usual parent–
> child interactions. This is more evident when there is a great differ-
> ence in the ages of the natural parent and the stepparent. The classic
> example is that of the middle-aged father with adolescent children
> who marries a woman who is closer in age to some of the children
> than to her husband (GAP, 1973, p. 95).

In most parts of the Western world a sexual relationship between a
stepparent and stepchild constitutes adultery but not, from a legal
point of view, incest. 'But, but, but,' says Maddox, 'however close in
age the stepson and stepmother, the oedipal thread in their relationship
remains. She is his father's wife, and, in consequence, something more
besides' (Maddox, 1975, p. 98).

We may trace many of the difficulties arising in the stepfamily as
a result of sexual conflict to the issue of identity once again. The
stepmother is a parent to her stepson but not quite a whole parent,
not quite the natural mother. If she were a whole parent the issue would
be clear, her obligations and role expectations would be defined clearly
and her legal position would be secure. It is perhaps for this reason
that many stepparents decide to adopt their stepchild if this is at all
possible. More than half of all adoptions in the USA today are adoptions
by relatives. In Britain one third of all adoptions are by stepfathers.

Whether or not these adoptions achieve anything other than the obvious legal clarifications is a controversial matter. There seem to be arguments for and against. Those for, centre mainly on the satisfactions gained, especially by the stepparent, in the feeling of being a complete and independent family unit. Those against argue that it is unjustifiable to cut a legitimate child off from one of its legitimate biological parents and one half of its entire family. Individual parents may bring forward many other arguments, and doubtless some cases could be found where adoption has been a success and others where it has merely exacerbated existing problems. However, the motivation to adopt probably comes often from a desire on the part of the stepparent to resolve those issues of unspecified roles and uncertainty about identity that have been examined above.

Aside from the specific issues presented to parents as they participate in this increasingly prevalent stepfamily situation, the analysis presented highlights some of the issues of sexuality, rivalry and envy that are part of the dynamics of all families, perhaps less overt, and less dramatic, but nevertheless present and necessary to cope with.

Illustration B: Families with a handicapped child

The term 'handicap' covers an enormous range of conditions. Some handicaps, such as the congenital absence of a finger or toe, or a cleft palate, are so minimal or so easily corrected by surgery that they are hardly even noticeable, let alone disabling; others, such as heart defects or amputations, may impinge on the person's life only in certain situations or at certain times; yet others may affect the total person all of the time – severe cases of cerebral palsy or cystic fibrosis, for example, or advanced cases of muscular dystrophy. Handicap, then, can be many things and have many meanings; it is not a simple, meaning-invariant phenomenon. For this reason structural variations in the family resulting from handicap can be traced only at the 'variant' end of a continuum on which families with minimally handicapped children may not be distinguishable from other sorts of family.

All children require physical and mental stimulation, though the spastic child may require more than most. All children need to be fed and have their bodily functions attended to, though the demands on parents of children with mouth and throat disorders or with an ileostomy or colostomy are greater in these respects than the demands on parents of ordinary children. There may well come a point when the exaggeration of ordinary childhood demands and the inflation of ordinary parental needs imposes a régime which is different in a qualitative sense as well as a quantitative one from the usual family régime. Parenting with handicapped children may well represent an extreme form of our society's ideal family type, at least in respect of the handicapped child – with a focus on child-orientation, child-dependence, parental sacrifice, etc., as discussed in Chapter 2. It may also be that in families with handicapped children sacrifices for the 'good of the child' really are important which may be less clearly so in general parenting situations. But the dividing line is not clear-cut and the special demands on these parents quite often appear to highlight parental needs and requirements which are found in other sorts of family situation where perhaps they pass unnoticed.

Some writers in the field (e.g. Hewett, 1970, and Gath, 1972) point to the 'ordinariness' in the experience of many parents with handicapped children, claiming that the extent and significance of any variation from the norm in their families, and the size of the problems faced by them, has generally been exaggerated in the literature. The Newsons make the point that the basic requirement of these parents: 'is not a massive input of psychiatric help for themselves, to enable them to "adjust" and "accept" and "resolve their guilt feelings": they want to be treated like ordinary people who have a highly practical problem' (Newson and Newson, 1976, p. 44). They say that: 'In talking to the children's parents, what struck us was not their difference from, but their likeness to "ordinary" families' (Newson and Newson, 1976, p. 44). Most writers, however, describe problems and difficulties which *are* specifically raised by handicap and consequently stress the differences between 'handicapped' and 'ordinary' families. We shall concentrate here on the 'problem' side of parenting in families with a handicapped child, though many of the problems we describe are faced to a greater or lesser extent by all parents, whatever sort of family they live in.

There often appears a constellation of disturbed and disturbing emotional reactions on the part of the parents when they first have confirmation that their child is abnormal. The exact response of any parent to an unfavourable diagnosis will depend upon a variety of background factors. Different writers have variously stressed the importance of social class, cultural background, religious affiliation and financial means, the parents' mode of coping with past crises, the support given by family members to each other, their previous experience of illness, and the special meaning the handicapped child has for them.

There is a general consensus that regardless of how these various factors are at work, the birth of a handicapped child represents a crisis in the lives of the parents and in the family as a whole (Davis, 1963; Farber, 1960; Kew, 1975; Menolascino, 1968; Olshansky, 1962). The nature of the crisis is characterized in various ways. Davis (1963) and Menolascino (1968) adopt a stage-analysis approach to crisis and the latter points to three distinct stages in the crisis facing parents of a handicapped child. These are (1) 'novelty shock crisis', in which the parents suffer from insufficient knowledge and understanding of handicap and frequently reject the handicapped child in an emotional sense; (2) 'crisis of personal values' in which the parents suffer from chronic sorrow owing to their inability to fit the child into the personal value system of the family – they have 'lost' the child they expected; (3) 'reality crisis' in which help is needed in solving the practical everyday problems of care and handling.

Burton (1974), Levinson (1967), Jordan (1961), McMichael (1971), Adams (1960), and Noland (1970), whilst not using the stage-analysis approach, all point to the prevalence amongst parents of strong emotional arousal in the period following diagnosis, the predominant emotions being guilt, shame, grief, hostility, and feelings of reprehension both towards the medical services and towards themselves and their marital partners. Olshansky (1962) enlarges on the concept of 'chronic sorrow' attendant on parents after the birth of a handicapped child, and Margaret Adams (1967) claims that 'pervasive sorrow and anxiety' is a constant background feature in families with a severely handicapped child.

Many writers (Bozemann, Orbach and Sutherland, 1955; Chodoff, Standford, Friedman and Hamburg, 1964; Davis, 1963; Kew, 1975; Levinson, 1967) report that some parents strongly resist accepting a bad diagnosis. This is sometimes carried to the point of flatly denying that there is anything wrong with their child. An American doctor, Abraham Levinson, cites a case in which:

> there was a child brought to me who was obviously retarded but his parents argued with me and tried to convince me that he was bright. I finally asked them why they brought the child to see me if nothing was wrong with him. Only then did they admit that they thought 'there might be a little something' the matter with him (Levinson, 1967, p. 18).

Levinson continues:

> Over and over again I have encountered that paradoxical reaction among parents. On the one hand, there is the refusal to accept the doctor's verdict and, on the other, there is a realisation that something is wrong with the child (Levinson, 1967, p. 19).

Many other examples of this sort of denial are found in the literature. In one case a mother put her son down for a place at a public school after she had been told that he was severely mentally retarded (Kew, 1975). Similarly, many parents are described as 'shopping around' from one doctor and hospital to another in the hope of finding a more acceptable diagnosis than the one they have already been given.

When parents do come to accept the reality of their child's condition they are frequently seen to react in one of two opposing ways; either by rejecting the child, expressing anger and bitterness towards him or her and perhaps sending the child physically away from the family into permanent care (Tropauer, 1970; Bozemann, 1955), or else by 'over-protecting' – attending to the child's every demand, placing him or her at the centre of family life and re-organizing their own lives around him. These two reactions are not always unrelated: Green and Solnit (1964) describe the process of parents becoming overprotective towards a handicapped child as an attempt to conceal and compensate for their latent feelings of hostility. As Burton said of families who have a child with cystic fibrosis: 'open expression of such resentment is rarely possible – for who could be angry with a dying child?' (Burton, 1974, p. 18). A number of writers (Burton, 1972; Davis, 1963; Kew, 1975) describe families in which a severely handicapped child, although perhaps unable to talk or move about, seems to dominate completely the activity and organization of the whole family group. A social worker describes one such family in the following way:

> The youngest child, Jimmy, is severely mentally and physically handicapped. He really is a vegetable. He lies on the settee in the middle of the living room all the time. Everything has to be done for him, yet the parents are totally devoted to him and get very angry if the older children don't pay what is considered to be sufficient attention to Jimmy. If one of the children leaves the house without saying goodbye to Jimmy, dad blows his top, whereas in fact it means nothing to Jimmy as he is incapable of understanding. The parents don't want the children to ignore him. Life is very much centred on Jimmy and meeting his needs (Kew, 1975, p. 76).

An important factor in determining parental response to the birth of a handicapped child is the expectations the parents had of their child prior to its birth. Some discrepancy always exists between a parent's expectations of a child and the 'real' child who is born. When a child turns out to be handicapped, this discrepancy is even greater than usual. Bernard Farber (1968) suggests that when a child is mentally retarded this will affect the parents in different ways according to their socio-economic background. For professional parents who are socially aspiring, the discrepancy between the mental retardation label and other labels ascribed to the family by society may be greater than for families from lower socio-economic backgrounds. Farber concluded from his research that because of this the higher the socio-economic status of the family, the greater the impact on family relationships of labelling a child as mentally retarded. For lower socio-economic status families he found that the label of retardation mattered less than the child-care problems associated with the condition.

Farber's work led him to another important conclusion about families with a severely retarded child, namely that the normal life cycle of these families is arrested by the presence of the retarded child. This 'arrest' is manifested in a number of ways. For a start there will be a revision of age- and sex-roles as the siblings in the family grow up, for although the retarded child grows older in a chronological sense, and may grow larger physically, he/she may remain a child aged two or three in a developmental sense. This means that children born after the retarded child will eventually catch up with and finally overtake him in terms of their mental and social development; there will be a constant redefinition of their roles *vis-à-vis* the retarded child as the real age gap between them increases.

The life-cycle arrest is also manifested in the demands made by the child on the parents. Parenting may be seen as a developmental task. As a child grows older his or her requirements gradually change in accordance with psycho-biological development. The role requirements of the parents therefore also change. In this way the parent–child relationship is a developing one. When a child is severely retarded, however, this developmental aspect of parenting in the overall life cycle of the family may be arrested; the parent remains the parent of a permanently 'small' child. Thus, whereas other parents see their children grow up and leave home, and perhaps experience being a grandparent, parents of the severely retarded may not be able to anticipate these later stages of the developmental cycle.

In what other ways may parenting with a handicapped child differ from parenting with normal children? A great deal of the writing in this field has focused on what Tizard and Grad (1961) have called 'the burden of care' which dominates many families with a severely retarded child at home. In 1964 Rutter *et al.* carried out a survey of 3,519 nine- to twelve-year-old children on the Isle of Wight which was designed to focus specifically on retarded and handicapped children. The authors reach the following conclusion about the burden of care in families with a handicapped child:

> All surveys, including this one, have shown that the families of handicapped children have a considerable burden to bear. In part this stems from the difficulties posed in the upbringing of a handi- capped child and in the family adjustments which have to be made, and in part from worry and uncertainty about what caused the condition, whether the parents were to blame and what steps should be taken to help the child (Rutter *et al.*, 1970, p. 375).

On a practical level the burden of care may be seen in terms of taking the child backwards and forwards to doctors and hospitals for seemingly endless appointments, coping with special feeding difficulties and special problems of soiling and wetting, finding housing which is suitable for the child (for example, on the ground floor with no access steps, doors and passages wide enough to take a wheelchair, bathroom, etc. able to facilitate adaptations), coping with all the financial hardship imposed by handicap, arranging for special day-care facilities and appropriate special education, buying or making special clothes to suit the particular needs of the child, providing transport for the immobile child both inside and outside the home, and in many other ways catering for the needs and requirements of the permanently dependent child. Apart from these difficulties, parents may find that they are unable to relate their present situation to their own childhood and their personal recollections of child-rearing and parenting. They may therefore have no model on which to base their own reactions and behaviour as parents, no point of reference from which they can begin to tackle the new situations they face. Furthermore they may have inadequate knowledge of where they can turn for help. There are very many services, benefits and organizations for the disabled and their families. It appears that many of those who could benefit from their use do not even know of their existence.

On the emotional side, there is accumulating evidence to suggest that the parents of handicapped children feel differently in certain respects about their children and about their role as parents than the parents of able-bodied children. Prechtl (1963), for example, conducted a project on the mother–child relationship in a large maternity hospital. A proportion of the babies from his very large sample were eventually diagnosed as minimally brain damaged, although Prechtl's study was conducted before such a diagnosis had been made. What Prechtl found was that after a few months mothers did not show a 'harmonious positive attitude to their baby' in seven out of eight of those cases where the baby was subsequently known to be brain damaged. He pointed out that 'in the first place they did not think that the source of the problem was the baby itself but rather that they were "mishandling" their child. In the second place the baby's behaviour failed to satisfy the mother's expectations.' Prechtl compared these study-group mothers with mothers whose babies were normal. He found that they 'showed a higher approval of activity by the child, fostered a greater dependency in him and were generally less rejecting of their own home making role than mothers whose babies were not brain-damaged.' He concludes that 'these findings give evidence of the fact that the mothers of abnormal babies, although they are not aware of it consciously, are more protective and dominant' to their child than mothers to normal babies.

In a study of 40 mentally handicapped children in home and hospital care in Hertfordshire, Walter Jaehnig and Peter Townsend found similar expressions of parental overprotectiveness in families with a handicapped child compared with 20 control families with non-handicapped children (Jaehnig and Townsend, 1973).

In his study of hearing impaired school-leavers, Michael Rodda similarly found that:

> The profoundly deaf child is likely to have a greater affectual relationship with his parents which could be associated with more feelings of protectivity in the latter. In contrast, the partially hearing child is likely to rely more upon adult persons outside the family to act as protective agents against the stresses engendered by living in a normally hearing community (Rodda, 1970, p. 157).

A similar conclusion was reached by Shere (1956), who studied thirty pairs of twins. Within each pair one child was cerebral palsied. Shere found some significant differences between the parents' attitudes to the cerebral palsied child and their attitude to the able-bodied twins: the parents generally expected the non-cerebral palsied twin to assume more responsibilities and to act older than his age or capabilities would warrant; they overprotected the cerebral palsied twin, permitting him little discretion in his activities; they tended to be more responsive to the problems of the cerebral palsied twin and oblivious to those of his twin. Differential attitudes and child-rearing practices towards able-bodied and handicapped children have been documented by other writers too. Davis (1963), in his study of polio victims and their families gives some vivid descriptions of these differences which support the view that parents tend to overindulge and overprotect their handicapped children and foster a greater degree of dependency in them. As noted earlier, a number of writers view this parental response in part as compensation for feelings of hostility and bitterness towards the handicapped child (Burton, 1975; Tropauer, 1970; Green and Solnit, 1964).

Another effect of handicap on parental experience is seen in the limitation of family size in families who have had a handicapped child. Holt (1958), Tizard and Grad (1961) and Burton (1972) have all shown that there is a tendency for family size to be restricted following the birth of a handicapped child. Out of 160 mothers in Holt's sample who could have had more children, 101 decided not to do so. The decisions of 90 of these families were held to be directly related to the presence of a retarded child in the family. Burton reported, after her study of cystic fibrosis children, that 46 per cent of the mothers in her sample were afraid of getting pregnant again in case they bore another disabled child.

The emotional side of the burden of care is perhaps summed up best by Lindy Burton in the phrase 'tolerating the intolerable'. She observes:

> Little is worse for parents than learning that their child has a life-threatening illness. The diagnosis itself implies pain and hopelessness, and seems to preclude all joyful expectations for a normal satisfying life together. As such it is responded to not just as a threat for the future but as a real and actual loss, beginning at the moment the news is broken (Burton, 1974, p. 16).

There are at least two dimensions to the 'loss' Burton refers to. It may refer, in an emotional context, to the normal child whom the parents expected, but whom they have now apparently 'lost'. And it may also refer directly to a loss for the parents themselves of 'a normal satisfying life together'. There is implicit in this idea some concept of an underlying parental need, although Burton does not specifically examine such a concept. Much of the writing in this field carries the implication that certain basic parental needs, collectively viewed as comprising a 'normal satisfying life together', are somehow at risk of being unfulfilled when parents give birth to a handicapped child; but these needs are rarely held up to scrutiny in their own right.

In this field, as in others, writers are more accustomed to thinking of parents being instrumental in the fulfilment of the needs of children, rather than vice versa. In addition, where there is a conflict of interests between a handicapped person and the able-bodied persons around him, there seems to be a natural or conditioned proclivity for observers to side with the handicapped person. Thus, just as parents often adopt a differential policy towards their handicapped and able-bodied children, so also the majority of writers on handicap have tended in the past, albeit implicitly, to view the needs of the handicapped members of a family as having priority over the needs of the other family members.

According to social work literature, one of the most pressing requirements of parents with a handicapped child is to come to terms with the discrepancy between their expectations of 'normal' parenthood and the reality of having to cope with a handicapped child. The same may be said of all parents, but in the case of handicap a number of specific subsidiary requirements may be identified. The first of these is for parents to be told in a realistic but sympathetic way about the nature of the child's condition. Many writers (Adams, 1960; Burton, 1974; Davis, 1963; Noland, 1970; Younghusband, Burchall, Davie and Kellmer Pringle, 1970) cite examples of parents who were told about the diagnosis by doctors who were too busy to be kind, or who felt the task was so 'unpleasant' (Davis, 1963) that they could not be wholly truthful.

'Doctors' ignorance or unwillingness to inform parents – it was sometimes difficult to tell which – was resented by parents', says Younghusband (1970) in her report. Sheila Hewett devotes a sizeable section
to this subject in her study (1970), and after pointing out some of the
difficulties of diagnosis says:

> The presentation of these complicated facts to worried parents in
> terms which they will be able to understand, calls for considerable
> tact and ingenuity on the part of doctors. All parents are different
> and all children are different (Hewett, 1970, p. 38).

She notes that parents often do not take in what the doctors tell them
and many need repeated explanations before the message is absorbed.
Sometimes there is little communication at all:

> some doctors still seemed to be reluctant to put a name to the
> children's condition. Only 7 of these 21 mothers were told what was
> wrong before the children were one year old, 3 of these before they
> were three months old. But still 3 mothers of these 21 younger
> children had found out *by chance* what was wrong – one had over-
> heard the word spastic when the consultant was talking to a colleague
> and the other two had read it on an appointment card and a referral
> note respectively (Hewett, 1970, p. 14).

Hewett found that 70 per cent of the 180 mothers she interviewed felt
that doctors should tell parents as soon as they suspect that something is
wrong, even though they cannot be sure exactly what it is.

The need for information and guidance extends beyond the diag-
nostic situation into many other areas of life. Rutter, Tizard and
Whitmore (1970) indicate a wide range of parental requirements on
the practical level of child-care, though most of the items they list
under the heading 'help for the child's family' are essentially requirements of the handicapped child himself rather than the family's:

> Many parents feel (quite rightly) that they do not receive the help
> they need. Time needs to be spent in explaining the nature of a
> child's condition, what to expect as he grows up, how the handicap
> will affect the child and his family, and what kind of improvement
> or progress is possible. Parents need to be helped to work out ways
> of dealing with the day to day problems imposed by a handicapped
> child – such as how to cope with tantrums, how much a cerebral
> palsied child should be encouraged to do things without assistance,
> and whether parents should try to teach the child at home. Of
> course, quite often no precise answers to these questions can be
> given, but this in no way diminishes the need for them to be as well
> informed as the situation allows. Advice and support are at least as

necessary when there is no specific treatment as when there is. This
is a continuing need which cannot be met by a single definitive
statement, however comprehensive. The nature of a child's handicap
changes as he gets older and parents should be helped to deal with
each new issue as it arises rather than wait for a crisis to occur
before seeking help. . . . Parents need to be advised on how to obtain
the most suitable schooling for their child, what alternatives are open
to them and to whom they should go for further advice. Practical
help may be needed with transport (to hospital or a special school),
with housing, financial matters, holiday arrangements and a host of
other items of this kind (Rutter *et al.*, 1970, pp. 375–6).

In so far as these prescriptions reflect the requirements of parents
rather than the requirements of their children, they relate to a felt
need of many parents in this situation to reduce their anxiety and
effort, to minimize the 'burden' encumbent upon them and thus to
have the potential for greater fulfilment in their own individual interests and activities. Thus often-repeated demands for baby-sitters,
home helps, pre-school playgroups, night attendants, rest-breaks, and
help with transport and holiday arrangements are all effectively
demands to free the parent from an excessive burden of child-care and
to facilitate the satisfaction of interests which the parent may have
quite outside of the context of rearing a handicapped child. The
Younghusband report refers to letters received from over 300 parents of
handicapped children. The authors analysed the needs which were
expressed in these letters. Nearly all of the letter-writers expressed felt
needs of some sort and most of these came under the category of
'personal and social needs'. The 'need for relief from the care of a
handicapped child at home was the most pressing of all personal and
social needs. It was evident in relation to one hundred and twenty
three of the children' (Younghusband, 1970, p. 44).

The felt needs and requirements which we have looked at so far in
relation to handicap have related largely to practical day to day aspects
of living. Much of the social work literature is more concerned with
the emotional aspects of parental requirements; indeed casework
practice in this area is largely based upon a set of assumptions about
the emotional 'needs' of parents following the birth of a handicapped
child.

One of the main assumptions for which there is ample evidence,
is that most parents need to shelter themselves from the pain involved
in accepting their child's diagnosis. Examples were given earlier of
parents who denied the diagnosis in one way or another. Levinson (1967)
and Davis (1963) are but two of many who describe ways in which
parents clutch at straws in a desperate effort to prolong their hope. A

parent says: 'Well, I'll tell you the truth. We didn't – we might have thought of polio, but we didn't want to. We just didn't want to think of it I guess, even though he wouldn't walk' (Davis, 1963, p. 27). Davis found that even after they had accepted the diagnosis parents still adopted 'strategies' by means of which they could derive hope.

The demoralizing imagery accompanying the diagnosis was very soon counterbalanced by second thoughts of a more optimistic nature. Even those parents who sought temporary refuge in questioning the diagnosis soon accepted its validity for all practical purposes and began to develop rudimentary anticipatory strategies for estimating the child's injury and prospects for recovery. These early optimistic reappraisals were usually expressed in such terms as 'it's not so bad as we first thought', 'He's got the will power to lick the thing', or quite simply, 'We believe that he'll come out of it all right' (Davis, 1963, p. 34).

What are such parents hoping for? The answer, perhaps, is not simply the shadowy concept of normality, but rather the capacity to derive enjoyment from their child, to find fulfilment in his growth and development, and through him to enrich the meaning and quality of their lives. In this way children may be instrumental in the fulfilment of parental needs and when parents see such fulfilment threatened by the disability of their child they try in an irrational but understandable way to keep alive their hopes that the child will, after all, be normal.

Parents of handicapped children have many more specific requirements and needs than we can mention here. Younghusband counted 660 'personal or social needs' which were either explicitly stated or implied in the letters she received from parents. A number of important needs relate to the parents' adjustment to the reality of their situation as they search for new meanings and sources of satisfaction in their experience of parenting. This process of adjustment, according to the social work literature, requires parents to discuss openly their feelings, both negative and positive, about handicap, the child and their hopes and fears for the future. In 'The Doomed Family', for example, Atkin says: 'The social worker should enable parents to begin sharing a maze of confused and jumbled thoughts whilst awaiting a medical verdict' (Atkin, 1974, p. 62). And Gordon says: 'Sustained contact with the parents is of paramount importance. . . . The aim should be to help these parents to an awareness of their own feelings through their relationship with a member of staff' (Gordon, 1974, p. 146). Patten (1974) claims that the many parents' associations which exist for parents of the handicapped have the primary function of fulfilling the parents' need to talk about their situation and their feelings about it. Many of the researchers in this field (Hewett, 1970; McMichael, 1971; Young-husband *et al.*, 1970) found the parents they interviewed eager rather than merely willing to talk about their experiences or, as in the Young-husband study, to write about them in letters of 'up to 24 pages in length'.

Clearly this need, like many of the others we have looked at, is not peculiar to parents of the handicapped. Some form of readjustment after birth is perhaps necessary for all parents and the need to 'accept the reality of their situation' by 'working through their feelings' is to a large extent universal amongst parents, although the need is heightened in parents of the handicapped in view of the greater dis-crepancy between the reality they face and the reality they had expected.

Other needs may be listed in relation to adjustment which also apply to the parents of normal children. There is the need, for example, to preserve a sense of stability, and equilibrium in a situation marked by crisis and change (Bozemann, Orbach and Sutherland, 1955; Chodoff, Standford, Friedman and Hamburg, 1964; Farber, 1960). In respect of the marital relationship, there may be a need for both parents to readjust together in their attempts to resolve their crisis (Kew, 1974). Or again, there is an apparent need of many parents to attribute blame, either to hospitals and doctors or to themselves or their families, when they experience feelings of dissatisfaction with the child they have produced.

In common with other parents, the parent of the handicapped child is subjected to social attitudes and pressures which can at times be a source of conflict by working against the fulfilment of the various needs outlined. There are, for example, strong social pressures in our society for parents to feel a deep sense of personal responsibility for their children and this is part of the reason behind the reported feelings of guilt suffered by parents of handicapped children (Adams, 1960; Burton, 1972, 1974; Davis, 1963; Farber, 1968; Kew, 1974, 1975; Mandelbaum, 1967; Noland, 1970; Younghusband *et al.*, 1970; Zuk, 1970). Some parents feel that something they have done, something that they *are*, may be the cause of the child's disability. Others feel guilty because there is a strong conflict between their need for a positive experience of parenthood which may lead them to have feelings of rejection towards their disabled child, at least initially, and the social pressures that they feel to accept and care for their child as a 'loving' parent should. Social pressures tend to assert certain values over certain others which are in conflict with them, and in this way the fulfilment of important parental needs may be blocked.

If these needs are to be met in the case of parents of handicapped children, they must first be distinguished from the needs and require-ments of the child. Only then can their respective needs be assessed and balanced off against one another, perhaps opening the way for parents to lead more satisfying lives, less troubled by the burden of care.

The two parenting situations we have examined here – stepparenting and parenting with a handicapped child – illustrate some of the different pressures and demands on parents who live in families with distinctive structural arrangements. They are not complete 'case studies' nor are these particular situations necessarily the most important or the most widespread variations, though large numbers of people are affected by each. We might have looked more closely at single-parent families, for example, or at parenting in communal family arrangements, or at any of the other variations mentioned briefly in this chapter. To the extent that the study of these variants illuminate generic issues for all parents, they contribute to our overall understanding of parents' preoccupations, needs and requirements.

In mapping the main parenting issues through the life cycle in succeeding chapters we do not try to describe their innumerable permutations as they affect the diversity of family types described here. For one thing space is too limited and paper is only two-dimensional. Also, we believe that despite wide variations in family context and life style, there are certain *generic* issues for *all* parents at specific phases of the life cycle. The felt needs and requirements of one parent may differ markedly from those of the next; our intention is not to catalogue these differences – rather to explore the issues themselves. Although, in the course of this life-cycle approach, we may appear to revert at times to an assumption of a modal family type in our treatment of these issues, this is not our intention. There is a view that, at present, a great deal of variation exists on an institutional/practical level which on an attitudinal/ideological level is not fully acknowledged; in other words there is frequently a lag between behaviour and the appropriate conceptual models or paradigms of family life to encompass it. There may also be a class discrepancy: middle-class, professional people may show early acceptance of the multiple-model orientation, but can this orientation filter to working-class people in the same way? These are, ultimately, empirical problems. In the chapters that follow, we shall highlight phase-specific issues that may be generic for parents of all kinds.

4

Parenting begins before birth

The life-cycle stage at which parenting usually commences is what we call the early establishment phase. At this time people are characteristically preoccupied with being productive. There are various interest channels through which this preoccupation may be expressed. Parenting represents one of these. Occupational work represents another. These are the two major alternative, often competing, channels through which people may express the dominant preoccupation of the phase. For many people one interest channel is overriding – at a given time or permanently.

In this perspective, parenting – like work – can be seen to take up some part of people's life space. It takes up more in some people's lives than in others. Some of this variation relates to the varying requirements of children of different ages, and the influence that, to varying extents through the life cycle, children meeting them has on parents' lives. In essence, then, parenting can take up parents' time and their emotional involvement less or more. In part, some parenting involvement will be child-directed, for children do require considerable basic care and attention by *any* acceptable definition of children's needs.

Nevertheless, comparable standards of child-care may be attained by various parenting patterns. Parents themselves have some choice in where they invest their energies, so that the extent to which parenting occupies them at any given stage is partly parent-directed. However, this room for manoeuvre is more real in some people's minds and sub-cultures and material conditions of living than in others.

This is one framework in which the aspirations and conflicts people experience in the early establishment phase (and later life-cycle stages) can be meaningfully understood. It takes into account the variety of individuals' goals. It also allows for the fact that some people, because of superior material conditions, have more effective life space than others. Above all, this framework takes into account those who are unable to parent or choose not to parent along with other adults. In reviewing the main alternative routes whereby people achieve the status of parenthood or non-parenthood, it is apparent that there is considerable public consciousness of these issues, as reflected in a substantial journalistic commentary on them.

Voluntary childlessness

The onset of parenting is a critical point in people's life careers. Life style strategies are worked out partly in relation to people's ideals for occupation and family, though working out these strategies is a more conscious process for some people than for others. Some people delay parenting, and some people may deliberately decide not to parent. Non-parenthood may become increasingly popular as a life-style option.

There are reasons in addition to the more obvious ones surrounding conflict between family and occupational involvement that unduly motivate some people against becoming parents. Some people do not anticipate any developmental potential for themselves in parenthood. Others may wish to evade a feeling of being defined in a life-cycle stage, and associated with a cohort, according to children's ages: 'If you have children you become placed in an age, encapsulated in a generation. If you don't have any, then you're as old as you feel' (Read, 1974).

For some the decision not to parent is very deliberate, and central to a rigid life strategy:

I think I'm very lucky, my husband understands me. But I also think that if he really wanted children, I wouldn't stand in the way of him getting rid of me and finding someone who would give him a child. Having children would destroy me . . . (Read, 1974).

It is equally clear, however, that for others the decision is not so inflexibly conceived. For such people, voluntary childlessness informs their life careers from time to time, and then retrospectively:

We didn't plan not to have children, not having them just emerged. When we first got married we weren't financially able to, and then I got involved in my job. . . . Not having children is a decision I could never make permanent, because it's such an emotional subject, but I think we must be the first generation who have the luxury to choose (Read, 1974).

The legitimacy of voluntary childlessness seems to be increasing; through example, through the consciousness-raising influence of agencies like NON and writers like Peck (1975), and perhaps also through growing social acceptance of variation.

Nevertheless, those who elect this life strategy may still experience considerable negative social pressure. Traditional opinions die hard, and the voluntarily childless may encounter continual disbelief that they have 'really' chosen their path, and disapproval if it is suspected that they have. The following remarks are typical of the traditional view, although their author is doubtless influenced by the involuntary childlessness he witnesses in his work as a physician in an infertility clinic.

> There are certainly some women who say they have no desire to become mothers and genuinely mean it; but they are a minority. Every month a young woman is reminded that her primary role in life is to bear children and even the most ardent advocate of Women's Lib sounds unconvincing if she denies wanting to achieve motherhood at least once in her lifetime (Newill, 1974, p. 14).

These attitudes are directed at childless women rather than men. One may say that there is a credibility gap in relation to childlessness as a chosen life course for women.

Contraception

The 'luxury to choose' hinges on a number of factors: the social legitimation of choice, improved technical means of contraception and knowledge about the techniques available. Studies of contraceptive use and resistance by British women (Cartwright, 1974, 1976; Bone, 1973) suggest that women's knowledge about contraception is most frequently gained from informal sources, which the women often feel to be inadequate. Reporting on a survey on a sample of 2,520 women carried out for the Department of Health and Social Security, Bone (1973) writes:

> A third of the single women said they had received no sex education at school and two thirds had received no information about intercourse from this source, whilst only a fifth recalled being told anything about contraception. Approaching three quarters of the women who had had some formal sex education felt it was inadequate and a small majority (58%) said they had learnt most of what they knew from friends (Bone, 1973, p. 7).

Many people appear to avoid or forestall making an actual choice – that is deliberately planning parenthood or non-parenthood. Thus, of the married women in Bone's sample (including divorced, separated, widowed and cohabiting women) who were fecund but neither pregnant nor planning to become so, 93 per cent were using some form of contraception, but one third of the total population who were not planning pregnancy were using withdrawal or no contraception at all. Of the most recent pregnancies of women who were fecund, 36 per cent were unplanned (in that conception occurred whilst the couple were using contraception or when they were 'taking a chance') and 51 per cent were either unplanned or originated before the couple had employed contraception at all.

There are varying professional views on this high proportion of 'unplanned' pregnancies. A common psychoanalytic view is that one or both parents 'really' (i.e. unconsciously) want a child no matter how much they claim otherwise. This deeper motivation is seen to underlie their 'carelessness'. Others such as Krista Luker (1976), however, have developed a risk-taking model to explain the 'unplanned' pregnancy whereby at conception the woman is viewed as being in a situation of conflicting demands. On the one hand are factors which militate against the effective use of contraceptives: such as the price of contraceptives, the difficulty of obtaining them as and when required, and the personal inconvenience of using them. Weighed against such factors, however, is the risk of an unwanted pregnancy. Luker suggests that faced by these conflicting demands, people often simply 'take a chance' on the basis of a simple cost-benefit analysis, hoping that they will 'get away with it'.

In support of the 'risk-taking' view of unplanned pregnancies Cartwright highlights the fact that some women do not take the pill even though they feel it is the most reliable and satisfactory method of birth control. She argues that:

> One possible reason why more people do not use the pill is that it is 'too reliable' for any who prefer to have some chance of becoming pregnant. In an attempt to identify such mothers they were all asked: 'Other things being equal, would you prefer a method to be absolutely 100% reliable or to have a small chance of failure?' Seven per cent of the mothers opted for a slight risk . . . so a few may be playing a contraceptive version of Russian roulette quite deliberately (Cartwright, 1976, pp. 60–1).

As can be seen below, none of the currently available means of contraception are felt to be completely satisfactory. Bone reports the widespread feeling that some methods are 'messy' or 'unreliable'; others are felt to interfere with love-making; some carry a risk of painful or damaging side effects. Table 6 shows the percentages of fecund women in Bone's sample expressing complete satisfaction with the method they were currently using. Bone concludes that:

> consistent with their greater satisfaction, fewer I.U.D. and pill users were contemplating a change of method and it is suggested that those who once try these two most effective methods are in fact less likely than people trying other methods to abandon them (Bone, 1973, pp. 5–6).

Table 6 *Percentages of fecund women satisfied with contraceptive methods*

Method	%age expressing complete satisfaction
condom	44
pill	69
coitus interruptus	38
safe period	42
diaphragm	41
IUD	78
spermicides	40
abstinence	22

Source: Abstracted from Bone, 1973, p. 27.

A similar conclusion is reached by Cartwright from her national survey of the mothers and fathers of a sample of legitimate live children in England and Wales (Cartwright, 1976). In her book she suggests that 'the pill, the I.U.D., and sterilization were underused in that more couples regarded them as satisfactory methods of birth control than were currently using them' (Cartwright, 1976, p. 59). Cartwright indicates, however, that the pattern of contraceptive usage is changing,

Table 7 *Methods of contraception ever used (mothers responding)*

	1967–8 %	1970 %	1973 %
pill	28	40	65
cap	17	17	10
IUD	3	4	8
sheath	67	68	69
chemicals on own	6	8	8
withdrawal	46	45	45
safe period	21	15	13
male sterilization	}2	}5	3 }7
female sterilization			4
other	7	4	5
none	7	6	3
number of mothers	1,482	232	1,464

Source: Cartwright, 1976, p. 13.

with increasing use of the pill and decreasing use of the cap and the safe period (Table 7). These figures lend support to the view that contraception is increasingly becoming 'her problem'. The assumption that 'if she does not wish to mother it is up to the female to ensure her own protection' can place a heavy burden on women. Our own fieldwork with adolescents in London, for example, suggests that many young girls are under strong social pressure to take the pill. A journalist in the *Guardian*, Carol Dix, highlighting the negative side effects of the pill – headaches, depression, nausea, asks:

> It is well over 10 years since the euphoria that greeted the new wonder-drug, the pill, and it is about now that, after much shopping around, a lot of women have had to face the alarming truth – not only is there no magic contraceptive but they may have been persuaded to use harmful techniques, believing that contraceptives are good for them because they are good for society. Has a figurative woollen cap been pulled over our eyes . . .? (Dix, 1974, p. 9).

Unplanned parenthood

Despite the promotion of contraceptive devices, and increased dissemination of contraceptive knowledge and pressures, unplanned pregnancies still occur. In Cartwright's study of legitimate births the proportion of mothers who said they were using some method of birth control around the time they became pregnant with the survey baby was 22 per cent. Although most couples took the news of an unplanned pregnancy in their stride, some did not. Asked to look back to the time when they had first discovered they were pregnant 13 per cent of all mothers said they regretted it happened at all and a further 14 per cent said they wished it had happened later. Bone reports a comparable finding: '17% of last pregnancies were regretted and 11% would have been more welcome later . . . 39% of unplanned pregnancies were reported as regretted' (Bone, 1973, p. 6). In relation to life careers the critical point is that *parenthood* resulting from unplanned pregnancies is not envisaged in prospect by definition. Although this *need* not be overwhelming, the outcome may be negative when people have had definite ideas about the preferred course of their lives – ideas that do not include parenthood, or immediate parenthood. Termination of the accidental pregnancy may be the least disruptive solution for some, but not for others, and the rearrangement of life plans and expectations to accommodate the ensuing parenthood may be catastrophic for some, whilst others will accommodate more easily or even with pleasure. Many people's life careers are considerably influenced by unplanned parenthood, and many may see this, in retrospect, as a 'blessing', perhaps not even a mixed one. None the less, considerable support is required for individuals who are likely to experience accidental parenthood as traumatic or unmanageable.

It is worthwhile pointing out that whilst unplanned parenthood is frequently thought of in relation to younger people – either young couples 'who wanted to wait for a few years', or 'to finish college', etc., or more pervasively, the young unmarried mum – it occurs in other sub-groups too. An unplanned child later on in marriage, for example, may completely alter a woman's plans to resume full-time paid employment after her older children are at school. It is assumed in the culture that not all 'after thoughts' are planned. Unplanned pregnancies can be still more disruptive for older women who are widowed or divorced.

Notice must also be drawn to the case of fathers. Whilst the young married man who did not manage to complete his degree or apprenticeship before becoming a father may elicit some sympathy, the case of the fathers of illegitimate children, whose parenthood is very frequently unplanned, has attracted little attention. Fathers of unplanned children frequently are fathers of illegitimate children; Dulan Barber's book, *Unmarried Fathers* (1975), draws attention to their situation. Barber interviewed a series of fathers of illegitimate children, and amongst the range of men's feelings he encountered, there was considerable longing to experience more involved parenthood with accidentally conceived children. But this is one group against whom the sanction and support for positive and active parenting seem to be stacked. One of Barber's respondents had a long and much publicized fight to keep his daughter, who is in care though he spends much time with her. He wanted full custody of the child, but while he was unemployed he was told he could not support her, and when he had a job he was told he could not look after her. Barber points out that the problem is not really one of the law discriminating against unmarried fathers, but that: 'It simply experiences great difficulty in seeing them as anything other than the reluctant recipients of Affiliation Orders' (Barber, 1975, p. 119).

Desire for parenthood: the ideal frustrated

Many people 'know' they want to parent, and decide to embark on this course. However, from common knowledge and from such fieldwork experience as there is with new parents, it seems that many people do not remotely anticipate the impact of parenthood on their lives. For some the ideals and reality mesh well, but for many they do not. For people who wish to parent, but find this channel blocked by infertility, ideals and reality are discrepant. The emotional, psychological and social pain frequently experienced in this situation is crystallized in the titles of two newspaper articles focusing on the topic, 'Barren Pains', describing the history of one woman's futile struggle for fertility (Lowry, 1975), and 'My mother-in-law looks at my stomach before she looks at my face', describing the relief infertile women may attain by participating in discussion groups. Newill believes that the needs and requirements of infertile people are not adequately met by the medical service at present.

It seems obvious that human fertility will eventually have to be recognized as a special branch of medicine in its own right. My ideal, therefore, is the creation of departments of human reproduction within teaching hospitals and the larger district general hospitals throughout the country, specializing entirely in research for practical work in all aspects of human fertility. These departments would run infertility clinics as well as contraceptive clinics, and would be staffed by doctors specializing entirely in fertility. At present there is no such department in this country; research is sporadic, and infertility work is confined to a few enthusiasts trained in various specialities (Newill, 1974, pp. 18–19).

A significant determinant of women's fertility is age. Newill assesses the significance of age as a fertility determinant, and suggests how, physiologically, the dice are loaded against people who choose to parent later rather than earlier.

It has been estimated, by a professor of gynaecology, that after ten years of marriage, couples who married between the ages of twenty-five and twenty-nine showed 14% infertility, those who married between thirty and thirty-four showed 23% and if they married after the age of thirty-five the percentage of infertility went up to 40. . . . This means that the older a woman is when she finds herself unable to conceive the sooner she should seek medical advice. . . . If she is a 'career woman' who married after the age of thirty with the intention of starting a family sometime in the future she would be well advised to try for her first child with little delay. Departments of gynaecology and infertility clinics are full of women who used contraceptives for years after marriage because they put their careers first or imagined they could not afford a child immediately. When they eventually decide to start a family the children, who would have arrived years before when the woman was younger, stubbornly refuse to be conceived when she is older and less fertile. Women are most fertile in their teens and many a schoolgirl discovers to her cost that she cannot lightly experiment with sexual intercourse and escape pregnancy (Newill, 1974, pp. 17–18).

Newill's position contains a bias against 'career women' and illustrates one of the ways in which the value dilemmas implied in the decision to parent may present very difficult conflicts. A woman's opportunities to continue a career at a reasonably congenial level after becoming a mother may be far greater if she was occupationally well-established before she had her children. How aware people are at present of these various facts is uncertain, and what weight they ascribe to them in reaching decisions on their life careers is unclear. Clearly some people take them into account, as illustrated in the following remarks of a voluntarily childless woman:

> We re-examine the situation from time to time, as I don't think it's something you can just decide for good. I don't think it can be, especially for a woman, because time runs out and then you find you can't have children whether you want them or not. But so far, when I've thought about having children, I've thought against it, but I do get that slight feeling in my throat that I'm going to run out of time and so I have to re-think (Read, 1974).

Other ways of starting families

Adoption is a resolution commonly chosen by infertile couples, although they do not, as is sometimes assumed, comprise the only type of adoptive parent. People with no fertility problem also adopt children, though this may more frequently be of successive rather than first children, and adoption agencies are sometimes biased against adoption by fertile couples. Considerable ambivalence seems to pertain towards adoption which is not 'necessary'.

Adoption by single parents tends to be more negatively sanctioned and seems to be tolerated only in exceptional circumstances. This is illustrated in the report of the first single parent to adopt a child in California after the state law then permitted adoption by single parents (Jenkins, 1974). The adoption agency concerned is reported as saying that the adoptive father was only awarded the adoption as the child concerned was extremely difficult to place, and had been previously rejected by several couples. A single adoptive father presumably arouses more ambivalence than single adoptive mothers, who have anyway constituted the majority of single adoptive parents in California. If variant situations like these are statistically insignificant, the insights they generate are not. The father concerned in this case wishes to parent, but explicitly not to marry. His solution to the problem was an adoption.

Some single women who wish to parent decide to have children of their own. Whilst Ashdown-Sharp's *The Single Woman's Guide to Pregnancy and Parenthood* (1975) is relevant also (and perhaps more so) to those for whom single maternity is not so deliberate, she considers issues and decisions that the unmarried pregnant woman is more likely to confront than the married couple. These include: whether or not to marry, whether or not to seek an abortion, whether or not to keep the pregnancy a secret from the father or from one's own parents, whether or not to seek adoption or fostering, how to ensure an adequate income. In addition, the single parent is in a different legal position from the married parent, in respect of allowances and rights and in respect of the cohabitation rule whereby the sexual life of an unmarried mother is open to investigation by social security officers and if the rule is found to apply her social security payments may be cut off.

The decision to parent

There is an enormous literature on the decision to parent, which constitutes a field of research in its own right. Parents of different types, ages, sexes, cultural backgrounds and situational circumstances set in motion the train of events that produces a child with different degrees of intention and realization of what they are doing. Sometimes the act is sanctioned by religious beliefs in the sanctity and purpose of the activity as a central life goal; sometimes it reflects rather, the wish to show one's sexuality, potency, or adequacy as a person. Sometimes the act is used in a Machiavellian way – to keep the woman at home (with 'one in the cooker'), or in the hope, sometimes unconsciously felt, that the 'new blessing' will save a crumbling marriage.

Among the various approaches to understanding the motivation for having or not having babies – psychological, social, cultural, economic and the like – a recent major effort has been launched that integrates the various approaches and tests them cross-culturally. Lois and Martin Hoffman, in their study of 'The Value of Children to Parents', have assessed the field and extracted nine basic values for which there is some research support, and which provide the basis for a framework for further study (Hoffman and Hoffman, 1973; also see Pohlman, 1969; GAP, 1975; Le Masters, 1970).

We paraphrase, and elaborate somewhat on the nine basic values outlined by the Hoffmans:

1 Validation of adult status and social identity. When people become parents, they are considered to be full and complete people, and to have valued social functions in the reproduction of the group. In most societies motherhood is woman's cardinal role, and therefore without it the person is not socially 'complete'.
2 Expansion of the self. By having a child, one links oneself to a person who will survive one, and who will probably also have children, and one thus achieves a measure of immortality.

3 Achievement of moral values: according to the culture, the achievement of goals valued by the group, giving care as a form of altruism, fulfilling a religious mission, contributing something to the group, and by exercising child-care duties responsibly one demonstrates one's virtue, sexual modesty, control of impulsivity, and so on.

4 The creation of a primary group tie that is larger than the couple bond; increasing the source of affection and loving ties.

5 Stimulation, novelty, fun – playing with the baby, enjoying it, learning with and from it.

6 Achievement, competence, creativity. Having made a baby, people feel satisfied with themselves; they did it; they had a part in a marvellous process, producing this beautiful and complex creature, with its continually unfolding array of surprises. In the secular society's framework, people feel the kind of creativity in themselves that formerly they stood in awe of God for having done.

7 Power and influence. The infant baby is more under one's control than any other person ever has been or ever again will be. For some people this is an operative motive.

8 Social comparison, competition. Through one's baby one compares oneself with others, and for some this is a primary motive. One may feel oneself, and be seen to have the most beautiful, cleanest, prettiest, healthiest, best behaved baby in the locality, and from this one may derive indirect satisfaction of one's own competitive strivings.

9 Economic utility. For many, a new baby is not only a new mouth to feed, but a new helper – in the house, on the farm, in the family business, in one's old age.

Which particular constellation of values individuals experience will depend not only on their personalities and their relationship and situation, but on the values which prevail in their social group. The Hoffmans have sought to understand people's fertility motivation both in terms of the values they place on having children, and a number of environmental factors including: alternative channels for satisfying these values; costs of having children (what must be lost or given up to have children) non-economic as well as economic ones; barriers to having children (e.g. housing shortages, poverty, illness); and facilitators to having children (e.g. prosperity, help, etc.). The Hoffmans consider that fertility motivation can be analysed in terms of how the value of having children interplays with the alternatives, and with the costs, barriers and facilitators in the situation to produce an actual motivation.

Reviewing this formulation, its compatibility with our own approach to the issue of how tasks are confronted in making a transition to parenthood is apparent. Our own formulation of the situation may be presented as follows.

People reach the point in their life cycle where they confront, explicitly or implicitly, the possibility of having a child. At this point in their lives they are likely to be preoccupied with productivity (i.e. expressing creative interests of some kind, in which occupation and parenting are the two major channels most people experience.)

For some people, the decision to parent, like a career decision (Feldman and Feldman, 1975) may be left to 'just happen'; for others it may be planned and scheduled – as a career in its own right, or to dovetail with a model in the couple's minds of one or both of their occupational careers. For still others, the decision may have an expedient character – to get housing or allowances; and for others it may reflect still other motivations from the range described. Whatever the underlying motivation of the decision, there is more likely to be a healthy and satisfying outcome if some of the consequences are faced.

Preparation for parenthood

There has been a good deal of romanticization about parenthood – what Arlene Skolnick aptly terms the parental mystique. This has gone hand in hand with the idealization of the nuclear family. Many of the issues we raise at this point are discussed in Skolnick's account of the costs of parenthood:

> In recent years there has begun to be a trend away from the notions of parenthood-as-fulfillment and of child rearing as part of the grand design of the social system. There is a growing awareness that even wanted and dearly loved children seem to bring heavy costs to parents (Skolnick, 1973, p. 304).

Skolnick deals not only with the financial costs of children, but spells out the *strains of parenthood*, which are emphasized in the *nuclear family situation* of social isolation: 'Our own society imposes great demands on parents while providing minimal institutional support to replace the kin and community assistance of former times' (Skolnick, 1973, p. 312). Some of these strains are more evident in families with pre-school children, and we shall discuss them in a later chapter. Many surround the transition to parenthood itself. The work of Le Masters (1968), Feldman (1971), Rossi (1974) and others has been pivotal in drawing professional attention to the emotional, psychological and physical strains of parenthood.

In a now historic paper, first published in 1957, Le Masters building on Hill, was one of the first to postulate parenthood as a crisis (Hill, 1949; Le Masters, 1957/68). By this Le Masters meant that the addition of the first child to an urban middle-class family represented a 'sharp or decisive change for which old patterns are inadequate', implying a difficult transition to the new situation. He stressed that this was common where children were planned and desired, the problem being that parents had 'almost completely romanticised parenthood', having little if any effective preparation for the parental role.

Le Masters mentions the following responses to parenthood that emerged from his study undertaken in 1953–6:

> The mothers reported the following feelings or experiences in adjusting to the first child: loss of sleep (especially during the early months); chronic 'tiredness' or exhaustion; extensive confinement to the home and the resulting curtailment of their social contacts; giving up the satisfaction and the income of outside employment; additional washing and ironing; guilt at not being a 'better' mother; the long hours and seven days (and nights) a week necessary in caring for an infant; decline in their housekeeping standards; and worry over their appearance (increased weight after pregnancy, etcetera).
>
> The fathers echoed most of the above problems but also added a few of their own: decline in sexual response of wife; economic pressure resulting from wife's retirement plus additional expenditures necessary for child; interference with social life; worry about a second pregnancy in the near future; and a general disenchantment with the parental role.
>
> The mothers with professional training and extensive professional work experience suffered 'extensive' or 'severe' crises in every case. These women were involved in two major adjustments simultaneously: (1) they are giving up an occupation which had deep significance for them; and (2) they were assuming the role of mother for the first time (Le Masters, 1957/68, p. 161).

From this exploratory study, Le Masters drew several – then radical – conclusions:

1 That parenthood (rather than marriage) is the real 'romantic complex' in our culture, a view expressed by many of his respondents.

2 'Couples are not trained for parenthood, that practically nothing in school, or out of school, got them ready to be fathers and mothers – *husbands* and *wives*, yes, but not *parents*.' Parents are caught unprepared, even though they have planned and waited for this event for years.

3 That couples find the transition to parenthood painful because the arrival of the first child rapidly changes their pair pattern of interaction into a triangle group system. 'Due to the fact that their

courtship and pre-parenthood pair relationship has persisted over a period of years, they find it difficult to give it up as a way of life' (Le Masters, 1957/68, p. 462). Either spouse may be jealous of the other's attentions to the baby. If they preserve their pair relationships, they are often thought of as poor parents.

4 That parenthood, rather than marriage, seems to mark the final transition to maturity and adult responsibility in our culture, suggests that 'the arrival of the first child forces young married couples to take the last painful step into the adult world' (Le Masters, 1957/68, p. 462).

Feldman's work considers the impact of children on the marital relationship even more focally. In a study by Feldman and Meyerowitz using questionnaire survey techniques on a sample of 400 primiparous couples drawn from several geographic areas in the USA, they assessed the effects of a first child on various aspects of the development of the marital relationship. One dimension they assessed was the expectation of satisfaction alongside the actual reported level of satisfaction at various stages of parenthood. They found marked differences between the sexes:

The period before pregnancy is recalled as being more positive than pregnancy. The decline in reported satisfaction during pregnancy is significantly more marked for the husband than for the wife. Wives expect further decline in satisfaction, while the husband expects a marked improvement after the first month with the baby (Meyerowitz and Feldman, 1966, p. 2).

On a measure on which the amount of time that things were 'going well' was assessed the authors found a steadily declining time during the early months of parenthood.

During pregnancy the mean % time that 'things were going well' was 85%. When the child was one month old a very slight decline was noted. At five months old the percentage had declined to almost 65% which suggests stress during the 2nd–5th months (Meyerowitz and Feldman, 1966, p. 2).

The authors identify unsatisfactory sexual relationships as presenting a major source of stress during this period, although the following were also important: inability to express feelings to the spouse, unshared leisure time, and inability to discuss the husbands' work. Significantly:

The respondents agreed strongly that having a baby made the marriage even better. But in response to specific questions they also agreed at a lower qualitative level with items stating 'our baby's needs conflict with our own desires', 'care of the baby limits the recreational activities we can do together', and 'when the baby is awake we find less time for each other'. But they disagreed with the statement that 'the baby's demands are a strain on the marital relationship' (Meyerowitz and Feldman, 1966, p. 5).

In general Feldman's work has shown that marital satisfaction tends to decline with first-time parenthood (Feldman, 1971). Disruption of the sexual relationship, chronic fatigue and exhaustion, feeling of nervousness and blueness, decline in verbal communication between spouses, decline in good humour, are common characteristics. The Clausens' work reports similar findings of fatigue and confusion in the wake of incessant child-centred demands on the time and energy of the parents of young children (Clausen and Clausen, 1973).

Some professionals feel that contemporary young adults have too little awareness of the burdensome aspects of parenting before they commit themselves to parenthood. Mia Kellmer Pringle is very aware of this deficit.

the current over-romanticised picture of parenthood, and of motherhood in particular – projected by the media and the advertising industry – ought to be changed. A more realistic and perhaps even daunting awareness needs to be created of the arduous demands which child rearing makes on the emotions, energy, time and finances, as well as the inevitable constraints on personal independence, freedom of movement and, indeed, one's whole way of life. Babies should be presented 'truthfully' warts and all – sometimes fretful and demanding, often wet, smelly, crying at night and 'unreasonable' – rather than with a permanent angelic dimply smile and sunny temper. Deglamourising parenthood in this way will not deter those who truly want to care for children but it may act as a brake on those with unrealistic expectations. . . . Several other notions, which have no foundation in fact, should also be dispelled: that having a child is the sole or most important or easiest way to feminine fulfilment; that a baby completes a home, rather like a T.V. set or fridge; that it will cement an unsatisfactory or failing marriage; that maternity has a therapeutic effect, particularly on girls who were themselves rejected in childhood; that a child belongs to his parents like their other possessions; and that he should be grateful to his parents even though he did not ask to be born (Kellmer Pringle, 1974, p. 156).

Le Masters has cited comparable beliefs prevalent in contemporary American culture, which may equally misinform a decision to parent, if too central to the motivation; some of them are that:

Rearing children is fun.
Children are sweet and cute.

Children will turn out well if they have 'good' parents.
Children appreciate all the advantages their parents give them.
Love is enough to sustain good parental performance.
All married couples should have children.
Childless married couples are frustrated and unhappy.
Children improve a marriage.
Child rearing is easier today because of modern medicine, modern
appliances, child psychology, etc. (Le Masters, 1970, pp. 18–29).

If people nowadays have too rosy a view of parenting *before they
parent*, this probably reflects societal tendencies rather than indicating
that the literature on parenting in particular is deficient. By the time
most people consciously start to read about parenthood issues – if they
do at all – their commitment to parenting has already been made. The
literature beamed at parents in the ante-natal situation is, therefore, not
relevant to the pre-conception situation. What agencies like the Family
Planning Association distribute, and what students are taught at school
is potentially more relevant.

The Department of Health and Social Security's book on *Preparation
for Parenthood* is a key document here, for, as an account of consultation
with agencies working in the field of preparation for parenthood, it
reflects both the present state of the field in the United Kingdom, and
directions in which professionals consider initiatives should be moving
(Department of Health and Social Security, 1974).

The consultation documents seem to have dealt more with *parentcraft*
than with parenting. The consultations were aimed at 'helping parents
to be better equipped to meet their responsibilities to their children'.
This was seen to necessitate a programme 'to try to impart awareness
and understanding of the developmental needs of children and the part
played by parents in meeting them' (DHSS, 1974, pp. 12 and 13). Once
the territory was defined in these terms, the main questions which
emerged related to the best way of promoting a programme so based:
whom to direct it at; at what stages in people's lives to direct it; what
methods to use; what knowledge to impart; and who to undertake this
programme? Although it was felt that a broad perspective was adopted
in the consultations (DHSS, 1974, p. 8), the perspective was, in our
terms, inevitably narrowed by the heavy emphasis on children's
developmental needs as the reference point.

Children's needs certainly influence parental experience. That is
why we consider parents' needs largely in relation to children's developmental phases. What is lacking in contemporary culture, however, is
sufficient awareness of people's *continuing developmental needs* – of
adults as well as children, and that includes parents. The consultation
documents reflected this deficiency rather than taking it on directly.

The Department of Health and Social Security programme of which the consultations form part has nevertheless promoted other work which opens the way to confronting the issues.

Talking of 'responsible parenthood', Kellmer Pringle remarks:

> Preparation for parenthood, including family planning, could make an important contribution. Modern parenthood is too demanding and complex a task to be performed well merely because we all have once been children ourselves. . . . An effective programme of preparation for parenthood would have to adopt a wide and comprehensive base. It should deal with the whole area of human relations and in particular with child development, first-hand experience of babies and young children should be an essential part of the programme; as should be an understanding of the ways in which the relations between a married couple are bound to change when they become parents.

> Responsible parenthood must come to mean that the parental life style has been freely and deliberately chosen in the full realisation of its demands (Kellmer Pringle, 1974, pp. 157–8).

This may seem a tall order, but in some ways it may be easier to meet than Kellmer Pringle implies. Although many characteristics are generic to the parental situation there is not, after all, a unique parental life style, and people have an increasing choice of life styles with which their parenting experience may be incorporated. Much of what we say in this book surrounds the variation that is possible.

In another respect Dr Pringle's agenda may not, however, be as feasible. *Can* people have a full realization of the parenting experience before they are immersed in it? At best the realization may be partial. Different devices, e.g. first-hand observation of babies, have been tried in an effort to increase the effectiveness of the anticipatory experience. But there are probably limits to what filters through to people before they experience the real situation themselves. It may be very difficult to envisage the fatigue of new parents responding to night-time feeds, for example, until one has the realization thrust on one. For many people the sensation of disturbed sleep recedes quickly as their infants, and they themselves, experience more restful nights. Conversely, it is difficult to envision the joy and delight of having a baby until one actually has one. Little is known about how fully people are able to anticipate the impact of parenting before they commit themselves to it. Focal research in this area may provide other insights too: like, how much do prospective parents think in terms of life with babies forever after when they decide to conceive, and how much do they realize – in advance – that babies, and they too, grow older. In short, whilst we think it desirable that prospective parents be able to anticipate some of the impact parenting will make on their lives, we think there may well be limits to this. Research in this area should be productive. Some research already indicates that mothers seek out advice when involved in particular stages from relevant experts; advice given at this time tends to be specially remembered (Maccoby *et al.*, 1962). A study by Robert Fein on men's experiences before and after the birth of a first child is a step in this direction (Fein, 1974a). A study in progress by Ann Oakley in West London aims also to throw some light on this area. We report on each of these studies later in this chapter.

Illuminating the birth experience

Though childbirth is doubtless still widely surrounded by a veil of secrecy, as the Newsons (1972) suggest, considerable demystification of the birth experience in our society has already taken place. Some of this will reach audiences not yet committed to parenting, via schools or the popular media. Some of this information has been popularly available only on a restricted basis, as with feature movies on giving birth.

The main thrust of consciousness-raising in relation to childbirth has taken place in hospitals and ante-natal classes held elsewhere. This is beamed at people who are already committed to parenthood, and at people who are receptive to getting a feel of what the experience may be like.

There is wide variation in the type and quality of the socio-psychological aspects of obstetric care available in the country. Some hospitals lay on talks, organize discussion groups for prospective parents, and arrange visits to labour and delivery rooms and maternity wards, familiarizing people with the equipment, physical layout, and ethos of the place. Few hospitals at present offer as much as this, and in some there is very little orientation to the transition. Crucial differences can lie behind apparently similar services. Talks or lectures on analgesia in labour, for example, can be highly prescriptive, or can explain alternatives to prospective parents and highlight their implications. The latter approach seems preferable in that it puts people in a better position to choose their own analgesic support, within clinically acceptable limits. It seems likely, however, that some people require a more directive approach.

Equally, there are wide variations in the service delivery offered during birth and the immediate post-partum period. One well known difference involves attitudes to fathers' presence: whether it is actively encouraged, grudgingly tolerated, or disallowed. Another important difference surrounds assistance with infant feeding: the extent to which parents are enabled to elect a preferred feeding method with a minimum of guilt, and given the support required to establish the feeding relationship on a confident footing. This has more important implications for breast feeding than is sometimes realized. In some situations parents will be left to sink or swim on their own; in others they are sensitively helped, and sometimes provided with detailed notes that beam right in to the microcosmic world of initial breast feeding, giving parents a reliable guide, explicating doubts they may be experiencing, and continually reminding them to ask for assistance should things not be working out well.

A lot of variation in quality hinges on who happens to be involved with parents in the care situation: e.g. the midwife concerned may be an empathetic person or not. A lot, too, depends on the structure of services locally available. How long are parents expected to stay in hospital: one week or forty-eight hours? or will they give birth at home? Services which seem complicated to administer are not necessarily so. It is possible, for example, for mothers and fathers to be encouraged to go out the evening before mother and baby leave the hospital. This may be an important time for the couple to learn that they can leave their baby in safe care and enjoy their relationship with each other. Frequently such issues are determined by considerations other than those likely to facilitate people's transition to the new parental situation. Once in a care situation, however, whether the parents are able to choose it or whether they are assigned to it, their experience is influenced by the explicit stances taken or overlooked by the hospital or health agency concerned, as well as by the personalities with whom they are in immediate contact.

A study of 54 primiparous women in London by Jane Hubert (1974), for example, revealed that in no case had any of the women seen a baby being born, and even amongst those who had attended classes too high a level of sophistication and knowledge was assumed. The majority of women were ill-prepared for labour. Hubert suggests that this affected their attitudes to the newborn child, and this was not helped by a general lack of communication from professionals.

What seems to be required at present, above all, is increased awareness amongst parents and prospective parents, and amongst professionals in the field of people's feelings about childbirth. Which feelings, if any, are generic to the experience? How do various people fare with alternative care approaches? This is an instance of the gap in contemporary knowledge about the contact points between care-givers and people in professional care situations. There are, however, signs that in the childbirth area, as in others, initiatives are afoot to improve the quality of that nexus.

In the USA the work of Niles Newton (1955, 1962) has been seminal, and in the UK Sheila Kitzinger's *Giving Birth* (1973) is a key work. It is subtitled 'The Parents' Emotions in Childbirth' and it aims directly to explore, 'with the help of labour reports written by women – and their husbands – soon after the event, what it *feels* like to have a baby, the complex emotions of pregnancy, the weeks after the baby comes, and the relationship between husband and wife through the whole process of child-bearing' (1973, italics original). The parents' accounts *do* convey a wide variety of possible experience in childbirth – emotional, physical and situational. One common factor between the respondents was that they had all attended Kitzinger's ante-natal classes, but the births took place in different settings. We quote two accounts here, one which shows the fulfilment a couple were able to attain in a self-consciously joint childbirth experience, whilst the other shows childbirth as an emotionally unexceptional experience. Appropriately for the experience of joint childbirth, each parent has written an account:

The mother writes:

> It was very much a joint effort. Without John I'm afraid I never would have made it. He played the most important part, and felt with me in a joint experience of the most important event in our lives. The tangible creation of our love was actually born, as well as conceived, in love. She is a very lucky baby, and so are we.

The father writes:

> I was awakened at approximately 3.00 a.m. by my wife in the bathroom. She told me she felt labour was beginning. I propped her up in bed. It took us all of half an hour to establish reasonable harmony of breathing with contractions. I breathed with her through all levels. I insisted that she breathe properly and relax; otherwise it would hurt. I did not remain a logical adviser, but rather a catalyst, acting through the spontaneity of love rather than logical detachment. I have the glorious realization that I have emotional harmony with my wife.
>
> We established harmony with the breathing, after which I left to call the midwife. I had Pippa on her side, she found this more comfortable, and was rubbing her back and breathing simultaneously with her when the midwife arrived. I was by this time wholly involved in the labour, and her breath was my breath. This was undistilled love, a oneness some only achieve through copulation. The midwife determined that the front part of the cervix was all that barred my baby's descent. She instructed my wife not to bear down but to continue to breathe with the contractions. We both continued, and when we blew out at the end of a contraction I gave her a puff from my cigarette.
>
> Now came the bearing down stage and the most painfully beautiful experience I have ever had. My wife was in a sitting position now. I had my right arm around her back with my hand under her arm supporting her, while her left arm was around my neck.

I knew there was no point in my saying, 'relax honey', I had to feel it with her. The perspiration was running down my back. I said, 'Come on honey, deep breath – now bear down!! Hold on, hold on!! Now breathe.' I could see a tiny portion of the baby's head lightly covered with black hair. The nurse made a small incision in the perineum. My wife and I took a breath and bore down. 'Bear down honey, it's coming! Bear down, bear down, hold on, hold on.' The baby's head popped out fully exposed to the neck. Along with it came the umbilical cord and nurse clamped it. My wife was told to pant and push gently on the next one.

The perspiration was rolling off my head. Then the glorious moment when the little being was wholly released from the vagina. The nurses turned the baby round. 'It's a girl, honey!' I shouted, 'It's a girl, honey!' I was beside myself with joy. I had given birth along with my wife. I was exhausted. It was glorious, just glorious.

Whoever said that a joint endeavour of husband and wife in natural childbirth was extremely fulfilling did not come anywhere near describing the ecstasy I experienced. We are so very happy. This experience has made a bond between us that no ordinary birth, nor in fact any other experience, could have done. We have a sense of rapport that goes far beyond anything I have ever experienced or observed. Emotional harmony, physical harmony, mental harmony. We have all three. Turbulent and passionate as it is – Yin and Yan – we are so blessed (Kitzinger, 1973, pp. 148–50).

The idealization of childbirth expressed above is by no means universal. Kitzinger recognizes this in her introduction to a contrasting experience:

Not all women, however well prepared, enjoy childbirth – and certainly a great many feel no special ecstasy. It is important to allow a woman her *own* feelings, and not to deny them their validity in any way by stimulating emotions. This mother found nothing 'spiritual' or 'revealing' in her labour, but felt it was a job well done (Kitzinger, 1973, p.11).

The mother concerned writes:

The general impression was that the methods of relaxation worked. I should have felt completely at sea without the knowledge, even though we had a most helpful and sympathetic midwife, and I had Julian's hand to hang on to. You will gather from this that I did not find it an uplifting experience, but I did get a lot of satisfaction from being able to control myself. I'm sure it was a very good thing for Serena. She is marvellous!

The doctor arrived at an awkward stage in the transition, when we were trying treating a contraction as first stage-type instead of looking for pushes. The shallow rapid breathing worked beautifully.
Doctor: Was *that* a contraction?
Midwife: Yes, a *good* one.
Doctor: Well, I'll read the Sunday paper in the next room until something more interesting (dramatic?) happens.
My husband reminded me of all the things I was forgetting, stuffed wet sponges in my mouth, gave me powerful mixes of PLJ and glucose (most refreshing) and startling accounts of first sight of the baby's hair. ('It looks the colour of a winkle – after all it *is* a marine animal still!') It must be a great deprivation not to have your husband with you (Kitzinger, 1973, pp. 77–8).

A *range* of this sort of account giving them an idea of possible courses of the childbirth experience, has much to offer imminent parents as an orientation device. The detailed reporting of parents' experiences has much to offer professionals, by way of yielding insights for more sensitive care. The breast-feeding notes mentioned earlier, for example, are obviously informed by talks with many mothers. Such studies could reach back earlier in the ante-natal period, and still earlier in some cases, and extend forwards into the post-natal situation, both immediate and extended.

Some professionals are well aware how much can be learned from patients directly, to inform the nature of the service offered. Jolly indicates how readily available some of the evidence is. He suggests what really needs to be known to predict future difficulties is what the pregnant woman really feels about the baby inside her:

Much can be learnt from the way the girl enters the doctor's surgery or the hospital clinic to determine whether or not she is pregnant. Some will radiate happiness whereas others will show how frightened they are lest they are pregnant. It is on this first ante-natal visit that so much must be learnt about the girl's feelings. This is the occasion when it is possible; later in pregnancy when so much else has happened it will be much more difficult. The doctor should find himself able to answer the question: 'What did his patient feel when she first knew she was pregnant?' (Jolly, 1975).

Pregnancy and childbirth are times when people tend to be specially open with information about their feelings, and are often eager to talk about their experiences and concerns. Care-givers are in a position to learn a good deal if they are prepared to listen. Some researchers are now directing studies towards systematic documentation of parents' feelings at this time (Newton, 1955; Newton and Newton, 1962).

The birth experience as a determinant of outcome

An ongoing study by Ann Oakley on how 50 contemporary British women (25 working-class and 25 middle-class) experience becoming a mother is distinguished by the particular emphasis she places on the women's treatment by medical personnel. In this study, the women's feelings about medical treatment received (in the clinic, hospital and general practice situations) are conceptualized as variables of potential relevance to the quality of her transition from a non-maternal to a maternal role. Other distinctive features include Oakley's focus on clinically 'normal' childbirth, with the welfare of the mother rather than infant as the primary research concern. She points out that in other studies where the mothers' attitudes and feelings have been the primary concern, the perspective adopted is often influenced by the psycho-analytic view in which the woman's level of psychosexual development and acceptance of the female role is stressed. Oakley's interviews with mothers having their first baby (two interviews during pregnancy, one after the birth, and one when the baby is five months old) should provide useful data.

Psychoanalytic view on variables critical to the outcome of pregnancy

The study of pregnancy and its outcome in relation to the mother–child relationship, has attracted considerable attention from psychoanalysts. Grete Bibring (1959; 1961), Therese Benedek (1970a), and Gerald Caplan (1959; 1961) have made major contributions. They share with others in the field, e.g. Pines (1972), a preventive psychiatric perspective, underpinned by psychoanalytic theory.

These clinicians have considered pregnancy focally in terms of women, and have attempted to describe generic characteristics of 'normal' pregnancy. It was observed that the behaviour of pregnant women was often similar to that found in severely disturbed patients: 'Magical thinking, premonitions, depressive reactions, primitive anxieties, introjective and paranoid mechanisms, frequently associated with the patient's relation to her own mother, seemed to prevail' (Bibring, 1959, p. 115). Pregnancy patients were perceived as responding particularly rapidly to therapeutic intervention. Researchers in the field postulated various theories about normal pregnancy as a time of 'normal crisis'.

Bibring's group, in line with the territory mapped by Erikson in *Childhood and Society* (1950), proposed the following formulation of pregnancy:

> as a crisis that affects all expectant mothers, no matter what their state of psychic health. Crises, as we see it, are turning points in the

life of the individual, leading to acute disequilibria which under favourable conditions result in specific maturational steps toward new functions. We find them as developmental phenomena at points of no return between one phase and the next when decisive changes deprive former central needs and modes of living of their significance, forcing the acceptance of highly charged new goals and functions (Bibring, 1959, p. 119).

This formulation related mainly to the intrapsychic elements of the transition to maternity, and to physiological ones. The social aspects of the role transition to parenthood were considered only marginally. The biases in the orientation were clearly illustrated in the following:

> Pregnancy, like puberty or menopause, is a period of crisis inducing profound psychological as well as somatic changes. These crises represent important developmental steps and have in common a series of characteristic phenomena. In pregnancy, as in puberty and menopause, new and increased libidinal and adjustive tasks confront the individual, leading to the revival and simultaneous emergence of unsettled conflicts from earlier developmental phases and to the loosening of partial or inadequate solutions of the past. This disturbance in the equilibrium of the personality is responsible for creating temporarily the picture of a more severe disintegration. The outcome of this crisis is of the greatest significance for the mastery of the thus initiated phase (maturity in puberty, aging in menopause, and motherhood in pregnancy) (Bibring, 1959, p. 116).

Whilst Bibring suggested that 'there is a disturbance, peculiar to the period of pregnancy, arising from the facts of pregnancy themselves, be they emotional, physiological, or social', she in fact dwelt in the psychological:

> Stress is inherent in all areas: in the endocrinological changes, in the activation of unconscious psychological conflicts pertaining to the factors involved in pregnancy, and in the intrapsychic reorganization of becoming a mother. A new organization of all forces must be made, and this necessity leads to the crisis of pregnancy. Within this crisis, of course, individual problems and neurotic conflicts of significance are highlighted.

> If one assumes then that pregnancy involves intense upheaval of psychological processes, the question may be raised of the possible effects this has on the attitude of mothers towards their infants. We may have to consider that in a number of cases reorganization of the psychic equilibrium has not yet taken place when the woman is confronted with the reality of the newborn and the further demands this places on her (Bibring, 1959, pp. 116–17).

Thus much of the weight of the outcome of pregnancy was attributed to the mother's intrapsychic experience of the transition. Other variables were relatively dismissed, including the mother's intrapsychic response to the social aspects of her transition to the maternal role. Social factors were marginal to the formulation, and were suggested to affect outcome in two respects. Bibring observed firstly that contemporary changes resulted in a lessening of supportive sources in society, making the mother reliant on the marital relationship for more support than it can often give. Second, she noted the declining attention to the irrational and emotional aspects of living, and thus 'appropriate expression and elaboration of her (the mother's) emotional involvement', in parallel with the increased emphasis on 'scientific' in contemporary society (Bibring, 1959, p. 118).

Benedek's contemporary writing on pregnancy built on her work over many years. In *Parenthood: Its Psychology and Psychopathology* (1970) she presented her views on the psychobiology of pregnancy. The aspects emphasized are self-evident from the terminology.

> Pregnancy is a 'critical phase' in the life of a woman. Using the term as ethologists use it, it implies that pregnancy, like puberty, is a biologically motivated step in the maturation of the individual which requires physiologic adjustments and psychologic adaptations to lead to a new level of integration that, normally, represents development (Benedek, 1970a, p. 137).

The social aspects of pregnancy as a status transition were not included in this formulation. Nevertheless, her emphasis on the physiological underpinnings of pregnancy was both distinctive and important.

Much is now known about the physical impact of pregnancy on women – e.g. increase in weight and size, the tendency towards varicose veins, fatigue, etc. This may be more extreme with subsequent rather than first pregnancies, as mothers with small children to care for often have little time or energy to care for themselves. More needs to be known of the impact of such physical changes on women's self conceptions.

Caplan's conceptualization of the psychology of pregnancy is the most inclusive. In *An Approach to Community Mental Health* (1961), Caplan defined crisis as a state of intrapsychic disequilibrium, and postulated pregnancy as a period of increased susceptibility to feelings of crisis. In such a period, he suggested one expects to find an increase in the individual's important problems on the one hand, and 'a weakening of the essential ego structure, so that the person cannot make use of his usual repertoire of problem-solving methods, or that his supports in his family, in his social environment, and in his culture, might be weakened' on the other (1961, p. 66). The person is thus likely to be less able to deal with the increased problems in hand.

Caplan observed that these conditions apply in pregnancy. There *are* important problems – among which is the woman moving to a new role, usually experienced as a greater change when a first baby is expected, but for some women, greater on the birth of their second child. In preparing for this new role, Caplan writes there is likely to be a revival of old ideas and fantasies of what the role will entail. Hence the woman is likely to become involved with feelings about her own mother, leading to complications if her relationship with her mother was a conflictual one. 'They are likely to modify her feelings about what will happen when she becomes a mother and, as it were, takes her mother's place. Will she become a better mother than her own mother was or will she be worse?' (Caplan, 1961, p. 67). Caplan emphasized that the increased susceptibility to crises hinges not only on psychological problems, but 'economic and social problems' too. Examples are where the woman has to interrupt her working life, or when there are housing problems associated with the expected child.

Caplan also observed an altered capacity to deal with problems, which were seen to be associated with the normal metabolic changes of pregnancy, a time of altered behaviour and emotional upsets. His third variable related to the weakening of external supports in dealing with the problems.

> The upsets in the pregnant woman, as a result of all that she is going through, are apt to produce upsets in the equilibrium of all members of her family, particularly her husband. The upsets produced in him are *upsets in his relationship with his wife*, so that very often he is less able to support her during this period than during their normal relationship when she is not pregnant (Caplan, 1961, p. 214).

This is at a time when, Caplan observed, the wife needs more psychological supplies than usually.

His view of pregnancy strongly indicated opportunities for mental health intervention. That is, that people are receptive to help with their problems at these times. First, in a crisis old problems surface and new ones arise. There is a chance for new solutions, which may be healthy or unhealthy. Caplan saw it as critical for a healthy solution that pregnant women be able to realize that when the baby comes along it will be 'an individual in its own right, separate and different from everyone else she has dealt with in her life in the past' (Caplan, 1961, p. 85).

Crisis also seems to facilitate intervention because of the situation being in a state of flux; the person is more susceptible to influence when he is in disequilibrium.

Therefore, we can say that the crises of pregnancy present us with a very good opportunity to affect, by minimal intervention, the future mental health of the woman. And since we are dealing here with a series of crises which are strung on the strand of the development of the relationship of this woman to her future child, this gives us an unequalled opportunity to influence the way she will develop in her relationship as a future mother to this child. Moreover, since the crises involve in an intimate way not only the woman but all the rest of the family, this gives us an opportunity to influence by the use of minimal effort, in order to improve the total family relationships of this little group of people. It is from these points of view that I am interested in the psychology of pregnancy (Caplan, 1961, p. 72; cf. Lomas, 1967).

Caplan, nevertheless, never shifted the focus in this process from the mother. According to his perspective, father may be involved, but there are limits to his involvement and he should not be pushed too far. His is a supportive, giving role in relation to his wife who receives. He may have upsets during the pregnancy, but these relate to his relationship with his wife, rather than his imminent parenthood.

In our culture husbands are not held in high esteem during pregnancy and delivery. Some people have attempted to remedy this by involving the husband actively in taking care of his pregnant wife and enlisting his collaboration in the delivery process. This is all to the good, as long as they do not push him too far, and expect from him more than certain husbands are able to do. . . . The expectant father is mostly a figure of ridicule in our culture.

This is extremely unfortunate, because from what I have been saying it is clear that he should have an important role in providing emotional supplies for his wife. He should be making sure that her 'battery is charged up' so that she can afterwards help her child. He has the task of giving her support during the crises of pregnancy so that her weakened ego can be strengthened by his. . . . The husband may also be upset; and in our culture this may lead to the beginnings of marital disharmony. This is especially so because of the changes in the wife's sexual appetite, if this happens to be a change for the worse. She becomes frigid and loses her desire; and at the same time she becomes irritable and sensitive and easily insulted. In these circumstances, if the husband does not understand what is going on, he is apt to feel that she no longer loves him, he may ascribe this to having made her pregnant, especially in view of her possible initial negative reaction to conception. He is apt to be quite sexually frustrated too, and either to have fantasies of infidelity or to go out and look for alternative satisfaction (Caplan, 1961, pp. 94–5).

The corpus of work described above has some serious limitations. One is its exclusion from the view of entry into parenthood of the social aspects of this transition. Caplan has gone the furthest of the psycho-analysts reviewed towards including social considerations in any systematic way, but in our view, the resultant scheme still leaves a disproportionately weighty burden for the 'outcome' on the mother's intrapsychic state. This is not surprising when one considers the context in which these professionals worked. They are all clinicians, and though in this instance their orientation was towards 'normal' pregnancy, they were used to dealing with pathology. A limitation related to overlooking the changing role aspects of the transition, and to the heavy focus on the mother's feelings of crisis in the here and now, was an implicit sugges-tion that the 'outcome' is an end product, having qualities of finality, and deterministic for the nature of the mother–child relationship thus established. Whilst this is partly so, we suggest that the post-partum period can also be fruitfully viewed as the start of another stage. A second group of limitations surrounds the exclusion of pivotal figures, other than the mother, from focal consideration in the transition – in particular, the father, and the infant. This ties in with a specific culture-bound view of the nature of the marital relationship. We now look at writings which go some way to filling these gaps.

Transition to parenthood: A critical status transition

Alice Rossi's conceptualization of the transition to parenthood goes a long way towards bringing into focus the social aspects of the process (1968–74). The main questions of her sociological analysis are: (1) What is involved in the transition to parenthood: what must be learned and what readjustments of other commitments must take place in order to move smoothly through the transition from a childless married state to parenthood? (2) What is the effect of parenthood on the adult: in what ways do parents, and in particular mothers, change as a result of their parental experiences.

Rossi's contribution is also distinctive in focusing on the adult parent, rather than the child, and retains an integrated and inclusive framework. This is in line with 'heightened contemporary interest in adult socialization' on the one hand and 'the growing concern of behavioural scientists with crossing levels of analysis to adequately comprehend social and individual phenomena and to build theories appropriate to a complex social system' on the other (Rossi, 1974, p. 105). Rossi specifies:

> In the past, social anthropologists focussed as purely on the level of prescriptive normative variables as psychologists had concentrated on intrapsychic processes at the individual level or sociologists on social-structural and institutional variables. . . .

It is no longer possible for a psychologist or a therapist to neglect the social environment of the individual subject or patient. . . . So too it is no longer possible for the sociologist to focus exclusively on the current family relationships of the individual (Rossi, 1974, p. 105).

Rossi, therefore built instead on a third strand of work which views parenthood as a *developmental stage* (Rapoport, 1963, 1964; Rapoport and Rapoport, 1964, 1965). Her use of transition – as a neutral term – is pointed. Previously, new developmental stages were commonly referred to as times of 'crisis' and, later, 'normal crises'. Rossi was concerned not to dichotomize normality and pathology, and to have a single framework for dealing with a range of outcomes: 'A conceptual system which can deal with both successful and unsuccessful role transitions, or positive and negative impact of parenthood upon adult men and women, is thus more powerful than one built to handle success but not failure or vice versa' (Rossi, 1974, p. 106).

The framework in which Rossi views the transition to parenthood specifies the stages in the development of the parental role, and compares that role with the two other major adult roles – in work and marriage. The stages defined in the development of all role cycles are: (a) anticipatory; (b) the honeymoon stage i.e. immediately after the role is assumed; (c) the plateau stage – or protracted middle period during which the role is fully exercised, and (d) disengagement – termination. Consistent with her concern with *transition to parenthood* Rossi focuses on the first two of these stages. She aims to identify the unique and most salient features of the parental role. Numerous important points surrounding the transition to parenthood are made.

Firstly, she emphasizes the considerable cultural pressure on young women to see maternity as necessary to a woman's fulfilment as an individual, and to secure her adult status. Rossi observes that the inception of pregnancy is not always voluntary, that 'it may be the unintended consequence of a sexual act that was recreative in intent rather than procreative' (1974, p. 107). Given this, and the cultural resistance to terminating pregnancies, she speculates on a high incidence of unwanted pregnancies in society, and draws attention to the relative lack of research into parental satisfaction:

> Only the extreme tip of the parental satisfaction continuum is clearly demarcated and researched, as in the growing concern with 'battered babies'. Cultural and psychological resistance to the image of a non-nurturant woman may afflict social scientists as well as the . . . public (Rossi, 1974, p. 107).

Rossi points to the timing of first pregnancies as critical to the way parental responsibilities are joined to the marital relationship. She charts the influence of widespread contraceptive usage and suggests that where pregnancy follows close on marriage, marriage is the major turning point in a woman's life. Rossi feels that the major transition point is increasingly the first pregnancy rather than marriage. Other researchers, like Oakley, share this view. We think it conceptually more precise to view both marriage and first (and subsequent) births as social and psychological *points of no return* for the primary incumbents of these experiences. They may be seen as transitions of similar significance, although the constellation of implications hinging on the first birth, is increasing in its impact on women's lives especially, whilst the implications hinging on marriage alone may be receding. First pregnancy is more of a transition point for women because it so often marks the transition to fulltime housewifery; both have to be coped with at once.

Where there is a break after marriage and before parenting, wives tend to work in occupations and husbands are usually still establishing themselves occupationally. Rossi believes that the fact that couples are on an equal footing in this early period 'presses for a greater egalitarian relationship between husband and wife in decision-making, commonality of experience, and sharing of household responsibilities' (1974, p. 107). Gavron (1966) has suggested, on the basis of British data, that in this new situation parents may establish some barriers between themselves and their children – 'a marital defence against the institution of parenthood' – replacing the typical coalition in more traditional families of mother and children against husband-father. Rossi notes the increasing commitment to both marital and parenthood roles before the husband's and often wife's, education is complete.

A special quality of the transition to parenthood surrounds its 'irrevocability'. Rossi crisply comments: 'We can have ex-spouses and ex-jobs, but not ex-children' (Rossi, 1974, p. 108). She thinks giving children for adoption is a rare way of undoing the commitment, with psychological withdrawal on the part of the parent a more common response. Here Rossi demonstrates how a focus on the parents generates new possibilities for understanding variations in children according to their sex–birth order position among their siblings. Her overarching point is that the transition to parenthood – or in this case motherhood – is not necessarily positive: 'For many women the personal outcome of experience in the parent role is not a higher level of maturation but the negative outcome of a depressed sense of self-worth, if not actual personality deterioration' (Rossi 1974, p. 109). She feels that there is ample evidence that for many women maternity has not provided opportunities for personal growth and development, on a qualitative level.

The possibility must be faced, and at some point researched, that women lose ground in personal development and self-esteem during the early and middle years of adulthood, whereas men gain ground in these respects during the same years. The retention of a high level of self-esteem may depend on the adequacy of earlier preparation for major adult roles in the occupational system, as it does for those women who opt to participate significantly in the work world. Training in the qualities and skills needed for family roles in contemporary society may be inadequate for both sexes, but the lowering of self-esteem occurs only among women because their primary adult roles are within the family system (Rossi, 1974, p. 109).

This issue is explored in Dana Breen's study of 50 women's first experiences of childbirth (Breen, 1975). Using repertory grid and projective techniques on mothers, Breen has researched some of the changes that take place for women before and after childbirth. She distinguishes between 'well-adjusted' and 'ill-adjusted' women by means of various tests and finds that the latter group is characterized by, *inter alia*, 'some sort of conflict between the way they see themselves and the way in which they construe the mothering role' (Breen, 1975, p. 122). Breen suggests that women in this group tend to have a more stereotyped, unrealistic and idealized view of the mother's role, which 'appears to be culturally determined during pregnancy'. Of 'well-adjusted' mothers, Breen writes:

> I think it is possible to say from looking at the findings I have presented that some women are well-adjusted in the sense that they experience no conflict with the social environment and the traditional roles it defines, but that others are well-adjusted in the broader, less constricted sense that they are at peace with a more personal definition of their role and that they are able to call forth a more realistic appraisal of their human environment where positive and negative qualities are integrated (Breen, 1975, p. 126).

Given the demands of the role transition involved, Rossi believes that contemporary preparation for parenthood is quite inadequate. She highlights four points (1974, p. 110):

1 Children have little opportunity to learn pragmatically in the subjects most relevant to family life – sex, home maintenance, child-care, interpersonal competence, empathy. She speculates that most American mothers may face maternity with no previous child-care experience 'beyond sporadic baby-sitting, perhaps a course in child psychology, or occasional care of younger siblings'.

2 There exists a lack of any realistic training for parenthood in the anticipatory stage of pregnancy. She feels the possibilities in the type of preparation that does exist – reading, consultations with friends, parents, spouse, and preparing a place and equipment for the baby, are limited.

3 When the baby does arrive, assumption of responsibility for it is abrupt. There is 'little intervening apprenticeship experience of slowly increasing responsibility. The new mother starts out immediately on 24-hour duty, with responsibility for a fragile and mysterious infant totally dependent on her care.'

4 There is also a lack of guidelines to successful parenthood in terms of values for child-raising, though parents are readily informed about their children's food, clothing and medical and related needs.

Rossi has probably gone the furthest in explicating the social aspects of the transition to parenthood. But even she looks at the transition very much in terms of motherhood rather than parenthood.

The present need is to develop frameworks which *systematize the integration of social and psychological phenomena of critical status transitions* and which are able to handle both the generic characteristics of all critical status transitions and the specific ones of particular transitions.

Some work towards this has already been done (Rapoport, 1963, 1964; Rapoport and Rapoport, 1964, 1965). Substantively this work dealt with the critical status transitions of getting married and becoming a parent. Some of the generic issues discussed in these studies include the emphasis on integrating the intrapsychic and social strands of life. For example, at critical status transitions, tasks have to be confronted irrespective of personality structure, and individuals can solve them in their own ways and develop as a result. Even if it is difficult for some people to accomplish the tasks because of their personalities, they may be helped by using their social resources, such as friends and/or health visitors. So it is important to look also at participation and resources in all spheres of life such as family and work: decisions and possibilities in one sphere will be influenced by the others.

A final relevant contribution – very important for later stages – is the way this work highlights the need to look ahead to subsequent stages, e.g. to parenthood once married. In general, outcomes to a particular transition are not only end products but the setting for stages to follow. People who have not managed well at one stage may still recoup at another.

Fathers and pregnancy

A major limitation of existing perspectives on the transition to parenthood is the exclusion of fathers from focal consideration. This is consistent with established views on fathering in psychoanalysis, as exemplified by Benedek (1970b) in her portrayal of 'fatherhood and providing', in which she talks of the affective qualities of 'fatherliness', as having an almost secondary nature.

What is genuine fatherliness? How does it come about? Fatherliness is an instinctively rooted character trend which enables the father to act toward his child or all children with immediate empathetic responsiveness. Fatherliness is not *rooted* as directly as fatherhood itself in the instinct for survival in the child, yet it is derivative of the reproductive drive organization (Benedek, 1970b, p. 175).

Where fathers have been looked at focally during pregnancy, the orientation has been to pathology, in contrast to the concern with women in normal pregnancy. An example that attempts to break with this tradition is the paper by Jessner *et al.* (1970) on 'The Development of Parental Attitudes during Pregnancy'. They challenge the conventional stereotype they observed of the new and expectant father: a role characterized by the maturational transition of youth into adult, and the phallic achievement of the boastful beaming father. In addition they note that the father is presented as a slightly comical figure – someone who has done his job and deserves praise, but must content himself with a supporting role while the real drama is enacted by wife and obstetrician during pregnancy and childbirth.

Jessner and his colleagues suggest there are signs that this is changing and that the following are relevant: (1) acceptance of previous psycho-analytic findings and recognition of the emotional importance of father-hood; (2) changing family structure in the new urban environment; (3) shifts in the cultural definition of masculinity. They observe that 'the evolving social structure of middle-class America redefines and emphasizes the participant role of the expectant father and the new father' (Jessner *et al.*, 1970, p. 231). Nevertheless they seemed to treat fathers on equal terms with mothers. Eager to protect fathers from the fate of another demanding stereotype, and cautious over limits to fathers' involvement, they stressed their differences from, rather than similarities with, mothers. 'Fatherliness is humanized by a new emphasis on participation, but if it is seen as identical with motherliness instead of complementary to it, there is distortion of the authentic paternal role' (Jessner, *et al.*, 1970, p. 232). Dorothy Burlingham (1973) has recently also made a move away from tradition in focusing on the pre-oedipal infant–father relationship.

A recent empirical study by Greenberg and Morris (1974) found that in a sample of 30 'first' fathers from 3 British maternity hospitals, fathers manifested 'engrossment' in their newborn infants, a sense of bonding, absorption, and preoccupation in their child. The researchers interpreted this as an innate potential 'released' in fathers by exposure to the infant.

The Newsons (1963/72, pp. 122–47) have looked at the part played by fathers in parenting with infants. Their work is more sociological;

they recorded the degree of participation in infant care by Nottingham fathers in the late 1950s. They assessed a participation rate for fathers by asking mothers whether fathers took part in: feeding; nappy changing; bathing; getting baby to sleep; attending to it at night; taking it out without mother; playing with the baby – often, sometimes or not at all. Their report was informative, and now provides a useful 'historical' data base in a changing domestic area.

Elements in the Newsons' assessment of father's participation suggest some generic problems of research in changing patterns of values and behaviour. In the case of fathers who were rarely at home because of work commitments, for example, the Newsons assessed their participation in infant care by rating them on the basis of their likelihood of helping when at home (Newson and Newson, 1963/72, p. 135). This may be a realistic basis on which to have rated participation of working-class fathers in Nottingham in the late 1950s, but it overlooks the possibility, however tentative in that case, that people may have some scope to choose how much and when they work. Approaching it in the way outlined ignores possibilities of change. Another example from the Newsons' data-interpretation which highlights the point of just where to break into assessing people's values, concerns who tends to children at night. The Newsons say it is often more convenient for mother to do this, because the cot is usually on the mother's side of the bed (Newson and Newson, 1963/72, p. 136). This leaves out the question of why the cot is always on the mother's side!

Values about men's and women's roles have changed a lot in the time since the Newsons' early work. This is particularly marked in the USA, a situation reflected in Robert Fein's work. In his study of 'Men's Experience Before and After the Birth of a First Child', Fein has tried to fill some of the gap in existing approaches (Fein, 1974a). He looked at a non-clinical sample of men entering parenthood, without reliance on a crisis perspective, and in a framework that brings out the fathers' strengths and weaknesses. His overall conclusions, from an exploratory field study with 30 middle-class American couples, interviewed before and after childbirth, are:

> That men experience a greater range of feelings and can participate more actively in infant care than previous literature on men's perinatal experiences has suggested ... it is useful to consider pregnancy, birth, and post-partum infant care in the context of a couple and not solely as an experience of the mother (Fein, 1974a).

Fein's descriptive analysis deals with prenatal experiences, the birth process, and post-natal experiences. When Fein first asked men to talk about their feelings in pregnancy, men often responded in terms of their wives' feelings, but when pressed to talk about their own feelings, many

were found to share those of their wives. Some of the men said they
thought of themselves as members of a 'pregnant couple'. Fein suggests
that pregnancy is a psychological reality for men, as he saw men participating in the pregnancy and preparing for the coming change in their
lives, though the degree of consciousness about these processes varied.
The four major areas of concern men described were: labour and
delivery; parenting; the amount of emotional and financial support they
would give and receive; and possible changes in their marriages and
life styles, though most men said their worries about the birth lessened
after attending childbirth education classes. Everyone in Fein's sample
attended such classes – most men had gone at their wives' initiative,
though some had encouraged their wives to go, and others had assumed
from the start that they were in the experience together.

Most men felt generally positive about approaching parenthood, with
moments of doubt. Fein encapsulates the ambivalence in observations
like: 'Most of the time I can't wait. And some mornings I get up and say
to myself, "sure I can wait. I wish I could wait longer" ' (Fein, 1974a,
p. 21). One of his respondents put it this way:

> There's a certain type of person in mental hospitals who is charac-
> terized by not being able to make connections between actions and
> their consequences, and that's exactly what I feel like. The fact that
> we made love one night, and that led to this, is very strange to me.
> The synapse is broken from the fact that Abby's that big to the fact
> that she's going to give birth. That just seems like another world.
> And then from giving birth to being parents. I can see us giving
> birth, 'nice job, Abby. Now just leave that over there with the nurse
> and we'll go home' (Fein, 1974a, p. 21).

Some men were worried about how to care for children. Many wished
to be emotionally closer to their children than their fathers had been to
them. But they felt they had almost no models for this from the culture
in which they had grown up. Hence they were trying to familiarize
themselves with children, most observing children more than previously,
some reading about child development and parenting, whilst some
practised parenting with pets. Others were concerned about insufficient
support after the birth, especially those whose families lived far away.
Some were worried too, by how the child would make them change or
restrict their life styles. Some men planned not to be in paid employment
after the birth to aid in this transition.

Most men said they expected at least occasional difficulty in the
postnatal period, with a 'we'll take one step at a time' attitude common.
Overall, men in the study prepared to face the coming weeks in their
lives with mixtures of anxiety, stoicism, excitement, and hope (Fein,
1974a, p. 25).

All Fein's male respondents were in the labour room for some time during childbirth; almost all participated actively in labour; most attended their babies' births.

> Men timed contractions, breathed along with their wives to help them stay 'on top' of contractions, massaged backs, brought ice chips and juice, translated and transmitted requests from their wives to doctors and nurses, gave constant caring attention and encouragement, and were consistent reminders to their wives when labor was most difficult that the women were not alone and that labour would end (Fein, 1974a, p. 25).

In an English study by Richman, Goldthorp and Simmons the place of men in the labour room and in the hospital generally was described quite differently. The authors describe the 'entrance trauma' many men felt in the hospital reception area: 'They emotively described their wife as "being taken from them" or "disappearing" with a "silent midwife" ' (Richman *et al.*, 1975, p. 144). Their description of the fathers' participation is in sharp contrast to that of Fein:

> In some ways the father's presence at birth can be likened to a small boy permitted to enter the sanctuary of the school staffroom. . . . He can be dismissed at will while the doctor makes an examination. His rights to be present are not only limited, but vague. During labour he often sleeps. At birth he is not certain what to do where to stand or put his hands (Richman *et al.*, 1975, p. 145).

Fein's respondents were surprised at how tired they felt after delivery. As did the parents' reactions recorded by Kitzinger (1973), so did the male's reactions at delivery in Fein's sample range from great emotion to detachment. Husbands and wives who were together during the birth found the experience important. Both men and women repeated that the emotional support of nursing staff was critical to them during the birth. It seemed to Fein that it was especially with the difficult labours that the support of medical staff was welcomed when given and missed when not. He compared the handling of two fathers, both of whose wives underwent emergency Caesarean operations, while they waited nervously. The more fortunate one reports:

> All of a sudden, the doctor walked into the waiting room, still dressed in his operating outfit. Walking quickly up to me, stopped, and said, 'What did you say you were going to name your son?' (Fein, 1974a, p. 28).

His counterpart waited and waited:

> All the nurses seemed so busy. One told me to be patient, that I'd be informed when there was news. Finally I called a friend to get a break from my worrying. He congratulated me and told me that he had

called the hospital and received the announcement that mother and son were well. The nurses and doctors had forgotten me (Fein, 1974a, p. 28).

In the study of Greenberg and Morris cited earlier, both fathers who witnessed the birth, as well as those who did not, reported feelings of engrossment with the infant (Greenberg and Morris, 1974). These included: the feeling that they could easily distinguish their baby from others; the feeling that their child was perfect; that they were strongly attracted to their infant and focused their attention on him or her, and that they felt extreme elation and increased self-esteem because of their child. There was, however, a trend that fathers who were present at their infant's birth felt more comfortable in holding their baby. The researchers suggest that current hospital practices may interfere with the 'release' of this paternal engrossment response. They recommend that fathers' visual and physical contact with the child should be encouraged as soon after the birth as possible.

A study by Parke and O'Leary (1975) which compared mothers' and fathers' behaviour towards newborn infants, included observations in both a university and a general metropolitan hospital. Each of the hospital samples was from a different socio-economic group. Nevertheless, the study showed no differences in the fathers' feelings and behaviour to the infant. Fathers were observed to be very active interactors with their infants, and to stimulate the child physically and verbally. Moreover, fathers' interaction with their newborn infants did not appear to depend on the mothers' presence.

It may be that fathers have greater opportunity to show fatherly feelings when childbirth takes place at home. One couple in Fein's sample, 'of the opinion that hospitals are places for illness and that birth is a process of health', delivered their baby at home. Fein conveys the pride the father experienced in taking his one-hour-old baby on a tour of their home, whilst mother and father shared a bed the night of the birth, with their child next to them.

Most men reported that the weeks after the birth were hard but not horrible. It emerged repeatedly how unprepared new parents were for the amount of work involved in caring for a small infant. By six weeks post-partum, most couples had established a relatively ordered pattern of home life and baby care, though specific arrangements varied considerably by couple, and the process of adjusting continued. The feelings of the first night home seem to have had a special stamp on the subsequent toning. The amount of post-natal help couples received from external sources varied, as did their child-care routines, in which 'the traditional model of mother primarily responsible for the care of the infant and father caring for mother and child was the rule' (Fein, 1974a, p. 31). There were, however, important exceptions to this.

Fein has identified several critical factors in post-partum adjustment. An obvious one is *family support* and several respondents reported thinking more about their parents and siblings since the birth of their own children than previously. *Work support* was a key variable to men grappling with the question of how to blend and balance family life and work life. Men reported receiving little emotional or material support from work for the transition. Where support was offered it was usually personal rather than institutional. None of Fein's male respondents received paid paternity leave. The quality of support from the workplace is conveyed by Fein's record of the following accounts.

> 'The women in the office were all excited,' said one man. 'The men asked about the baby but weren't really interested.' Another man spoke with disappointment about the attitude at his job toward fatherhood. 'There's a feeling of "so what's a baby, just make sure you're on time." ' Contrasting this experience, a social worker said that his schedule was adjusted over the summer so that he could spend more time with his wife and child. 'People at work really love the baby', he noted. 'Sometimes it feels like one big family.' Many men seemed to take a stoical attitude toward the lack of support from work. 'I didn't expect much and I didn't get much' summed up many feelings (Fein, 1974a, pp. 34–35).

Home-based employment was the ideal seen to facilitate many needs and requirements:

> Ideas of flexible hours for parents with young children, paternity leave, and tax incentives for businesses and corporations to develop ways to support family life received solid backing from men in the study (though no men said they expected to see any major changes along these lines in the near future). . . . Control over their time and 'slack in the system' were two related factors that seemed to contribute to minimizing the stress and difficulty to post-partum adjustment (Fein, 1974a, p. 35).

This was highlighted by the negative experience of one male respondent whose job required him to work not only night shifts but occasional overtime shifts as well. The Newsons' observations on the impact of shift-work in Nottingham are in contrast. They suggest that the shift-worker is more likely to become highly domesticated and participant than the worker who keeps conventional 9 to 5 hours (Newson and Newson, 1963/72).

Other factors which were recognized as important in the adjustment were the *health of the baby*, and something which one of Fein's respondents called *'not fighting it'*, that is, yielding to the life-style implications of the new reality, according to whatever pattern evolves.

Fein looked focally at the *men's feelings* in the post-partum period, and found that feelings of exclusion from family life were fairly common. Work required men to be away from 'the vital work at home' more often than some wished. Many respondents mentioned the decrease in the amount of time they could now spend together with their spouses alone. This was a major change in the post-partum period, and wives as well as husbands wished they had more time to spend alone with their partners. One wife complained: 'He comes in after work and, before saying any-thing to me, runs to the baby and starts playing with him' (Fein, 1974a, p. 38). Some men felt disappointed that their babies did not smile at them; some were frustrated that they could not breast feed their babies, speaking of 'breast envy'. Overall, Fein felt that some men experienced feelings of deprivation or 'neediness' through a combination of having to care for their wives and infants, and receiving less attention them-selves than they had prior to the birth. In contrast, others had positive feelings of inclusion in the family life. The feelings of exclusion and jealousy Fein describes are less likely to occur where father's place in the household is clearly defined and protected, as in the situation the Newsons describe for working-class families in Nottingham. They report that fathers there feel a right to be part of the normal domestic scene, and that domestic patterns are fitted around them (Newson and Newson, 1963/72, p. 218).

Fein talked to his respondents on the changes they felt in becoming parents. These frequently hinged on facing the realities of the post-natal division of labour. Fein observes that the meaning of becoming parents was a complex and special experience to fathers – both practi-cally and emotionally. A feeling of becoming a middle generation was a common current in the interviews, and several couples pointed out to Fein that the first six weeks of life with their infants was just the beginning: ' "If you really want to know how we're doing", said one man, "come back in a year" ' (Fein, 1974a, p. 43).

The baby's influence

Treating infants' health as a variable in post-partum adjustment, implies recognition that they are variable on arrival in the world. There has previously been an awareness that the baby has some influence on parental experience, but not until recently has it been conceptualized as a central variable in the transition to parenthood. Lomas, for example, has pointed out that factors other than the physiological or psycho-logical make-up of the mother have been neglected in considerations of post-partum breakdown. He suggests that the innate temperament of the baby should be considered along with factors like the setting of the confinement. 'It would be interesting to know, for instance, whether there is a correlation between breakdown of the mother and a tempestuous disposition in the baby . . .' (Lomas, 1967, p. 132). Gerald Caplan (1961) went further than this in taking cognizance of the baby's influence. He acknowledged that the mother–child relationship was a circular process involving two (sic) people, each of whom contributes to it:

> It does not just come from the mother. The kind of baby, the sex of the baby, the appearance of the baby, the reaction pattern of the baby, all these kinds of things, which no one can predict in advance, will influence how the mother will feel towards it (Caplan, 1961, p. 86).

Nevertheless, he then proceeds:

> But you can predict what the mother is going to feed into the mother–child relationship, by listening to how the mother talks about three different topics during pregnancy (Caplan, 1961, p. 86).

These comprise: the woman's attitudes towards the conception and the pregnancy itself; the woman's attitude towards the foetus; and what the woman says about her fantasies about the baby to be. Thus, having made the baby's influence potentially salient to outcome, Caplan reduces the significance of the interactive process he has suggested, giving greater emphasis to what the mother starts off with in her head.

Until very recently, the prevalent view has been what Betty Cogswell (1969) describes as one of 'uni-directional socialization'. She explains what this widespread popular and sociological myth entails:

> Those who utilize the uni-directional model assume *a priori*, and often with ideological fervor, that socialization occurs within a pattern of superordination-subordination, whereby new learning proceeds from fountainhead to empty head, from giver to receiver, from parent to child. Parents and other agents are thought to control the process, and through their communication and behaviour to mold the pliable novice. The novice is viewed as an object to be acted upon, a willing and passive recipient in the socialization process (Cogswell, 1969, p.1).

Cogswell records a number of historical, ideological and social reasons for the development and perpetuation of the uni-directional model, but her point is to present research findings – her own and others – which support the notion that socialization is effected through reciprocal influence between both novice and agent. The essence in relation to parents and children is that parents have a 'repertory of actions to accomplish each of their objectives', rather than a set of fixed techniques. Activation of elements in the repertory requires both cultural pressures and stimulation from the child. She cites Bell (1968) who suggests on these lines that parents invoke two types of repertories: 'upper limit control behaviour', which reduces and redirects behaviour of the child which exceeds parental standards of intensity, frequency, and competence for the child's age period; and 'lower limit control behaviour', which stimulates child behaviour which is below parental standards. Parents exhibiting such behaviour tend to be regarded as being 'in control' and the importance of the child's stimulation of their behaviour is therefore generally overlooked.

Research evidence which confirms that some babies are 'easy' and some 'difficult' or anyway different, and which indicates that these variations have important implications for parental responses, and thus the child's, i.e. the whole parent–child interaction, is accumulating (Campbell, 1972; Lewis and Rosenblum, 1974). A major study which redefines the issues in this way is *The Effect of the Infant on its Caregiver*, edited by Lewis and Rosenblum (1974). Although this work is traditional in focusing on the interaction between the child and the mother (rather than both parents), the authors draw attention to the fact that:

> There have been few voices stressing the necessity of observing both partners in this dyadic bond – it is important that we now focus attention on the impact of the infant as *a source of* the formation, regulation and indeed even the malevolent distortion of the care-giver's behaviour (Lewis and Rosenblum, 1974, p. 9).

Contrary to the view of uni-directional socialization, the authors propose categorically: 'We have begun to see in quite explicit terms that the infant even at birth is no mere passive recipient of stimulation from those around him, ready to be moulded like clay on the potter's wheel' (Lewis and Rosenblum, 1974, p. 9). The authors argue that the child affects the parent by means of such variables as its sex, physical stature, state or arousal level just as much as the parent affects the child. They demonstrate this by means of various methods, for example by varying different aspects of the infant along some known and defined dimension and observing the resultant effect on the care-giver.

In a study with blind and sighted infants Fraiberg found that the blind child's inability to see affects its pattern of smiling from as early as two months old and this in turn has a marked effect on the behaviour of the mother.

> For the mother of the blind baby, the selective response smile to her voice signified 'knowing' and 'preference' and, the first fears of 'How will he know me?' were diminished by appearance of the universal sign.... But the smile was not automatic. In our records and on film we

see the mother coaxing a smile. Sometimes several repetitions of her voice were needed before the smile appeared. Clearly something was needed that was not automatically given. Then, in our records of this period we begin to see that the most reliable stimulus for evoking a smile or laughter in the blind baby is gross tactile or kinesthetic stimulation. As observers we were initally puzzled and concerned by the amount of bouncing, joggling, tickling, and muzzling that all of our parents, without exception, engaged in with the babies. In several cases we judged the amount of such stimulation as excessive by any standards. We had rarely seen among parents of sighted babies, in such a range of homes, so much dependence upon gross body stimulation. Then we began to understand; these games provided an almost certain stimulus for a smile, while the parents' voices alone provided at best an irregular stimulus. The parents' own need for the response smile, which is normally guaranteed with the sighted child at this age, led them to these alternative routes in which a smile could be evoked with a high degree of reliability (Fraiberg, 1974, pp. 222–3).

Fraiberg suggests that alternative 'languages' of communication can quickly become available to both parent and child in this situation. Thus parents may become sensitized to the use of body movement instead of facial expression. Lewis and Rosenblum stress the need to explore the use and organization of various sense modalities as they occur in 'normal' development of the parent–child relationship as well as in such 'extreme' situations, but they endorse this view of the interactive nature of parent–child behaviour. They argue that although the effects of parent on child and child on parent may usefully be reduced to their component elements, the interaction must ultimately be regarded as a dynamic developmental system. For them 'the phenomenon under study is dyadic in nature, and only through dyadic study can we come to assess the nature of each participant's contribution.' For these authors there is ongoing effectiveness: 'a chain which must be studied in terms of its integrity rather than through its component elements.' They concede, however, that reduction to such elements especially, in view of the bias over the past few decades, to the component elements of the child's effect on its care-giver – can be a useful and important step in understanding the dyadic system.

The work of Lewis and Rosenblum and of others, using ethological methods such as Martin Richards and Judith Bernal suggests that 'ordinary' babies vary in many ways which affect the parental experience in potentially radical ways. Research by Richards and Bernal (1971) on night waking in infants during the first 14 months of life reveals wide differences in patterns of sleeping and crying between different groups

of babies. Various tests were applied outside the mother–child interaction system which suggest that these differences are not purely a
response in the child to variations in parental treatment. The effect on a
parent of a restless child who cries easily and sleeps for short periods
only or who is relatively difficult to feed can clearly be exhausting and
depressing, or at very least demanding, and may differ considerably
from the experience of the parent of a 'passive', 'sleepy', 'contented'
child.

In the highlighting of infants' responses to stimuli, the implicit
assumption has gained ground amongst professionals concerned with
child development that parents *should* maximize the stimulation of the
child to ensure rapid and early development of cognitive and motor
activities. In this way pressure is put on parents (and in the main this
still tends to mean mothers) to work from the earliest days on the task of
'socializing' the child. Newson and Shotter, for example, in an article
headed 'Adults can help a child to learn the use of his own gestures?'
make the following statement:

> It may be that children's humanity has to be *made* during interactions
> between them and those who already possess it. . . . It is this system
> of goals-at-which-to-aim-while-conducting-one's-life that must be
> transmitted to children by their parents. Lacking knowledge of such
> a system of man-made goals, our children would not know how to live;
> it is in such systems that our humanity seems to consist, and their
> construction in the child seems to begin almost from the moment of
> birth (Newson and Shotter, 1974, p. 347).

The value of early development and the broader issues subsumed under
question 'socialization for what?' are rarely made explicit.

An interesting facet of Cogswell's contribution, if one accepts that
parents and children do influence each other, and that children determine to some degree the nature of their own socialization, is the question:
What can happen when parents overrate their position in their
relationship with their child?

> The consequences are dual. They may be beneficial to the parent but
> most detrimental to the child. For general acceptance of the uni-
> directional model provides implicit societal sanction for insecure
> parents to play god to their children, or to compete with them in ways
> and in areas where the child cannot possibly win. Thus their own
> insecure egos may be bolstered, but at the expense of the child's
> freshly emerging self-confidence. . . . How much more desirable is
> the conscious nurturance of the reciprocal relationship between parent
> and child which exists in fact. The child could be spared feelings,
> possibly lifelong, of inadequacy and dependency, while the parent

hopefully could appreciate the child's contribution to his own growth and development and to the parents (Cogswell, 1969, pp. 12-13).

Cogswell suggests there are valuable benefits to be derived from taking the behaviour of the child into full account and living out a reciprocal model of socialization. One is of direct benefit to parents:

A positive consequence of the reciprocal model, if parents recognize its function, is that it provides psyche income whereby parents can concentrate on their lives without feeling guilty about jeopardizing the children's socialization. Moreover, they can direct energy and time to solving family problems, especially those of the whole group, with the assurance that minimal catalytic activity invokes the reciprocal process of continuing socialization (Cogswell, 1969, p. 14).

Another advantage is that the child – and later adult – has an opportunity to develop first-hand skills in the novice role. Cogswell observes:

Throughout the literature on socialization I have never seen a reference to skills inherent in this role. I am not referring to intelligence or creativity or physical capacity. What I am suggesting is that there are a set of social skills attached to the role of novice which can enhance movement through a socialization system, as well as enhance potential outcomes . . . (Cogswell, 1969, p. 15).

We have drawn explicit attention to the influence of children so that they may be seen alongside mothers and fathers as pivotal in the outcome of their births. This corrects, in some measure, the perspective that overemphasizes the role of the mother's intrapsychic state on the outcome of her pregnancy for both herself and child. We now see, moreover, that enlarging the perspective may enhance the quality of the experience. The quality of outcomes, for mother, father and child, for this and for subsequent stages of the family cycle, are affected by what happens at this stage.

Successful outcomes of entry to parenthood: confronting the issues that lie ahead

The problem of assessing the relevance of knowledge and insight to the management of actual tasks of parenting remains a fascinating and unsolved one.

We refer again to Fein's respondent who at six weeks post-partum said that Fein should return a year later to evaluate how they were doing. Indications from other outcome studies (such as those done in Caplan's unit), would suggest that this couple, though sceptical, stood a good chance for a favourable outcome, because they were planning ahead. Whilst still in the 'honeymoon phase' they had an awareness that life goes on and new issues follow. We do not here discuss the pros and cons of various forms of division of labour between the spouses. The assessment and adoption of a particular pattern, with its strains and benefits, is something that parents often wish to work out for themselves and not have prescribed for them. We wish to describe the options; what issues, constraints, costs and benefits they entail, so that parents may confront themselves what lies ahead. Parents may then be better equipped to face the question of what type of marriage and family life to have. While it is not possible, and perhaps not even desirable to be conscious of all the implications of alternatives at this stage, decisions about life-style patterns are in fact taken, and they affect not only the current stage, but what follows. There are different ways of approaching this. Some may refrain from decisions on specifics, leaving flexibility and room to manoeuvre in evolving solutions appropriate to their child and themselves. Others may seek clarification and attempt contingency planning. But sooner or later the issues that lie ahead must be confronted. Babies grow older; so do parents; another stage follows. Situations change in their meanings, implications and demands, so that advance preparation that is too rigid can lead to grief. On the other hand, too little advance preparation, leaving events to 'fate' and the 'inevitable', may leave parents and families unprepared to make their lives satisfying – and the awareness of what 'might have been' a good experience comes too late.

We move on to the next chapters with the view that anticipatory work is as relevant here as in the birth process: some parents, who have not found babies their 'scene', may find enjoyment in interaction with small children. Others, who enjoy babies, may need to anticipate another kind of transition if they are to sustain a constructive and mutually rewarding relationship with their children. The Newsons have suggested that middle-class mothers tend not to enjoy their children's infancy stage (Newson and Newson, 1963/72). This is consistent with our findings in the PEP graduates' survey, where infant care was linked (as shown by statistical cluster analysis) with 'cleaning' in the minds of British graduates (Fogarty et al., 1971, p. 245). In her American study, which was the base for some of the British work, Rossi found it more linked to 'feeding' in the repertoire of domestic tasks. This is possibly associated with the impression that Americans are not only enjoined to have fun with their babies, but actually do this through focusing on the oral aspect of infant care.

In general, whichever orientation particular parents have – and there are significant intra-societal variations – it seems justified on available evidence to argue that their experience as parents will be enhanced by the awareness in each phase that a different stage will follow. If the current stage is experienced as gratifying, a continuation may be enhanced by anticipating the changes that must occur in order to minimize a clinging to or idealizing the past. If the current stage is frustrating, the guilt and strain may be lightened by the realization of changes to come.

We have not, in this chapter, given direct attention to the medical factors which may militate against the kind of expression of parents' needs that have been described. These factors include the traditions and training experiences of medical professionals, and achievements in technical care as measured by such indicators as morbidity and mortality statistics. There is also the medical-legal constraint, particularly in the USA, where having the husband's presence makes for a potentially hostile witness who could stimulate litigation for malpractice if anything went wrong. While recognizing these issues, we have concentrated on the focus of the book, and tried to identify patterns emerging in recent research. We believe that by taking these findings into account many of the issues can be resolved in ways that are more orientated to parents' needs than they are at present.

We now consider issues in child development that parents face in the next life cycle stage: the early and middle years of active parenting.

5

Parental issues in child development

Pre-school to puberty

This is a book about parents and their needs, not focally about the needs of children. Yet, as parents, people are concerned with their children's needs, and the developmental events and issues that are presented to them as children grow. Because of this, we focus here on children in the period of their greatest developmental change in the family context – namely, the stage between early infancy (which was described in the last chapter) and puberty, which will be described in Chapter 7. In most of the chapters based on the life-cycle framework, we deal with both children's life events and parents' dilemmas in attempting to integrate them into their own lives. Here, because there is such an enormous literature and so many aspects and phases to the development, we group together relevant issues about children's development; we consider their parents' life situations to which these issues are being assimilated in the next chapter.

Indeed the literature for this period is so voluminous, and the events so variegated that it might have been sensible to further sub-divide the chapters, into four or more. We refrained from doing so despite the length of the chapters for two reasons. First, we do not wish to focus too much on the children's situation, except in so far as it is crucial *for parents*. Second, we did not wish to re-enforce the tendency to see school entry as a fixed point in the life cycle before which it is unnatural or harmful for parents to have other people care for their children. By considering the whole time span of early and middle childhood we hope to deal with the issues raised by school-entry in perspective, as an event in a class of events having to do with the development of independence and autonomy in the child.

In considering child-development issues of concern to parents, there are many ways to sort them. The different 'schools' of developmental psychology illustrate this. Those that concern themselves with intellectual and cognitive development, choose different landmarks from those concerned with language development, the development of social skills or the capacity to adapt to the ecology of life in which the child finds itself. Those concerned with motivation and the development of the personality use still different dimensions and mark out the growth process with different events.

Amongst the professionals there are Skinnerians, Pavlovians, Lewinians, Freudians – and a host of others, whether aligned by the names of their founding fathers or by the schools of thought and subject matter derived from their work. Reviews of the literature in the various fields of child development seek to keep abreast of them for specialists (cf. for example, Koch, 1959; Hoffman and Hoffman, 1964; Mussen, 1960; Goslin, 1969; Mussen, Conger and Kagan, 1969; Kellmer Pringle, 1974). While parents in our society are, to some degree, concerned with the same set of issues – from bladder control to vocabulary building – some of the specialists' ways of considering them are more closely linked to parents' own perceptions and their own attempts to understand what they are experiencing, as well as their efforts to satisfy their own felt needs.

In making the choice of topics within which we organize the discussion of children's development and its impact on parents, we have selected issues which seem to be *both* generally perceived by parents as important to them and to be widely recognized by authoritative writers on children as key developmental issues. This duality of approach is necessary in our society because of the existence of child-development experts. In simpler societies, where each parent is his own authority and specialists are involved in relatively fewer issues, the task of selecting the significant events would be easier, being based on the events recognized in the culture. While each parent in our own society is, in a sense, the one whose view prevails as to what the child is feeling, wanting, needing, doing, parents also rely, in varying degrees, on experts to guide them. In presenting material in this chapter, we use categories that emerge from what we know of parental concerns, and then discuss them in terms of the writings of the experts. There is very little of a folk-science of parents' views of these issues, comparable for example to what has been described for simpler and more homogeneous societies in the analyses of the cultural context of child-rearing practices (cf. for example, Kardiner and associates, 1945; Gorer and Rickman, 1950; Whiting and Child, 1953; Mead 1953; Inkeles and Levinson, 1954).

In the simpler societies that have been analysed by anthropologists and their associates in the child-development fields, issues such as how to feed and bathe an infant, how to handle toilet-training, masturbation, sexual play, aggressiveness and so on, are responded to relatively consistently by adults according to the norms and practices of their culture. Parents have internalized these as part of their individual personality structures as a result of the patterning in socialization practices that exist in such societies. While there are individual differences within all societies, even the simplest and most homogeneous, there are patterned tendencies within the simpler societies for parents to define the concept of human nature in one way or another and to respond to characteristic child-development events according to their cultural conceptions. The Hopi child is systematically inhibited in the expression of aggression while the Plains Indian child is titillated and his aggressivenesss encouraged.

In our own society there are many variations, as we have indicated, and few clear cultural directives in child-rearing. Individual families create, in the privacy of their diverse conditions of housing and social life, an amalgam of child-rearing practices based on their individual experiences as children in families, their interpretation of the many sources of advice on child-rearing that they receive – from kin, friends, neighbours, the mass media, expert accounts – and discussions. This does not mean that there is no patterning within our own society. As we argued in the chapter on social expectations of parenthood, there are indications that some authoritative views become more influential than others. Also, there are patterns by age groupings, by social class, by ethnic group and by social setting (e.g. rural/urban/suburban) which are bases for patterned variation.

For example, looking at the age factor, it is clear that children between the toddler stage and puberty are present in most British and American households during the time parents are between their twenties and forties. As Table 8 shows, for British households using the wife's age as the index, there are children in this phase present amongst younger families, and some amongst older families, but the heaviest clustering is in the period when the wife is between 25 and 45 years old.

Indications of social class differences and regional differences are seen in the studies by Young and Willmott (1957), Bott (1957), Bernstein (1963), Stacey (1960) as well as in the longitudinal reports of Davie, Butler and Goldstein (1972) and Douglas (1968). Many of the same variations by social class, ethnic group and specific family problem or structure, exist in Britain in similar form as in the USA. For example, there is a tendency in both countries for middle-class parents to have permissive values (Sears, Maccoby and Levin, 1957; Newson and Newson, 1970); for public provision of alternative child care to be associated with deprivation (Schorr, 1975; Tizard and Moss, 1976); for dual-worker families to be 'overloaded' (Rapoport and Rapoport, 1971/76; Holmstrom, 1972); for families with handicapped children to experience characteristic strains in dealing with the implications of their special situation (Koch and Dobson, 1966; Hermelin and O'Connor, 1970; Rutter, 1968; Wing, 1969; Kew, 1975).

Table 8 *Women with children in household under age 14 (UK) as percentage of all women in age group*

Women's age	Number of children in household			
	1	2	3	4+
15–17	1·4	nil	nil	nil
18–24	18·6	11·1	2·6	0·6
25–34	20·0	35·6	16·9	8·0
35–44	24·1	28·5	13·3	7·4
45–54	17·3	5·9	1·5	0·4
55–59	1·9	0·1	0·1	nil
60+	0·1	nil	nil	nil

Source: Based on General Household Survey, 1973, p. 71.

But we are a long way from having a parentology. We know that parents cannot avoid becoming involved to some degree in the challenges presented by the child – though there are great variations both within and between societies in this. The child-centred parent who is responsive to every word, facial expression, cry or step of the child is at one extreme – and the neglectful, indifferent, perhaps abusive parent at the other. Amongst 'ordinary' parents there is a wide range of philosophies of child-care, of psychologies of human nature, of goals of life and the aims of interpersonal influence in child-rearing. Parental 'interest' in the child has been found in a number of studies to be an important differentiating factor; and this, in turn, may relate not only to the state of economic strain and deprivation the family experiences, but to such demographic factors as the number of children in the family (Nisbet, 1968).

Within the constraints of their life conditions – economically, ecologically, educationally, demographically – families do something to cope with child-care. Somewhere in the picture an element of expert advice and guidance filters in; sometimes this is used heavily, sometimes it is given scant attention.

There are different sorts of expert materials – ranging from the technical reports of specialists published in their own professional journals through articles by specialists or intermediaries of one kind or another in the media. There is also a range of publications by specialists directed at the public. Some of these provide practical guides for parents, e.g. Dr Spock's and Dr Jolly's (1975) compendia of practical advice for parents particularly in relation to medical issues. Others are orientated to helping parents to understand their children within the context of a particular orientation – e.g. the Tavistock series of booklets explaining for parents the age-specific behaviour of their children (O'Shaughnessy, 1969; Osborne, 1969; Dare, 1969; Rosenbluth, 1969). These booklets deal with 'normal' problems such as temper tantrums, nightmares, fears and phobias, as well as issues such as going away from home, the arrival of siblings, language development, and so on.

But one is left with many child development issues where there is discrepant and changing information from experts. This leaves open the question of what is the appropriate response, from both parental and child points of view. For example, when a child experiences difficulties in verbalizing, one point of view would have it that there are developmental anomalies in the maturation of the vocal mechanisms. Another might emphasize the possibility that there are psychological inhibitions preventing the inbuilt propensities for language development from unfolding (Chomsky, 1968); still another might stress the notion that inadmissible feelings or stressful conflicts are being indirectly expressed. An accurate differential diagnosis can be of crucial importance to both parent and child so that the parent responds in the appropriate way. But often it is difficult to make such a diagnosis, the differentials being in the professional viewpoints rather than in the child. There is little to indicate in such situations how parents select their models for defining the child's behaviour, or what difference it makes.

Cook-Gumperz studied parent–child communication over issues of control of the child's behaviour; she accepts the idea that 'any parental theory is better than none', and adds that 'an explanation of the parental theory which accompanies the parents' actions is better than none' (Cook-Gumperz, 1973, p. 130). This is an area worthy of further exploration.

For the time being, we examine the relevance of this kind of a position by discussing some major issues presented by children in the two phases dealt with in this chapter.

Issues in pre-school (early childhood) development

One of the issues now considered of major importance in the child's pre-school development is what we term *separation/autonomy*. The development of autonomy in the child is part of the growth process; the guidance and regulation of this process through the management of separations is an element of parenting. The topic forms a focus of attention for developmental psychologists and psychiatrists as well as social scientists concerned with the effects of institutions other than the family on pre-school development. According to researchers such as the Newsons and Gorer (1973) who have reported on the actual concerns of parents, this is a topic of widespread parental concern as well, particularly in respect of the child's development of autonomy. Josephine Klein (1965) considers autonomy to be one of the principal British values, as indicated in the community studies that she reviews.

Encouraging autonomy in the child means tolerating separations – a process which has become fraught with anxiety in our society. It has appeared to be more focal in the professional literature recently. C. W. Valentine, formerly president of the British Psychological Society, did not mention the issue in his book *The Normal Child*, which has gone through four printings since its first appearance in 1956 (Valentine, 1962). Now attention is given to the process as a potential source of deprivation in modern reviews such as that by Van der Eyken (1967/74).

The great emphasis given to this topic now results from two kinds of phenomena. First there are the findings and interpretations of Bowlby and a group of other researchers who were impressed with the apparently deleterious effects on personality development of childhood separations experienced during the Second World War. These have been mentioned several times already and, as noted, have continued to be influential even among younger psychologists, though the data and interpretations are now more critically assessed by writers like Rutter (1972), Yudkin (1967) and Casler (1961). It is now usually broken down in research into analytic components such as perceptual stimulus/deprivation (Hutt and Hutt, 1973, pp. 245–7).

The second set of forces which has given this issue its special contemporary salience is the social change associated with alterations in men's and women's roles. As more and more women wish to work even while their children are at a pre-school age, and as there are few signs as yet that there are adequate child-care facilities or that fathers are ready, willing or able to redress the balance of parenting responsibilities within the home, there is intense concern with alternatives. What alternative care facilities are both feasible and acceptable to parents who care about their children's healthy development? As parents seek a greater measure of autonomy for themselves, the issue becomes one of how much separation and under what kinds of care auspices can this be accomplished responsibly. This has acted as a spur to the interest in the separation/autonomy issue.

There are indications from research, as well as from the testimonials of conscientious parents who have tried alternative care arrangements, that properly managed separations need not be harmful, may be beneficial, and should be viewed in a context of assessing quality as well as quantity of care.

Schaffer and Emerson (1964), in a study of children's first attachments, found that almost one third of most children's first attachments are made to people other than the primary caretaker (ordinarily the mother). This is most frequently the father. Though the father is traditionally seen as a relatively shadowy and unimportant figure except as a support to the mother, Schaffer and Emerson found that by the age of eighteen months 75 per cent of children protested on temporary separation from the father. In one example cited by Friedlander *et al.* (1972), a Spanish-speaking father talked to his child for less than 5 per cent of the child's 'listening time', but although this was the only Spanish to which he was exposed, by one year the child had acquired a rudimentary grasp of the language.

These sorts of studies prompted Richards (1975, p. 3) to say that: 'If we are to gain a full understanding of the development of children in our culture we must study their relatinoship with both mothers and fathers (as well as other people).' The importance of fathers to children cannot be assessed by the amount of time they spend together. Richards suggests that fathers in our society could be much more involved than they are in the rearing of their children.

Since Bowlby's early work (1951) his own attention has focused more on the attachment mechanism. He has found it useful to ground his theories in animal behaviour, and has marshalled further evidence for his thesis that impairment in the capacity to form affectional bonds is likely to be associated with life-long disturbances of personality functioning (Bowlby, 1969, p. 14). In his most recent publications, Bowlby does not seem to have changed his orientation, retaining cautious wordings but implying that an attachment to one mother-figure is crucial. Others, developing this vein of thought have tried to show the hazards of separations, particularly in anxiety-rousing situations (Robertson, 1962). The importance of stimulation in the inter-action between mother and child rather than sheer presence, has been emphasized by several researchers (Casler, 1961, 1968; Provence and Lipton, 1963; Ainsworth, 1962).

Bowlby's work has had a tremendous influence, not only on mothers and on hospital administrators (as we indicated in Chapter 2) but in the research world as well, particularly in experimental psychology and ethology. It had a marked effect on psychological theories 'and drew attention to the need to explain the characteristics of the child's bond with his mother' (Foss, 1972/74).

As Foss went on to say in his introduction to Rutter's book which reconsidered maternal deprivation theory, the work of Bowlby has also been seminal in arousing an 'anti' response. A spate of works both by professionals and more recently by women's movement advocates range from the 'not proven' stance to active disclaimers (Wootton, 1959; Rutter, 1972; Morgan, 1975).

Rutter's book (1972) reviews available literature and concludes that

the case for Bowlby's stance – in its fullest form of concentrating an
infant's attachment needs to a single figure, ordinarily the mother – is
not scientifically supported. Schaffer, publishing a year earlier, concluded that while attachment is crucial, the actual breadth of attachment is a function of the social setting in which the child lives. Writing
as early as 1959, Wootton criticized the Bowlby thesis on the same
grounds.

Recent ethological studies have underscored this point by demonstrations with animals. Some studies by 'human ethologists' combine
experimental with naturalistic methods. Rheingold and Eckerman
(1971, p. 75) for example, studied a series of infants in laboratory
situations which simulated typical instances of separation dilemmas.
They found that if the child voluntarily separated from the parent into
a safe and enjoyable setting there was no stress:

> infants left their mothers and with no distress entered a new environ-
> ment, whether or not it contained a toy. When toys were added to
> the environment, infants who previously had no toy entered faster,
> stayed there longer, and played with the toys more than infants
> who previously had a toy. Furthermore, when the new environments
> contained three toys rather than one, the infants travelled farther
> from their mothers and stayed away longer, playing with the toys.

The infants crept into the experiment environment of this study
and moved about freely, with no distress, contrasted sharply with
the marked distress and almost complete inhibition of locomotion
shown by infants *placed* alone in the same environment in a previous
study.

Research of this kind indicates that the question of separation/auto-
nomy and its management breaks down not only into dimensions of a
child's susceptibility (e.g. in relation to perceptual stimulation) but
also into dimensions of the environment that bear on deprivation
experiences. Crucial in this is the handling of the actual separation
(degrees of coercion, etc.). The institutions into which war-time
children were evacuated may not have been as capable of providing
acceptable caring environment as are contemporary nurseries. The
Tizards, studying contrasting environments provided by nursery
schools (where the child remains at home) and residential nurseries of
a modern, familistic kind, found no basis to expect that nursery-reared
children would be severely disturbed. At the same time, they found
that nursery children were more shy with strangers, more 'constricted'
and 'immature' in their social behaviour, and more 'diffuse' in their
attachments – not surprising considering the greater range of care-
giving figures in that setting. They conclude that multiple care-giving
could, under other circumstances, be even more personal than in the

nurseries they observed, and that it is not the institution *per se* but its particular composition and functioning that produces the observed results (Tizard and Tizard, 1971).

But, with experience of the potentially deleterious consequences of parental deprivation in the background, the new interest in alternatives is accompanied by an insistence that standards of care be monitored and enriched (Jackson and Jones, 1971; Jackson, 1973).

This area is likely to merit considerable further research; it is of interest in two quite distinct ways to the challenges that parents experience in relation to separations from their children in pre-school years. First, further knowledge is likely to offer guidance for parents making decisions about nursery schools, playgroups and the like. Second, it is likely to offer guidance for the social-psychological archi-tects of nursery schools in their training of staff and development of child-care programmes. In both respects, normalizing the use of these supplementary and alternative forms of child-care is likely to have an important influence on children, and therefore on the adults they become. Bowlby inspired the fear that too much separation of the child too soon meant that society would be at risk of a large infusion of people growing up with defective consciences. On the other extreme has been the hazard indicated in earlier research of the 'over-protective mother' who does not give the child enough autonomy early on. This anxiety takes the form of the fear that the children, and the adults they become, would be crippled by an excessively harsh conscience and conformist bent. The issue today, both in research and in practice is to locate the optimal balance of protectiveness within the family and separation from the parents – for the child's healthy development and for the parents' needs.

One line of investigation implies the need for a new look at fathers. We have already mentioned Schaffer and Emerson's (1964) finding that the most frequent 'other' figure to elicit attachment behaviour from young children, is their father. Why then is there so little information and research on fathers and their young children? Richards (1975) feels that this has something to do with the way research is organized to take place within office hours – that is when fathers are not at home. While this is so, research workers in other areas of investigation have found it possible to alter their working hours to suit the demands of the situation. It seems to us that there has not been much support in the social environment to investigate father–child relationships – both actual and potential. The myths of motherhood and the biological base for the domestic division of labour may have to recede further before fathering is actively sanctioned by society. Even fairly comprehensive and up-to-date reviews of the literature such as that of Penelope Leach (1975) do not contain references to father in the index, and Van der

Eyken's (1974) list of organizations 'which take an interest in the provision for the pre-school child' is couched in terms of provision for 'the child and its mother' (p. 244). Bronfenbrenner's (1974/76) recommendations make the same point – reflecting conventional assumptions about family structure.

The part played by mothers in the development of their young children has been so emphasized that virtually every other relationship – actual or potential – has been relegated to the background. This includes relationships with siblings. There is evidence, for example, that siblings (like other familiar figures) reduce children's distress in unfamiliar situations. Heinicke and Westheimer (1966), in studying children entering a residential nursery, found a reduction of stress in those admitted with a sibling, even where the sibling was not old enough to look after the child. Rutter (1972/74, pp. 38–9) summarizes the available evidence succinctly:

> It is important to note . . . that bonds form with people who have no caretaking role towards the child and the presence of a peer or sibling reduces stress in similar fashion to the presence of a parent-surrogate. On the whole children are less distressed with their mother than with some other person so it would be equally wrong to conclude that any individual does equally well. But there is no evidence that it is being a mother that is important. On the basis of the very scanty available evidence it seems more likely that the stress-reducing properties of the accompanying person are related to the strength of bond formation. It may be hypothesised that where the bond is strongest with the mother she will have the greatest stress-reducing properties, where bonds are stronger with someone else she will not.

Concern is developing among theoreticians and researchers of child development about the focus that has been given to the influence of mothers to the exclusion of fathers, siblings, peers and other adults. Even some psychoanalysts, who until recently have been concerned almost entirely with the mother's reactions and handling of the young child, show signs of new thinking on this issue. The basis for the new thinking is the counterpoint to the mothering emphasis provided in the concept of a '*drive for individuation*', from the toddler stage onwards. While conventionally the recognition of this drive in the child has been regarded as a requirement of good mothering, it has been a less focal theme until recently. It is still, however, seen as a maternal responsibility. Mahler, Pine and Bergman (1970), for example, note that mothers must 'grow in their maternal role to a higher level and to achieve greater distance from the child, compatible with the changes in their individuating child' (pp. 259–60).

This formulation still implies that the main responsibility is on the mother without reference to other potential relationships with the 'individuating child'.

Phyllis Greenacre (1966), another psychoanalytic writer, has on the other hand pointed to the importance of companionship with father from the child's second year – the year in which the child's horizons widen so much. And Dorothy Burlingham (1973) has recently stressed that 'the child's relationship to a second person, the father, is instrumental in helping to bring about the progress toward individuation', although she points out that in psychoanalytic writings, 'the preoedipal father is accorded a minor role' (p. 24). While psychoanalytic writings have a lot to say about the relationship of son to father – real and fantasied – Burlingham notes that there is little documentation about the relationship of father to child, the father's fantasies in the period between impregnation and birth, and during the first weeks of the infant's life; the father's hopes and expectations concerning the child's growth and development; his jealousies of the mother's preoccupation with the infant; the arousal of his own feminine attitudes; the impact on all these attitudes of his own latent memories of his own father relationships (1973, p. 30).

In her considerations of some of these elements, Burlingham points out that though it is 'normally' expected that the infant's early tie to its mother will be stronger than that to its father, this is not always so and the child may turn to its father to provide what the mother does not. From her experiences at the Hampstead Baby Clinic, Burlingham concludes that 'on the whole attitudes have changed dramatically in the present generation of young parents who experience it as wholly natural for both partners to take turns in looking after the infant's needs, and not to distinguish between a maternal and paternal role in this respect' (1973, p. 33). Up to this point, Burlingham gives the impression that lack of distinction between maternal and paternal roles in child-care is being normalized in our society. However, the implications of this attitude are difficult for her to sustain. While she allows for the possibility that if the infant's care is taken over by the father, its development may be satisfactory, she indicates some surprise when it was found that such an infant by the age of fourteen months was 'developing *remarkably* well' (p. 34). Burlingham then goes on to relate such caring behaviour in fathers to their marital choices:

In some instances the choice of partner in marriage was found to be based on the father's maternal attitudes and their corresponding absence in the mother; this gave the husband the opportunity to take over a role which coincided with his wishes. From the beginning it resulted in interferences with the mother's management, criticism of the way she handled the child, and competition with her in the care of the infant (Burlingham, 1973, p. 34).

These difficulties in altering conventional patterns may be due to innate drives, as has been held in the past; they may be due to unconscious mating choices as Burlingham suggests; or, we suggest, they may be due to attempts to change established patterns of life in affectually loaded spheres. A more generalist psychiatrist, Howells (1969) suggests something along this line, as do social psychologists like the Newsons. Elizabeth Newson (1963/72, p. 30) when discussing four-year-old behaviour, points out that:

> even in this age of vastly increased involvement of fathers, where young children are concerned mothers remain more vulnerable to social criticism. This is because of social expectations: in the end, criticism of the upbringing of a young child is still primarily aimed at the mothers. Fathers are not expected to take public responsibility for either the behaviour or the appearance of very young children, and blame will be transferred to the mother even where father has voluntarily accepted the major involvement.

The Newsons' observations, together with those we made in studying dual-career families, suggest that at this point in history families require to have as many reliable resources as possible available to help with the management of separations. This is seen not merely as being a prerequisite for their meeting their own needs without being irresponsible toward their children, but as instrumental also in the encouragement of autonomy in their children (Rapoport and Rapoport, 1971/76).

A second issue which is topical both for parents in this early stage and for researchers in the child-development field, is that of how to respond to *aggression* in the child. The traditional view of children's aggressiveness in our society was essentially moralistic. Children's tantrums, their self-assertiveness, etc. were considered 'naughty', 'bad', or selfish – and parents were expected to punish them so that they could be trained out of these undesirable habits and into more desirable ones. Early observations by traditional-minded psychologists yielded observations such as: 'the typical two year old [shows] much "snatch and grab" in play, with frequent kicking and pulling of hair, while the four year old is usually quarrelsome with much boasting' (Valentine, 1962, p. 74, citing Gesell). The traditional tendency was to seek to tame these anarchic animal instincts. More recently the prevailing orientation has been a much more permissive one, stemming from psychoanalytic clinical experiences with the pathogenic character of inhibitions of Victorian family life where children were to be seen and not heard.

In the USA, where this trend went to its most extreme limit, areggs-sive behaviour (breaking toys, furniture), deliberate naughtiness, roughness, striking, biting or kicking other children or adults, throwing, slamming, stubborn resistance, shouting – later with abusive language and so on, was considered essential for self-actualization. It was also considered adaptive in a competitive society.

But in this respect, as in the others, there have been variations and changes noted in research conducted on the topic over the past couple of decades. In both Britain and the USA it was amongst the middle-class parents that the greatest permissiveness has been observed – presumably in reaction against their Victorian backgrounds (Sears, Maccoby and Levin, 1957; Newson and Newson, 1970). Middle-class parents have been more inclined to use verbal reasoning as the favoured form of control, to attempt to clarify and understand the motivation underlying the observed behaviour, and to withhold rewards, including love and affection, as the favoured punishment. Working-class parents, in contrast, have tended more to use counter-aggression (including scolding and physical punishment) and to emphasize the immediate consequences of the act rather than understanding its motivation (Klein, 1970, p. 476).

In contemporary writings there is a shift toward greater firmness as a desirable response to a child's aggressiveness. Adolescent confusion and violence, disrespect for authority and lack of acceptance of realistic goals and values is thought of as stemming in part from the permissive attitude of parents toward anti-social behaviour in their young children a generation ago. Therefore, Spock, and others writing about the phenomenon of aggression and its management, have called for a retreat from permissiveness, defined as harmful in its extreme in the same way as the older harshness and constriction was in its extreme:

Excessive . . . harshness is unfavourable. However, most parental characteristics do not fall into such simple moral categories. Take, for example, parents' ambition for their children. It sometimes puts an unusual strain on a particular child and thereby produces symp-toms. But it's essential to realize that parental ambition in the broad sense is what has accounted for all the advances in civiliza-tion . . . [or] when parents emphasize right and wrong, especially at certain stages of development, it sometimes helps to produce a compulsive (overscrupulous) personality in a pararticul child. But unless there is a majority of moralistic people in every country in every generation, there can be no justice. In fact, there can be no society (Spock, 1974, p. 146).

In Britain, Dr Jolly stays close to the mundane world of common-sense care in the home and accordingly discusses these issues only indirectly. He notes that parents' responses to their children's behaviour generally are affected by their early family experiences which in turn vary according to social class. In urging parents to try to transcend whatever their background inclinations may have been that might interfere with considering the differences among children (temperamental as well as developmental stage) he notes the importance of communication with the child, explaining why a line is being taken, and doing some thinking and planning about the child's feelings and likely responses in order to forestall trouble. He notes that most *moderate* methods of discipline have times and places when they are helpful and, like Spock, that it is the extremes of over-disciplined and under-disciplined children that are undesirable (Jolly, 1975, Ch. 19).

Middle-class parents feel more that they can influence the child and shape its development, whereas working-class parents (particularly more deprived ones) tend to feel more frustrated and irritable, and at the extremes feel a general sense of alienation, fatalism and powerlessness to influence events generally. Aggression in their children may only be expressing what they as adults feel but are constrained to try to control; and this may add to their difficulties (Kagan, 1971, p. 187).

The Newsons report a correlation between social class and the use of 'smacking' as a punishment method for aggression. They report the further finding that tantrums in children are related to the use of corporal punishment methods. The greatest frequency of both are in the families of manual workers. A vicious circle may ensue. In cases of gross aggression, parents seek to halt the behaviour – and if they fail to do so, they may 'give up' or have the child taken from them. The vicious cycle is seen also intergenerationally. A number of studies show that children who experienced aggression as a punishment (or who internalized it as a mode of interaction through viewing aggressive scenes by parents or others) have a greater tendency themselves to become violent parents (Gelles, 1972; Scott, 1975).

In available research, Sears, Maccoby and Levin (1957) examined the issue of effectiveness of discipline and found that the parents who frequently report using corporal punishment *which they combine with reasoning* are those who experience a feeling of being able to control the child. Those who only beat the child experience further frustration. And there are indications that punishment at home may be responded to covertly and with displacement by further aggression in permissive settings outside the home.

Mussen, Conger and Kagan (1969, p. 285) conclude that current research shows that either too much permissiveness (which has the effect of being experienced as rewarding aggression) or too harsh or inconsistent punishment may exacerbate the child's tendency to be aggressive.

There is little data on the part these and other pieces of scientific information play in governing parental response to their children's aggression. Aside from the question of differentials in access to this kind of information and incapacity to assess it, there are differences in the significance of aggression to different sub-groups. Lower-class use of physical punishment is based to some extent on traditional beliefs and values which legitimate this pattern ('spare the rod and spoil the child'). But many statistical reports group different sorts of manual workers' families together to display distributions; solid, respectable working-class parents along with people living under severe deprivations and frustrating material conditions. The latter are, in many cases, responding as much to their own frustrations as to a set of principles about child-rearing. The introduction of new knowledge about the effects of physical punishment to a family near their threshold of tolerance for any kind of frustration, and perhaps under the influence of alcohol, is of dubious effectiveness, as Gelles (1972) and others studying violence in the family have pointed out.

Though an extreme example of the phenomenon under scrutiny, violence highlights some of the issues in the management of aggression generally. Aside from the point that violence is transmitted intergenerationally, as already indicated, current research points specifically (again) to deficiencies in fathering (Hyman and Mitchell, 1975; Court, 1970). Hyman and Mitchell, for example, in a study comparing the families of twenty battered children seen by the National Society for the Prevention of Cruelty to Children research unit, with twenty parents who were not known to be batterers, found that the battering parents were less adept at verbal skills (i.e. scored lower on 'verbal intelligence') and on abstract reasoning, and had a lower capacity to plan and control impulse discharge. Battering fathers, in particular, were found to be deficient in their capacity to give warmth and to participate in interpersonal relationships, as well as in their general capacity to be enthusiastic and to enjoy life. Their overall tendency to be introverted and to resort to a life of fantasy leads to the conclusion that 'In particular the inaccessibility of the fathers has emerged very strongly . . .' (Hyman and Mitchell, 1975, p. 296).

In summary, the definition of aggressiveness in children is a function of sub-cultural definitions of normality and desirability of different sorts of behaviour; the prescriptions for parental response to aggressiveness are also so influenced. Parents are most likely to impose either excessive or deficient controls on children's aggressive behaviour under a number of conditions:

1 A child-rearing philosophy that such control is desirable for the child (as with the traditional over-control ideologies prevalent in Freud's time and illustrated in the Schreber case; and with the recent over-permissiveness ideologies prevalent in the period following the Second World War).

2 A set of sub-cultural norms which by extrapolation sanction physical punishment on the one side (spare the rod and spoil the child) or neglect on the other.

3 Personal needs which overpower a parent's perspective and judgment and lead to manipulating the child to express the parent's needs, e.g. for power (by over-controlling the child), for expression of aggression (by encouraging antisocial behaviour), and so on.

4 Situations which override personal differences of an individual nature, e.g. in extremes of poverty, crowding, deprivation, alienation and oppression. They may lead to uncontrolled and inconsistent parental regulation, or apathetic disregard for the child's behaviour and a corresponding lack of discrimination about the meaning and function of aggressiveness in the child.

Issues of how to handle separation and aggression are explicitly recognized in one form or another as important by parents. The third issue – that of *gender identity in the child* – is still for many parents peripheral or unrecognized. Nevertheless, as it is increasingly in the consciousness of parents, and an issue that both research and social action groups emphasize in the pre-school phase of a child's development, we give it some attention here. It is particularly appropriate to do so despite its relatively low salience for most ordinary parents, because so much of this book's point of view hinges on the question of how sex-roles in parenting are changing or could change.

Research perspectives on the child's formation of a gender identity, particularly in relation to the part parents play at this stage, are as various as those of parents. Rather than being divided according to social class, ethnic group or other such variables, researchers' differences in viewpoint emerge from the different academic 'schools'.

There is agreement that in our society children in the pre-school period show different patterns of behaviour by sex. Boys are generally more active, aggressive, more 'naughty' and destructive, rougher and more 'thing-oriented'. Girls are generally more compliant, passive, more expressive emotionally, mature earlier in verbal and communication skills and are more 'people-oriented'. There is a vast and controversial research literature on these issues, with data of varying degrees of 'hardness' supported by one or another theoretical position. This literature is reviewed in different places and with different biases

(Hutt, 1972; Maccoby, 1966; Maccoby and Jacklin, 1974; Kagan, 1971).

Research on children's development of sex-typed behaviour ranges from those studies which support the view of biological determination of the observed differences to those studies which support the view that differences are due to conditioning and modelling in the social environment in which the children are reared. A third view is one that gives a part of the observable effect to each and argues in a value-framework for the transcendence of both cultural and biological givens. This view will not be mentioned here but it is more relevant to the chapter on parenting with adolescent children.

The most extreme position in favour of the power of socio-cultural determinants comes, paradoxically, from a medical school research team. John Money and the Hampsons have studied the development of hermaphrodites located through the research unit in endocrinology at the Johns Hopkins Medical School. These people, though few in numbers in the population, are important because they are of indeterminate gender in their external morphological characteristics. Accordingly, hospital staff tend to assign them to one or another gender at birth, and it is in that way that they are reared by their families and communities. Recently it has become possible to derive a 'true' gender-typing of hermaphrodites by chromosome tests. The studies by Money and the Hampsons have shown that there is a closer correlation between the social sex-typing of their subjects on follow-up than between the genetic sex-typing made possible by the new techniques of bio-genetic analysis. On the basis of these findings they conclude that individuals are born 'psycho-sexually neutral', and learn sex-differences in attitude and behaviour through experiences with sex-role expectations as they grow up. They conclude that *the first three years of life set an individual's orientation to gender roles in a way not dissimilar to the imprinting process* observed in animal development (Money, Hampson and Hampson, 1955 and 1957).

At the other extreme is the view which gives primacy to the biological, genetic and hormonal composition of the individual members of the two genders. This view departs from the position that the biological evolution of the species has produced a binary sex-typing within species to provide not only the mechanism of reproduction, but a wider range of contrasting and complementary ways than one type might have to foster adaptation and survival. This view includes a range of people who are strange bedfellows academically. On the one hand there are the orthodox psychoanalysts, who follow Freud in arguing that 'anatomy is destiny'. A recent modification of this view is that of Erikson, who argues that women – having within themselves the womb and the power to bear offspring for chosen men – are built fundamentally to concern themselves with inner space, and the psycho-biological commitment to give birth to and care for infants (Erikson, 1968).

This statement of Erikson corrected an imbalance in Freud's view, which attributed too much weight not only to the male and his phallic preoccupations, but to the way in which the female was assumed to feel deficient by comparison, her 'penis envy'. However, it remains a view which attributes a more direct relationship between body structure and social role than many contemporary researchers would allow, even within psychoanalysis, as Jean Miller (1973; 1976) has shown.

On the other hand, many conventional experimental psychologists also argue in favour of a biological basis for sex-role typing, primarily on the basis of 'facts' observable in empirical research. Hutt, for example, contests the interpretations placed by Money and the Hampsons on their data. She argues that hermaphrodites are freaks and that in the other 99 per cent of humans the differences are much more marked biologically; that hermaphrodites represent a deficiency in exposure to androgenic influences (i.e. that the individual will have more of the feminine elements of biological makeup); and that in any case the data, while indicating that individuals (especially the more accommodating feminized ones) *can* adapt to either sex role, do not indicate whether they are *best* placed in this way for their own satisfactory development (Hutt, 1973, pp. 70–2).

Hutt (1972, p. 133), after mobilizing available biological and psychological materials to support her thesis that sex differences are not only determined by historically derived conditions of contemporary life but are in fact more 'natural' and adaptive, concludes that human genetic factors have produced a species in which:

> the conformity and consistency of the female makes her a reliable and dependable source of nurture for the infant in its protracted dependency; for more effective communication and socialization a greater emphasis and reliance on linguistic skills and moral propensities has proved valuable; for the exploring and resource-hunting male in turn, a facility for dealing with spatial and conceptual relationships for reasoning, for divergence in thought and action, has proved equally useful. Many of these features are not of contemporary origin, but have both a phylogenetic and ontogenetic history.

The greater emphasis on learning of sex roles has been associated with anthropologists on the one hand, illustrated by the influential early work of Margaret Mead, and by learning theorists in psychology. An early statement of the learning theory position is that of Mowrer, who, in 1950, discussed the process of sex-typing in children's development:

In the ideal family constellation, a little boy finds it very natural and highly rewarding to model himself in his father's image. The father is gratified to see this recreation of his own qualities, attitudes and masculinity, and the mother, loving the father, finds such a course of development acceptable in her son. Tentative explorations, conscious and unconscious, in the direction of being 'like mother' quickly convinces the boy that this is not his proper or approved destiny, and he speedily reverts to his identification with father. In the well ordered, psychologically healthy household, much the same picture, in reverse, holds for the little girl.

Mowrer's view of what sort of factors disrupted this ideal cultural pattern in the 1950s centred on irregularities such as parental discord (which put the child in a position of alienating the love of the opposite-sex parent if it identified with the same-sex parent), or where a parent was weak or missing, and the natural tendency to identify with the same-sex parent was not facilitated or rewarded.

More recent research, particularly associated with experiments in learning theory, has introduced a further sense of complexity into the picture. Gender identity is established by age five or six and little boys know they will grow up to be men and little girls know they will grow up to be women. But it is now recognized that there is more to it than a simple matching of self to the attributes of the same-sex parent (Kohlberg, 1966). Children consider themselves to be like the parent of the opposite sex to a far greater degree than was at first visualized in early formulations, even in intact and 'normally functioning' family settings. One set of findings suggests that the process of cross-sex identifications is somewhat asymmetrical, with more girls adopting in their self-conception elements of their fathers than the other way round. Mussen, Conger and Kagan (1969, p. 273) suggest that this tendency relates less to anything intrinsic in boys and girls than to the fact that in our society males are perceived to have more power, and this creates a greater tendency to orientate oneself toward the male. Other research supports the plausibility of this line of argument. For example, Koch (1959) found that girls with older brothers show tomboy traits to a greater extent than do boys with older sisters, though the latter tendency is also present. Several observers have noted that in our society, with its emphasis on masculinity, tomboys experience less by way of negative social sanction than do 'sissies' (e.g. Brown, 1965). And Bandura and his associates, in a series of experiments on the development of aggressive behaviour based on childhood experiences, established that though pre-school boys were more likely than girls to imitate models showing aggressive behaviour in films to which they had been exposed, these effects were conditioned by expectations of reward or punishment for such behaviour. When the different experimental groups were shown not only aggressive behaviour, but aggression rewarded, they responded nearly equally in the degree of subsequent aggression shown. The implication is that the more aggressive responses of boys than girls in the less thoroughly conceptualized experiments were in fact conditioned by the boys' general experience of being rewarded for such behaviour. In contrast, girls tend to have such behaviour suppressed in ordinary situations (Bandura and Walters, 1963; Bandura, 1965).

Maccoby and Jacklin, in a wide-ranging review of the available literature on the psychology of sex differences, conclude that it is difficult to be definitive on whether biological difference brings about the stimulation of different behaviour patterns in parents or the other way round; there are indications of both tendencies and also there are indications that perceptions and norms about what attributes are associated with little girls or little boys are subject to cultural variation and change. Parents vary not only in their detailed conceptions of what the two sexes are like but more importantly in relation to which elements are considered important and how parents ought to respond to them (Maccoby and Jacklin, 1974, Ch. 9).

An interesting element of the research reported and analysed by Maccoby and Jacklin relates to the distinction made between what is considered 'natural' in boys and girls and what is considered 'desirable'. We give an illustration here of how this relates to the sex-typing issue, and then return to it in our discussion of values in child-rearing. A study by Lambert *et al.* (1971) compares English-speaking Canadians with French-speaking Canadians. Studying seventy-three parents of six-year-old children and using techniques developed by Maccoby and Rothbart earlier they found a number of elements consistent with stereotyped conceptions of sex-differences, and a number which were different – but with the added dimension of the direction of socialization taken into account. Maccoby and Jacklin (1974, pp. 343–4) bring this out as follows:

these groups of parents thought the typical behaviour of boys and girls was different on many items, but their values concerning how the two sexes ought to behave were quite similar. Boys were described as being more likely to be rough at play, be noisy, defend themselves, defy punishment, be physically active, be competitive, do dangerous things, and enjoy mechanical things. Girls were described as being more likely to be helpful around the house, be neat and clean, be quiet and reserved, be sensitive to the feelings of others, be well mannered, be a tattletale, cry or get upset, and be easily frightened. But when asked which of these characteristics they thought it was important for boys and girls to have (or *not* to have) parents said they thought it was important for *both* boys and girls to be neat and clean, to be helpful around the house, to be able to take care of themselves, and not be easily angered, not to do dangerous things, not to cry, and to be thoughtful and considerate of others. Surprisingly, it was also thought important for both boys and girls to defend themselves from attack and to be competitive.

A number of other studies indicate similar tendencies to recognize a value component as well as a naturalistic observation component in making sense of child-developmental issues in this area.

Pleck, whose view represents another attempt at synthesis of psycho-biological and cultural formulations, suggests that any consideration of new sex role models should be based on a foundation of observations about actual developmental patterns as well as on values. Starting with the suggestion of Kohlberg (1966) and Block (1973) that sex-role development has much in common with intellectual, ego and moral developmental processes, each of which is subject to modification on a psychobiological base, Pleck (1975, p. 172) suggests that children go through phases of sex-role development from an amorphous first stage to one where they learn the rules of the game of sex-role differentiation as defined in our culture, and conform to them somewhat rigidly. He argues that it is only after they are able to transcend this stage they they may develop a more neutral conception which can reflect their individual needs and temperaments rather than being forced to fit stereotypes.

Pleck's statement represents a value as well as reflecting the actuality of the human potential for bisexuality in that he is seeking a way of facilitating individual self-actualization regardless of gender, and his argument assumes that a falsely stereotyped sex-role context for development distorts this. The implication for parents is that if they wish to shape the young child's experience toward an ultimately more satisfying developmental pattern, they should disregard many of the traditional cultural ideas of what is normal for a boy and what is normal for a girl and respond to the individual's specific tendencies. While this formulation is controversial, it provides a valid counter-formulation to that proposed by Hutt, which suggests that while individuals can be shaped in various ways, they will be happiest if they are shaped to fit the 'true' biological base of the two sexes.

The view proposed by a number of writers favouring an androgynous model of sex-role typing (i.e. one that transcends conventional stereo-types and relates to the individual's developmental tendencies regard-less of gender) (Osofsky and Osofsky, 1972; Rossi, 1964a; Rowe, 1974) is different only in degree from the earthy advice of Drs Jolly and Spock, who argue for the consideration of individual differences.

Parents themselves are not likely to be engaged in the analytical process of weighing up genetic, environmental, and other influences on their own and their children's interactions – though this is more likely to occur with highly educated, self-consciously rational parents. But, to the extent that they can transcend stereotypes and dogmas about sex-roles, the emerging view is that they are more likely to facilitate rather than impede the development of a satisfactory identity.

Issues in school-age (middle childhood) development

It is generally recognized that the divisions of developmental stages are based on both social criteria and inherent psychobiological developmental criteria, and that there is an interplay between the two. Parents orientate their policies to conceptions of the child's stage of development. The school syllabi, methods and administrative breaking points are also geared to a conception of natural growth stages. But these conceptions, including the concept of childhood itself, how long it lasts and what behaviour is expected of children in different age categories, is a product of social historical factors (Aries, 1962).

From a family's point of view the features of industrial society that affect how this stage of life unfolds are the absence of the father from the home for most of the child's waking hours in pre-school years, followed by the absence of the child from the home for increasing blocks of time following school entry. The delegation of what had been a family function to an external societal institution – the school system – has been seen in various ways, both by researchers and by families. On the one hand it is part of the 'stripping' of families of their traditional functions, along with the specialization that has put medical care in the hands of doctors, food production in the hands of farmers, entertainment in the hands of professional entertainers and so on. On the other hand, educational institutions provide a structure for the child's day that relieves parents of some of the care responsibility; they provide training in the development of skills which lie beyond the competence of most families and thereby help families to realize their aspirations for their children.

Whether a particular family sees the child's entry into school as a loss or a relief, and whether the child itself is excited or terrified at the separation from family figures, children are required to enter school by their sixth year. Many parental responses to their children's pre-school developmental issues relate to the feeling that when their children enter school they will be judged as parents as well as their children being judged as scholars (Newson and Newson, 1975).

School-entry brings with it a new set of experiences, which join with the developmental experiences occurring independently of school, and together affect the lives of parents as well as their children. From age about six to eleven, the parent may feel increasingly that other forces are at work in the child: the school, the peer group, and the child's own developing personality.

The work of Piaget, and of those influenced by his approach, has detailed how the child develops a number of skills quite dramatically during this period. Its linguistic communicative skills, having already emerged from an 'egocentric' to a more 'sociocentric' bias, and its cognitive capacities, having moved from the pre-conceptual and intuitive form of thinking and reasoning to one that applies logic to 'concrete operations'. Later, a more abstract and formal operations stage emerges as a basis for logical thinking; and, correspondingly, a more rigid conception of morality ('moral realism') which is orientated to the expected responses of an authority figure, gives way to an internalized conception of the rules and moral judgments involved in social life ('moral relativism')(Piaget, 1932/48; Inhelder and Piaget, 1958). According to the Piagetian view of the developing child, which has had wide influence especially in educational settings, there is a natural unfolding of stages which may be facilitated or hampered by social interaction but which are epigenetic. Subsequent American work by Kohlberg (1964) and Mussen, Conger and Kagan (1969) have added to the description and classification of stages, the dimension of the child's *feelings* about experiences. Feelings of guilt and anxiety as well as of satisfaction and pride may be present, and unless recognized may become problematic.

To the extent that a parent holds a view of the child's development as going through a natural sequence of stages with associated problematic issues (as distinct from the earlier view that good or bad habits are products of good or bad training), different tactics are selected to match the child's stage of development as well as the nature of the act itself. Kohlberg (1964, p. 423) observes, on the basis of experimental studies:

A technique effective in prohibiting cheating may be ineffective in prohibiting disobedience. . . . A technique such as physical punishment effective in preventing cheating at age five in the home may be ineffective in preventing it later (at age twelve) in the home or in the school.

In general he argues for the parent making an 'appropriate match' between the adult's moral judgment and reasoning and the child's. But while

there is a great deal of consensus among parents of all social classes as to their ideals of character for their children as adults, [there is] a great deal of variation and confusion in translating these into expectations for young children's conduct.

Kohlberg does not conclude that anything a parent feels to be right had equal validity. Rather, he notes that though uncertainty of outcome tempts one to do what is convenient at the moment, it is important (particularly in moral development) that there be a *consistent* orientating of behaviour to 'ideals of character and maturity in the future' (p. 426). He cites Bronfenbrenner's (1962) analysis of the Russian moulding of character, particularly in schools, as consistent with this principle.

The psychoanalytic view of the development of the child has given its primary attention to the less manifest elements of development (the less cognitive/intellectual elements) and concentrated on the fantasies of the immature mind, the feelings and drives associated with instinctual life – love, hate, fear, anxiety, envy and rivalry. The difficulties of the psychoanalytic model, as a way of relating to children's development for *parents* (rather than for psychoanalysts in their consulting rooms) is that it has the obverse deficiencies to those of the more cognitive schools.

In the psychoanalytic perspective, the child enters a phase in which instinctual drives of sexuality and aggression are constrained in the interests of the child's becoming more civilized. This occurs via education and a process of 'sublimation' of the instinctual drives. Freud wrote, giving the initial impetus to the formulation of the *latency period*, which has governed psychoanalytic thinking ever since:

[Latency] represents an educational ideal from which individual development usually diverges at some point and often to a considerable degree. From time to time a fragmentary manifestation of sexuality which has evaded sublimation may break through; or some sexual activity may persist through the whole duration of the latency period until the sexual instinct emerges with greater intensity at puberty. In so far as educators pay any attention at all to infantile sexuality, they behave exactly as though they shared our views as to the construction of the moral defensive forces at the cost of sexuality and as though they knew that sexual activity makes a child ineducable (Freud 1905/53, Standard edition, Vol. VII, p. 179).

While the Piagetian view holds that children are ready to develop by school-entry time because their cognitive apparatus has matured sufficiently to cope with the learning challenges, Freud's holds that children are ready because they can tame their body functions sufficiently to relegate them to a latent role – underneath observed patterns of behaviour, but covert and therefore relatively inaccessible to observation and study.

We know little about how parents feel about the separations involved or about the experience of parenting during this early school period. The Newsons (1976) report that Nottingham parents do not portray their seven-year-olds as conspicuously quiet, but indicate as much turbulence as at earlier ages; they query the utility of the concept of latency. The latency concept is questioned more generally as being culture-bound. The exemption of children from participation in household work and from exposure to adult occupational problems and issues is considered by some observers to reflect a particular historical situation rather than intrinsic properties of children.

Skolnick (1973, p. 326) draws attention to the anthropological critique of the whole modern idea of childhood:

> In general the anthropologists have attacked two ideas: the universal developmental stages and the incompetence of children. Mary Ellen Goodman (1970), for example, argues that the data of anthropology refute two fallacies of American child rearing and pedagogy: 1) the fallacy of universal age/stage linkages, and 2) the fallacy of under-estimation – the assumption that children are incompetent . . . (more specifically) a supposedly universal stage of development which anthropologists have failed to find in other cultures is that of latency . . . in some cultures genital sexual behaviour is continuous from infancy through adulthood.

In most societies lacking schools or workforces structured in the way ours has been since the Industrial Revolution, children work in varying degrees, usually alongside their parents, from the age of three onwards (Stephens, 1963, p. 386).

Though the school becomes an important influence in controlling the child's behaviour and training its skills, the literature indicates that parents remain the most important figures in teaching the child how to live (e.g. Mussen *et al.*, 1969, p. 534). It also implies that parents face a new kind of challenge in their parenting – that of incorporating into the relationship with their children the fact that others are important – particularly teachers and peers. Many parental guidance texts take the latter into account as they urge parents to 'provide opportunities for healthy exploration of the environment' (Hawkes and Pease, 1962); 'children must be allowed to grow at their own rate and in their own style rather than be called on to fulfil the ambitions of parents' (Williams and Stith, 1974, p. 446). The latter authors go on to note that for children in this phase:

> While adults are sometimes necessary, children have achieved enough trust, autonomy, and initiative that they want to become involved in

a world where adults are usually not welcome . . . children rebel against cuddling, are more restless, usually are dirty, snaggle-toothed, and speak a language adults find too difficult to understand. At home, vocalization assumes new patterns – children talk back and accuse parents of unfairness, chores are forgotten, they fail to show up in time for dinner, embark enthusiastically on projects only to have to be prodded to finish them. Some children disdain from taking baths and keeping their rooms clean. . . . In the fourth, fifth and sixth grades, problem behaviour reaches a peak: teasing, discourtesy, scuffling, rebelliousness, carelessness, untidiness and disobedience. These children are frequently irritable, easily offended and often discouraged.

This is, in general, the period in which child-centred parents are addressed by a wide range of child-guidance specialists and exhorted to be tolerant, respectful, genuine, honest, consistent, loving, flexible, firm, loyal, humble, even-tempered, full of fun, and so on (Obsatz, 1967; Williams and Stith, 1974; Hawkes and Pease, 1962).

Le Masters (1974) expresses the view that many expectations of parents of latency children are 'myths', just as the idealization of parenthood is a cultural myth (cf. p. 144). He lists the following popular myths that contradict the everyday experiences of parents and observations by sociologists, psychologists and others studying either child-development or family life at this phase:

1 Rearing children is fun.
2 Children will turn out well if they have 'good' parents.
3 Today's parents are not as good as those of yesterday.
4 Child-rearing today is easier due to modern medicine, modern appliances, child psychology, etc.
5 Children will not get into trouble if they have been told the facts of life (about sex).
6 Love is enough to sustain good parental performance.
7 There are no bad children – only bad parents.
8 Children improve a marriage.

Studies based on observation and sensitive interviewing, such as the Newsons' study of the seven-year-old in the urban environment (1976), tend to dispel these myths by painting a rounded and realistic picture of the young child's experience and behaviour. One of the main characteristics of the seven-year-old to emerge from the Newsons' study is their developing sense of initiative. At this age the child has already developed cognitively to a point where he can engage in what Piaget called conceptual thinking: he sees how to make classes of things and understands the relationship between them. We can consider this further in relation to the three issues which concern parents particularly saliently in this phase and which are also foci of research: *social and moral development; achievement performance;* and the *consolidation of gender identity.*

Children become focally concerned with social and moral develop- ment issues during their school age, when their peers and teachers, as formal authorities, become more important to them. They are con- cerned about whom they are meeting at school, who is telling them what to do and what others are being told to do, who is nice to play with and who is horrid, what to do about the bully who pushes other boys around, or lifts up the girls' skirts, whether getting onto the football team or into the school play is important and why. They want to be liked by others and become concerned with why others do or do not like them, and how they compare with other children in this regard. Their parents are likely to be interested to some extent in what form these social experiences take – is the child behaving well, making friends, being taken advantage of, coming under good or bad influences in the friendships that are being developed? In some instances the greater involvement with peers is a relatively easy experience for all concerned. Sometimes, however, the formation of these relationships can be problematic and the parents may become more involved and concerned about them.

Research on these issues has been encompassed in a number of frameworks. Some of it has been studied as 'moral development' – or how the child develops social rules, judgments about what is right or wrong in specific social contexts and a sense of internal standards to guide behaviour (Piaget, 1932; Kohlberg, 1964, 1968; Wilson, Williams and Sugarman, 1967).

We have already indicated that the approach taken by Piaget to the development of stages of moral growth contrasts with the approach of psychoanalytic writers who emphasize covert processes like 'superego development'. What is clear in both is that the child's social or moral development is shaped by interaction with others and not entirely from an automatic and direct unfolding of a biologically programmed competence. Kohlberg expresses this view, in the light of a consideration of the full range of research evidence, as follows:

the emphasis on social interaction [in moral development] does not mean that stages of moral judgement directly represent the teaching of values by parents or direct 'introjection' of values by the child. Theories of moral stages view the influence of parental training and discipline as only a part of the world or social order perceived by the child. The child can internalize the moral values of his parents and culture and make them his own only as he comes to relate these values to a comprehended social order and to his own goals as a social self (Kohlberg, 1968, p. 491).

Research in America by Kohlberg and others, and in Britain by Sugarman (1973), for example, finds social class differences in the *rate* of social development of children. But, children of all classes show the *type* of developmental stages observed by Piaget (toward a less rigid, more reciprocating and relativistic sense of equitable justice). Peer-group influences, popularity, and family factors (communication, warmth, sharing in decisions, etc.) are found to affect the child's overall rate and extent of moral development.

It is the child's capacity to form affectional relationships with others that governs its ability to take roles, and this appears to be at the heart of moral development. Parents provide one basis, but not necessarily the only one, for this process. Opie and Opie (1959) document peer influences at this phase. Various sociologists have emphasized role-playing as a key process. Some of the writers influenced by the symbolic interactionist school of social psychological theory (e.g. G. H. Mead) use what Goffman calls a 'dramaturgical model' (Goffman, 1959). Goffman sees social life as analogous to theatre, with frontstage and backstage behaviour situations, roles, audience, performance styles and skills and so on. The child at this stage of its development is learning to differentiate more roles and, as Mead pointed out, is developing its ability to visualize his or her own 'performance' from the standpoint of other people both in and out of school.

The child also learns situationally appropriate behaviour which, as Harré (1975) has pointed out, has elements of ritual. Extending the point of view of Richards (1974), Shotter (1973) and Newson and Shotter (1974) that mother–child interaction has social as well as cognitive and emotional dimensions, Harré argues (1975, p. 159) for a multidimensional perspective to the child's development and therefore the parents' response to events in it:

> A schoolchild, aged between five and twelve, can . . . be thought to be operating in five distinct social worlds, each with its own accepted personas, its own rules and conventions, its own vocabulary, and even its own naming system. These are the child–child world of the playground, the teacher–child world in class, the teacher–child world out of class, the home world and the local society.

According to this view, the child–child world of the playground becomes a crucial arena for developing social competence adaptive for subsequent adult life.

Parents respond to issues presented by their children according to their own assessment of the child's social and moral development, and of the relative weight of different influences in it. But here again, little is known either of what parents have in mind when they are 'parenting' in this dimension, or of what difference it makes to the child's social development – other than that it does seem to make a difference if parents have *some* conceptual framework. But more research is needed on this.

An increasingly salient issue for parents as the child is absorbed into the world of schooling is *achievement*. It increases in its importance particularly if there is streaming or selection within the school system.

Whether in relation to peers and their 'pecking orders', to teachers and their score-charts, or to parents, the child is likely to become involved in this issue of achievement. How much emphasis to put on doing well; how much to care about excelling or performing up to expected standards, and in which areas of activity inevitably become concerns even if only to be rejected as unimportant.

The development of an achievement motive within an individual has been studied from many perspectives by David McClelland and his colleagues (McClelland, 1953; Rosen, 1956. Also see Kahl, 1965; Strodtbeck, 1963, and Turner, 1964). Certain characteristics of parent–child interaction have been found to contribute to the formulation of this motive before it takes specific shape in relation to vocational or organizational success strivings. High standards of expectations for self-reliance and mastery coupled with warmth and encouragement seem to be critical to its development, as is appropriate timing to gear in with the child's developing capacities and the provision of opportunities for practice.

Longitudinal studies both in England and the USA show that there is a self-perpetuating process of performance in which early signs of mastery and performance motivation become powerful predictors of later performance (Moss and Kagan, 1961; Douglas, 1968). Achievement motivation seems to emerge – whether spontaneously or under pressure – in boys earlier and more intensely than in girls. But it is mothers rather than fathers who seem to be instrumental in fostering it.

Mussen and his colleagues (1969, p. 462) conclude from the range of available studies that two factors are crucial in the development of achievement motivation:

1) the desire to please parents who encourage this motive (particularly if the parent actually emphasizes the value of intellectual mastery in preference to other interests and values).
2) an identification with parents who are effective models for intellectual mastery (particularly if the parents are not over-powering or autocratic).

As Josephine Klein (1965, p. 508) points out:

parents who want to encourage their children to take an independent
interest in things have to take a deal of trouble . . . [and] . . . a parent
who takes trouble to arrange the child's experience in this carefully
graded way is bound to interact a good deal with the child.

She regards this as analogous to the Bowlby hypothesis about maternal
deprivation – only on the credit side of the parental influences affecting
child development; and links the general syndrome as described by
McClelland to that of the elaborated language codes described by
Bernstein (1961). She also notes that reports on parental behaviour in
deprived settings indicate that mothers in such settings are often too
anxious to be nurturant (and their children are, accordingly, less
confident in facing problems), and that less nurturant mothers have
neither the time nor the patience always to respond willingly to their
children's needs. Finney (1961) notes that children from settings of
this kind tend to develop various attitudes incompatible with high
achievement.

In general, these studies concentrate on academic achievement, and
are couched in terms congenial with middle-class values. There is very
little on achievement in other areas – sport, interpersonal relations,
etc. Floud, Halsey and Martin (1956) document how this variable is,
accordingly, distributed along class lines. Using IQ scores and a
number of other indices of achievement, students whose fathers are in
higher social status occupations were found to do significantly better
than those from lower-class backgrounds. Citing a number of British
studies, Klein documents the importance of social class and social
mobility orientation as a factor associated with the achievement issue
(Mogey, 1956; Stacey, 1960). Jackson and Marsden (1962), Spinley
(1954), Bott (1957), Young and Willmott (1957), Gorer (1955),
Lockwood (1958), and others who have accumulated community-based
data show the same tendency – for middle-class families to value
education, social mobility and individual achievement, and for working-
class families to vary according to whether they were mobile. The more
mobile, 'status dissenting' families aspire to middle-class patterns,
though they do not always know how to implement it. The more
'status assenting' working-class families do not, for a range of reasons, value
those patterns and neither encourage it nor model it for their children.

Sugarman, in a study of 540 London fourth-form boys, analysed the
inter-relations between father's occupation, values and academic
achievement of the boys – including in his sample two grammar
schools and two secondary modern schools. While these boys were at
the high end of the developmental period with which we are concerned,
Sugarman analyses the factors leading up to their achievement orientations by the time they reach fourth-form. He found that a cluster of

values associated with middle-class culture are most predictive of achievement orientation – whether the boys came from middle-class homes or from homes of manual workers. The key value variable seems to be future orientation – i.e. 'the degree to which they are oriented to preparing for the future and to making sacrifices for it' (Sugarman, 1966, p. 298). He argued that the home 'is probably the major influence on pupils' values' though there are school and peer influences too. An interesting feature of Sugarman's analysis is that he shows how variations within social class can operate to produce the observed effects. While there is a tendency for middle-class families to value achievement and to orientate their children to the future, these values may be found in working-class homes as well, and not all middle-class families display these traits.

As indicated above, *consolidation of gender identity* is also a salient issue in this phase. A child knows by the time of school entry that it is of one or the other sex. There is considerable evidence that fundamental sex-typed attitudes and behaviour patterns are already firmly implanted by the age of five. The period that follows is one of consolidation of gender identity. This is cemented by the overlay of domestic models with those of the educational system, with its differential by sex-typed books, games, sports, standards for behaviour, expectations for performance. These appear to be changing, with coeducation and the movement to de-stereotype the content of books, etc. But the un-weaving and re-weaving of a culture that has been centuries in the making is a lengthy process, and by and large the process of consolidation of conventional sex-role stereotypes and standards continues in this phase.

Characteristically it begins with the model of sex-roles perceived by the child at home – initially pre-school, but appreciated more fully in the school period. Lynn points out social class differences in the American context:

The father's work status helps determine whether children cling to narrow masculine and feminine definitions and at what age they begin to differentiate themselves by sex. In contrast to the high status father the working man presents a masculine model that is more clearly differentiated from the feminine one; for example, he is likely to condone aggression, a traditionally masculine attribute. His work is especially attractive to young boys, who understand and find intrinsically interesting such activities as building a house or repairing a car. The high status father, although he presents a subtler model of masculinity, becomes more attractive as a standard for the boy as he matures and becomes aware of his father's status and prestige. . . . Compared to the high status father the working father is more intolerant of his girl's tomboyishness and is more restrictive and punitive with her. In this way he defines her feminine role narrowly, but he is less likely than the high status father to engage in the kind of intimate flirtatious interaction that, because it gratifies, reinforces the girl's coquettish femininity (Lynn, 1974, p. 80).

Rabban (1950) had earlier found that it was because of working-class parents' more clearly defined sex-roles, that children from working-class families differentiated themselves by sex at an earlier age than the children of middle-class parents.

As for mothering, femininity and the associated traits of nurturance, affection, etc. that were established in the family according to the conventional model, they are also consolidated in the child's 'mental map' during this school period. Recent research testing the empirical basis for the Parsonian model in the mental imagery of children has sustained the picture of mothers being seen as more nurturant and fathers more instrumental and also more punitive (Kagan, 1956; Bronfenbrenner, 1961; Droppleman and Schaefer, 1963; Ucko and Moore, 1963; Meissner, 1965).

The results of these studies must be taken sceptically, and there are some signs that the images of parental role models that become part of the child's mental map are subject to change. Ucko and Moore (1963) for example, found that while four-year-old children of both sexes indicated in doll-play experiments that they considered the mother doll as the more helpful parent, six-year-old boys show the father as more helpful. What is not known is whether this reflects a broader view of the parents' worlds which becomes possible for the school-age child, or whether fathers actually take a greater interest in their sons following school entry. There may be other factors. In any case, images in the children's minds which become models for their own subsequent parenting behaviour, are not biologically fixed. They are subject to change both as circumstances change in the person's life, and historically as the models themselves change. Educational change as well as family change – sometimes one more than the other, sometimes the reverse – can alter an individual's gender identity, not in a fundamental sense, but in the sense of the ideas, norms and standards associated with it.

Kagan, summarizing a number of American studies on sex-role identity acquisition and its consequences, concludes that:

> By the time [the child] is seven, he is intensely committed to molding his behavior in concordance with cultural standards appropriate for his biological sex and he shows uneasiness, anxiety, and even anger when he is in danger of behaving in ways regarded as characteristic of the opposite sex (Kagan, 1964, p. 162).

The importance of establishing a solid gender identity goes beyond the immediate interests and activities in school – but extends mentally to sexuality and vocation as the child extrapolates his experience and feelings into future aspirations (Rapoport *et al.*, 1976).

Parents see this happening. They are part of it. They may approve or disapprove, and seek to correct imbalances or dissonances, but little is known of how their effort weighs against other influences in relation to their child's psychosexual development or their own comfort. Once again, this is a rich area for further investigation, involving the concordance among parental, educational and peer interactions with the increasingly autonomous child.

Value issues in child-rearing and in research

As indicated in the beginning of this chapter, we consider the value issue as crucial. First, though our society is complex and differentiated, there are value elements in the culture and sub-cultures which affect how a child's behaviour is defined and how parents should respond to it. Their interpretation of children's behaviour – e.g. of aggression, in peer-group relations, in school performance, etc. – is to some extent a function of how our society interprets and evaluates the behaviour patterns conventionally associated with boys and with girls. Second, in adopting a tactic for response to a child's behaviour, parents are to some extent influenced by their values. This is particularly true for those parents who are not so preoccupied with survival issues. When they decide how to respond to sexuality, aggressiveness, achievement orientation, and so on, they are (implicitly or explicitly) asking themselves 'toward what goals are the child-rearing practices directed?' 'What sort of person would we like this child to become?' 'Of what value will it be if we allow this or constrain it – e.g. in terms of the child's eventual capacity to function in society?'

These issues are often disregarded in the literature on child development and child-rearing. There is insufficient knowledge about which early experience produces which later patterns of functioning. The focus of most research and guidance books is on a shorter time span. There are, however, some exceptions. Notable among these is Bronfenbrenner (1971) who explicitly raises the question when he considers the contrast between American national character and Russian national character, and seeks to relate it to their child-rearing practices.

At a more fundamental level, there are new studies which begin with the question of the value of children to people. Lois Hoffman's current research (1975) aims to clarify the relationship between specific value orientations to having children and the cultural contexts in which the values occur – on a world wide contemporary basis. Berelson (1974), in a review of the reasons for wanting children, that have been prevalent within our own society, argues that we evolved from a phase of relative

indifference toward children to one of being 'child-centred'. Acco
to Berelson we seem now to be entering a new phase of 'rationalit)
responsibility', in which problems are recognized and capac
cultivated – with parenting becoming a talent like playing the piano,
doing mathematics or playing tennis. He does not take on, explicitly,
the issue of how to establish criteria for gauging competence or success
at child-rearing but quotes Wordsworth in accepting the over-riding
value of *revitalization* as at the heart of parents' involvement in their
children's growth:

> A child, more than all other gifts
> That earth can offer to declining man,
> Brings hope with it, and forward-looking thoughts.

In post-Second World War Britain, the relationship between the
social values of the day and the professional conceptualization of
parenting with young children is clear in the following observation by
Winnicott:

> The aim of infant care is not limited to the establishment of health,
> but includes the provision of conditions for the richest possible
> experience, with long-term results in increased depth and value in
> the character and personality of the individual (Winnicott, 1964/73,
> p. 57).

It seems, however, that there is a problem in identifying requirements of this sort as children's 'needs' without pointing out simultaneously that people have continuing developmental needs. It is no
longer adequate to look at the requirements of children and parents
separately. By the time that Kellmer Pringle, for example, produced
her perspective on *Children's Needs* (1974), there was a generation of
parents who had themselves been reared *à la* Bowlby and Winnicott.
It seems fairly inescapable that these parents share the 'needs' she
identified: for love and security; for new experiences; for praise and
recognition; and for responsibility. The more cynical were calling these
new adults 'Spock-marked' as a result of their parents being so child-
centred. At a time when children's needs appear to be more and more
finely identified, demanding higher and higher standards of child-
rearing practice, the lines on which this is done, its underlying assumptions, and its implications for parents require careful attention. In the
recent past, with its child-focused ideology, it has been widely felt that
children's development potential should be maximized. The value
position that seems to be gaining currency now is one of balance.
Parents should be free to choose how much they wish to invest their
own energies in facilitating their children's development as against
their own – within limits. But parents will be in a better position to

choose if they know more about their own development potential and problems as well as their children's.

Even within the ideological focus on children's 'needs', accumulating research 'evidence' indicates that children's 'needs' have been defined in pretty open-ended terms, to maximize their opportunities for development: physically, intellectually, educationally, emotionally and socially (Kellmer Pringle, 1974). The issue of how these values fit with other values – of society and of the parents – is rarely considered explicitly. 'No sacrifice is too great when it comes to one's children.' In this social climate, the fact that parents have needs of their own is often overlooked. Where they are concerned, fulfilment of parents' needs tends to be regarded as selfish, especially if this detracts in any way from the meeting of children's needs as they are defined at present. It is this constellation of ideas that is currently being reconsidered – both factually and in value terms.

One factual basis for reconsideration is the assumption that a child who is indulged and gratified as an infant will mature in such a way as to be able and willing to gratify others, i.e. its own children. This implies the management of the *discontinuity somewhere in the life of the child*. In childhood everything is to be beamed in on the person, in parenthood he or she is expected to surrender this position of apparent privilege, and switch to one of giving, to directing all to the child. Adolescence is the mediating period after which the person is expected to become 'mature', i.e. capable of exchanging a situation of getting-it-all to one of giving-it-all. But the real crunch comes with parenthood. The assumption that a child who has been *highly* gratified and stimulated will be capable of this transition because it is the person who feels good about himself who can give to others is an arguable one. If the child-rearing is *too* gratifying it may alternatively be seen as stimulating omnipotent fantasies, and creating an unrealistically demanding child. Such a child feels subjective deprivation when anything is deficient from the ideal; and, as most of life is somewhat deficient in this way, there may be chronic anger, disappointment or depression. If a parent has been socialized for this sort of life expectation, being abruptly faced by a completely different set of conditions may be stressful (Rossi, 1968). The experience of having been so gratified may give the individual greater inner resources to bestow the benefits on another, particularly if it is a wanted child with whom the parent can identify. But this may be simplistic. First, one must consider the longer time span beyond the duration of the early gratifying phases of parenthood. Parents who may be able to give up fulfilling their own needs in the early years of parenthood may find it difficult to sustain this year after year. And they may find it difficult to recoup when their parenting functions recede. Second, the degree of sacrifice that some parents experience in the present may invest the whole experience with an element of stress that makes it difficult to give emotionally, despite being on hand all the time.

Another issue is the place of achievement motivation, future orientation, deferral of gratification and other aspects of this constellation of values in the life of the family. Parents may have worked to one set of values but urge their children to adopt another. They may place unrealistic or conflicting demands on them. Awareness of such issues is increased through research, even if the research itself cannot contribute directly to the resolution of value dilemmas.

But research itself is subject to value issues and biases which may divert it from relevance to the experience of parents. Biases introduced by clinical experience, by the limitations of survey methodology or by the laboratory-experimental method (what Liam Hudson (1972) calls 'The Cult of the Fact') are all illustrative of this. We have illustrated some of the problems of clinical bias in the work of Bowlby and Winnicott.

There is also survey bias. Some of the reports of the National Child Development Study, for example, were designed to analyse the effects of certain parental and family factors on children's development. Davie, Butler and Goldstein (1972) assessed the children in the study sample in terms of 'attainment tests' of reading and arithmetic ability and graded them according to a scale of X months' ability. They then related the possible effects on children of what they call 'parent-centred' variables: e.g. family size; parents' education and social origins; parental interest in their children's education; whether the parents were living in one- or two-parent situations; whether there was a working mother. The researchers had some reservation about this procedure, pointing out that the current education system itself (and hence attainment tests of the sort they have used) 'contains a built-in bias in favour of middle-class children' who 'find in the school situation basically the same scale of values as they experience at home'. Nevertheless, the authors legitimate their adoption of this strategy in the following way:

The implications of this are not that most judgements and measures of children's development are worthless. Teachers, research workers and others must use some framework as a basis for evaluation. That the framework embodies ideas, attitudes and expectations which are more commonly met in middle-class homes and therefore amongst middle-class children, is perhaps inevitable in our society. However, the fact of this framework must be borne in mind in interpreting the results. If our 'yardsticks' are a little bent, this does not mean we should throw them away – especially if we have no others. But their 'curvilinear characteristics' should not be overlooked (Davie, Butler and Goldstein, 1972, p. 29).

Difficult as it is, it is necessary to confront these value issues, even when a choice of methods is made that seems to be the best available compromise. It is important to remain alive to the fact that competition and achievement are values, not biologically fixed variables.

In considering the issue of conditions under which competition and achievement are congruent with, or antithetical to, collaboration and enjoyment, Philip Slater (1970) has argued that they have become antithetical in contemporary American life. The cut-throat, achievement-oriented society has produced breathless people running faster and ever faster, and there is a deficit of co-operation and human fulfilment. When parents are spurring on eager toddlers, are they teaching them basic motivating values that are likely to be carried into adult life to the toddlers' ultimate misery?

Perhaps it is not desirable that parents become too self-conscious about their interaction with their children. But researchers and other experts whose 'evidence' helps to generate parental expectations should bring the values implicit in what they advocate to closer scrutiny. When Kellmer Pringle (1974, p. 100) makes observations about the pressures that parents put on their children to control their bladders from a very early age, she is describing competitive values present in our society and manifested in these parents. In criticizing these pressures as onerous to the child, it would be useful to discuss the issues for the parents as well. These touch not only on their own self-images and relationships to others in their social networks, but also on their goals and values for the child. Presenting a child with an onerous socialization demand is part of the everyday chore-work of parenting. What makes bladder control so special and how does it fit with other tactics and values in child-rearing? Researchers, in discussing these issues, can usefully recognize their own values as well as their more factual contribution to the issues.

For example, it seems essential, in analysing the data on the effects of mothers' working, to express caution about the finding that those children whose mothers worked full-time before they started school have 'lost' approximately three months in reading age at the age of seven. There are so many intervening variables – of family size, housing situation, parental relationship, level of education, etc., that to assign weight to one variable in such a multivariant situation is spurious. Similarly with the finding that a seven-year-old in a one- or two-child family compared to one in a five or more child family has a 'gain' in reading age of approximately twelve months. Various interpretations of these data are possible as well as various value implications.

Striking a suitable balance is difficult, as the authors of the National Child Development report agree. What is highlighted here is a critical dilemma, and one which many parents experience, some more consciously and acutely than others. Most people have ideas about the kind of society they would prefer to live in, and many people share similar values about the good society. At the same time, what many parents desire for their own children reflects values which are discrepant from their social ideal. A common example of this occurs when socialist parents send their own children to private schools. The gratification and delight that parents derive from their children's eagerness and growth, the joy they get from facilitating their children, often overrides more general abstract motives. So we have parents who want to be part of an equitable world, but who cannot resist trying to rear 'special' children. And, when middle-class care-givers and teachers use their own values to assess the behaviour of working-class children, parents may find themselves being told that to be 'good parents', responsible and adequately functioning, they must live out a scale of values that is alien to them.

In his recent book, Spock (1974) reflects the value dilemmas in child management for contemporary parents. He argues that we are at a point in history in which young people must establish their own value hierarchies, and perhaps the role of parents should be to equip them to cope with these issues. He feels that they may be better equipped to do so if values of a humanistic, co-operation kind are inculcated, rather than acquisitive, competitive values:

> [The] philosophy of each for himself worked fairly well during the rugged past, when the frontier was being pushed back and the country was being developed. But I think that it is not adequate for solving some of the most urgent problems of today (Spock, 1974, p. 41).

He feels that parental hesitancy to do what they feel is best for their children had as one of its roots the earlier American wish that children be different from and better than their parents. They deliberately withheld their experiences and themselves as models because they felt fearful that they could not help their children to excel. Expert exhortations have aggravated this tendency, and American parents are characteristically self-effacing and guilt-ridden as they see their children develop problems. He argues in favour of relaxation of parental inhibitions and guilt, and the striking of new, appropriate balances between self-expression and self-abnegation. He says (1974, p. 135) that if children are allowed from their earliest years to assume that their wishes come first, they may grow up to be tyrants.

Though the British scene is different in many respects from the American – it also has many similarities. Dr Jolly (1975) though working in a more circumscribed framework of a paediatrician's role takes a similar line about values as parents search for solutions to such issues as separation and achievement. He aims to increase parental awareness of how parents and developing children interact with one another over the everyday growth and illness events of childhood to produce results which are desirable and enjoyable for both, or antithetical to these goals.

A new book, edited by Nathan Talbot on *Raising Children in Modern America* (1974/76), seeks to strike a middle ground between the more practical-minded works such as that of Jolly and the earlier Spock, and more value-oriented works such as the later Spock, Winnicott and Bronfenbrenner. It is policy-oriented and multi-disciplinary in its research orientation: it is critical of 'major shortcomings in current child-rearing arrangements and practices' but at the same time it 'seeks constructive solutions' (1976, p. 491).

Spock, Jolly and Talbot – different as they are within the paediatric profession – have in common their efforts at encouraging the generation and dissemination of information that can be used by society, parents and by growing children themselves, to realize their ideal values in life. The newer emphasis is to use expert information and guidance not abjectly, but in a framework of parental self-reliance.

6

The early and middle years of active parenting

The parental phase we deal with in this chapter is a protracted one, which parents experience from the time their first (and perhaps only) child emerges from early infancy, till the time that their first child reaches adolescence. It is a phase in which adults generally are likely to be preoccupied with productivity and performance, and building up life investments.

Using Rossi's (1968/74) terminology for sub-phases in a role cycle (anticipatory, honeymoon, plateau and disengagement or termination), it is the *plateau* phase of the parental role that we focus on in this chapter. The Group for the Advancement of Psychiatry (1975, p. 23), who use similar terminology, define the plateau phase as the 'long middle period of the parental cycle' which follows on the earlier 'honeymoon' phase.

Rossi (1968/74, p. 106) notes that the termination of the 'honeymoon' phase is not as easily defined as its inception. There is no culturally defined event or ritual to mark a transition from the 'honeymoon' to the 'plateau' phase of parenting; so it is marked by subjective experiences in parenting.

Parents seem to feel that they have reached a new phase in parenting when some arbitrary event, significant to them, occurs – such as the child being able to walk unsupported, or to respond to a question with a full sentence answer. The transition to the phase is generally marked by a greater capacity for autonomy exhibited – sometimes demanded – by the child, with a parallel experience of increased separateness (not necessarily distance) on the parents' part. The time at which the earlier phase seems to round off in parents' own experience, taking on a coherent image for them and giving way to what follows, may come sooner or later. For many it will occur in the child's first year, though for some in the second year or later; its timing is likely to vary with the birth order of the child.

Most parents have more than one child, and the impact of having several children at different stages of their own development is likely to be important. It is also important to consider the birth order of the child in relation to parenting problems. Both professional and popular literature has frequently noted ways in which first children have a different life-experience from subsequent children. Less attention has been given to the relevance of the child's birth order for the parent. Sometimes it is mentioned that the first child is the one the parent 'learns on', and therefore serves as a 'pathmaker' (Senn *et al.*, 1968) in the experience of parenting. Much less has been said about subsequent children. Marjorie Janis's (1964) study, *A Two-year-old Goes to Nursery School* is an exception. This is the youngest child of three, and the book highlights the implications of this last child's critical transition for the mother's wish to return to work.

In the last chapter we focused on some of the developmental issues presented by children as they progressed from diaper-wearing toddlers to pre-pubertal children (e.g. pre-school separations from the home, experiences with sex-typing and discipline, school entry and achievement experiences). In this chapter we shall focus on *parents*: their preoccupations, felt needs, interests and requirements as they proceed through these years of life and incorporate these child-initiated events into their more general life space and experience. At some point in the phase that concerns us here, parents are likely to experience some combination of critical status transitions characteristic of the phase. One of the most significant contemporary transitions is the mother's return to work. Though not universal for mothers, it is now statistically normative, and the issue of whether or 'not to return and when, is likely to be a salient one for nearly all mothers. The decision may follow on as an outcome of other parents' experience: a child entering nursery school; a child entering primary school; a child completing primary school, etc. Father's job changes are other likely critical status transitions. So is the birth of subsequent children. Moving house, often to a different neighbourhood, or away from the city centre to the suburbs, is common in this phase, and often associated with the birth of a subsequent child or change of a job. The significance of this transition and the adjustment required for all family members is often underrated by families themselves. If the move involves change of neighbourhood and less contact with established ties, the lack of available supports can make this transition specially difficult to deal with, particularly for wives and children (Seidenberg, 1975). Each of these events presents an opportunity to parents, more so than at other times, of altering the paths of their life careers and rearranging their life styles.

Children at different stages of development each have needs that taken altogether will produce different family constellations for parenting. For example, parenting with two pre-schoolers, then two in school and a new-born infant, then two in primary school and one already in secondary school will be the developing scene in a three-child closely spaced family. The scene obviously differs from a family whose first child remains an only child.

The early and middle years of active parenting that we review in this chapter coincide with what we previously called the early and mid-establishment phases:

> The [overall] phase is long and variegated, occuring roughly between the ages of 25 and 55, depending on the stage of family and work cycles. The central preoccupation of people is with making commitments that constitute *satisfying life investments* (Rapoport and Rapoport, 1975, p. 186).

In the late establishment phase, which will be discussed in Chapter 7, there is a greater preoccupation with the yields of these life investments – but during this phase people, both men and women, are preoccupied with making them – *being productive* and *performing well* in their chosen lines of effort. Though in some contexts it is useful to limit the idea of productivity to economics, in the life experience of men and women *as parents* a broader definition is warranted. Productivity may be expressed in having and rearing children, in creating and sustaining a home, in preparing for and functioning in a job, in other activities in the community. For some individuals it will take place in a wide and variegated spectrum of activities, for others a relatively narrow and specialized band. For all, the issues focus on choices, strategies and allocation of energy and commitments in the different life spheres.

In the early part of this 'plateau' in parenting there may be considerable strain. Financial strain is widely recognized. Though most fathers concentrate their energies on getting and holding a job and/or developing a career during this phase, the economic demands on the family are high relative to earnings. As Abrams has shown (1963), finances tend to be 'tight' in this phase of the family cycle. But it is not only a matter of finances. John and Suzanne Clausen (1973, p. 189) whose research focuses on the family dynamics of a cohort of California children followed up from their birth in the 1940s, write:

> Especially during the early years, children connote broken sleep, noise, confusion and when there are several, congestion. Mothers of young children put in an inordinately long work week and tend to be confined to the home much of the time. The early years of motherhood are frequently remembered as the period when one constantly yearned for a full night's sleep and for a day free of demands. In our longitudinal data at the Institute of Human Development, mothers with three or more children fairly closely spaced, looking back at the

early years of motherhood, from the perspective of the late 40s, are
likely to recall those early years as years of extreme exhaustion and
discouragement.

The exact array of stresses and strains will depend not only on the
personalities of mothers, fathers and children, but on the structure of
their family life. Families in which there are two parents face different
problems and have different resources from single-parent families;
families in which both parents work have a different situation from
those in which only the father works; families in which fathers are
available and familistic in value orientation as well as having occupational commitments have a different set of conditions from those in
which the father is often away and perhaps more committed to the
satisfactions of work or career than to those of domestic life.

In Chapter 3 we drew attention to the wide diversity of family
structural types. This range of variation occurs within all phases of
parenthood, including the phase we are concerned with here. For the
purpose of this chapter, however, it is useful to distinguish between three
main modes of family organization which relate to the parental issues
which are salient during the phase – particularly the relation between
work and family – namely, the conventional, the new-conventional
and the dual-worker modes.

We refer to families in which the male is the provider and female the
home-maker as *conventional* (Fogarty *et al.*, 1971; Rapoport and
Rapoport, 1975). Here women have their children early and assume full
responsibility for them. This is *their* channel for expressing their
preoccupation with productivity. The husband, as provider, is involved
in his occupation. Whether he has the kind of job he enjoys or not,
whether he is involved in a competitive struggle to establish himself
occupationally or not, it is through his occupation that he is likely to
express his preoccupations with productivity during the early part of
this period. Both mothers and fathers have characteristic problems and
rewards, according to how they structure their lives in this period. For
the father a potential problem is how to reconcile the demands on time
and energy stemming from occupational work (which are characteristically higher for this period) with the demands arising at home. If he
responds to work demands fully, he may feel that he is failing to help his
wife and that he is missing out on the enjoyable aspects of the child's
development. The special vulnerability of the wife in the *conventional
family* for this period has been more widely documented than that of the
husband. The bored and trapped feelings of housewives described by
many writers may be exacerbated when the school system takes over a
major share of the child's care. The wife may experience withdrawal of
a function that has hitherto been her main *raison d'être*. Women in this

position may feel like the redundant worker and may react with feelings of depression, or they may develop new interests or revive old ones.

An increasing proportion of mothers decide some time during this phase to return to paid employment or study; this we call the *new-conventional pattern*. The woman may re-enter at any time during the early parenting phase or indeed in another phase before or after. The decision process may entail considerable strain, as re-entry to the workplace poses special problems.

The wife in the *continuous dual-worker* family has never really left her occupational role, even following childbirth. Here both spouses work continuously at their occupations, as well as in domestic roles. Couples vary in how committed each partner is to occupation and family, and in how full-time and egalitarian the situation in fact is (Rapoport and Rapoport, 1971/76). The characteristic problems encountered by dual-worker families centre on the management of overloads, and the effective mobilization of supports and resources to make the pattern work.

We do not intend that these 'types' be considered as exhaustive or as rigidly binding. Families change their structure in the course of the family cycle, and different families are to some extent characterized by different patterns, e.g. by class or local community. Young and Willmott (1973) have described one sort of patterning that may be associated with the long-term historical process in which we are involved – toward symmetry. In the progression through recent history in our society, families have evolved from a dominant form of family structure in which only the husband is the breadwinner, to one in which both husband and wife have two meaningful roles, one inside the home and the other in the external occupational world. Young and Willmott suggest that many of the observable stresses stem from the change process which involves dislocation of existing patterns.

In the sections to follow, we explore the ways in which work and other options and constraints affect parenting. We consider the issues of the early and middle years of parenting under two major headings: *Parents' experience in this phase*; and *Parenting and institutions outside the family*.

Parents' experience in this phase

There is now considerable writing that looks beyond the prevailing – or eroding – image of parenthood as happy fulfilment in this phase. There is a middle ground of research and personal/professional writings that document something intermediate between the obsolescent romantic myth on the one side, and the angry, despairing requiem for the family on the other. Skolnick (1973, p. 310) observes that we have reached a point where it is possible to take a more subtle and differentiated view – one that goes beyond myth-busting. The difficulties making family life manageable, let alone enjoyable, go beyond the modification of idealized expectations which stand in the way of fulfilment in the event. There are strains in family living that have to do with occupational demands, with noise, pollution and crowding attendant on urbanization and industrialization, and with dehumanizing cultural tendencies and role expectations.

Jessie Bernard's recent reviews (1972, 1975) of the accumulating literature detailing facets of these strains have pulled together a convincing demonstration that the gender differences in experience of this phase are part of a pervasive and structurally patterned phenomenon. She has argued that marriage should not be assumed to be a unitary phenomenon, but consists of the joining of two sets of experience, the wife's and the husband's. The differences between 'her' marriage and 'his' marriage are not only profound, but are subject to cultural prescriptions and therefore subject to change. This is indicated in the statistics which show that distress associated with the single state formerly supported the view that marriage was something that was 'good' for women, but less so for men. Contemporary statistics (see below) indicate that the reverse is more prevalent today. Marriage is a better experience for fathers than for mothers.

This is not to say that the male role is lacking in strains, or that there are no happy housewives in this phase of active parenting. There is much variation. We suggest that an approach is required that allows both an appreciation of variation and a sensitivity to underlying dynamics which give any given pattern its meaning in experience and in society. Minority phenomena at one point in time – dual-career families, single-parent families, captive housewives, male liberationists – not only contain a range of personal meanings for those manifesting the patterns, but may reflect different currents in the change process that gives them a wider significance as indicators than their sheer numbers would suggest. We describe the contemporary picture of parental occupations, felt needs and requirements during the plateau phase of parenting indicating illustratively where possible, how the developmental challenges presented by the child (described in the preceding chapter) impinge on parents' lives at this phase. In the final section of the chapter we shall consider some of the ways in which families and institutions outside the family are evolving new patterns of relationship in response to some of these needs.

Contemporary issues in mothers' experience

The plateau phase of parenting is one in which the conventional image or ideas of the happy and fulfilled mother and children at the centre of the family stage has been dominant. The other is expected by this time to have mastered the stresses and strains of absorbing a child (then another child) into the couple relationship, and will have emerged from the first joys associated with the honeymoon phase of motherhood with a sense of competence in her role, and will have worked out a way of managing the tasks that confront her. It is the phase in which the parental role is 'fully exercised' (Rossi, 1964b).

Stereotypically, this is a happy period in which satisfying routines are established and satisfactions of the mother's preoccupations with productivity are found in responding to and shaping the children's development – seen as a never-ending, constantly-stimulating sequence of interesting and exciting challenges. Many of the motivations for having children mentioned in the idealized literature on parenthood are available for enjoyment, and the correspondence for many women between their ideals and their experiences is sufficiently close so that they can reply to survey questionnaires that they are content to answer stereotypically that they are happy. In the PEP survey of British university graduates eight years out of university, most of them in the earlier part of this phase of the family cycle, 60 per cent of the respondents, across all categories of married people (male/female, with and without children) report their marriages to be 'very happy', with a further 30 per cent of the men and 25 per cent of the women stating that they are 'pretty happy' (Fogarty *et al.*, 1971, p. 253). The order of differences between men and women reporting 'mixed feelings' is similar, with 16 per cent of married women and 10 per cent of married men indicating this response. Other surveys in the USA indicate a similar response to questions in the survey context (Orden and Bradburn, 1968). We shall return to this in the next section on the marital relationship.

It is acknowledged that there is a bias toward overstating the level of satisfactions, and that there is a build-up during this phase of covert dissatisfactions, gradually making themselves explicit, both in word and in deed. Rollins and Feldman (1970) and Blood and Wolfe (1960) also report this pattern and they confirm the imbalance of negative experiences for women.

We concentrate here not on the overt manifestations of the positive, idealized conceptions and experiences of parenting for women in this phase. They are well enough known, and they may remain not only the overt expression of experience but the genuine deeper experiences for many through this phase of parenting. We suggest that it is also useful to consider the less idealized experiences in some detail to balance the idealized conventional presentations, and because they have in fact reached such proportions that they are in some sub-populations the dominant experience.

There has gradually emerged a picture of the housewife/mother at this phase which is so pervasively indicated to be unsatisfactory that it can no longer be attributed to sensationalist journalism, neurotic feminism, biased sampling or any other such legitimately sceptical responses to the earlier indicators, like Friedan's angry book on the Feminine Mystique, taking to task the American consumption-orientated culture for attempting to con housewives into being satisfied with material comforts. Literature from medical practice (Lovshin, 1959; Norris, 1964) has documented the 'tired housewife syndrome' as relating neither to organic illness nor psychoneurosis, but to overloads and strains in the role – producing feelings of loneliness, self-deprecation, depressive and psychosomatic symptoms.

Pohlman (1969, p. 153) notes that the very isolation of young mothers produces a self-perpetuating effect, as each feels alone in her predicament:

> It seems illogical that each of many thousands of mothers should conclude she has some peculiar individual problem, and should go through a period of soul-searching and hostility and repression and guilt in her relations to her children.

Epidemiological literature documents the increasing prevalence of depressive symptoms, suicidal attempts and other associated complaints among women in all advanced industrial settings (Guttentag and Salasin, 1975).

Linden Hilgendorf and Barry Irving, in a re-analysis of data from the National Stress Study conducted by the Tavistock Institute, indicated that in Britain the most vulnerable sub-population for psychosomatic stress symptoms (e.g. pains and ailments, shortness of breath, palpitations, sleep disturbances) is married women 35 +, at home and with no hobbies. Married men under 35 are the least vulnerable (cited by Rapoport *et al.*, 1975). This is confirmed by the General Household Survey, which shows the greater prevalence of psychiatric symptoms among women than men (OPCS, 1973, p. 231).

The literature of sociology has concentrated on the structured constraints in family life, as well as the larger societal inequalities and discriminatory practices militating against self-fulfilment in women – with a notable pioneering study in Britain by Hannah Gavron (1966), paralleling the more impressionistic powerfully influential American book by Betty Friedan. Later a number of American studies (Lopata, 1971; Epstein, 1971) have elaborated and qualified the theme.

Both in the USA and the UK it is suggested that marital violence and child-abuse may be related not only to physical and economic deprivation, but to some of the psychological deprivations that may be associated with the mother's role in this period even in families with a high level of affluence (Elmer *et al.*, 1967; Hyman and Mitchell, 1975; Scott, 1973; Kempe and Helfer, 1972; Skinner and Castle, 1969; Gil, 1973; Court and Robinson, 1970).

Time-budget studies in a number of countries (e.g. Szalai, 1972; Walker, 1976; Haavio-Mannila, 1972) indicate that strains on house-wives only increase if they choose to work – a solution increasingly prevalent for all sorts of reasons as we shall indicate below. These studies were made in the 1960s, and it was a general experience that their husbands did not increase their participation commensurately to offset the withdrawal of women's activities in household work when they take on outside employment. Data collected today shows some signs of change, though as we shall indicate below in our discussion of fathers' experience, the surface has only been scratched.

Having established the character of mothers' 'at risk' situation at this stage, and that there are indications that the risks are structured into their social roles as wives and mothers, it is useful to examine in greater detail some of the qualitative studies and reports that illuminate their personal experiences. It is through focusing on the experiences of mothers, approached by different research methods (including self-reports) in different contexts that the statistical tendencies reported can be interpreted and a better understanding for both the scientific and the policy issues can be sought. This is important because of the tendency on the part of some people to see the distress responses as atypical, a minority reaction due to weakness or neuroticism, or other such reactions. We suggest that they represent indicators of a process which have more widespread significance and implications.

We begin with Gavron's study. She was one of the early researchers in Britain to draw attention to the plight of the house-bound mother, and her work was generated prior to the emergence of the newer feminist consciousness. Her study, based on two sub-samples (one of 48 middle-class mothers and one of 48 working-class mothers) in Kentish Town, London, has had a wide influence within sociology as well as amongst other professionals. This is due not so much to the quality of her data or the sophistication of her analysis: these were fairly rudimentary. But, what came across powerfully in her formulation was the insight derived from conceptualizing the predicament of modern women as entrapped people, suffering the consequences of having chosen a valued option in a situation that entailed excessive constraints, particularly but not exclusively for the more highly educated.

Couching her analysis in sociological terms, Gavron observed that 'the problem of women represents a network of conflicting roles which interact with each other thereby aggravating the situation' (1966, p. 142). In spelling these out (p. 143) she indicated discontinuities of the type we highlight in our critique of current child development models:

It has been seen how the ideologies that today surround parenthood conflict greatly with the values and expectations that women held before becoming parents. It has been noted that the set of ideas that support our present system of education which attempts to offer equal opportunity to all children to prepare for becoming instrumental members of a work orientated society conflict considerably with the roles and functions of motherhood as conceived by the self-same society. The ideology of the modern family demands high standards of care, living and involvement which inevitably restrict the freedom that the 'new woman' has been encouraged to expect from her childhood and education. In the work situation many of the attitudes to women are again based firmly on past ideologies which ignore the realities of the present.

Accordingly, Gavron's policy recommendations called for a fundamental reassessment of occupational, domestic, and community role definitions, together with an educational thrust to allow for greater integration of women and children into all phases of social life, avoiding their encapsulation in an environment which is productive of psychosocial deprivation.

In the decade that has ensued, a massive literature, both in the UK and the USA, has detailed and documented many aspects of the problems outlined by Gavron. Suzanne Gail, a university lecturer who withdrew from employment to concentrate on child-rearing, became distressed at the accompanying experiences. She used her skills as a writer to describe some of the personal dimensions of her predicament. She wrote (p. 152) the following in a collection of papers on different occupations edited by Ronald Fraser (1968): 'it never occurs to anybody that young educated mothers are a social problem, and could be given some help in readjusting, some alleviation of the drudgery even if only for the children's sake.' She emphasized how the dissatisfactions of her situation rebounded on her relationship with both husband and child, and believed that her child would benefit from a nursery class 'where he was given something constructive to do, and more company of his own age'.

In her cry of pain, indicating her tensions, difficulties in concentration – so powerfully induced by the tasks of incessant child-care that even when she had some free moments she could not immediately mobilize her mental abilities – she summarized the feelings and constraints of many women. She also pointed to structural deficiencies of the housewife/mother role. If a mother is so called upon to concentrate her needs for self-fulfilment on child-rearing, the small helpless child is likely to become the object of a kind of 'tyranny, or of smothering affections that asks the child to be a substitute for all she has missed' (p. 153).

We have already indicated some of the difficulties confronting a young mother if she takes outside employment and a way of dealing with some of these problems, and we shall return to this again below. But it is useful here to illustrate some of the feelings involved and the conflicts in felt needs. A workshop conducted by some staff members of the Tavistock Institute is illuminating. This is a group of professionals who, like Gail, are articulate and involved in understanding the issues and, in this case, are specialists in the human development and related fields. Acutely aware of the requirements of high-quality child-care, they noted both that this has traditionally been the mother's province but that there should be acceptable functional equivalents not beyond their ingenuity as sensitive and resourceful people to devise. However, their observations confirm the difficulties for mothers in transcending the conventional patterns, *particularly* the more conscientious mothers: Elisabeth Henderson and Margaret Rustin (1975, pp. 3–4) report on the Tavistock staff group's attempt to form a viable alternative:

> Involved in these arrangements – bringing a caretaker into the house, taking the child to someone else, involving a triangular journey, sharing arrangements with other families, playgroups, etc. – is often a deep sense of psychological strain. A number of women who reported their experiences said that despite making alternative arrangements, they felt ultimately responsible for the child's care. Particularly where there was anxiety about arrangements dovetailing properly, the mothers felt prey to continuous nagging anxiety about the satisfactoriness of the arrangements – often being preoccupied about them, checking and re-checking them – so the mother found it difficult to devote her mind to work.

For some people the experience of being a housewife involves disjunctive, antithetical elements rather than a satisfying whole round of work activities. Not only are domestic activities discordant in the experience with child-rearing activities, but for a mother with a permissive ideology, the conflict between any attempt to create a beautiful environment in the home and to encourage free expressiveness in a young child are at odds with one another – particularly for people living in restricted physical spaces. It is difficult to 'shake free' one's conception of domestic standards, however much one may accept the idea of sacrificing physical standards in favour of the child's expressiveness. And many people would not wish to make this kind of choice.

Ann Oakley's (1974a, 1974b) recent work follows through on some of the implications of these points, and has provided further illumination of several issues for wives and mothers at this phase. Oakley's work makes it clear that the conflicts of the burdened housewife/mother are not simply mental frustrations of middle-class women whose aspirations

have been raised, but are more fundamental than that. In her sample of
40 London housewives between twenty and thirty years old and divided
between working-class and middle-class mothers, she pursues some of
the issues raised by Gavron in greater depth and in detail. Analysing the
housewife role in comparable terms to those used for other occupations,
she compares being a housewife with being a factory worker, drawing on
the analysis used by Goldthorpe and his colleagues (1968). Using three
key variables – monotony, fragmentation of tasks, and pressures for
speed in performance – she found that on all three variables the women
described their work in similar terms to Goldthorpe's factory workers,
except that their view of their job was even more so, as is shown in
Table 9 (1974a, p. 87).

Table 9 *The experience of monotony, fragmentation and
speed in work: housewives and factory workers compared*

| | Percentages experiencing | | |
Workers	monotony	fragmentation	speed
Housewives	75	90	50
Factory workers	41	70	31
Assembly line workers	67	86	36

Oakley (p. 81) found that dissatisfaction was much higher amongst
those who described their work as monotonous. 'Eighty per cent of the
women who said "yes" to the monotony question are dissatisfied with
housework, compared with forty per cent of those who said "no".'

In relation to fragmentation, she concluded that nearly all (90 per
cent) housewives experience their work as 'subdivided into a series of
unconnected tasks not requiring the worker's full attention'. The
experience of time pressure was also more frequently reported by the
housewives in Oakley's sample than by Goldthorpe's factory workers.

Another element in the stress situation experienced by housewives is
that of social isolation. Gavron indicated this in her study and in
numerous studies subsequently it has come to be focused on as a major
element in producing the symptoms of distress across the social class
spectrum. Pohlman (1969, p. 153) argues that a 'culture-wide problem'
of this kind 'suggests the need for rational leadership to try to rearrange
matters within the culture to alleviate' it.

Within the housewife role there are differences in the nature of the
tasks and in people's orientations to them, as we have already indicated,
but it seems from recent research that some elements in the role tend to

be universally disliked – especially cleaning. Other elements, especially playing with children, tend to be universally liked. Oakley (1972) had earlier indicated how the widespread pattern of men helping out a bit, particularly amongst middle-class husbands, may actually be counter-productive in that the wife is left with a less enjoyable mixture of domestic activities. This is because the husbands, when they help, tend to take over the more enjoyable elements, leaving the wives with the lion's share of the less enjoyable ones.

A number of recent studies seem to indicate that marital role is a more powerful determinant than social class or gender of the strains described in the housewife's role. Gove and Tudor (1973) reviewed the large literature on sex-roles and mental illness, and concluded that women's higher illness rates relate to marriage not gender as the contrasts between men and women emerge for married individuals, not single ones – across the class spectrum. They found contrasts between middle- and working-class wives, but the net effects were comparable. While working-class wives had more economic stresses to cope with, middle-class wives had greater frustrations at being strait-jacketed by the housewife role after having been educated for a broader range of interests and activities.

The Thomas Coram Research Unit (1975) have studied mothers' mental states, using as indicators functional impairment, subjective emotional state, and interviewers' assessments of their behaviour. They found in a mixed social class sample that half of 142 mothers experienced moderate or severe mental distress during the year preceding interview. In the same period, 67 per cent of the mothers visited a general practitioner or doctor for some reason; 23 per cent described having possible psychiatric symptoms, such as feeling depressed or anxious. Twenty-one per cent of mothers report having taken tranquillizers or sleeping pills.

Naomi Richman (1975) investigated a series of 80 British mothers with three-year-old children manifesting behaviour problems and a control group of 80 mothers without such problem children. She also found no significant differences in mothers' mental states by social class. Moreover, she found no significant differences between the families with problem children and those without. This indicates that the mothers' depression in these families could not be assigned only or primarily to the extra demands of problem behaviour in their young children. She based her assessments on criteria such as disturbance of appetite, sleep difficulties, weight loss, impairment of concentration and inability to carry out ordinary activities, sad moods, feelings of worth-lessness, suicidal thoughts and attempts, etc. and additionally she took into account differences in experience of stressful life events as cor-rections for variations within the sample, and concluded that the primary exacerbating factor differentiating depressed from non-depressed mothers were money problems (particularly in relation to unemployment) and housing. She noted that housing is a particularly important factor, and that mothers are more likely to be depressed if they live in flats rather than houses.

These findings raise the issue of the relevance of social class as a variable; though they are not indicators of social class in a strict sense, there is a loose relationship between housing types and social class, and unemployment and social class. Furthermore, George Brown and his colleagues (1975) found in another London series of 320 married women in this age group a cluster of factors which cumulatively produce depressive symptoms, and that they are most evident among working-class women. The four factors which they find contribute to women's vulnerability are: early loss of mother (before age eleven), three or more children under age fourteen, lack of a confiding relationship with husband or boyfriend, and not going out to work.

The prevalence of these different stressful life events in one or another social class group is something which, like housing and unemployment, is only a loose relationship. Whatever it was that caused Brown's young mothers to have lost their mothers early more frequently if they were from working-class than from middle-class backgrounds may not remain in operation for another cohort. Certainly the larger family size and the lack of a confiding relationship between husband and wife have been associated in the past with working-class background. But studies show not only that working-class families are more conventional-minded in these respects (Newson and Newson, 1963/72), but that they are subject to change.

In a Chicago study conducted by the same market research organization that produced the early studies in the 1950s by Rainwater and others on poor families, the authors conclude not only that the degree of discontent with conventional women's roles is very pervasive in the USA but that there is a convergence between middle- and working-class attitudes. They argue that the principal difference between middle-class and working-class wives is that they arrive at their discontent through different channels – the middle-class wives want to accentuate existing patterns of self-development, training, education and occupational commitment; the working-class wives are changing their orientation entirely. Theirs is a qualitative change: 'Starting from scratch, as it were, and embarking on novel pathways. Mothers' examples and the experience of formal education have helped to prepare them for resistance rather than for adjustment to social change' (Social Research Inc., 1973, p. 29). Because of the general economic upgrading of working-class life as well as the alterations in consciousness – the two being interrelated – women's consciousness-raising has been directed to non-maternal aspects of their predicament (Social Research Inc., 1973, p. 40):

The stark poverty, the lack of adequate housing and furnishing and clothing (and sometimes food), the absence of special treats and indulgences, the presence of sick, tired, alcoholic, or harsh parents who could offer little interpersonal warmth or security – things of this sort, not uncommon in the past, have become relatively uncommon in working class households of today, and it is giving the women a sense of confidence and of having made a change for the better.

The authors argue that improvement in material conditions has not, in these circumstances, led to a passive contentment, but rather to questioning the *status quo*, a more active and critical approach to the tasks of improving the quality of life, a more vigorous search for new options and new life styles which now seem within their grasp rather than hopelessly out of it.

It would seem that it is more useful to consider the various elements of stress and strain – such as the actual structured characteristics of the role of housewife, and the actual prevalence of life events (Dohrenwends, 1974) – rather than thinking in social class terms. Not only are there these demonstrable and crucial intra-class variations – in housing, employment, etc., – but they are subject to change. The crucial differences, say in how a young mother handles the issues of separation from her child, disciplining aggressive behaviour, or the formation of sex-role conceptions – as well as in relation to the overall signs of strain that she manifests – are likely to relate to whether or not she is fully engaged in the housewife role, whether she has a regular paid occupation as well or another kind of outside interest, and whether she is parenting on her own or with a spouse in residence. In all of these situations, the couple relationship or its absence is pivotal, and this is what we shall consider next.

Changing issues in the couple relationship

The distress felt by so many mothers from different backgrounds and circumstances, has repercussions not only for themselves but for their marriages. Even for those who accept conventional role models as guides and standards for their lives, the constraints they experience may have consequences for the relationship; there are some issues which are endemic to long-term intense relationships after a period of several years. Bernard (1975b, p. 66) notes that taking all of these things together:

> this period in the life cycle [when children are from age 6 to 14] is the nadir of general marital satisfaction in the marriage of both husband and wife. Everything seems to be wrong. Positive companionship is reported at its lowest level, as is also satisfaction with children. Understandably, therefore, negative feelings are at their highest.

The wife is usually in her thirties, probably swamped by the demands being made on her from all sides; and her husband is probably devoting most of his energies to his profession. No wonder relationships between husband and wife suffer.

Similar observations have been made by clinicians, students of divorce and informed observers of family life.

Rollins and Feldman (1970) summarizing their own longitudinal study of marital satisfaction among 799 middle-class married couples in New York State, report that marital satisfaction tends to decline with each year of marriage, particularly following the advent of children. As we have already indicated, they find that this is much more pronounced for wives than for husbands, but it affects the marital relationship and it is exacerbated by the presence of dependent children in the family.

The Kinsey reports, elaborated subsequently by Masters and Johnson and others, document the decline in sexual interest and sexual activity (at least within the marriage) with each year of married life.

A number of studies are now available which document that the myth of happy families in this phase is really only applicable to a proportion of couples, a proportion that declines for each year of marriage until the children have left home. Some of them will be described in the next chapter.

Weissman (1974) has shown that difficulties in marital relations are related to the depressive state which is generated in so many women during this phase. There have been a number of attempts to explain how these discontents become entrenched in the marital relationship. Mismatches of personalities or social backgrounds exacerbate annoyance over 'personal habits'; loss of companionship and leisure for the wife lead to irritability; having too much involvement by 'in-laws' or too little contact with kin lead to specific problems; or difficulties over income and the management of money are notable flash-points, and ordinary events in family life – including the birth of children, children with defects, responsibility for the care of aged parents – may contribute to an accumulating stress pattern in the marriage (Blood 1969, pp. 349–78; Dominian, 1969; Chester, 1972; Levinger, 1965).

Some observers have emphasized the dysfunctional aspects of the romantic conception of marriage that has been prevalent in our society, leading to inevitable disillusionment and disenchantment in those marriages where a new and more enduring basis for the relationship is not developed, such as shared interests (Le Masters, 1974).

It is our view, in agreement with Skolnick (1973) that the present-day family, particularly at this phase of parenting, is confronted with a number of issues that go beyond that of overcoming a romanticized image of marriage and the family. They even go beyond the points made

by Skolnick, of coping with the stresses and strains of an urban industrial society which is noxious and dehumanizing in many ways. They
involve the additional strain of coping with unknown situations, which
have no rituals or patterned guidelines, which are at the same time
highly valued and unknown, which are irreversible and likely to mobilize anxiety and conflict in making the innumerable decisions that are
required in the areas outlined in the last chapter – independence and
autonomy training, sex-role and gender conceptions training, handling
aggression and discipline, moral and social development, achievement
motivation and performance – these and the other issues posed for
parents by the growing child engage the parent in an exhausting series of
conflicts and decision which cannot help but be stressful. Gelles (1972)
and other students of marital violence attribute to the lack of prepared-
ness of modern parents for the tasks they confront a major share of
causal determinacy of outbursts of uncontrolled anger.

The principal safety valve prior to having children is that of early
divorce. While that remains a safety valve for the years of active
parenting that follow, the presence of children is an inhibitor to divorce
and also an ameliorating factor in marital dissatisfaction (in addition to
imposing further strains). So, the factors making for satisfaction or
dissatisfaction in marriage at this phase are complex – and as well as
the external events and circumstances already noted, there is the factor
through time of the differences in growth rates and potentials of the
two partners, a factor considered to be of major significance by
Bohannan (1970) in divorce.

In addition to divorce, splitting up, arranging alternative forms of
stimulation and intimate relationship – which have been described by
writers like the Constantines (1972), the O'Neills (1972), the Francoeurs
(1974), Ramey (1975) and Bell (1975) as characteristic of this phase,
there are a number of indications of purposeful attempts to modify
marriage and parenting institutions. One set of these involves attempts
at experimental living arrangements which are communal in some
sense. This is a highly variegated set of experiments which may have
many lessons to provide for the future; but as they are still highly
volatile and tiny in proportions, we shall not consider them further
here – having outlined some of their characteristics in Chapter 3. We
shall, however, describe some of the studies that have recently been
made on attempts to modify the couple relationship within the framework of the family as we know it, and attempt to assess their contribution to our understanding of how parents' felt needs may be getting
met in new ways, by new models and concepts of family life and of the
roles of parents. The approach to this new understanding is proceeding,
as in other areas, by different methods. Conceptual clarification (e.g.
Scanzoni's (1972) analysis of sexual bargaining, and Safilios-Rothschild's

(1975a) analysis of the nature of interpersonal power in the marital relationship); by survey research (e.g. Orden and Bradburn's findings leading to the proposition that the element of choice is crucial in relation to coping with the stresses engendered by both spouses carrying occupational as well as domestic responsibilities), by intensive case studies of families pioneering new patterns (as in the work of the Rapoports, 1971/76; Poloma and Garland, 1971; Holmstrom, 1972; and Epstein, 1971; Grönseth, 1975); and by personal and clinical impressions of professional observers of the issues of changing couple relationships (e.g. Millar, 1975; and Miller, 1972).

Millar, a Canadian psychiatrist, gives advice on the management of the marital relationship. One excerpt is worth citing because it bears on one of the issues we indicated in the last chapter as arising in the nature of children's development and at the same time impinging on parental efforts to develop their own lives and their relationship. Millar discusses the issue of disciplining children. In gearing his advice to the conventional family situation, he observes that the usual situation is that mother does most of the disciplining and fathers participate now and then.

He gets to be the good and giving one who takes the kids to do fun things on the weekend, and she gets to be the ogre.

Does it have to be this way? To some extent, yes. More fathers than mothers work outside the home, and they're just not around when the bulk of child management is taking place. Fathers' share can never be 50 per cent . . . but then, that's not what's needed anyway. What is needed is that children have more than one experience of adult authority. They need to know clearly that *parents* (not just cranky mothers) have certain expectations of them. Mothers don't always want the job divided down the middle, but they do want their husbands to understand how hard it is to be kind, and tough, and fair, and firm, and loving . . . 20 times a day. And they want a little help with it. . . .

It *is* possible to get a husband involved in parenting, but you have to go about it thoughtfully. The first job is making him see that you are hurting: that trying to nurture, communicate with and discipline the children without more help from him is getting a bit overwhelming. Since he married you, there's a pretty good chance that he cares. Pick your time carefully. The poorest time to get anybody to see you are hurting is when *they* are, which in the average family, is 6 p.m. The kids are tired and hungry, and father wants to relax after another day in the shark tank. You've been rehearsing all day how you're going to get a decision out of him about piano lessons, braces and Mary's nose-picking. Everybody's looking to get, and nobody's in a state to give . . . [but fathers can and need to learn that they] can't be silent partners in parenting these days. Life is too complex, discipline is too tough to handle all by yourself. Kids need decent limits, humanely enforced. It grows them up. Two parents can do a lot more effective job of this if they try, are a little patient with each other, and don't lose sight of the unwritten contract that brought them into this home, and gave them these children. They can do the job together. Their kids are counting on it (Millar, 1975, pp. 86–7).

Millar is not advocating as revolutionary a stance as are some members of the men's movement. He is accepting a conventional marital structure, and suggesting how mothers and fathers can spread the load of interaction with their children just a little.

Many fathers do not wish to share the load and are not convinced that it is essential for them to do so. Many writers and sociologists have put forward their accounts and analyses on the basis of an assumption that most fathers will not be either able to change or willing to. Ann Oakley's analysis (1974b) does not seem to envision this as a realistic possibility in any major way, and Shirley Conran's bestseller *Superwoman* (1975) was explicitly based on the assumption that whatever the long-run prognosis might be, most women in the here and now will have to learn to cope more efficiently themselves with the tasks of homemaking if they are to survive psychologically.

There are many indications that there is a wide range of phenomena between the unwilling and uninterested husband who wishes to retain a conventional model for his home and hearth and the radical egalitarian couples – to be described below – who feel that an equitable life style can be attained only through equal sharing. Miller (1972) an American sociologist and proponent of equality (particularly in economic fields), and husband of psychoanalyst Jean Miller, proponent of revision and reform of psychoanalytic concepts implying sex inequality, has published a description of his personal struggles to live up to his ideals in his marriage. He admits that he is confused about how the complex fo values involved are to be clarified, and reluctantly classifies himself as a 'lapsed egalitarian'. He feels (p. 247) that for many men like himself – middle-class professionals of idealistic bent – the concept of equality is eminently acceptable, but its practice is more of a strain than they bargained for:

Probably the most important factor which accounts for the direction we took was our amazing naivete about the impact of having children – a naivete incidentally which I see today having a similarly devastating effect on many young parents. We just had no idea how much time and emotion children captured and how they simply

changed your lives. . . . Our first son was superactive and did not
sleep through the night. We were both exhausted. My wife insisted
that I not leave everything to her; she fought with me to participate
in the care of our son and apartment. I took the 2 a.m. and 6 a.m.
feedings and changings, for our ideology did not allow me to just help
out; I had to 'share' and really participate in the whole thing. I
resented that degree of involvement; it seemed to interfere terribly
with the work I desperately wanted to achieve.

So he became a backslider on his ideals, feeling guilty but not out of
step with his age-mates and colleagues, most of whom had not even
made the degree of effort to accommodate to the demands of parenting
at this stage of their careers that he had.

Bailyn (1970) delineated various types of husband–wife patterns of
commitment to family roles relative to occupational roles. Amongst
the series of 200 British couples of whom at least the woman was a
graduate whom she studied, the pattern that she terms the 'co-ordinate
pattern' is one that seems most highly related to marital satisfaction as
our society evolves toward a more egalitarian structuring of sex roles.
She sees the co-ordinate pattern as stressful in various ways, but also
capable of producing satisfactions which make the strains more tolerable:

the factors associated with happy co-ordinate marriages are more
managerial ones, those that ease the physical burdens of integrating
the realms of family and work. The proportion of happy marriages
in this pattern is greater when the wife is not alone responsible for
the care of the house and the children and, perhaps not unrelated,
when income is high . . . [it has been reasoned that] the co-ordinate
pattern represents a true integration of the realms of family and work
for both husband and wife and is in no way a mere reversal of
traditional family roles. [The data] supports this line of reasoning.
In contrast to the conventional pattern, happiness of co-ordinate
marriages increases as the husband's work satisfaction increases.
Also . . . the proportion of happy co-ordinate marriages is particularly great when high income is combined with high ambition
of the husband: 83% of these couples have very happy marriages.
Thus, the family-orientation of the husband whose co-ordinate
marriage is successful is not a substitute for work; on the contrary,
work is both important and satisfactory to such a man and his family
emphasis is based on choice, not on default (Bailyn, 1970, pp. 105–8).

A number of accounts now exist of sub-groups in which the marital
couple have sought ways of managing some of these issues. Two
research reports of such situations with more extensive role changes
will be described. They are the studies by Laura Lein and her

colleagues at Harvard, and by Erik Grönseth and his colleagues in Norway.

Laura Lein and her colleagues (1974, 1975) have analysed the patterns of 14 middle-income families with pre-school children in which both parents are in paid employment. They identified three broad alternative patterns in the division of responsibility among the couples studied: (1) the wife does most of the household and child-care tasks; (2) the couple share most child-care but not housework; or (3) the couple share most child-care and housework.

Lein and her colleagues (1974, p. 183) found that where domestic work sharing is achieved, usually with flexible occupational patterns, many men spend more time in child-rearing as well as in domestic work and that many of these fathers enjoy their new roles more than they anticipated.

> With the wife out of the home for part of the day, or as often happens, for the evenings, the husband finds himself responsible for many child-care tasks. Several husbands in our sample have discovered, sometimes to their own surprise, that they enjoy the extra time with the children and the added sense of more actively participating in their development. In fact, some have found that they are skilled and competent in these tasks.

Grönseth (1975), with the backing of the Norway Family Council, studied 16 work-sharing families, plus 7 families who wanted to adopt the pattern but found no employment possibilities and five ordinary families who served as a conventional comparison group. The definition of work-sharing families was that both husband and wife had to be part-time workers of not less than sixteen hours and not more than twenty-eight hours a week, and that they share domestic as well as economic provider roles. The spouses could work in the same or different places, and could combine their jobs or hours of working at them in various ways.

Most of the women in Grönseth's sample of work-sharing families were neither professional nor highly committed to a career, and they wanted time commitment to their occupation limited while their children were young. They felt the need *not* to work full-time. The men in the work-sharing couples, Grönseth reports, respected their wives' desires and tended to be either anti-career or to have a moderated career orientation. One reason given by most of the husbands and nearly all the wives for having chosen the work-sharing pattern was because they wished to be the principal child-minders of their children, and they wished to share this task between them. In short, Grönseth suggests that the combination of factors that produced work-sharing couples was wives' moderate career aspirations coupled with husbands' familistic orientations, plus a shared child-centred orientation.

Grönseth reports the following felt gains in the lives of the work-sharing couples he studied.

1 The couples all felt they had gained something by this arrangement in relation to enriching their life experience and shared interests. This finding is also reported in a number of other studies of egalitarian marriages (Gurin *et al.*, 1960; Chilman and Meyer, 1966; Levinger, 1964; Rapoport, Rapoport and Thiessen, 1974).

2 The couples reported improved sexual relationships. Other studies (Farrell, 1974) have argued that this would occur if men and women related to one another as co-equals, but some authorities have argued, as we have noted above in Chapter 2, that egalitarian marriage would produce impotence. Grönseth directly counters images of impotence and the emasculated male, by producing data about the couples' sexual lives which supports at least the existence of perceived enrichment in this area.

3 All of the work-sharing couples reported as a benefit of the pattern that they were able to spend more time together. This finding is felt to be the most specific to couples adopting this part-time work-sharing pattern. Other dual-worker or dual-career studies have emphasized the overloads and difficulties for these couples to find time to spend together. To the extent that spending time together is a felt need for couples in this phase – as much of the research has indicated – the work-sharing pattern seems uniquely geared to meet it.

It would seem on the basis of available research on changing conceptions of parenting in relation to the couple relationship at this phase, that at least three elements are crucial if the couple relationship is to function as a reasonably satisfactory and satisfying partnership for parenting:

1 That the pattern that is adopted be a chosen one rather than one into which the couple has been involuntarily catapulted. It would seem that couples need reaffirmation of the chosen elements of their situation – in the marital choice, the choice to have children, the choice of whether or not to work and how much commitment to put into occupational work *vis-à-vis* domestic work. In instances where there is no choice – involuntary redundancy, accidental pregnancy, reluctant employment or undesirable jobs, the obstacles to finding couple satisfaction and harmony are more difficult, though by no means impossible.

2 The feeling that whatever mutual support is being given is fair and equitable, and is the best that can be done under the circumstances. Whether the sharing is on the basis of a conventional division of labour or a fully egalitarian work-sharing pattern, the

crucial element for the couples concerned is that the pattern is supported to the best of the ability of each member given the existing constraints. This emphasizes the importance of an awareness of one another's constraints as well as positive values and wishes.

3 The presence of a mental model according to which the couple is able to assess how well their own experience is matching up to what they want and consider desirable in the marriage. There has been a great deal of discussion of the deleterious effects of an over-idealized and role-specialized conception of marriage in relation to the demands of child-rearing. Reacting *against* the perceived negative elements of the conventional family situation is now recognized as not enough. Assessment of alternative patterns – their social/psychological costs and benefits is increasingly called for.

In this context, the focus which is now being turned onto the father's role is crucial. The mother's role conceptions have produced the prime impetus to change – because of a configuration of experiences, dissatisfaction with the conventional pattern, new opportunities, in education and employment, birth control, and new models of marital and couple relationships. Initially, as Glazer-Malbin (1975) has pointed out, there emerged a gap between the evidence being produced by accounts of variant patterns of one kind or another, and the gross data of domestic division of labour produced by the various time-budget studies such as those of Katherine Walker (1976) and Szalai (1972). The former suggest ferment and change in couple relationships; the latter suggest a static quality as far as men are concerned, with all the changes adding up to an increase in the burdens on women. What signs exist that the men in fact may be changing or are interested or potentially able to change?

Contemporary issues in fathers' experience

Throughout the book we have emphasized the prevailing conception of father's role as peripheral in the family: an important support for mother but not really an essential ingredient in the everyday parenting aspects of the family life. He is useful as a model for his sons, as a provider, occasionally as a disciplinarian within the family, and as a facilitator of the mother – in giving her the necessary technology and keeping it in good repair to keep the household running. We have mentioned in various contexts how family experts, both in research and in the care-giving professions have tended to address their work to mothers. Researchers have assumed that mothers could speak for father and so they have generally neglected to interview fathers; and advice handbooks on child-rearing have almost always been addressed to mothers. What seems gradually to have emerged is a polarizing effect between mothers and fathers, in which the disadvantages for both have become clearer.

One kind of polarization emerges as a consequence of the father's occupation, which keeps him away from home for extended periods of time. There is a considerable literature now on the undesirable consequences of 'father absence', e.g. among seamen, long-distance lorry drivers, airline pilots, spiralist managers and the like. A literature has accumulated which argues to the point that paternal deprivation, as well as maternal deprivation, can be harmful to children, particularly growing boys. In the USA the Gluecks (1950) and McCords (1962, 1969) emphasized the importance of defective fathering in the background of juvenile delinquency. Fathers who were criminals, absent, violent, or negligent were found more often in the family backgrounds of delinquent than of normal children. In Britain, Robert Andry (1960) made a start in this area, and his findings have more recently been confirmed and enlarged by West and Farrington (1973). Andry interviewed two samples of respondents: 80 male delinquents aged twelve to fifteen and 80 males aged twelve to fifteen with no such delinquent record (all working-class) and the parents of each. He concludes from his study (1960, p. 127):

> delinquent boys (suffering neither from mental defects nor diseases, nor from broken homes) tend to perceive greater defects in their fathers' roles than in their mothers' roles, whereas non-delinquents tend to perceive the roles of both parents as being adequate. (Further, this seems confirmed in the main by both parents.) Thus the prime differentiating feature between delinquents and non-delinquents, as far as parental role playing is concerned, is the delinquents' perception of their fathers' role as being negative.

Andry emphasized lack of love from fathers and lack of training and discipline as crucial elements for boys.

Anderson (1968) found that loss of a father during the early years of childhood was more likely to be associated with male juvenile delinquency than the loss of a father during later years of childhood – a finding that was endorsed by Kelly and Baer (1969). Siegman (1966) found that male medical students whose fathers were away in the army for at least one year during the student's early childhood admitted to more anti-social behaviour.

The interrelationship of variables (for example father absence and poverty) means that it is not always easy to assess the relevance of father absence as such to specific sorts of childhood behaviour. Relevant in this respect is the fact that a fatherless home is also a home with a husbandless mother. Parker and Kleiner (1966), for example, interviewed American black urban mothers with and without husbands and found that those lacking husbands seemed worse off psychologically and were not so goal-oriented as mothers with husbands. This might affect the children as much as the absence of a father. However, while many writers accept the correlation between father absence and juvenile delinquency (e.g. Lynn, 1974), the reasons for the correlation are controversial. Herzog and Sudia (1970) point out that four major explanations can be offered for the association. These are that delinquency in boys results from a masculine protest against feminine domination; that the child has inadequate supervision; that the child suffers from the absence of a male model, and finally, from the loss of family cohesion.

Most of the available research on fathering focuses on paternal behaviour in terms of its effects on children, rather than its possible meaning in the marital relationship or to fathers themselves. It also tends to be confined to more extreme situations than those occurring in most families, e.g. where there is complete absence of fathers, either through occupational requirements, or through emergencies like wars, or for any of the reasons behind the existence of single-parent mother households. There is also a certain literature on defective fathering in the background of schizophrenia (Lidz, 1957), and violence (Gelles, 1972).

As for 'ordinary' households, the tendency has been, as documented above, to assume that if a man is a good provider he is a good father, to use Biller's expression (1970). It has only been recently that these assumptions have been subjected to a new look.

Gaynor Cohen's recent report on *Absentee Husbands in Spiralist Families* is an example of a study of fathers in ordinary families. Based on a fieldwork study in a middle-class estate of 700 houses in southwest London, her study reports on interviews with 42 families. The majority of families had primary or pre-school age children, and the general character of the estate was conventional – not unlike the suburb described two decades ago in Canada, Crestwood Heights (Seeley *et al.*, 1956). Most of the women were not in paid employment, and their commitments were primarily to the care of their home and the upbringing of their children. Their husbands, mostly in their mid to late thirties, were responsive to the income and career pressures characteristic of the early and middle establishment period. Cohen (1975, p. 2) writes:

> Almost all of them felt that they were at a crucial stage in the development of their careers and were optimistic about their chances of future

success, provided they devoted their time and energy to their work. Their careers necessitated a great deal of mobility not merely residentially, but within the job itself. This meant prolonged absences from the home. Only 9 per cent of those interviewed claimed that their hours were regular and involved little travelling. For most, their jobs involved a considerable amount of travel. Some of them were away from home regularly for one or two nights a week, with long working days in between. Others were away from home for varying lengths of time – from two to ten weeks – sometimes as frequently as three or four times a year. There was clearly a connection between mobility within the job and the status of the job, the higher the status, the more frequent the absence from home tends to be.

She noted that father absence is more prevalent than it may appear from the above because even men who were not employed by large organizations were often absent during the day and early evening, at meetings, courses and other activities regarded as beneficial not only to themselves but to the family.

Tom Crabtree, an educational psychologist, makes similar observations in 'Father away – and a family without faces'. In a *Guardian* (1976, p. 11) article based on his clinical experience he used the concept of paternal deprivation, and reported that it transcends social class lines:

> There was, I'm glad to say, no class distinction among the paternally deprived, one job's as effective as another: the children still don't see much of dad. The fathers I saw included a doctor, a farm labourer, a teacher, a waiter, a policeman, and a bricklayer.
>
> I'd expected to see long-distance lorry drivers and sailors. What I saw were factory workers and salesmen, and one milkman. . . .
>
> These children are not the 720,000 mentioned in the Finer Report whose fathers are not living with them. That's absence. I'm referring to intermittent presence, concealed desertion, paper fathers – call it what you will.

Crabtree drew attention to the implications for children of father absence. Gaynor Cohen emphasized the implications for wives. She argued that the husband's absence removed from the wives a vital source of support at a time when the latter were faced with the heavy burdens of bringing up young children. These burdens fell in two main areas: the general management of home and family life; and the child-rearing process. Cohen suggested that the wives formed support groups amongst themselves to counter the problem of isolation and that the estate environment afforded special opportunities for this strategy, an element of estate living much appreciated by the wives.

One of the points made implicitly in Cohen's study, and explicitly in a number of other studies of mid-career development of managers (e.g. Rapoport, 1970; BIM 1973) is that there is a trade-off that occurs at this point. The husband steps up his occupational investment to provide a better standard of life for the family, while decreasing his actual involvement in their everyday life. His wife and family in return put up with the loneliness, frustrations of coping single-handedly with the tasks of domestic life. Mobility is seen as a necessary evil, states Cohen (1975, p. 4); more family life or more money is the question posed by Crabtree (1976, p. 11).

If this set of trade-offs wears well with the family, and conventionally it has done more or less, the forces for divergent involvements of husband and wife become collusive. The husband derives most of his gratifications from his occupation, the wife enjoys the benefits of his efforts and learns to cope better without him under foot. A culture that values material objects, consumer goods, social status and its symbols, encourages this pattern of father being taken out of close family involvement in this phase of active parenting.

Two lines of development in men's roles have recently begun to unsettle this pattern, aside from the manifest and complex pressures on them from women. These pressures have been pivotal, and we say they are complex because they include both the militant pressures to change and the pressures that come from men's concern *for* women, their distress and the inequity of their predicament. One has to do with men's dissatisfactions with the rewards available to them in a lifestyle so concentrated on work and its accompaniments. The second, a complementary factor, has to do with the possible awakenings in men of a desire for more involvement with their wives and children.

Concern, at first at a philosophical level by writers like Marcuse, with the 'unidimensional' personality that is produced when a person is too specialized in one kind of activity, set the stage for later writings like that of Fasteau (1974) who emphasized the dehumanizing effect on men that participation in a technologically oriented, competitive occupational world produces. More recently this malaise has been translated into specific and tangible manifestations. Haward's (1973) research on airline pilots, for example, has yielded the conclusion that domestic worries are linked with impaired flying efficiency, serving to account not only for the pilot's disturbance but for putting others at risk through increased accident rates. Missing one's family, feeling out of touch with what is going on, missing important occasions like children's birthdays, feeling redundant when one is at home – all these things may result not only in pilots seeking gratification outside the family, but to their feeling distressed and overwhelmed with the unsatisfying elements in their situation, and their performance being impaired.

The second stream of writing, both from within the social sciences and from informed observers, is based on a new value position of giving a more meaningful share in the child-rearing process to father. These writers stress that this requires liberation from the emotionally constricting demands of the 'masculinity' models and values, and a widespread change in attitudes towards the male's commitment to work.

Farrell (1974, p. 21) a principal spokesman for this viewpoint, writes:

> Men's involvement in breaking out of the straitjacket of sex roles is essential because of the way it confines men at the same time as it confines women. As soon as men define themselves as the only ones capable of handling certain situations, of being aggressive, of earning the most money, then . . . he defines himself as *having* to earn the most money, and that definition still further defines him as a person who cannot afford too much time with his wife, children, petty discipline or housework.

Farrell's aim has been to enable men to redefine their masculinity and thus open up for themselves the possibility, for example, of increased involvement in child-rearing as a channel for their own increased fulfilment. He also sees this as something of a precondition for relieving the strain on women: 'Equal responsibility for child care is now seen only as a women's liberation goal, but it is impossible to achieve unless men view the responsibility as part of their freedom to be less job-oriented and more child-oriented.'

From a research perspective Joseph Pleck (1975) has explored the available data on men's family roles – the nature of their participation in child-care and housework, the factors which limit their participation, the consequences of limited participation, and also their potential for role change. Reviewing time-budget studies he concludes that men's 'family work' averages in the USA between 62 and 96 minutes per day, of which child-care constitutes a relatively small part. However, he rejects the notion of a biological basis for male or female participation in parenting, arguing that claims to the contrary are based on inconclusive data. A number of studies now exist such as the important early work by Greenberg and Morris (1974). Fathers of newborn children were observed to manifest 'engrossment' in their infants, and a sense of bonding, absorption and preoccupation in their child in a way which was no different from that of the mothers. Robert Fein's work described in Chapter 4, indicates the existence of a similar phenomenon. In a direct comparison between the behaviour of fathers and mothers towards their newborn infants, Parke and O'Leary (1975) have also found much greater overlap than is conventionally assumed, and concluded that the only behaviour that fathers manifested less frequently than mothers was smiling. Pleck (1975, pp. 1–2) concludes, therefore, that men in general have the *capacity* for child-rearing just as women do, though there are, obviously, individual differences among members of both genders: 'Later parental differentiation in childcare must occur in spite of, not because of, men's early dispositions about children'. He argues that while men's family roles are to some extent limited by the nature of their work roles, this is not a fully adequate explanation. On the other hand, he considers that sex-stereotyped ideology about family–work relations undermines men's family role.

Writers such as Dulan Barber and Maureen Green have argued similar points of view in Britain, and James Levine (1976) has written a book based on the most recent American research which is the clearest available statement supporting the idea of the nurturant potential of males. Barber produces a wealth of descriptive data to argue the case for *Unmarried Fathers*, based on the notion that fathers can care for children too. This is a point earlier made by George and Wilding (1972). They argued that fathers in fact care for children in greater numbers than often realized, in spite of having to go against the grain of various social agencies and practices.

Maureen Green (1976) in her book *Goodbye Father* portrayed fathers as somewhat lost and left out of the scene where the valued action is (namely interaction with the children). This has been produced, she argues, by the recent overemphasis on mothering.

Some fathers not only find themselves in the single-father situation described by Dulan Barber through divorce or desertion, but are catapulted into a fathering role by unemployment, particularly when their wives are employed – an increasingly common configuration in the contemporary situation of high unemployment accompanied by high married women's employment. This has its difficulties, as have been described by Leathley, an unemployed executive, in terms reminiscent of Michael Miller's attempts to do what is not accepted for males:

I collect the children from school, and I feel an outsider there . . . because all the mothers seem to know each other. Then Joyce comes home, and there seem to be so many things she has to do for the children that they only want her to do that I feel even more spare. It's all very well to say that I'm giving way to self pity, but so would anyone if there's no prospect of getting back to my old position as head of the family, and all the time I can see that actually they can do very well without me. It makes you think what the bloody man's there for at all, when all's said and done, except to provide and I've failed at that.

But many fathers, as Green, Barber, Levine and the other writers document, find unexpected enjoyment in active parenting. Others, suddenly deprived by divorce or separation, of the enjoyment they had been building up half-unawares, become active in organizations like Families Need Fathers to attempt to regain some of the parenting prerogatives they have lost.

James Levine's book (1976) is the most recent and closely argued case for fathering to be revitalized, *not* only because women are demanding it, *not* only because it could happen to the best of men, *not* only because the children need it, and *not* only because otherwise fathers will be left out in the cold – but because men can parent too. Levine sees parenting as an option available both to men and to women, one that both can enjoy and that in any given family ought to be developed in the way that suits the temperaments of the individuals concerned, rather then being divided into specialized traditional moulds. The real constraints are not biological imperatives nor organizational requirements, but ideas and concepts, textbooks and laws, images and expectations – all of which are alterable through purposive action of men and women. Interviewing, living with, observing 120 men across the USA in all walks of life, men who care for children in one role or another (teachers, parents, nurses, paediatricians), Levine focused on child-rearing within the family because, he argued, 'the fulcrum for any major change in the roles of men and women [is] *who* will care for the children'.

Parenting and institutions outside the family

Because of the history of the academic disciplines and of specialisms within organizations – which we have discussed early in the book – there has been a tendency for both specialists and functionaries to look at specific institutions and their goals as though they were closed systems. The requirements of factories, schools, recreational facilities, hospitals and other specialist organizations – even in a self-consciously service-oriented society – tend to be seen in their own terms. But, for parents they are there for their, the parents' use, sometimes obligatory (as with schools), sometimes optionally (as with pre-school playgroups).

As we are in a society that is changing fairly rapidly and fundamentally, and as we are writing in a framework that explicitly questions whether social institutions are meeting human (in this case parents') needs, we shall look at the important institutions bearing on the predicament of parents in this phase and attempt to sort out some of the salient issues. Four such institutional spheres seem crucial for parenting patterns: employment outside the home, the use of child-care facilities, relations with schools, and the use of leisure and recreational facilities.

Parents and employment outside the home

It has been axiomatic in our society that men work full-time all through the phase of active parenting, and, as we have indicated, there is a certain legitimation for fathers' commitments to work and career to be intensified in this period in order to meet the family's valued needs for housing, consumer goods and long-term economic foundations. At the same time, there have been discernible shifts away from the model of fathers being sole providers. Mothers have entered employment outside the home for a range of reasons including many non-economic ones, and for a longer span of their marital careers than ever before, even while they have pre-school children. In Britain, for every 1,000 mothers with children in 1971, 187 were employed and a further 15 were economically active but out of employment. Over one third of these mothers were effectively full-time workers. According to the published census data based on a 10 per cent sample of the 1961 and 1971 censuses, the increase in employment rates for mothers of young children has been faster than for all married women under sixty, and it seems to be rising still. This phenomenon is also reported in the USA (Waite, 1976; Carter and Glick, 1976). However, the problems about mothers taking employment outside the home – and the issues are not only for mothers but for their husbands and employers also – have not receded in anything like a way commensurate with their increased economic activity. Many questions recur: whether they will be able to handle their jobs, physically and psychologically; whether their expectable absences will be augmented by their children's as well as their own illnesses and accidents; whether they will become pregnant and have to drop out; whether their husbands will move away and take them along; whether their children and/or their marriages will be harmed by their working, etc. These risks and associated strains are weighed up in each family against the risks of staying at home. The latter may be considerable, particularly if the wife is qualified, if there is more than one child, or if the housing situation is isolating.

Which felt needs are satisfied by deciding one way, and which by deciding another way? Some of the points to be made repeat ones already made. But they have different salience in different sub-groups of the population. Wortis (1974) in an explicit assessment of mother's needs, notes that mothers in this phase express: *boredom* – and the need for more stimulation and variety; *isolation* – and the need for social contact; a *desire to get back to work* – and use of their skills. Safilios-Rothschild (1974, p. 19) stresses their need for *self-actualization* – and the positive benefits for the family as well as for the individual. Many writers emphasize the expressed importance of the *economic gains*, not only in sheer cash terms, but to relieve the financial dependency on the husband, a factor mentioned in the study by Tizard *et al.* (1976).

Many writers emphasize the anxiety that working mothers feel about making the right arrangements for their children's well-being, and avoiding harming them. Yarrow and her colleagues (1962) found that contrary to common belief, working mothers had better rather than worse experiences with controlling their children and developing a satisfactory relationship with them. The impression that mothers experience relief of many of their depressive symptoms when they take up employment outside the home, with obvious implications for mother–child relations, has also been confirmed by George Brown and his colleagues and Tizard and his colleagues. This depends, however, on the job to some extent. Adding a job which is alienating to a domestic situation which is oppressive is no adequate solution.

But Jessie Bernard notes that some mothers, in doing this social-psychological cost accounting, find that 'the price [of staying at home] is right', and they settle for the irritations and dissatisfactions which, for them, are more acceptable than the irritations and dissatisfactions of other options. Some mothers remain at home because there is no realistic option for occupational work outside it – the job market is not inviting, their domestic supports are not adequate, their motivations to *make* things work out in favour of taking employment not that powerful. Amongst mothers who remain at home, some meet the needs that employment would meet, but in other ways. Cohen's study of women's support-group formation in a middle-class suburban housing estate is one illustration. Bringing in impersonal news of the outside world via the media, however, does not seem to cut down the sense of isolation, as Myrdal and Klein (1968, p. 148) observed in their early study:

> The isolated woman at home may well be kept 'in touch' with events, but she feels that the events are not in touch with her, that they happen without her participation. The wealth of information which is brought to her without any effort on her part does not lose its vicariousness. It increases rather than allays her sense of isolation and of being left out.

While sociability may be found in the local community, in the form of women's groups and the relatives close by, this may allow only a more limited range of contacts than may be wished for. However, for many the available channels may suffice. Isolation and confinement to a small range of social contacts may also be dealt with by increasing voluntary activities; Loeser (1974) notes that volunteering can give many of the same intrinsic satisfactions as paid employment outside the home, can serve as a stepping stone to a career in paid employment, and can provide additional specific gratification that many available paid occupations lack – for example allowing for work with a high moral purpose, or work that is critical of established institutions. The issues underlying discontent among many housewives may not be salient for all. Financial dependency, for example, may be an irritant to independent-minded egalitarian women, but it may be accepted as a natural accompaniment of marriage for others, as a reasonable form of job for a woman, even though the security of tenure is diminished.

As the 'work outside the home' issue is unfolding, it is extending beyond the pivotal question that has preoccupied many mothers of whether to work or not. The issue widens to include questions like what sort of work to do, and when to return to work outside the home. The issue may be related to the whole family situation, and the potentials of fathers' and mothers' work considered together in relation to family programmes. These may include facilitating fathers achieving higher qualifications, in which case mothers' work will be for a time the main source of the family's economic provision; or there may be an agreed phasing of acquisition of consumer goods – with an all out push for basic goods early on in the phase with both parents working, followed by an agreed relaxation by one or both at a later point. In other families there may be an agreement in favour of parsimony and spartan life style, as in the couples described by Grönseth, with attention focused on infants rather than goods and the assumption that if goods are wanted at all, they can come later.

Some of the possibilities discussed in this theoretical way do not fit well with the realities of many people's situations. Frequently there is little choice for men, and still less for women. There *are* imperatives in some occupations and organizations that are real and inflexible. Sometimes there are no occupational options for either the father or the mother. Fathers who wish to take on more active parenting in this phase, and to support their wives who may wish to do more work outside the home, may find constraints on them that are not only confined to the agreed work day, but that require trips away at weekends, or overtime demands by persons and forces that do not consider specific family situations. What is difficult to assess in a general way is how much of this is a residue of old attitudes and practices, used in the industrial relations situation and/or in the marital situation to rationalize leaving things as they always have been. One American study (Renshaw, 1976) with a large multinational corporation indicates that the stresses of international job transfer, extensive travel and job change can be managed more adaptively for both organizational and familial functioning if the communication and interaction amongst the various individuals concerned is optimized. This allows for the feeling that one can influence the process at least in some way or to some extent, countering the depressive and alienating effects of feeling in the grip of impersonal forces – which may be as debilitating for managerial families as are some of the assembly-line processes for workers (see also Culbert and Renshaw, 1972; Seidenberg, 1973).

Leaving aside the costs and benefits to mothers of taking a particular job or not at a particular time, and the flexibility or constraints in fathers' conceptions and the realities of their occupational jobs, the single factor of greatest concern to many parents in adopting a stance on the issues relating to parents' employment outside the home is the effects on children. 'What about the children' means not only who will look after them when mother and father are at work, but what will be the consequences for the growth and development? Will they feel abandoned and unwanted or will they feel more independent and respected? Will they feel more that it is their family as well as their parents if they are expected to pitch in and do domestic work to help take up the slack, or will they feel exploited and overloaded given the strains of school work etc.? Will they have an enriched range of parental role models and experiences, or will they be confused with two heads of the household and two providers?

A spate of studies, in England and America, have asked some of these questions. Reviews of the literature by Wortis (1974), Yarrow (1962), Yudkin and Holme (1963), Hoffman and Nye (1974), Howe (1972), Moore (1964), and Rutter (1972 and 1974) give a general verdict of 'not proven' for the more alarmist formulations of damaging consequences to children if mother works. Hoffman's review is extremely comprehensive, including British as well as American sources, and examines five hypotheses using published literature as data: (1) the working mother provides a different role model than the non-working mother; (2) employment affects the mother's emotional state – sometimes providing satisfactions, sometimes role-strain, and sometimes guilt – and this, in turn, influences the mother–child interaction; (3) the different situational demands as well as the emotional state of the working mother will affect child-rearing practices; (4) working mothers provide less adequate supervision; and (5) the working mother's absence will result in emotional and possible cognitive deprivation for the child. Hoffman concludes that accumulated evidence, although patchy and inadequate, offers some support for the first four hypotheses; but that *empirical studies of school-aged children yield no evidence for a theory of deprivation resulting from maternal employment; and that there are not adequate data on the effects of maternal employment on the infant.*

On the basis of this not-proven conclusion, some mothers (and some policy makers) may conclude that it is in order for mothers to take employment provided that they wish to and that they make adequate care arrangements for their children. Others may conclude the reverse, on the basis that the risks are too high. 'Unproven' does not mean 'no risk'.

The view that mothers' work is important not only to meet the parents' felt needs but for the child as well is voiced in some quarters, but even less demonstrated in detail. Safilios-Rothschild (1974, p. 19) mentions the advantages for children of being 'freed from the mother's possible neurotic tendencies and conflicts, of the limited educational, cultural and time resources, as in the case of lower class mothers'. Some observers have attributed to the mother and child entrapment together in the home some of the motive power for child-abuse incidents, particularly when the mother is frustrated and overloaded (Skolnick, 1973). And Yudkin and Holme remark that the confinement of a child to his mother's company for the first five years of life constitutes a form of isolation and deprivation that could increase the stress of making a transition into school, create problems in later life in questing for such a close and intense relationship, and impair the child's capacity to form a range of relationships (1963, pp. 137–8).

In the National Child Development Study (Davie, Butler and Goldstein, 1972) the researchers noted that anxiety that has been roused recently by the numbers of mothers taking work outside the home is based on the assumption that mothers belong at home and that their constant presence is essential for the healthy development of their children, particularly in the early years. They make a detailed attempt to sort out the elements that go into favourable and unfavourable conditions for mothers combining work outside the home with parenting – including the presence of domestic help, the presence of a spouse in the home, the size of the family, and so on. They gather detailed data on mothers' work prior to the child's school entry and found that about 10 per cent of mothers worked full-time prior to their child's school entry, and another 40 per cent (approximately) worked part-time, temporarily, or only afterwards; they found no signs of ill effects on the child from mothers working, but expressed caution about covert or delayed possible effects. The small signs of retardation in reading age detected – though of perhaps complex aetiology – are given full attention rather than minimized. This would lead to the adoption of a very cautionary attitude in some circles.

The general drift of professional opinion, both of researchers and clinicians, is however in the other direction. Spock, for example, notes a major shift in his own orientation from his earlier child-care manual in which he not only assumed that mothers should always be at home, but cast numerous aspersions on those mothers who felt that they had to go out to work, making him an early *bête noire* of the women's liberation movement. In his most recent work (1974, pp. 226–7) he notes

instead the power of the egalitarian ideals in our society, and observes
some of the inequities of the conventional homemaker role. He calls,
in essence, for role-sharing:

> For whatever reasons – desire for a career, need for money, enjoy-
> ment of company – more and more women are taking jobs and I
> assume that this trend will continue.
>
> But if more and more women want to have uninterrupted careers,
> and if they and their husbands want to have children, too, how will
> the children be cared for? Young couples – and also unmarried
> young people who are thinking ahead – give various answers. They
> say, on general principles (and I agree) that when mothers work
> outside, fathers should shoulder 50 percent of the housework and
> child care. And if careers have to be limited temporarily to provide
> parental care for young children, equal consideration should be given
> to limiting the careers of both father and mother. They ask for
> day-care centers provided by the state for all-day care of children
> from birth until they can attend school at six years of age; staggered
> work hours for the father and mother so that there always can be a
> parent at home; a number of families living together in a commune
> where domestic work and child care are shared sociably or where the
> women who prefer to stay at home can care for the children while
> others may go out to work. They suggest that in some families the
> father might stay home permanently while the mother works.
>
> In a society changing as rapidly as ours is now it is inevitable that
> the roles of both sexes, the relationships between them and also
> child-rearing will shift. I consider it a good sign that young people
> want to think realistically and idealistically about such matters.

The work of researchers like Jack Tizard, who have conducted an
appraisal of nursery provision, may be seen in a similar light (Tizard
et al., 1976). The issue is not whether mothers should work or not, but
rather, if they do choose to work – as so many do – how can one assume
that the resources for supplementary child-care available are adequate
to meet the needs of developing children?

Child-care: the requirements for a range of options

Issues of child-care are proliferating. From a position that all care by
non-biologically related persons outside the parental home is bad for
the child, a current position argues for the advantages of different kinds
of care, and the necessity for defining and enforcing standards.

We consider care provision for young children not only in relation
to children's centres of various sorts, including schools, but also,
theoretically at least, in relation to places children attend as part of

everyday life, like shops and hospitals, and to life at home. To the extent that the care of children – or parenting – is recognized as a community responsibility, as well as a parental one, the options for more responsive provision increase. Though a high priority for many parents, the recognition of caring requirements in so wide a range of contexts as this position implies is low priority as a national programme and amongst established formal institutions like factories and hospitals. However, the movement for more varied and diffused day-care is likely to grow. We review its central ideas that are propounded by researchers, pressure group proponents and parents themselves.

It is important to distinguish between 'care' in the sense of looking after a child physically and assuring that it is kept safely and reasonably comfortable, and 'care' in the sense of giving something additional to nurture its development. A caring ethos can be present in many settings such as supermarkets, doctors' consulting rooms, etc. By sensitive orientation and responsiveness to the felt needs both of child and parent, services could be geared to make experiences like shopping and attending ante-natal clinics, also caring ones.

Another important distinction is between care which is arranged in reaction to a problematic family situation, and care that is deliberately arranged to enhance children's and parents' life experience. Esther Goody (1975), in a comparison of West African and West Indian fostering practices, contrasts the 'purposive fostering' in the former practice to the 'crisis fostering' practised by the latter. The distinction carries over into the practices of the two sub-groups in London, and has generic applicability to others.

Paediatrician, Mary Howells (1970, p. 53) argues from first principles, that 'the means of child care are less important than the needs of child care. Parenting is more important than parents.'

Proliferating nurturance in society requires that people in institutions and outside them, become more caring whether they are parents or not, whether they are performing in prescribed child-care roles or not, and in relation to their own children as well as others. A child psychologist (Grams, 1975, p. 7) expands on the implications:

> The future may see more frequent decisions to provide children with optimal parenting, utilizing a combination of parenting persons. Included may be the child's father and mother, as well as a variety of parent surrogates. Some may be siblings or other relatives, and some may be individuals who choose to work as parent substitutes on an individual basis in the child's home or with groups of children in a child care centre.

It is not uncommon in today's world for parents to have no informal help available, in the form of relatives, neighbours or friends, to share in parenting. In these cases, paid day-care is the major option. This takes place on both a personal and institutional basis. Paid day-care is not necessarily harmful for children (as in the institutions studied by Bowlby and others during the Second World War) and may be valuable as a way of diluting the intensity of parental involvement in the child. A variety of care is theoretically attainable – and to some extent actually available today. While there is pressure for standardization of day-care, there are wide differences on the parents' side as to aspirations, felt needs and requirements for their children's care.

Many parents want only brief respites for relaxation or visits to service personnel, like dentists, or hairdressers. There are others who require sustained and dependable supplementary care. While much of the literature has emphasized the importance of day-care in counteracting mothers' isolation, it is now apparent that many mothers wish to have some time for themselves, as relief from the incessant and intensive interaction that children bring. Fathers, too, may have needs which can be met through child-care provisions, particularly as more of them accept parenting responsibilities. Susan Golden (1975, p. 133) who conducted an intensive study of the intricacies of work–family interplay in two young American families, observes:

> It has become more difficult for men to get time alone and away from the pressures of both work and family. Women are now getting this time with the support of the women's liberation movement. They are demanding that men take over the children, most frequently on weekends. This time is also his only allotted free time. With the full burden of child-care shifting from the woman to the joint shoulders of man and wife, the system sometimes gets off balance and the man's needs are occasionally lost in the shuffle.

This is a less recognizable British syndrome, though Maureen Green's book (1976) points to something akin to it. In general, to the extent that parents share child-rearing and to the extent that they incorporate it into a round of daily life rather than confining it to a home-base, these issues are likely to impinge on both mothers and fathers. Gavron and Skolnick have both noted the absence of provision in public places for children to *be*, let alone be integrated into adult activities. One mother, quoted by Skolnick, speaks of having to move around on eight legs from drugstore to newsstand to fishmarket, now that she has three children. Skolnick notes (1973, p. 309): 'The inconvenience this middle-class mother experiences are magnified to greater torment for the poor, who must spend hours waiting with their children in welfare offices, hospitals, clinics and the courts.'

One type of solution involves making the places parents have to attend as part of everyday life more oriented to young children. The lack of suitable provision at certain places where young children are known to attend heavily is quite remarkable in our society. Shops are a prime example, both department stores and supermarkets. Whilst they rely on the 'housewife' for their turnover, they usually fail to provide even minimum measures that would facilitate everyone's comfortable functioning, especially people with young children. The store that provides changing facilities for young children is exceptional. It is quite common for stores and most supermarkets to provide no ordinary toilet facilities. Whilst shopping trolleys in which toddlers can sit are now ubiquitous in supermarkets (with some effort to provide also attachable bassinets for babies), it is not uncommon for little other help – like packing and transporting purchases – to be made available to parents with young children. Ante-natal clinics (and medical clinics generally), dental surgeries waiting areas, exhibition galleries, schools, offices, shops and public services generally do not provide for the children who inevitably attend these places in the company of adults.

Many parents are reluctant to let the care of their children be shared, even where opportunities are available or could be rented. In part this relates to parental concern about standards of child-care. For some parents reluctance to leave the child is the natural response to any separation anxiety shown by the child. Parents' own separation anxiety is also a factor. The GAP Committee (1973, p. 25) observe:

> At the pre-school period, parents often do not realize that separation anxiety can be as difficult for them as it is for the child. Parents are told to allow the child to assert himself, to explore, to show initiative, but at the same time they have to set limits and be present when the child needs them. They can become confused and frightened because the child no longer seems to need them so much. The child imitates them, and when they are able to accept this initial separation, so can he.

However, many parents cling to their children, wanting to confine their children's development to their inputs exclusively. The GAP Committee note this possessiveness and comment that many parents emphasize that the child belongs to them and that they should have the credit for bringing it up. As Grams notes, some parents believe that they can best help their child in a competitive world only by giving them the very best they have, which tends to mean all their time and energy. They resist the child's socialization being diffused among other inputs, even at the risk that the child will not turn out well, in which case they will feel they need to bear all the guilt. In contrast, other parents feel that enrichment comes into a family with the child's increased range of experience in the outside world, as with a parent who has a job and an interesting round of daily experiences to bring back into the family. In addition, there is the possibility that a child whose care is shared is protected from the excesses of over-involvement, which may include child-abuse. Whether formulated in these cost-benefit rational terms, or in terms of more inchoate inner feelings of resistance against giving up the care of one's own child to someone else, even partially – as expressed by such 'liberal' reflective thinkers as Suzanne Gail and the Newsons, there are obviously problems on the parents' side as well as on the side of the state and the component institutions which are potential providers of optional care facilities.

The larger social arguments in favour of increasing day-care provision are not confined to meeting parents' needs, or helping the economy by allowing parents to be more productive economically in occupational employment. They also include the consideration, which Wortis emphasizes (1974, pp. 373–4) of rearing individuals who are better citizens, more capable of sharing, more co-operative:

> The new, radical generation of parents do not want dumping grounds for their children, but rather centers of exciting educational activity and play in which children and adults share collectively in the process of growing up. Dissatisfied with the racist, sexist, and middle-class biased education that children receive in public (state) schools, the radical day care movement wants day care that is organised and controlled by the people in their communities who wish to create a more democratic, equalitarian society for their children.

Wortis aspires to a particular sort of society, to which the care groups she describes above seemed suitably oriented. What she envisages may be less possible if children are confined to their families early in life, or if established care institutions are uncritically accepted. Spock, however, observes a dilemma common amongst people with this value orientation (1974, p. 234): 'I doubt that most of the young idealists who propose nurseries would really be satisfied with average children.'

Spock is personally disinclined towards early day care. Nevertheless he now acknowledges the responsibility to think constructively about increased day care, given the strength of parents' movement for it. There are signs that, given safeguards, this shift in attitude is occurring amongst other professionals who deal with children.

Jack Tizard and his colleagues (1976) in their comprehensive review of the issues involved in nursery provision, put forth a multifaceted case for an increase of nursery services in Britain. They suggest that the long-term educational and social benefits that some people attribute to early education and good child-care are not as convincing as many believe. Their own argument rests on short-term criteria, and provides so clear a perspective for integrating parents' needs and children's needs – even where these may differ – that we quote from it at length.

A point they repeat throughout their book is the requirement for varied provision, the requirement to create options. They write (pp. 26–8):

> the primary reason for providing good care for young children is, in our view, a short-term one. Good services increase the possibilities for happiness and well-being of young children and their families; and these immediate benefits are worthwhile and important. Given the amount of unhappiness and stress among young children and parents, at what should be a happy and enriching time of life, action to improve their lot is to be welcomed.
>
> Secondly, in developing pre-school provision, we think that much more attention must be paid to changes occurring in society and to what people want. In other words the services should offer parents and children realistic alternatives from which to select those that best satisfy their changing needs and aspirations.
>
> If offered a choice, it is clear that some mothers and fathers would wish to share child care, housework and employment, whilst others would wish to take it in turn over the years to accept the main responsibility for these various activities. In other families, the mother would choose to retain the major responsibility for the children and home, though she might also wish to work away from home, at least part-time. In still other families traditional parent roles might be exchanged. Finally, the mother – or for that matter the father – might remain at home full-time; or both parents might work full-time. Each of these ways of life offers its own rewards and exacts its own costs – and what will suit one family will not suit another. We wish to see parental choices made explicit and available.
>
> Choices for parents imply choices for children – and our belief is that the choices for very young children are likely to be best made by their parents. Of course society can and should assist parents to make wise choices just as society can and should intervene when parents do harm to their children. But in general, we see society's role as facilitative rather than restrictive; and we advocate an adequate provision of services because it is only in this way that we can offer real choices.
>
> Many people who would agree in principle with this viewpoint oppose the expansion of out-of-the-home daytime services for young children because they believe that it is harmful for young children to spend all day, or even a few hours, in the care of adults who are not their primary parent figures. This view has for long been used as an argument against nursery expansion. . . .
>
> We think that the issues of maternal deprivation and maternal separation have become clouded by confusions between day care

and residential care, and by unwarranted generalisations made on the basis of research carried out in institutions in which the quality of care is very poor. Our own view is that day care of good quality (and we can specify what we mean by that) is likely to benefit rather than harm young children . . . .

We . . . make explicit our view about the effects upon children attending a good day care centre. To start with there is, for example, widespread agreement that from the age of about three nearly all children enjoy and benefit from the association with other young children; and there is abundant evidence that most cope happily with full-time nursery schooling even without their mothers. Where opinion differs are as to the effects of nursery attendance upon younger children, and as to the value of nursery care which lasts throughout a full working day.

We believe that many younger children would benefit from attendance at a well-run nursery centre for part or even most of the day; and we think very few indeed would be harmed by it (they could be kept at home if they weren't happy). This does not mean that we think that all young children *ought* to attend a nursery centre, any more than we think all mothers ought to go out to work. Probably many more mothers *would* go out to work if they knew their children were being properly cared for in their absence. Probably, too, many more children would spend longer periods in day care if day care services were available. But many mothers would prefer, as the playgroup movement has shown, to share their delight in bringing up young children with other mothers and other children. And many others would keep their children at home. What we are saying is that good services make it possible for parents to make such choices; in doing so they promote well-being in a way that cannot be attained by other means.

The Neighborhood Daycare Service in the USA is an attempt to provide a child-care service, tailored to the needs of individual parents, by utilizing the neighbourhood itself instead of relying on a trained professional workforce. Arthur Emlen (1970) has studied the workings of this service. He described how the service acts as a catalyst in the formation of neighbourhood care arrangements, and provides information, referrals and consultations as required. Local families themselves find amongst them people who are prepared, for an arranged remuneration, to take on care-giving roles. The families themselves devise a structure of neighbourhood care arrangements to fit their needs. Emlen concludes from an analysis of the detailed functioning of fifteen such neighbourhood care committees and their work that in a given year '482 requests for day care [come] from 346 users for 554 children', not including the care-givers' own children who are often involved in the arrangements. Local mothers who serve as paid care-givers treat it as a job, but do not, in Emlen's experience, adopt a mercenary attitude. They are, rather, people who find the work gratifying, and who are able to do this as their own particular way of resolving the work–family dilemmas prevalent in our society. In many cases care-givers' clients were also their friends. Emlen found advantages and disadvantages either way. He concludes that in any given case the question of care-giving with friends or with strangers, simply becomes part of the local situation which requires management for specific issues. Overall Emlen concludes that the conception and experience of these private arrangements, stimulated and provided with consulta-tive back-up by public service agencies, but predominantly kept on a 'non-professional' neighbouring basis, are highly favourable. His evaluation was focused on parents' needs rather than children's, the study being concentrated at that level and within too brief a time span to assess the longer term impact on the children. However, the parents were expressing a conscientious concern for the care of their children by their actions and in the presence of local social controls. To this extent, it seems reasonable to take their satisfaction with arrangements as some preliminary indicators of the programme's positive effects. This would require confirmation by further study.

In Britain there are similar experiments, such as the Dartmouth Park Hill experiment in London, which has been flooded with appli-cants to participate in this parent-controlled day-care centre. The service is primarily voluntary, with one paid employee. Parents share the care-giving, and there is an explicit ideology of encouraging children to take an active part in daily chores. The age range is from two to five years, the earlier age groups being excluded because of statutory rulings governing staff and premises for infant care rather than because the centre disclaims the relevance of their work for younger children. The problem of full-time working parents, including single parents, is handled by accepting a limited proportion of children from families who are unable to participate fully in the rota system. This element is replaced by the paid helper. Like the ideological groups described above by Wortis for the USA, the Dartmouth Park group also has a social reform orientation (Children's Community Centre, 1974, p. 7):

We do not want to reproduce the social relationships present in society at large, and are trying to develop different ways for children to relate to each other and to adults. We want to work against the competition and individualism that capitalism encourages and thrives on. . . . We hope to work against the notion of the survival of the fittest and the domination of the weak by the strong, in particular because girls tend to come off worse in physical fights. We refuse to believe that competition, hierarchies and authorities are all part of 'human nature', and believe that it *is* possible to rear different kinds of people: people who can work together (at school they call it 'cheating'); who support and care for each other and who are sensitive to each other's needs.

These ideas are built into the organization and running of the centre as far as possible with, for example, the children's books being chosen to avoid the traditional sex-role stereotyping that is mirrored and propagated in many children's books. The centre is seen as a place not only where parents may obtain relief from the burden of continuous child-care in the home, and children find a new, diverse range of experience, but it is also a community centre where parents may develop their neighbourhood interests and extend their contacts throughout the community in which they live. To this extent it is both a meeting place for parents and a point of departure for other community projects.

The wider Pre-School Playgroup Movement has flourished in Britain. The first playgroup was started in 1960. By 1972, the latest date for which figures are available, the number of playgroups in England was put at 15,266 (Hansard, June 1976). Lady Plowden has described the Playgroup Movement as a 'cycle of opportunity', particularly for those parents and children in deprived areas. She sees a number of positive advantages to be gained from the pre-school playgroup, and thought of it partly as offering the mother the chance to understand and enjoy the development of her children. The Pre-School Playgroup Association (1973, p. 3) writes about its work:

> There is something that cannot be gained from outside the school door. But it *can* be experienced inside the playgroup, where mothers can see their children learning and share the excitement and satisfaction with them. From there, the experience, with all the new opportunities for learning that it brings, can be taken back into the home.

There are some specialist-type playgroups, like the Langtry Road Family Care Centre in London, started under the aegis of the social services department to fulfil a therapeutic purpose, offsetting as much as possible risks in the parental environment of children in the local area. These are professional efforts, with varying degrees of parental participation. Most playgroups, however, are oriented to development rather than therapy or specialist care. Financial arrangements, staffing and staff–parent relationships vary with local conditions. Tizard and his colleagues observe (1976, p. 79) that commendable as playgroups may be for mothers who are primarily homemakers, they are 'an irrelevance to mothers who have to go out to work full time through economic necessity'. If one adds to this mothers who choose to work full-time in order to realize their own developmental requirements and/or to contribute to the economic requirements of the country, playgroups in their present format are seen to meet a limited, if very significant, range of felt needs.

Only during wartime has a really comprehensive system of day-care provision been made available in Britain. Since the Second World War, there has been a fading-out of state-financed facilities of this kind, with a recent revival of interest and some action in this direction. Brenda Crowe (1975), in a review of available day-care facilities in contemporary Britain, urges a 'do it yourself' approach, more or less on the neighbourhood care lines described above. A recent feature article in a Sunday pictorial adopted a similar view (*Sunday Times Magazine*, February 1976, p. 11).

The provision of day-care in workplaces for children of employees is very patchy. In universities day-care facilities for children of students and staff are sometimes provided, and also used for purposes of child observation by students of human development. Some hospitals provide crèches so that trained nurses who are in short supply can return to employment while their children are still young. One commercial organization, Kindergartens for Commerce, aims to provide packaged playgroups, with information, equipment, consultation and staff for industrial and commercial organizations wishing to attract and hold parents, particularly mothers in the present context, who might otherwise be lost to the workforce.

For parents who lack any of the options described, but who wish to work, by far the most common arrangement is to use a private child-minder. In 1973 Brian Jackson, director of the Child Minding Research Unit, estimated that 100,000 children were being illegally minded. In 1974 he revised his estimate to 330,000. The true figure is impossible to substantiate, however, since a great many child-minders are used informally, or function illegally.

To operate legally child-minders must be registered, have their premises inspected and operate within a fairly stringent code of practice. Not all illegal child-minders are bad, although overcrowding and sub-standard care exist. The discrepancy between demand and provision continues to create this undesirable situation.

Margaret Bone (1975) reports in a survey of day-care facilities and pre-school children conducted by the Government Social Survey that 32 per cent of British pre-school children were reported to be receiving day care in 1974, but that an additional 33 per cent *wanted* it but were not receiving it. By age four 91 per cent of the parents of pre-school children wanted such services. Single-parent mothers and working mothers were categories in which the desire and use for such services were particularly high. Both are increasing categories in the population.

Day-care provision is still, therefore, much more limited than is currently required to meet both parents' and children's needs. The problem is of such magnitude that it will require not only the decisive government interventions called for by Tizard and his colleagues (1976, p. 28) but also a variety of locally-created options. These could serve the needs not only of parents and their children who require day-care services, but also facilitate, albeit indirectly, an improved atmosphere of collaboration in local communities.

Parenting and schools

The child-care issues dealt with so far in this section are specially salient for parents in the earlier years of the active parenting phase but many continue in some form when children enter primary school. The school day does not usually coincide with an adult's full-time working day; school holidays are longer and more frequent than the leave allowed from most occupational jobs; parents have commitments at weekends, like major shopping expeditions, which may be difficult to accomplish with children; both parents and children are sometimes ill. Care problems arise from these factors even once the children are at school.

Several issues have been recognized particularly in relation to *parenting with children at primary school*. The Newsons convey the way in which children's school entry is widely felt as a major contact point through children with an outside institution (Newson and Newson, 1968/70). They report that the pace of the child's socialization tends to be accelerated in the period preceding school entry, as parents grow anxious in anticipation about *their* standards of child-raising being judged by the child's behaviour and level of performance at school.

Improving the relationship between *home and primary school* has been a central concern of British educators since the publication of the Plowden report (1968, p. vii). The report emphasized 'the importance of the role of the parents and how their attitude to and interest in education of their child appeared to be the single factor in the circumstances of the home which contributed most to the child's progress at school.'

Research on the subject which has since appeared focuses, on the whole, on the child and on the factors in the child's home environment which affect his or her school performance in one way or another. Less common is a focus on the parents and on parents' experiences and needs *vis-à-vis* their child's involvement in the educational system. Parent/school interaction is more accepted and more written-about in the context of primary school education than previously, and there are a number of publications on the link between parent and primary school which highlight parental experience.

Some of the research in the 1950s and 1960s emphasized the separation between home and school, the 'wall between family and school' (Bronfenbrenner, 1974, p. 101). In Britain, in particular, where the historical background leading to the extreme emphasis on the autonomy and separateness of educational institutions is more deeply rooted in the issues of church and state relationships and relationships between the social class groups, the wall has been a formidable one.

In the past decade many studies – both from the parents' perspective and from the point of view of educators – have led to a number of changes involving parents. Research in both Britain and the USA has underscored the importance of family influences in educational performance (Moynihan, 1965; Musgrove, 1964; Davie *et al.*, 1972; Douglas, 1964; Halsey, 1972; Porter, 1974). At the same time they highlighted the structural barriers experienced – primarily, but far from exclusively, by working-class parents – between improving the interplay between home and school. It was generally acknowledged that this interplay was a necessary, if not a sufficient condition to improving the educational performance of the child – e.g. in relation to levels of aspiration (McClelland, 1953). These are of elaborated linguistic codes (Bernstein, 1965) and social adjustment generally. Young and McGeeney (1968) in an interesting piece of educational action research in a London Educational Priority Area, were able to document a number of situations in which parental feelings were both present and important. Ordinarily these feelings had been kept covert, while parents complied in a relatively docile manner with a range of authoritarian barriers and prescriptions erected by the school. Alternatively, they stayed away. Examples were signs instructing parents to keep within certain bounds, or not to come without appointments, or to participate in parent–teacher meetings passively by listening to the delivery of prepared blocks of information, or being spoken to by teachers in an infantilizing manner, or being excluded from interaction with or knowledge of the work of the school's governing body, etc. Taken together, these measures were seen to contribute to parents' feelings of impotence, withdrawal or confusion in relation to their children's school experiences, and sometimes anger at the teachers who express such excluding and controlling attitudes. Aside from the indirect effects those phenomena may have on the children's orientations to education, they affect their relationships with their parents (Jackson and Marsden, 1962).

Bronfenbrenner has also noted not only the separateness of schools as a problem for children and parents, but their structure and rather subtle covert stance – of 'downgrading the role of parents' by seeking to establish and sustain the authority of the teachers. There are, of course, complex issues here, and to some extent the goals of education in an egalitarian society require teachers to strive to overcome influences of parents which run counter to these goals. In abstract social justice terms, as Rawls has argued (1972), the family as a social institution presents impediments which other institutions, such as schools, must work to counteract. On the other hand, from parents' viewpoints, and recognizing that schools and educational theories are amenable to change, the need is often felt in this phase of parenting to work out a more viable relationship with the school, in whose context the child is developing significant patterns of achievement orientation, social and moral standards and sex-role identity.

However, viewpoints and practices are moving toward both a greater sense of alliance between parents and teachers (cf. by encouraging participation by parents in all sorts of school activities (McGeeney, 1969)) and new kinds of alliances – as with the varieties of de-schooling efforts (Lister, 1974).

This trend towards de-emphasizing the boundaries between primary school and home, parent and teacher, has spread throughout Britain and the USA in the last decade, and the principle of welcoming parent participation in school is now quite widely accepted. Nevertheless, there is still a tendency to define the problem either in relation to the children (in terms of producing the optimum conditions for the child's ability to learn), or for society. Even Litwak and Meyer (1967), whose American study was a pioneering effort to discover appropriate links between home and school, discuss the advantages of an 'open-door' policy instead of the traditional 'locked-door' policy for the school in relation to their educational goals. The discussion takes place in an appropriately entitled chapter 'The School and Family: Linking Organisations and External Primary Groups', but the entire discussion revolves around the question 'If some type of relationship is desirable to enhance education, how can that relationship be achieved?' rather than a consideration of parents' or children's needs.

An important recent development is seen in the work of Hope Leichter (1974, p. 175), who with a number of colleagues has made explicit the educational aspects of family living. She writes:

> The family is an arena in which virtually the entire range of human experience can take place. Warfare, violence, love, tenderness, honesty, deceit, private property, communal sharing, power manipulation, informed consent, formal status hierarchies, egalitarian decision-making – all can be found within the setting of the family. And so, also, can a variety of educational encounters, ranging from conscious, systematic instruction to repetitive, moment-to-moment influences at the margins of awareness.

Still relatively focused on the education of children, the approach nevertheless has importance for parenting in two ways. It emphasized parents' *continuing* importance as educators – a necessary correction to the erroneous impression that delegation of some educational functions to specialists strips the family entirely of its influence in this regard. And, secondly, it gives a modern recognition to the complexity of interaction processes in *actual* families, as distinct from an idealized model of the authoritarian family of the past. In Leichter's 'Family as Educator', parents can be educated by children as well as the reverse (1974, pp. 15–23); siblings can have a range of influences among themselves as well as in relation to their parents; parents can educate one another; and all these things can affect the relations of parents as well as children to the schools outside.

Parents and leisure

The early and middle years of active parenting tend to be distinctive in the leisure lives of most people. Children and the home are positive centres of interest. This, in addition to the constraints on parents of young children, marks out the early establishment phase as one in which such leisure activity as there is tends to take place around the home.

Because the early years of parenting are usually financially tight, and because husbands and wives, whatever their pattern, tend to be stretched physically to meet occupational and child-rearing demands, there tends to be a drop-off in other activities outside the home, first in women, then for the men (Sillitoe, 1969). In the PEP study of over 2,000 British graduates, Thiessen and the Rapoports (1977) found that the transition to parenthood has a powerful effect on young couples' recreation patterns, particularly curtailing women's leisure activities.

Many parents have difficulty in working out suitable baby-sitting arrangements and may feel reluctant to leave their young children with babysitters at all. The Newsons (1963/72, pp. 141–2) report on baby-sitting practices in their study of parenting with one-year-olds but not in their studies of parenting with four-year-olds and seven-year-olds, which would have been more relevant for this chapter. Nevertheless, their information on parents of one-year-olds (many of whom had older children as well) suggests what may be ongoing patterns with young children:

> We asked the mothers: 'Do you and your husband ever manage to leave the baby so that you can both go out?' and followed this by asking what normally happened to the baby in such circumstances.
> Over the total sample, and without reference to the provision made

for the child's care, we found that 22 per cent of these parents were able to arrange an evening out together once a week or more often. Thirty-eight per cent occasionally left the children in the evening; and 40 per cent had been out together either once only or not at all since the one-year-old's birth. Between social classes there were considerable differences on the question of whether or not parents went out together at all, although class seemed to have little bearing on how often they went . . . there was a very definite class trend, ranging consistently from the 25 per cent of professional workers who never left the baby with a sitter to 59 per cent in the unskilled labouring class.

We did not ask why those who stay at home do so, but we were often told spontaneously. The most obvious reason, which was not in fact given very frequently, is lack of opportunity: that there is no baby-sitter available.

Leaving aside the tendency for conventional couples to have segregated leisure patterns (Bell and Healey, 1973), the Newsons (1963/72, p. 212) point out that many parents who have a more joint or companionate conception find it difficult to arrange outings as a couple:

Being able to ask the husband to baby-sit, however, offers no answer to the problem of how to share with him those outside social and cultural activities which may well have brought the couple together in the first place: occasions which can only be properly enjoyed when they can 'escape' together without the children. The only solution here is to have a baby-sitter; and in practice few couples with very young children can arrange to go out together as often as once a week.

As well as the differences between a more conventional and a more modern companionate conception of the marriage, class differences are likely to affect parents' feelings about sharing leisure interests and activities. The Newsons (pp. 212–13) report a linear relationship by class, with couples going out together 'occasionally' directly linked to class. Couples going out together very frequently (once or more per week), however, are more likely to be found at the high end (because they can afford it) and at the low end of the class scale (because they tend to have other adults living in the same house) (Table 10).

In the early part of this phase, many parents find their opportunities for going out together more restricted than when their first child was tiny. Taking children with them on 'adult outings' becomes more difficult as they grow too large for carry-cots, too wakeful for night-time transporting and easy resettling, and too eagerly social to give up participating with the people around them. For many people a characteristic of a leisure experience involves a break from daily

Table 10 *Couples who go out together frequently, occasionally or very rarely: analysed by social class*

	I and II	III WC	III Man.	IV	V	All Classes
	%	%	%	%	%	%
1 or more p.w.	21	17	23	22	19	22
Occasionally	54	47	35	36	22	38
1 or less p.a.	25	36	42	42	59	40

Source: Newson and Newson, 1963 edn, p. 212.

routine – from child-care and children's conversation. If parents have to take their children with them when visiting in the evenings, for example, they may feel a main purpose of the outing is defeated.

Day-time leisure with small children can also create considerable tension. Many parents find that the interests of very young children do not coincide with the kinds of events that they need and enjoy, whether visiting friends or museums, sport, or the arts. Their noisiness and restlessness, slow pace, rapid fatigue or ceaseless energy, inability to sit still, and numerous similar and conflicting characteristics of young children dampen many parents' enjoyment of leisure activities, and perhaps make them feel that the net balance of pleasure over strain is not positive. Though women drop outside leisure and recreational activities earlier than men in the parenting cycle, men too tend increasingly to withdraw into the home at this phase. This does not necessarily mean an increase in joint activities unless television-viewing is to be considered joint. Do-it-yourself decorating, home improvement and pottering around with the car increases for men at this point (Morrell Publications, 1973). Women's main physical activities – dancing and sport – drop off at marriage, following which they begin to cultivate 'crafts and hobbies', particularly knitting, sewing and other home-making arts (Sillitoe, 1969). After that, in the phase with which we are concerned, they become nearly totally involved in child-care. Later, when parents no longer feel so 'strapped for funds', and as children grow older and are in school, there comes a period when parents' activities and children's activities can be integrated in a satisfying way that neither is likely to find as satisfactory in the phase to follow.

We observed in *Leisure and the Family Life Cycle* (1975, p. 216) that: 'The challenge that seems to face most families is how to solve a pattern of activities and gratifications in their free and holiday time that will allow a mutually acceptable combination of shared and independent pursuits of enjoyment.'

This is more easily said than done. Fathers who think that they can make an instant relationship with their children on the annual family holiday are often destined to be frustrated. Parents who have not managed to sustain any personally meaningful leisure-time interests find it difficult to summon up instant enjoyments, let alone shared ones.

As noted earlier in this chapter, the Tavistock National Stress Study revealed that lack of hobbies was an exacerbating factor to people already vulnerable for symptoms indicating low life satisfaction. Another risk is too great an involvement in vicarious or passive spectator activities, particularly for those whose leisure activity is overwhelmingly home-based. Addictive television-viewing is the particular problem in this setting. First black and white, then colour television have claimed increasing proportions of the 'leisure pound' in the 1960s (Morrell Publications, 1973). Black and white sets are consequently available very cheaply second-hand, and found as second sets in homes with modest incomes. The life-cycle curve of nightly television-viewing, which is, of course an imperfect indicator to non-selective viewing, was found in the Tavistock Stress Study to follow the pattern described in Table 11.

Table 11 *Watch television every night (Tavistock sample 1965) percentages by age (men and women)*

Age	%
21–24	33·1
25–34	47·5
35–44	49·3
45–49	42·6
50–64	51·2
65+	40·0
Total N = 1,798	

This curve suggests the high plateau between the ages of 25 and 44, followed by a slight dip and then a sharply rising curve into the sixties. The peak represents the period in which there are children at home, the dip perhaps heralds the departure of the children. The subsequent rise suggests the different kind of interest in television in the later phases, going over into retirement.

Negative implications of addictive television-viewing tend to be considered mostly in relation to children. There are, however, negative associations for adults whose television-viewing follows similar patterns. The Tavistock study showed that women are more likely to be nightly viewers than men. Nightly viewing was negatively correlated with having a hobby. It was positively correlated, not only with 'no hobbies' but with stress symptoms. Even its anodyne function, therefore, is ineffectual for captive housewives. Steady, probably unselective, television-viewing as a 'free time' activity seems, like gambling, to be more associated with the lower, less educated, lower-occupation-skill groups.

There are several implications for more improved leisure provision. Recognition that parents with very young children may have different needs and requirements from families with school-age children is a starting point. Family structure varies according to numerous other dimensions that influence parents' leisure behaviour as well. Nevertheless, there are some respects in which family life-cycle factors tend to cut across other variables.

Many parents' leisure participation will be influenced by the baby-sitting arrangements they are able to make. For many the provision of crèche or play facilities at adult leisure activity locations is one suitable way of approaching the problem. This is at present done by some London Adult Education Institutes, providing a genuine option for mothers to attend classes. Some parents, especially those with slightly older children, like to undertake some leisure activities *with* their children. There are frequently bureaucratic obstacles to this in the form of separate adult and children's provision; but more responsive centres are facilitating attendance at some activities on a family basis. It is important that leisure providers do not think of the requirements as mutually exclusive alternatives. The same parent may have both needs: to pursue an interest seriously, independently and uninterruptedly; and to become involved with his older child in a pursuit which both of them can find meaningful.

The timing and siting of leisure facilities can also be very important to parents. Given the home-centred character of the phase, leisure facilities close to homes and open during hours when parents are able to either cover for one another or arrange other relief coverage can make a substantial difference in these years of active parenting. To an extent this has been recognized by some leisure providers, but there are many instances where parents' needs and requirements in this respect are ignored. Signs and by-laws prohibiting ball games, car-washing, and exercising pets still abound on public housing estates. The tendency to provide bigger and better facilities, involving their location at considerable distance from many homes, rather than providing more, less elaborate facilities on a more widely diffused basis is also prominent. Obviously, specialist facilities are also desirable, but if in times of relative scarcity when the chips are down, facilities of both sorts cannot be provided, provision at very local levels would perhaps benefit those who at present show the lowest levels of leisure participation.

The potentials for very local provision easily accessible to a cluster of households are great. More could be provided on public housing estates if the design and the management were suitably planned. London's garden squares are reminders of the social alternatives attainable even with high density living. Several squares contain shared children's play equipment, tennis courts and so on. These are not always built into new developments and more is possible. Many condominiums in the USA contain athletic facilities, communal barbecues, saunas, etc. There is considerable scope in such settings for informal sociability, close enough to people's homes to eliminate many of the barriers to getting out. There is scope for increased home-centred social provision as an antidote to the feelings of entrapment associated with highly privatized family life. But these are not the only meaningful forms of leisure to meet parents' needs at this stage. Variety and options are crucial.

7

Parenting with adolescent children

In this chapter we map out the main contours of the phase in which people parent with adolescent children. The phase has considerable overlap with other phases. Not only do parents often have older and younger children, but this phase marks the transition between the more active years of parenting and the parenting of adult children which follows. Parenting with adolescent children usually occurs when parents are at mid-life, in an experiential if not also a chronological sense.

In looking at the salient issues of mid-life for parents as people, we concentrate first, as in the other chapters, on phase-specific issues in parents' own lives. Some issues, less specific to this phase, will not be dealt with in this chapter if they have been focused on already, though they apply to many parents in this phase. For example, parenting and employment outside the home has been extensively discussed in the last chapter.

We then review social and psychological issues for the children, as experts in adolescent development have written about them. This parallels the presentation of child development issues focal for the previous parental phase, that were dealt with in Chapter 5.

Third, we consider the impact on the parents' couple relationship, and consider some of the specific issues of parenting with adolescent children. We suggest that parents' experiences in this phase have important similarities with those of their adolescent children; this may stimulate reverberations between the respective experiences of parents and children, often giving the phase a special, somewhat electric quality. Finally, we suggest that the changing trends in the life styles adopted by today's parents provide different models for their adolescent children. Such change, especially in relation to sex roles, is likely to be reflected in the life styles created by rising cohorts of young adults, and is likely to affect their decisions about their own marriages and parenting. For example, more men and women than previously may decide not to parent.

Parents as people at mid-life

By and large parents of adolescent children are at a stage of their own life loosely referred to as 'mid-life'. They may arrive at the point where their first child reaches adolescence when they themselves are anywhere from about thirty to fifty-five. Their exact age depends on many factors, such as how old each parent was at marriage, whether it was a first or subsequent marriage, what their experiences were in relation to family planning and so on. This 'middle-aged' phase can last a very long time, depending on how many children succeed the first one and how they were spaced.

Neugarten (1968) observes, however, that

> The major life events that characterise the middle part of the life-span . . . reaching the peak of one's occupational career, the launching of children from home, the death of parents . . . while they tend to proceed in a roughly predictable sequence, occur at varying intervals of time.

To this we would add . . . and in varying manners with varying outcomes.

Middle-aged parents are likely to be as established economically as they ever will be, and at the peak of their earning power. They are still usually in good health.

But this may not be a period of tranquillity. Individuals who are parents at mid-life are sometimes referred to as the 'middle generation' because usually their own parents are still alive and they may experience obligations in both directions (Franzblau, 1971; Hall, 1904; Miller, 1969). They may be disturbed and depressed because the pressures on them are frustrating and they may feel 'caught' between the demands of aged parents on one side and rebellious children on the other, with less chance for self-realization than they would like at this point in their lives. Unlike their children, they are expected to be strong, to cope, to have no 'problems', or indeed 'needs'. They often seem to exist to carry the burdens of others on their shoulders. Chilman (1968, p. 307) describes this as follows:

> From the viewpoint of the middle-aged parent, one does, indeed, seem to be caught in the middle of three generational cycles; between the increasingly complex, costly and disturbing needs of adolescents . . . who are bursting with desire for entrance into the adult world and the increasing problems and needs of the grandparents, who generally, are bursting with desire not to leave their full status in the adult world. The middle-aged adult, who may feel that her own status is threatened somewhat by her own development stage, is apt to feel further threatened by the competing, but somewhat similar claims of both the older and younger generations.

These 'middle years', as the GAP report (1973) calls them, coincide roughly with the mid-establishment phase of the family life cycle (Rapoport, Rapoport and Strelitz, 1975, pp. 210–11). Our usage of 'mid-establishment' should not be confused with other usages of the very elastic term 'middle'. For Hill and Rodgers, for example, the 'middle years' designate the period when the husband is between fifty-two and sixty-five and the family has 'launched its adolescent(s)'. They call this the 'post-parental' period. It is 'middle' only in the sense of being between the phases where the children are at home and dependent, and the phase of occupational retirement of the family provider(s). In the mid-establishment phase as we use the term, parents are preoccupied with the yields they are experiencing in relation to their *life investments*. Whereas people in earlier parts of the establishment phase emphasize the making of life investments, those in mid and later phases tend to emphasize their *critical evaluation*: have they been satisfying? Are they paying off – psychologically, interpersonally, and in terms of how well the children seem to have developed? The GAP Committee observe that 'the search for meaning to life appears during this time' (GAP, 1973, p. 113).

In a sense there is an inversion of the preoccupations that held in the earlier sub-phase. Whereas the tendency in the earlier phases was for the economics of the family to be 'tight', this phase is one in which there tends to be a firmer footing economically for the family, but an accumulation of strains, boredom or fatigue. By the time the first child in a family reaches adolescence, most parents are at a plateau of material achievement, but they will have gone through strenuous efforts to reach this.

For people who have remained married to their original spouse, the marriage may have endured for perhaps twenty years, and this in itself can present problems. It is a period in which there may be turmoil, restlessness and disruption. This critical aspect of the phase is communicated in what the GAP committee wrote (GAP, 1973, pp. 119–20):

> For both husband and wife, the middle years are often a time of taking inventory, assessing what has been accomplished and what the resources are with which to face the future. This may raise upsetting questions. The man may ask 'If I had done it differently twenty years ago, where would I be now?' The wife remembers that she rejected the proposal of the man who is now president of her husband's company.

This is conspicuously American middle-class in its content, and to some extent 'dated' in its sex-role stereotyping, but the essential underlying process of assessment is valid. The issue centres on what balance will emerge between the feelings of disappointment and those of enjoyment.

The GAP Committee (1973, p. 121) also indicate the positive potentials of this period, despite its negative aspects for many parents:

> The gruelling race to find a mate and establish a career – has been run; children no longer demand around-the-clock care; and social life is no longer dictated by the caprices of baby-sitters or the unpredictability of childhood diseases. . . . There is time now for enjoyment.

Nevertheless, the changes that occur at mid-life are likely to influence parents as people beyond simply allowing them to redirect their energies. Complex biological changes occur at this period of life. Changes in the central nervous system and in the hormonal system affect the body form, activity, and sexual interest. People progressing through this phase, whether or not they are parents, are likely to experience diminished acuity of sight and hearing, in speed of response, in absorption of new information, and in general level of sexual drive (Welford, 1958; Birren, 1960).

The awareness growing inside individuals of both sexes at this phase of life that they are mortal and perhaps on the 'downhill' side of their life cycles (at least in so far as physical capacities are concerned) can create considerable turbulence. It may take on the character of a personal crisis. In the sense in which it is salient in this chapter, the so called 'mid-life' crisis was first conceptualized by Elliott Jaques (1965). The concept is akin to the psychobiological crisis of 'generativity' earlier posited by Erikson (1950).

Jaques argued that at mid-life there is a developmental crisis which reactivates an earlier 'depressive' dilemma of personality development. According to how the earlier crisis was resolved and what resources are available in dealing with the reawakening of it in mid-life, the individual may enter a period of relative stagnation from a creative point of view (i.e. revert to a depressive 'position') or he may undergo a creative renaissance. He demonstrated these two possible outcomes in the works of great creative artists and writers, comparing their productivity prior to the mid-life crisis at, say, the age of forty with their situation after. Erikson's formulation also derives from psycho-analytic conceptions of the nature of personality development through a period of successive crises, the resolution of each of which is determined in part by the modes of resolution of prior dilemmas. On the other hand, he assigns a somewhat different emphasis to the dynamics of the particular life-cycle crises which people at mid-life may experience. In moving through these periods and working through the process that Maslow (1962) referred to as 'self-actualization', the

individual has to come to grips with somewhat different focal preoccupations at different stages. After having worked through, in
some degree, the earlier issues of 'basic trust', 'identity', and 'intimacy',
men in this phase come to grips with issues of 'generativity', which
may be spurred, as Jaques also suggests, by an awareness of death and
the depressive impact of this awareness.

The concept of the 'mid-life crisis' and its dynamics is now widely
recognized, but it has been considered particularly in relation to men
and their occupational interests. For example, it was used in a study
of mid-career development of managers. Rapoport (1970) traced the
different patterns of managerial career development that emerged as
successful managers confronted the choice between moving upward
into positions of heavier responsibility and remaining at a plateau of
moderate achievement. The former option, though bringing new
rewards (as well as strains), tends to entail a lessening of family
involvements.

Orville Brim (1976), reviewing the American literature on the male
mid-life crisis, concluded that while profound personality changes are
likely to occur for most men at this stage of life, the precise nature,
timing and outcome of the changes depend on an array of personal,
interpersonal and contextual conditions and events.

Daniel Levinson and his colleagues (1974, 1976) have completed one
of the few holistic studies attempting to encompass the range of bio-
psycho-social factors that affect male development at mid-life. On
the basis of depth interviews and tests conducted over a two-year
period with 40 men in various occupations around their early forties,
Levinson concluded that the mid-life transition is inevitable and
involves characteristic psychosocial processes that require working
through. It is inevitable because of the reality of bodily decline, the
necessity of confronting a generation gap between one's own age-mates
and oncoming younger people now asserting their autonomy, and a
crystallization of life accomplishments making it difficult to avoid a
realization of disparities between what one is and what one had dreamt
of becoming. It involves a focal process of coming to grips with three
key issues: acceptance of mortality, revision of one's self-conception as
an older rather than a younger person, and integration into one's
intimate life of a new conception of the male-female relationship, less
based on the dependency or the lasciviousness of earlier modes. To
the extent that these issues are satisfactorily dealt with, the turbulence
sometimes manifested at this phase may subside, and restabilization
occur.

We know little about what factors in the social environment are
important as a counterweight to the forces of biological decline. However, we are beginning to have some idea of how the experience may

be responded to by sex, chronological age, cohort and sub-culture. For men, for example, with increasingly rapid technological and organizational changes in the occupational sphere, the age at which they may feel they have reached their peak of occupational achievement may be lower than previously. At the point that it occurs, people may feel depressed at a sense of futility in life; they may embark on a second career, or change their life styles completely by opting out of the occupational ladder altogether, or they may recreate their current interests. For men in occupations which require competitive effort to make their way up organizational ladders, this may be a period of choice – between moving upward into more taxing senior positions with greater rewards of pay, power and prestige (though feeling perhaps that one is not as fit or as driven for such things as previously) *vs* de-emphasizing work aspirations in favour of rewards in family life or other interests.

In some cases the choices are 'primary', in the sense that they are 'freely' made from among available alternatives. In other cases they may be secondary. A manager, for example, may turn to the humanistic or family-orientated values after feeling that he has failed, or may fail at occupational advancement. This distinction between primary and secondary choice is important. The family-oriented managers who choose to become more involved in family life as a secondary option may become irritable or depressed (Evan, 1961; Bailyn, 1974). Those who choose it as a primary option, emphasizing 'humanistic' values rather than success, may have higher levels of satisfaction than their more 'successful' colleagues (Rapoport, 1970).

It is not only for managers that these issues are important. Many occupations are organized hierarchically. Much more is known, though, about the work careers of senior managers and professionals than of other workers. We need research on the frustrations of other people who feel trapped in their occupations at this stage of life; what options they realistically have and what values and constraints govern their choices.

For women at mid-life the current cultural ethos has changed. To some extent the biological manifestations of mid-life are being medically controlled, so that the previously dominating emphasis on the powerful effects of the menopause is less relevant. Psychological manifestations of mid-life, such as feelings of uselessness and redundancy, are seen as subject to similar determinants as those studied in males. Changes in occupational role pattern – for example, if conventional mothers feel themselves needed less as active parents – are seen as important factors. Women who have no alternative interest in occupational and other spheres have been shown to suffer more from such symptoms. Conversely, research indicates that those who confront the issues earlier and develop active interests outside the home, whether in paid occupations or otherwise, fare better psychologically, as we documented in the preceding chapter.

Women at this stage of their lives characteristically feel themselves to be faced with a fairly fundamental choice situation. While few would argue that adolescent children require no parenting (and many would argue that they require *more* attention than the more dependent and vulnerable infants), they do not require the same kind of parenting that most authorities and most people feel younger children require. This implies for most mothers that if they have not already entered employment outside the home, they may have this option reactivated. They may continue the home-maker option, enter paid work, or concentrate on voluntary work. The choice depends to some extent on prior patterns – but it is not necessarily a simple movement into employment from having concentrated at home. Some women, having been employed earlier, may for a variety of reasons choose to concentrate on the home during the period of their children's adolescence. Difficulties may arise which the mother feels require her attention; or she may see the impending departure of her children as rushing upon her and she may decide that the relationships during these years are too precious to allow to slip by on the edges of her working life.

However, the larger social trends in our society, as well as general patterning of family life-cycle involvements, seem to favour the choice of the paid worker option during this phase. We seem to have reached what Jessie Bernard has called a 'tipping point', where a new statistical norm is established – and it is now normative for most married women with children in the age group that we are talking about to go out to work. While women aged twenty-five to thirty-four with young dependent children drop out of economic activity in relatively great proportions (though over 30 per cent of them remain employed), women in the age groups over thirty-five show marked increases. In the analysis of *Social Trends* provided by the Central Statistical Office (1974) this is attributed to the fact that this is a period in which children remain financially dependent on their parents but 'cease to require constant attention'.

Though the return to work is difficult, there are many features of the contemporary situation which ease it. More women are doing it, and it is increasingly expected. It is often encouraged by one's children – who may point out scornfully that the mother is going all 'cabbagy' (Rapoport *et al.*, 1975). Many women wish to undertake a new occupation, their interests having changed in the interim. Fisher and Le Gros Clark (1960, 1966), in a study of a small sample of middle-aged women in an Essex town, found that of the 53 who returned to work after an absence for domestic reasons, only 16 entered the same type of job as they had previously held, when they were nearly all office workers. Most of the others took jobs calling on the skills they had acquired as wives and mothers – dealing with people, sales, hospital and other service occupations. This was, however, partly a function of the situation – a small Essex town with limited opportunities. A larger study by the Government Social Survey and a number of other studies found that a much higher proportion of women in this age group who intend to return to work wish either to take training to develop a skill or interest they had earlier established, or to take up again where they had left off. In general the higher the level of skill or education, the greater the zeal for further development. Many researchers, including Le Gros Clark (1960, 1966), Seear (1971) and Briggs (DHSS, 1972) emphasize the pool of talent available in mature women. But there is a gap between wishes and actual possibilities. In his recommendations to the Department of Health on nursing, Briggs recommended different training regimens according to the re-entrant's social and family circumstances. The Department of Employment (1975, p. 57) has reviewed all available data on these topics and concluded that: 'anyone who turns his back on [the strong and irreversible trend toward employment of married women] is opting out of a large and expanding field of labour supply.'

But there are many conflicts and difficulties in arranging re-entry to work. Alice Rossi compared it with the re-entry phenomenon in space ships – the friction may burn one up unless well protected; and Jessie Bernard compared the pains experienced with the 'bends' that divers experience if they surface too quickly. But, despite the difficulties, a large percentage of married women in the USA and Britain return to work at this phase of the family life cycle. Husbands' attitudes can be critical in encouraging or impeding this transition (Hunt, 1968; Fogarty, Rapoport and Rapoport, 1971).

Women who choose to be primarily homemakers even with their children grown, may find interest within the home to express themselves. Others may develop an interest they had long cherished in fantasy but had not been able to pursue – writing a book, painting, studying a language or literature, taking up an activity such as yoga. Adult education classes and institutions like the British Open University with its flexible regimens and low travel demands facilitate the pursuit of these interests and retraining requirements.

Many wives at this stage take up a voluntary activity. Voluntary community activities may be favoured by women who prefer not to be tied down by a job or to be part of an organizational system, yet who wish to employ their energies constructively and who do not require remuneration. However, Ferriss (1971) suggests that this is a less popular choice and has not grown rapidly. There are some signs that, both in the USA and Britain, there has been a recent resurgence of interest in the potential value of voluntary work (Loeser, 1974; Aves, 1976).

The key issue among mothers of decision from among options is not a simple intellectual exercise. There is often considerable anguish and conflict in mothers – about whether to go out or to stay at home. Home-oriented mothers, formerly the most highly-praised and sanctioned, are now somewhat 'put down' because of the newer cultural emphasis on women's emancipation. On the other hand, the work-oriented mother may experience an unwanted level of stress, feeling exploited both at work and at home. By this phase she may regret having missed opportunities for closer involvement in her children's lives.

The conflicts and strains experienced will affect mothers' perceived needs at this period. Whatever options are chosen, there arises the issue of re-orienting herself to a new configuration of life interests as the children pass through adolescence to adulthood and leave the home.

Issues of adolescent development: some professional viewpoints

There have been many approaches to understanding the issues of family life with an adolescent child. As already indicated, it is only recently that adolescence (and childhood in general) has come to be recognized as a distinctive phase, let alone a problematic one. Formerly, in historically known societies in Europe, young people reaching physical maturity would work on the family farm or enterprise, marry or leave to find work elsewhere. This is confirmed in the cross-cultural studies of many anthropologists, most notable of which have been those of Margaret Mead (1939). She contrasted the turbulence of American society, with its discontinuities of socialization between child and adult roles, with the Samoans, who slipped smoothly into adulthood when their bodies were ready, pointing up the fact that adolescence as we know it is a cultural creation.

On the other hand, it has been widely observed, following Van Gennep (1909/1960) that many societies ritualize the passage of individuals from a childhood status to an adult one. Work by Gluckman (1962) and Whiting (1958) has specified the functions of such rituals and the conditions under which they are likely to be found. They provide cognitive and emotional supports bridging discontinuities in social roles.

Sociological approaches

Talcott Parsons (1964), Robert Merton (1957) and Kingsley Davis (1940) have provided influential analyses of the social structural conditions confronting adolescents in Western society. From these theorists we can draw a classical picture of the sociological approach to adolescence. The theoretical framework used is that of structural-functional analysis, which consists primarily of an equilibrium model of both family and society. The fundamental elements of the model are social *roles*. The developmental process of adolescence is seen as one of *socialization* to the legitimate and established structure of roles. The *qualities* of the parent–adolescent relationships or the issues important to the *people* involved in them tend to be less emphasized. Dahrendorf (1958) compares such functional sociological theorists with Utopian writers: both conceive of society as a social system in a state of equilibrium. And, as Skolnick has pointed out, both have been concerned with the problem of social replacement. They conceive of socialization as a regular patterned process that maintains the *status quo*, with a built-in assumption of changelessness (Skolnick, 1973, p. 356).

For Parsons (1942 and 1964, p. 253) the role structure of the family is symmetrical and balanced with its two principal axes of male–female and parent–child. He has maintained that the principal basis for sex discrimination in families is in the family's necessary articulation with the larger society's roles, which it reflects. But, he writes that in

> the transition from childhood to adolescence new features appear which disturb the symmetry of sex roles while still a second set of factors appears with marriage and the acquisition of full adult status and responsibilities.

The assumption in this, and other classical sociological writings on this topic is that an untroubled steady state tends to exist and the fundamental conditions of social role definitions are sustained – i.e. that mothers are homemakers concentrating on expressive roles in the family and that fathers are out providing economically and achieving a social status for the family members. In this model, the main element of conflict recognized is around male adolescence. Parsons explains the greater prevalence of 'problems' with boys at adolescence as stemming from the fact that girls are socialized within the home to their adult roles as wives and mothers. Their role models are their own mothers who are, as he saw it, 'continually about the house', visible and busy, and presumably satisfied with their roles so that they can serve as suitable models for their daughters. What mothers do is tangible and understandable to their children. The daughters are seen as able to rehearse their adult roles by participating 'actively and usefully in such activities'. For boys, on the other hand, the situation is different. Occupation is a key element in males' ultimate adult roles but their fathers are not available or visible to them in the conduct of these roles and thus the boy is only semi-socialized for his main adult role. Parsons

(1964, p, 252) writes: 'This leaves the boy without a tangible meaningful model to emulate and without the possibility of a gradual initiation
into the activities of the adult male role.' While sociologists have
tended not to concentrate on adolescent–parent relationships directly,
some have written about *intergenerational conflict*, and *generational
continuity*. Eisenstadt (1956) has analysed the turbulence in this set of
relationships as characteristic of intergeneration processes in all known
historical and ethnographic situations. He sees it as part of the process
of social continuity – in which culture is transmitted not only by direct
indoctrination but also by novices rebelling temporarily so as to gain
some distance from their family perspective and to incorporate into
themselves as their own the social roles and values they have learned.
This is how generational replacement has been perceived to occur in
a way that is functional for the society as a whole.

Because there is a discontinuity, particularly for boys, and because
our society does not provide rituals of passage comparable to those of an
African warrior society with its social and surgical initiation rites at
puberty, the conventional view suggests that boys at adolescence tend
to create their own transitional peer groups – or to invest emotionally
in peer-group culture – what Coleman (1961) has called 'adolescent
society'. Girls' peer groups in this sense are less discussed by these
writers.

Kingsley Davis (1940), writing at about the same time as Parsons
(1942), did emphasize social complexity and social change as major
sources of parent–child conflict. He saw the potential for conflict as
arising partly out of biological and psychological differences between
organisms of different ages, and partly from the power relations
between parents and children. Davis portrayed parental authority as
extremely powerful, inescapable, and as lasting throughout the family
life span. He further felt that conflicting social norms, and the contrast
between ideals and reality, provide additional built-in sources of parent–
child conflict. This becomes particularly important at adolescence when
the semi-adult is searching around for ideals which can be incorporated personally. The hypocrisy that adolescents see in their parents'
inconsistent or compromising behaviour creates a credibility gap.
Davis's views foreshadowed some of the more modern literature on
adolescence that came to the fore in the late 1960s. Keniston (1971)
describes how this problem is better dealt with in traditional societies
which change slowly; such societies 'institutionalize hypocrisy' by
building into the culture occasions or rationales for violating the rules.
When social change is rapid, the institutionalization may break down
because there is a lag in the development of new rules or events to
justify such inconsistencies. This adversely affects the quality of
parent–adolescent relationships.

But peer groups can be malfunctional as well as functional, both for individuals and for society. Merton (1957), in his paper on 'Social Structure and Anomie', provides a framework for considering what happens to boys in the type of family system described by Parsons (1942). If adolescents, particularly boys, are blocked in obtaining their social mobility goals in the family they may turn to channels outside the family. Many of these are 'deviant' channels in which social goals are restructured. This has related to the fact that the dominant goal in our society (especially for males) is 'success', a goal that tends to generate an unlimited amount of aspiration. Given that the aspirations can never fully be realized in the family itself, the individual turns outside. Legitimate social channels for realizing the success goals are more limited than the numbers of people who aspire to them, so 'deviant' channels are sought. Merton set out the framework and most research on delinquency and deviance at adolescence has followed through the implications of it (Cohen, 1965; Downes, 1966). Adolescence, by implication, is a phase of development at which there is a high societal risk for problems of deviancy and delinquency.

Much of the research on adolescent delinquency has concentrated on working-class gangs. One controversy is whether adolescent delinquency in such settings represents deviant solutions to a dilemma posed by middle-class success goals plus inadequate working-class means for achieving them, or simply the illicit expression of different kinds of goals – those of physical prowess, defiance of the authorities, etc. – characteristic of lower-class culture (Miller, 1958; Cloward and Ohlin, 1964).

But the study of adolescent culture and society has revealed variations in the structure and composition of adolescent groups. Peter Willmott (1963), in a study of adolescents in the East End of London, observed that in the apparent separateness and rebelliousness of many youth gangs there is a continuity and the learning of a social solidarity that will serve them well as men, as fellow-workers and members of trades unions, and as good neighbours in a tight-knit working-class neighbourhood.

Another dimension of the sociological interest in adolescence is around *sexual activities*. Courtship is a phase in the family cycle that occurs universally, and is a standard element in studies of cross-cultural studies of kinship and the family (Turner, 1969).

While incest taboos universally require that sexual interests be directed outside the family at this stage, the search for a romantic love partner as it is seen in Western societies is a relatively new and unique phenomenon, as Goode (1964) has shown. Most research, however, has avoided the use of 'love' as a concept in favour of such operationalizable variables as length of acquaintance. Slater and

Woodside (1951), for example, studied London couples with a view to correlating their courtship history with their subsequent marital happiness, and found that among the 18 per cent of their 'normal' married couples who had known one another for less than a year before marriage the chances of marital happiness were significantly less than among those who had longer personal acquaintance. The modal period was between one and four years, accounting for 61 per cent of the marriages. Other variables studied have included courting behaviour, pre-marital sexual behaviour and (more recently) leisure behaviour of the young. But, as Cyril Smith (1968, pp. 1–4) notes, adults' interest in adolescents has often been ambivalent and the underlying points of departure in research are sometimes poles apart:

> Most people who write about adolescence have an axe to grind. They are either concerned with proving that youth is overindulged . . . or that they are hard done by. . . . There can be no doubt about the interest which adults show in what adolescents do . . . youth provides excitement . . . youth is envied because life seems to be much more fun for the young today, not only in contrast to the life their parents like to think they endured . . . but also . . . in contrast with the lives which the middle-aged are currently experiencing. . . . Envy very easily breeds resentment, and resentment is a fertile ground for projecting the troubles of this world upon the young. It is a short step from reasoning that the high spirits of the young lead them to damage public property to forming a habit of assuming that all vandalism is committed by teenagers.

Accordingly, the social analysis of parenting at adolescence tends to centre on parents as role models on the one hand and on parents as exercisers of social control on the other. Parents are studied in terms of their attempts to screen the friends of their children (particularly their daughters) and their setting limits for time-keeping and other activities. Conventionally, concerns about boys and girls have been different. The concern of parents for their adolescent girls primarily centred around sexuality, with assault or unwanted pregnancy the anxiety and courtship and marriage the desired outcome. Research portrays the discomfort of parents with the topic of sexuality and their embarrassment about it. The sexual behaviour, particularly of a daughter, was often seen to reflect on the reputation of the parents. With boys, parents' anxieties seem to centre on the company they are keeping, whether they will get into trouble or have accidents; and their hopes and aspirations about attaining a suitable occupational placement (Brannen, 1975; Thomas and Wetherell, 1974; Maizels, 1970). One of the persistent issues tackled by sociological theorists and researchers that demonstrates some of the problems of this particular perspective has to do with the 'generation gap', whether it exists or not, under what conditions, and in response to what determinants. As noted above, an earlier position was that the generation gap is a cultural creation in our society, due to discontinuities between child and adult roles which are not adequately bridged by rituals of passage. However, even earlier writers such as Kingsley Davis (1940) observed that inter-generational conflict should be understood partly in terms of intrinsic processes associated with social complexity and change. This contrasted with the Parsonian view, which emphasized elements intrinsic to maturation, as the individual being socialized came to accept the parents' frailties as human qualities rather than as hypocritical betrayals.

In general, the concept of 'generation gap', as Skolnick (1973, pp. 358 ff) has demonstrated, has been a confused one. There is confusion amongst experts as to what is meant by the term generation gap, and what purpose is served by its use. The rebelliousness of youth, for example, can be used to indicate a universal in the socializa-tion process or in individual development, or to show a specific characteristic of 'our culture'. Or it may be most usefully understood in relation to quite specific historical circumstances, as in the rebel-liousness of youth in the 1960s. Margaret Mead (1971, p. 50), moving with the times, presented the following reformulation of the nature of this specific generation gap:

> It isn't about parents not getting along with children or children rebelling or changing styles of morality. It is simply that at the time of World War II the whole world became one, so that there is a complete difference between all young people and all older people.

What was important about all this was that while many sociologists became aware that prevailing models of socialization did not fit the complex realities of intergenerational relations in contemporary society, they have not easily been able to abandon them. Shorter (1975, pp. 269 ff) has attempted to come to grips with this issue by applying a historical perspective. He feels a major shift in the relations between the generations took place in the late 1960s and early 1970s. He sees contemporary adolescents as *indifferent* to their family's identity in a new way. This indifference shows up in the unsystematic character of the discontinuity of values from parents to children:

> The chances that adolescent children will have the same views as their parents about love and sex, politics and economics, are sig-nificantly poorer now than before. . . . The new development is that *adolescent* children have begun to manifest a massive uninterest in their parents' values and in their own identities as guardians-apparent of the family line.

Shorter (p. 270) maintains that this discontinuity of interests and values is not a 'generation gap' in the classical sense, because

The generations are not 'in conflict', nor is the typical young person likely to find himself seething with rage towards his mother and father. Everything we know about how often young couples continue to visit their parents suggest the ludicrousness of generation-gap alarmism.

Shorter sees the discontinuities as more subtle with peer groups becoming more important in the task of adolescent socialization. Many studies of parent–adolescent relations in France, Germany, Denmark and the USA report the resurgence of the peer group and slackening of family influence. Data since 1965 indicate that adolescents increasingly turn to a subculture that is independent of the dominant culture rather than either conforming to it or opposing it as such; they prefer companionship with friends rather than family members (Vincent, 1971).

To summarize and extrapolate: many sociologists see parents as having the primary responsibility for socializing children to adult society. They share this function with schools (for a period of the child's life) who have responsibility for the cognitive development of the child and the child's preparation for the assumption of competent adult vocational roles. At adolescence, individuals become more autonomous forces in families expressing not only their own individuality but their disagreement with the values, roles or life styles of their parents. This creates a tension or 'gap' between the generations which is often troublesome in families.

The nature of the troublesome elements in family life as the adolescent's physical and psychological maturation presents a new force in the home is complex. It includes an element of sexuality with attendant anxieties about how it should be managed; an element of challenge to authority; and mixtures of pride, vicarious joy or sadness at an impending change of relationships in the family, including leaving home. Whatever the difficulties, it has emphasized that the tensions and rebelliousness may be socially functional, in that it allows the adolescent to leave the family setting and enter the wider society where he or she may activate internalized social norms and contribute to social continuity despite the rebellious behaviour in the family. It should be noted that major rebelliousness has tended to be considered a masculine phenomenon by most sociological writers, particularly when it carries over into the external society. Parents have tended to be more concerned with violence in boys and their capacity to enter the occupational system advantageously; while that with girls involves the control of their sexuality.

But this classical picture, while having useful elements, in attempting to understand young people's behaviour in sociological perspective is based on a relatively static view of society with a relatively fixed segregation between the sexes and unchanging patterns of relationship between family and society. It is less useful in conceptualizing what we observe today of changes going on in all these areas and young people's orientations to the changes.

Social-psychological and developmental frameworks

The developmental approach to adolescence – with its phase-specific concerns – has come from psychologists. Developmental psychologists and psychoanalysts have concentrated on adolescence as a stage at which the individual reaches full physical maturity and becomes engaged in the process of achieving psychological and social maturity. The original concept of adolescence, envisioned by the American psychologist G. Stanley Hall was multi-dimensional. His book (1904) was entitled *Adolescence: its Psychology and its Relations to Physiology, Anthropology, Sociology, Sex, Crime, Religion and Education*. But actual 'schools' of psychology have been more segmented in their treatment. The view of all the psychological approaches is, however, from the individual outward. Freud published on adolescence shortly afterward, stating the 'psychosexual' model and adolescence has been of considerable interest to psychoanalysts since. The definition of adolescence by Peter Blos (1962) is perhaps most succinct and representative of the classical psychoanalytic model. He sees adolescence as a 'process of adaptation to puberty'. Derek Miller subdivides adolescence into three stages, which vary according to individual and cultural circumstances: an early stage, from eleven or twelve to fourteen or fifteen, in which the fact of puberty dominates the awareness of the individual; a middle stage, from fourteen or fifteen to seventeen or eighteen, in which the individual becomes concerned with his or her identifications and how to achieve self-realization; and a late stage from seventeen or so to nineteen or twenty, in which the individual becomes engaged in training for adult roles.

The above conceptions are related to, but less widely influential perhaps than, that of Erikson. Erikson (1950, 1959) views the phase as one of the sequence of stages through the life cycle in which the individual undergoes critical heightening of a phase-specific challenge. In this case it is the challenge of *identity vs identity diffusion*. As with other life challenges, the character of the resolution of the crisis it creates is determined by psycho-biological processes but affected by cultural and environmental conditions.

The adolescent, in breaking out of childhood roles, becomes preoccupied with establishing for him/herself a satisfactory answer to the question 'Who am I?' In the search for an answer to this question, a variety of possible identities are tried out, experiences in different roles are sought, different kinds of relationships are experimented with, and the adolescent explores his/her own mental and physical properties and limits in a more active way than previously. If the young person fails to clarify and give structure to his personal identity, he is likely to experience depression and despair, a sense of meaninglessness, self-depreciation and dissociation – symptoms of identity diffusion. Erikson does not suggest that a positive outcome to the identity crises implies that the young person will persist with the same idea of 'Who am I?' for the rest of his life. The quest may never be completely resolved and questions of self-definition effloresce again in crises later in life, as we see in parents of adolescents. Erikson suggests only that the identity-formation issues are most acute and salient in the adolescent crises.

As compared with Erikson, Blos gives greater emphasis to the inner struggles, with the control of the new types and levels of instinctual expressions, of sexuality and aggressiveness. Miller gives relatively greater attention to the environmental circumstances. He notes that in seeking to achieve autonomy, an adolescent cannot be too attached to his parents *or* to his peer group, and he stresses the importance of a balance. Optimally, there should be a range of external relationships available, together with the cultivation of the capacity to make relationships with non-family members (Miller, 1974). Some modern psychoanalysts have carried the tendency to include the interplay of external and internal forces further – e.g. the formulation of Hansburg (1972) who interprets adolescent disturbance in terms of 'object loss' (the 'objects' being nurturing parents, teachers, the school, or the self as a child). But the centre of gravity of the psychoanalytic preoccupation is still in the individual (Anna Freud, 1958; Laufer, 1969).

Academic psychologists have concentrated on cognitive and behavioural development (e.g. Inhelder and Piaget, 1958). Adolescents show an increased capacity for hypothetico-deductive reasoning and conceptualization. They are more capable of organizing their own behaviour to control and channel aggression and to adopt appropriate adult roles for avoiding punishments and for maximizing rewards (Bandura and Walters, 1959). One concept which is used by social learning theorists is that of *developmental task*, and in this there is a *rapprochement* with sociological theorists of the family who use the concept of task in relation to status transitions in the family cycle (Duvall, 1962; Rapoport, 1963).

Having discussed some of the issues of mid-life for parents and the developmental issues of adolescence that impinge on the parents, we turn now to parents' experiences as a couple.

Impact on the parents' couple relationship

Parents at this phase are likely to be experiencing, as individuals, some of the mid-life processes described above. At the same time, their children, as adolescents, are likely to be experiencing some of the turmoil associated with the quest for personal identity in a world that is complex and changing and prone to disturbing environmental events and influences of various kinds. Before turning to the implications of all this for parenting, it is important to note that there is a cluster of studies that bear on the couple relationship at this phase. There is still a good deal of work to be done on this topic before it can be stated how much of the phenomena observed relate directly to the impact of adolescents and their problems, and how much relate to other forces. However, the general picture emerging from a number of sources seems to sustain the proposition that marriages are under greater strain at this point than at any time since the initial impact of accommodating to intimate living together.

Pineo (1961), in his follow-up of Chicago families married in the 1940s, terms the general process observed 'disenchantment'. Marriages by this time will have been under-way for twenty years or more; with earlier marriage and better health and longevity prospects, parents may not feel as old and worn out at this point as in previous societies. On the contrary, they may have stored up a sufficient body of frustrations and fantasies of alternative arrangements as to provide an impetus for wishing to have a fling, seek rejuvenation or another chance at a happy couple relationship with someone else. Previously, this was more common for males who, in the conventional pattern, would often complain that while they had grown their wives had remained at home stagnating with routine chores and babytalk. There are some signs that modern women at mid-life are seeking comparable alternatives for themselves.

Whatever the potentials in the future, as sex-role conceptions and patterns of economic provision change, the present picture is one in which marriages by this stage, if they hold together at all, are often 'hollow'. Accumulated strains tend to be handled within the relationship by insulation of one spouse from the other. A façade of well-being is preserved in the family routines, both before the children and before outsiders. In Pineo's follow-up study, he found a consistent pattern of change over the twenty years of marriage, showing gradual decline in sexual relations, in companionship, in demonstrations of affection, and in the sharing of interests. A number of other studies report similar patterns to those of Pineo. Blood and Wolfe (1960) in Detroit and Feldman (1964) in Upstate New York report similar trends. Soddy and his colleagues (1967, p. 410), reviewing the situation across the spectrum of advanced nations and cultures suggest that: 'Unless better means of adjusting for mistakes in choice of marriage partner are available than is the rule at present, the potential stresses in society from discordant marriages are bound to rise.'

Another interpretation of this phenomenon of disenchantment attributes a greater element to the impact of adolescent problems and processes on the couple. Many marital couples manage to cover over difficulties in their relationship at earlier stages, but when confronted with some of the problems – rejection of parental values, testing of limits of control, experimentation with sexuality, drugs, variant life styles, and so on – latent problems within the individuals and in the couple relationship may come to the surface and become problematic.

Beric Wright, in a study of stresses experienced by senior British managers, provides some insight into this. He notes that the main causes of stresses amongst managers coming for treatment in the clinic concerned were reported to be domestic rather than occupational. Wright sees this as not so much because managers lack occupational stress as because they find themselves in a situation where they have learned to 'understand the work situation better than . . . the domestic one which tended to be taken for granted and given inadequate nourishment' (Wright, 1975, p.125). He notes (p. 129) that this is particularly marked at the point when the children are adolescents:

> Parents are suddenly confronted with a problem area which they do not understand and to which their lack of involvement is clearly a contributory factor. . . . In addition and without overt problems it is not fair (and mothers constantly complain about this) to leave all or most of the child management to mother. Father does no disciplining, comes home and 'spoils' and tends to leave mother out on a limb as rather a dragon.

Many researchers of marital relationships at this phase have emphasized the importance of the sexual aspect, either as an indicator of the state of the relationship or as a channel for influencing it. Masters and Johnson (1966), for example, approach sexuality in the latter way, prescribing variety in sexual foreplay and positions as a way of remedying the boredom and disenchantment characterizing many long-lasting marriages. Other writers, such as Toffler (1970), recommend serial marriages, while still others such as the O'Neills (1972) and James Ramey (1975) expound on the favourable potentials in 'opening' the marital relationship beyond the bounds allowed by conventional norms or life-long monogamy. Ramey's research suggests that for many people the cultivation of 'intimate networks' stimulates and re-enforces the central core of the marital relationship rather than undermining it. But a good deal of research has still to be done to provide specification of circumstances under which particular effects occur and to separate short-term from long-term effects.

Between the more permissive orientations and the more repressive ones which emphasize the naturalness and inevitability of diminution and loss of sexual interest in this phase of life, there is a range of prescriptions for counselling, therapy, and social interventions in different professional frameworks (Dominian, 1969). Differences in orientation are due not only to contrasting values of the various ethnic and religious sub-groups in our society, but to the interpretation of specific data. Different age-cohort experiences, for example, and structural situations give different meanings to specific data.

Divorce statistics offer an interesting case in point. Chester and his colleagues (1977) have documented how all European countries have seen not only a rise in overall frequency of divorce, but in the tendency for divorce rates to increase in long-lasting marriages. Previous studies emphasized the peaking of divorce frequencies early in the marriage, with continuous decline thereafter. Very brief marriages are really, Chester suggests, 'aborted' marriages. But there are other patterns as well. Some marriages ending in divorce have been due to cohort effects of marriages contracted during the Second World War. Allowing for this, Chester indicates a new trend toward rising divorce rates in longer-lasting marriages. The statistically modal age of the wife at divorce now tends to be about thirty – early in the phase we are considering. Taking into account many elements contributing to this average – such as the ages increase in late-life divorce rates, changing patterns of marriage and fertility, etc. – we are left still with the impression that duration of marriage is decreasing in power as a factor in marital stability.

Chester notes (p. 68), however, that the pattern of increase in overall proportions of long-term marriages now terminating in divorce could in principle reflect the manifestation of formerly covert difficulties in the relationship because of more liberal divorce legislation. Though his conceptual framework does not allow for the direct analysis of underlying family dynamics, he concludes that in his opinion 'all the evidence suggests that in recent times there has been a real rather than an illusory increase in break-up of marriage' (p. 68), and that there is a secondary peak of divorces in marriages that have lasted up to twenty years (p. 71), the first peak being in marriages lasting up to four years. Given the lag between *de facto* break-up of a marriage and divorce, it seems reasonable to conclude that some of the contributing factors to the second peak in rate of divorce relate to the problems that have been described in this chapter.

As a consequence of the spread of divorce frequencies into longer lasting marriages, many parents of adolescent children find themselves in a single-parenting situation. Maddox (1975, pp. 59–60) suggests that in addition to the other problems confronting single parents, new norms for handling sexuality are required, particularly in this phase:

> Should the sex life of the unmarried parent be concealed from the children? There is far less consensus on this issue than there is on divorce or premarital intercourse. A child psychiatrist in Manhattan told me that he is often confronted, especially at vacation times, by a parent and lover who do not know what to do. They don't want to be hypocrites or prudes and they don't want to sleep apart for the whole of a Christmas or summer holiday. On the other hand, they know that children do not like to be forcibly reminded of their parents' sexuality (think of your own parents), and they do not want to upset a child already unsettled by a divorce. His advice may not seem very helpful. 'I tell them, "Do what you feel is right",' he says.
>
> What feels right depends in part – but only in part – on the ages of the children and what they have been taught about sex. Obviously, if they are adolescent and have not been exhorted to remain virgin until marriage, the parent will probably decide that what is permitted the child should be permitted the parent. And if the child has been brought up to remain chaste, the parent will probably want at least to appear to do the same while unmarried. But the conflict is real and deep between those who feel that children should know that the parent is a human being who likes someone to share his bed, regularly or occasionally, and those who feel that bed symbolizes union and that a child can only handle the emotions aroused by the parent's sexuality if he thinks that some kind of permanence is involved.

Extramarital liaisons need not be catastrophic to any of the parties involved, neither need divorce. However, Jessie Bernard (1975b) notes that when the husband's 'daytime wife', his secretary, is used for sexual gratification as well as other forms of service the wife may become increasingly antagonized, but underneath it all they are *both* the victims.

The research literature which emphasizes the drop in marital satisfaction and the correlative increase in divorce in marriages which have survived to this stage is not countered by a corresponding literature on revitalization of marriages, other than the studies cited which tend to focus on sexual activity. There are some indications, through the world of commercial leisure provision and its advertising media, that there is a portion of the leisure and recreational market which is geared to parents' wish to regenerate the pleasurable aspects of their relationship at this stage. Advertisements stress the importance of getting away from the children, getting to know one another again in a romantic setting, letting others make the decisions for one's daily routines and concentrating on one another. Emphasis is not on a whole-family-all-together type of holiday every time (though this may remain for one of the holidays), but on briefer more frequent holidays, some of which are *without* the children, so that the parents can cultivate their relationship.

Issues in parenting

The adolescent children have grown into young people, developing their own firm and specific identities, restlessly searching for stimulation and new experience, testing the limits that their parents and others will tolerate and the consequences of taking various risks. We wish to examine some of the specific issues in parenting, some of the dynamics in the relationships between parents and children that arise in this situation.

Parenting with adolescent children is decidedly *not* the relief it may have been assumed to be in earlier times when children took on adult roles earlier and norms favouring expressiveness of various kinds were less in evidence. Though children may not require detailed, day by day physical care in the same way as in infancy, there may be heavy demands for parental involvement of another kind. Different facets of this have been dealt with in research and clinical discussions, and different emphases have been adopted. Some psychoanalysts, for example, have not only taken the adolescent's turmoil to be akin to a psychiatric disturbance (the cure for which is the passage of time) but the correlative disturbance of the parents to be an expectable accompaniment, often also needing treatment.

It is only recently that there have been concerted efforts to analyse the *interlocking* nature of parents' and adolescents' needs at this stage, and to understand them in terms of normal psychodynamic development. The nature of the interlocking preoccupations is complex and is likely to vary with a number of factors, including the sex of the parent and of the child. The efflorescence of sexuality in the adolescent has repercussions on parents who may be on the wane in this respect, and more or less uncomfortable about it. Similarly, the fluctuations between exaggerated independence and child-like dependence in the child may have particularly acute repercussions for parents who, at mid-life, may be seeking new patterns of independence or dependence for themselves in relation to their families. The adolescent's wish to 'fly', to find adventure and new experience may repercuss particularly poignantly on the psychic equilibrium of parents who feel trapped in the ruts of their social roles and responsibilities. There is more to it than this. The accelerated rate of social and technological change creates a special set of problems in the parent–adolescent child relationship which may threaten parental authority when it is already being precariously stretched. Parents may feel it particularly difficult to be self-confident in their encounters with their children who seem so mature, so competent, so sexually precocious and independent-minded, with values of their own which may be sharply at variance with them. The GAP Committee observe (1973, p. 26):

> The accelerated rate of change in our society has made the adjustments of teen-ager and parents even more difficult. . . . The generation gap, or generational differences, in cultural values, knowledge, and outlook tend to be magnified. If parents look only to their own experiences for guidance in understanding their teen-ager's needs, they are almost bound to encounter frustration, bewilderment, and disappointment. As a consequence of being exposed to the concerns of their adolescent children, many parents have undertaken an agonizing reappraisal of a number of their own attitudes and beliefs.

Parents who can open themselves to influence by their adolescent children in respect of some of their expectations may find the experience very rewarding. Those who do not find some of their adolescent's ideas compelling in themselves may still tolerate behaviour and attitudes from their children that conflict with parental expectations. This may be rationalized in terms of the child's individuality, or in terms of his or her identity formation. There are, however, many parents who find the expression of behaviour that conflicts with their expectations very distressing. It may be that they 'confuse the rebellion in manners for a rebellion in morals' (GAP, 1973, p. 43), or alternatively they may personalize their children's deprecation of parental standards and authority as attacks directed at them as individual parents and people.

A major element in parent–child relations in this phase is the requirement of parents to facilitate their adolescent children's launching. From the adolescent's point of view, it may be difficult to seek adequate guidance and direction without feeling it to indicate a lack of competence; to seek support and reassurance needed without feeling smothered; to seek one's own patterns, without feeling selfish.

Whilst many parents will themselves feel the need to do the best for their children in this critical period, there are often difficulties in doing so. Parents may feel themselves to be better placed than others to lead their children towards a valid assessment of options. But they may be rejected by their children as out of touch, and they may feel unable to influence their children and so may withdraw rather than risk conflict.

Some parents create difficulties by projecting their own particular ambitions onto their adolescent children. They may feel they have not accomplished their own goals and wish to help their children to make better use of their opportunities. Or they may feel that their accomplishments must be taken up and carried on by their children. Apart from the difficulties and pressures such projections create for the developing adolescent, parents themselves may be disappointed. The GAP Committee (1973, p. 43) observe:

> Around the issue of going to college, some parents expect the adolescent vicariously to accomplish for them or successfully to compete for them. Rebellion against such pressures again causes some parents to expect the worst. It is helpful if parents do not lose faith in themselves or in the child's potential. They should expect the adolescent to behave consistently with society, to develop a reasonable degree of independence, to make educational and vocational choices within his competence and his interests, and to develop a healthy social and sexual identification. Optimistic expectations are often an expression of the parent's trust in himself, whereas pessimistic expectations may be feelings of distrust of one's self projected onto the child.

Another issue which may develop in parenting with adolescents relates to difficulties in undoing the past. There is an increasing amount of information now available to document the idea that many problems of adolescents are exacerbated by their earlier experiences in the home—separations, lack of love, lack of harmony, lack of communication, lack of organized control and so on. It may be painful for parents to learn when their children are adolescents and begin showing signs of difficulties caused by events in childhood, particularly if they are events over which there is no possibility of any corrective action being taken.

The study of adolescent problems – for example, juvenile delinquency, promiscuity, or psychiatric disorder – suggest that there are two types of background factor; one that may be dealt with by administrative intervention (given appropriate resources) and one that is less amenable to such intervention. Examples of the first are family size, poverty, poor material conditions of housing and deficiencies in parenting behaviour. Examples of the second are mental deficiency, history of family criminality or psychiatric disorder.

The type of situation most frequently found among parents of problematic adolescents centres on psychosocial deficiencies: in love from mother and/or father, in patterns of family communications, in training and role modelling, and in maintaining a reasonably happy and harmonious emotional atmosphere in the family (Glueck and Glueck,

1950; Andry, 1960; McCord and Thurber, 1962; Shields, 1962; West and Farrington, 1973; Wilson, 1975). One difficulty that is apparent on a widespread basis is that it is precisely in families which are deficient in these ways that there may be the greatest difficulty in taking counter-measures to correct the undesirable effects of earlier experience.

Recently, attention has been focused on another dimension of parenting that may be particularly difficult to undo, even for 'ordinary' parents. This is the background to over-permissiveness and over-indulgence which Spock (1974) observes coming to fruition in rising cohorts of American adolescents. Maintaining a satisfactory balance of discipline with adolescent children emerging from this kind of early experience can be very difficult. The issues are complex and often paradoxical. The child who presses hard on his parents to allow him to do something he/she feels underneath he/she is not yet ready for is perhaps as relieved as the parents when the line is drawn and accepted. The parent who apologizes when he or she is 'wrong' may experience an increase in esteem from the child rather than, as he feared, a loss.

Many specific questions recur in parenting with adolescent children, and there is no clear-cut indication of the way these should be handled, or indeed, that they should always be handled in the same way. Sometimes there are clear divergences of parents' needs from children's needs. Where these cannot be reconciled, the resolution inevitably takes the interests of one party into account more than the interests of another. The felt needs of the adolescent need not always be the decisive element, even where the child's best interests are of paramount value.

The specific questions that recur in the caring experience may be focused quite differently for the parents and the adolescents. From our previous studies of parent–adolescent relations (Rapoport, 1975), the following consensus seems to prevail at present.

Setting limits is a key concern to parents. From their viewpoint, recurrent questions include: How permissive to be? In what way? Should there be phases of relaxation of limits? Are the different kinds of limits for hours? money? friends? use of stimulants? sex? etc. Where should one be adamant; where should one relax? From the adolescent's perspective, the focal questions regarding limits may be different. How far to press the boundaries set by parents? How daring to be about doing things *probably* disapproved of? What to battle over and what to bend with?

Confrontations over limits are perhaps the most frequent and problematic in the lives of parents of adolescent children. For the parent: how late to allow the young person to come in? What behaviour is tolerable in 'cheeking' the parent? What amount of travel, where and

with whom is allowable on holidays? What degree of informality or
peculiarity of dress to allow, and so on. The adolescent may be bigger,
stronger, better-educated and even in some instances high-earning and
more competent occupationally than the parent. Yet, in this phase when
(s)he is still living at home (s)he is under parental authority. Whether
justifiably or not, parents feel that their judgment ought to be applied
for the protection of the child in many situations where the child
considers that he or she knows better.

Characteristically, when disagreements are intense the tendency is
toward conflict or withdrawal. Overt conflict generally means a family
row. The consequences of a row can be disastrous or the air may be
cleared and a new basis of relationships in the family evolved. Byng-Hall
(1975) describes how a characteristic family row over issues of social
control with an adolescent child may be managed constructively or
become enmeshed in a recurrent and self-defeating pattern of neurotic
interaction.

The limits issue may play itself out over a number of different topics:
drugs, sex, friends, hours kept, participation in social movements or
activities. In the USA, and perhaps increasingly in Europe as well, the
explosive quality of the confrontation, when it occurs, is increased
through the circumstances of social mobility. Families move residence
a great deal more than they used to and this may pose special difficulties
for the young people. They may have difficulty in making the adjustments necessary for a new school curriculum (this is more pronounced,
obviously, for the less academic-minded); they may have problems
about forming new friendships (this is more pronounced to the extent
that they are lacking in social attractiveness, or in social skills including
sport and other interests). Above all, there may be difficulties associated
with achieving and sustaining a good interactive relationship with their
parents. The latter may at this point be preoccupied with their own
problems of adjustment—to new jobs, homes and social circumstances.
Young people often, under these conditions, resort to extreme measures,
including drugs, running away from home, associating with groups that
seek excitement in delinquent ways (Seidenberg, 1973).

In Britain there is also a good deal of tension over the use of motor-
bikes, the choice of friends, the hours of returning home. Cyril Smith
(1968, p. 70) describes the issues of social control which parents face,
and notes:

> Parents show an intense interest in their children's friends, especially
> of their daughter's boy friends. Chaperonage may have largely
> disappeared but parents still have their say about when their children
> are allowed out for courting and where. Such control is naturally
> greater with pubescent children than it is with young adults, and a

recent survey of youth in a small Lancashire town showed that the majority of fourteen year old girls are made to stay in by their parents for some nights of the week, and most nights they are expected to be home before ten.

Fogelman (1976, p. 36), in a report of the National Children's Bureau follow-up of their 1958 cohort of children, now aged sixteen, indicates that the most frequent sources of disagreement between parents and children at this phase are 'Dress or hairstyle' ('Sometimes or often', 46 per cent) and 'Time of coming in at night or going to bed' (34 per cent). The latter in particular, is associated with setting limits to behaviour that parents feel puts their children at risk.

Lidz and other psychiatrists have noted that the issues of setting limits is very widely experienced but the form it takes varies. The question of how far parents should trust their children is an excruciatingly difficult one at this phase, because they feel acutely aware of the risks to which their children often seem oblivious: 'Their trust in the child they have raised and in their own capacities to raise a child undergoes its most severe test' (Lidz, 1968, p. 329). Lidz (p. 328) observes that the adolescent may press the limits very hard in other ways as well:

> Typically, the youth begins to search out flaws in his parents. The process may start with a basic disillusionment in learning about their sexual life—their hypocrisy in practising what they have forbidden—but he seeks shortcomings that he can attack openly and resent rationally. The criticism of the parents' behaviour, and even more the attacks on their character constitute a serious blow to the parents' authority and self-esteem.

They may also *reject their parents*. This may be specially likely if they become involved in social mobility, as Jackson and Marsden (1962) noted in their study of education and social class. Sometimes there is a vicious cycle of rejection and counter-rejection in which the young person is ejected from the household, or takes himself off, drifting into urban areas in search of jobs.

Many rebellious adolescents who remain in the family 'suss out' their parents, searching with the unerring instinct of one who knows intimately the points of particular vulnerability. The channels and form through which this process occurs varies with the sub-culture and environmental setting. An action that may suffice in a highly norm-bound goldfish bowl may pass quite unnoticed in a metropolitan setting. However, hitting at aspects of the parents' own identity is widespread and may make for a hurtful experience for the parents. If the father is a policeman, for example, the rebellious son wields a specially potent weapon when he flirts with delinquent peer groups, because of the vulnerability of his father in the community. Young girls whose consciousness may have been aroused by the ideals of the women's movement may attack their fathers for male chauvinism (and their mothers for spineless acquiescence). The daughter of a clergyman who becomes pregnant or contracts venereal disease would be another case in point. Children of eminently reasonable and permissive, trusting parents have often to press the limits particularly vigorously to get a rise out of their parents. By then it may be too late to intervene effectively as many a shocked parent from a busy professional family has learned to his distress when the child has been picked up by the police, or is in a ward for drug addicts.

The GAP Committee (1973, pp. 51–2) describe the process whereby rejection of parents, and parents' values, may serve to let the adolescent grow:

> Often his rebellion is against what he *thought* was taught him, not what he actually was taught. Sometimes he rebels because what he has been taught is different from what is practised. In general, he is basically rejecting not a mature religious belief, but his own childhood conceptions. Many years may pass before he realizes that his rebellion was not so much against parents, church, or culture as against his own immaturity. However, few things are so upsetting to parents as an adolescent, struggling with emancipation, who attacks their treasured value system. It may shake the parents' security and cause the child to be experienced as obnoxious.

They (GAP, 1973, pp. 52–3) explain in detail the process of parental rejection and personal development as it may work via the channel of *religion* in families where that channel is meaningful:

> Particularly difficult for parents to weather with a sense of perspective is the adolescent stage of atheism. . . . Usually this involves the young person's relationship to his father and to the being he calls God. In the small child the religious experience is closely bound up with his experiences with his parents. God is thought of in essentially the same way as the father. . . . If development proceeds normally, the young person learns to separate the two; parents are seen as less divine and more human, and God becomes less identified with the father. This separation is one of the tasks of adolescence; in the process the adolescent may reject God or father or both. This is a normal phase and usually transient. Even when it is of relatively short duration it is trying and perplexing to the parents. As the child works through his rebellion and gains a firmer idea of his own identity, he arrives at a new relationship with both God and father.

In contemporary secular society, the reaction of the adolescent may be against parental agnosticism and in favour of a fundamentalist religion, perhaps one remote from anything the parent might have espoused.

Derek Miller (1974, p. 98) observes that late adolescents in particular often reject parental beliefs and attitudes if they feel these have been imposed for hypocritical reasons.

Clinical, anecdotal and qualitative accounts of confrontations between adolescents and their parents provide a great deal of material documenting the difficulties of this period. The turbulence, conflict, discord and unhappiness that can come if confrontations are not well handled are legion. Adolescents accuse their parents of being authoritarian, antiquated, chauvinistic, hypocritical or stupid, and the result may be unhappy for both – however 'functional' a breakaway element in the relationship may be at this point. Some degree of tension is important for both young person and parent to 'distance' themselves from their earlier modes of relationship – appropriate between parents and younger children. But if this exceeds the optimal point, the consequences may embitter the lives of each party, as well as the relationship.

One psychiatrist, writing about a positive outcome to a confrontation over one of the most difficult issues in contemporary American adolescent–parent relationships – drug use – describes her own experience, both professional and as a mother. In the introduction she writes as a parent to other parents:

Parents like you and me are frequently bewildered by the changing world. Our children are facing different problems than we did, in a world with a seeming breakdown of morals and values, without the familiar guideposts that helped us through our own adolescent years (Densen-Gerber and Bader, 1972, p. 12).

Her daughter, Trissa Austin Bader, writes in response to the mother's question about what parents should know about drugs:

Two different things. Young people my age need to know one thing, parents another. Parents need to know how to keep their children from taking drugs. First, they should pay attention to them as people instead of worrying about little things – for example, whether their little girl is in a white dress which might become spotted . . . [and] you'd have to give the facts of what drugs can do; such as, they will kill you eventually. Perhaps not kill you, but maybe cause you to jump off a bridge and be crippled for the rest of your life. . . . It's not enough to just hear parents say, 'Oh, no, they're terrible, don't get mixed up with them, and that's that.' Children want to know why (Densen-Gerber and Bader, 1972, pp. 20–1).

The mother adds, from her experience, that provision of information is not enough. Limits have to be set, and policies developed.

In general, research from a number of fields has re-enforced the idea that a satisfactory outcome to parent–adolescent confrontations is likely to emerge only through a satisfactory blending of the twin elements of *love* and *discipline* (Glueck and Glueck, 1950; West, 1967; Andry, 1962). But this is partly a matter of feeling and expression, partly a matter of technique: *how* to communicate?

There is often a feeling on both sides of the parent–child relationship at this phase of an impasse in *communications*. Key questions from the parents' viewpoint may include: How much to probe into the children's private lives? How much to discuss one's own personal problems with them? How to make one's own viewpoints understood without simply becoming dogmatic, which may lead to a foreclosure of communications? From the adolescent's viewpoint, the pressing question may be: How much to tell parents about what actually goes on (especially when it may be near or over the limits set)?

Another issue centres on the question of *participation*. Parental concerns may include: How much to allow children's participation in family decision-making? How much to expect their participation in the family chores? What to do together; what separately? The adolescents' questions may be: How much to participate? Do I have to? Will it be boring? What will I get out of it? What would I otherwise be doing? Will I miss anything? Will I be letting anyone down if I don't participate?

Another set of questions recur for parents around the issue of organizing the activities of, or *programming* their adolescents. How much to structure the child's activities? How much guidance to offer without being asked? When? How? From their children's perspective, the questions are: How to define and respond to parental organizing efforts: Is it controlling? fussing? protecting? caring? Is it belittling or insulting if a parent intervenes or is helpful? Does acceptance imply incompetence?

Parents of adolescents are often concerned about appropriate *distancing*. When to keep 'hands off'? How to stay clear without implying you do not care? Adolescents are often concerned to press for distance. How and when to opt out of family things? How to distinguish between 'their' (parental) concerns and 'my' concerns without too much guilt or anger? Once having opted for distance, is it a sign of weakness to want to come back into the fold? This is an era in which both parents' and adolescents' felt needs oscillate, and divergence and disappointment is likely. At the same time, the need to recuperate from strains or disappointments, to rehearse for new sallies into the world outside and to regroup one's resources is acknowledged to be an important element in the family enabling process (Rapoport *et al.*, 1975).

Throughout the experience of parenting with adolescents, the two sets of lifelines intersect and reverberate most often in relation to *values*. We noted above the dynamics that often occur through the channel of religious values. Another major channel in which parents' values are tested in caring for adolescents is *sexuality*. This is an area in which parents often feel especially confused about their responsibilities in relation to their children. Whilst the wider society to which the adolescent is becoming orientated may focus attention on genital sexuality, parents may feel more comfortable to play this down. It is not only because contemporary parents were reared in an earlier era of more repressive sexual morality, or even because they feel their own sexuality to be on the wane and are therefore made envious and uncomfortable in the face of their children's. It is partly because contemporary youngsters link sexuality to the development of the person and of the capacity for interpersonal relationships in a way that is new and difficult for many parents to accept. It is at this phase of parenting that the most difficult dilemmas may arise in parenting, to reconcile general abstract values with specific values as parents in particular situations.

The GAP Committee's perspective on the role of the parent in relation to general life values, which we see as the core of the experience of parenting with adolescents, is well-rounded and compatible with our orientation. We quote their view at length (GAP, 1973, p. 63).

In the area of values, it is necessary for the parents to establish a working set of values for themselves – not 'super-modern' or 'loose-minded' but open-minded. Parents need not accept valuelessness as a way of life. They have a right and duty to advocate particular values and expectations; they have the right to attempt to pass these values on to their children. However, they must respect the child's right to go through a phase of living in which he contradicts parental or societal values or establishes different values. This is not a negative reflection upon parents. It is in the nature of the child–parent relationship and at times may reflect positively upon the parents' rearing of the child.

Communication, which is a positive value, can go a long way, but there may come a point when communication has to come to an end and action take place.

The problem of the relationship between actions and values often becomes acute, both for parents and their adolescent children at this stage. Parents may recognize that their earlier failures to act may be interpreted by their children to mean that they have not cared; and a new form of struggle may occur to reassert parental influence against forces in their children's lives which have gained in strength. The children are likely to have involved themselves in groups and activities which bolster specific values, which may or may not be compatible with their parents.

Condry and Siman (1974) in a study of forty-one adolescent peer groups in New York, distinguish three different types of activities, each reflecting a set of values; *socially constructive activities* (e.g. doing useful work for the community); *neutral activities* (e.g. listening to records); and *anti-social activities* (e.g. doing something illegal). They also obtained information on the young people's perceptions of their parental values in relation to these activities, and found that the gap increased in the order of divergence from socially valued activities. The researchers concluded, in the face of the fact that so many young people were participating in these sub-groups that the power of the peer-group influences were greater at this stage than the parents.

Bronfenbrenner, noting that the increase in delinquent activity in the past decade has been very steep among people in this age group, searches for factors in the social environment which alienate young people from socially valued activities, usually mediated by their parents. Citing the White House Conference on Children (1970), and particularly the report of the committee under his chairmanship, Bronfenbrenner (1974, pp. 161–2) makes the following summary of elements in the contemporary situation which counteract any parental effort to be influential with their children:

> In today's world parents find themselves at the mercy of a society which imposes pressures and priorities that allow neither time nor place for meaningful activities and relations between children and adults, which downgrade the role of parents and the functions of parenthood, and which prevent the parent from doing things he wants to do as a guide, friend and companion to his children. . . .
>
> In our modern way of life, children are deprived not only of parents but of people in general. A host of factors conspires to isolate children from the rest of society. The fragmentation of the extended family, the separation of residential and business areas, the disappearance of neighbourhood, zoning ordinances, occupational mobility, child labor laws, the abolishment of the apprentice system, consolidated schools, television, separate patterns of social life for different age groups, the working mother, the delegation of child care to specialists – all these manifestations of progress operate to decrease opportunity and incentive for meaningful contact between children and persons older, or younger, than themselves. . . .
>
> *We are experiencing a breakdown in the process of making human beings human.* By isolating our children from the rest of society, we abandon them to a world devoid of adults and ruled by the destructive

impulses and compelling pressures both of the age-segregated peer group and the aggressive and exploitive television screen, we leave our children bereft of standards and support and our own lives impoverished and corrupted.

This reversal of priorities, which amounts to a betrayal of our children, underlies the growing disillusionment and alienation among young people in all segments of American society. Those who grew up in settings where children and families still counted are able to react to their frustration in positive ways – through constructive protest, participation, and public service. Those who come from circumstances in which the family could not function, be it in slum or suburb, can only strike out against an environment they have experienced as indifferent, callous, cruel, and unresponsive. This report does not condone the destruction and violence manifested by young people in widely disparate sections of our society; it merely points to the roots of a process which, if not reversed . . . can have only one result: the far more rapid and pervasive growth of alienation, apathy, drugs, delinquency, and violence among the young, and not so young, in all segments of our national life. We face the prospect of a society which resents its own children and fears its youth. . . . What is needed is a change in our patterns of living which will once again bring people back into the lives of children and children back into the lives of people.

While many of these 'roots of alienation' apply to the whole range of parenting phases, they have a particular relevance to parenting with adolescent children, as the problems come to a head at this point and parents feel particularly powerless. Many express the feeling that they have 'given up' on their children by this time, and may rely on the social services or the police to control their adolescents who are beyond their capacity. The literature increasingly indicates parental concern about the management of adolescent reactions of various kinds – from withdrawal to overt rebelliousness. This is a point at which professional supports are needed but are likely to have to take a variety of unorthodox forms to reach young people who have got into trouble (Tyler, 1976). There is relatively little information about how parents handle their problems at this stage. There are suggestions that siblings may play an important part as intermediaries (Rapoport, 1975), and there are indications that often the parents themselves experience a crisis at this point.

Changing models: today's parents, today's adolescents, tomorrow's parents

The differing value systems of parents and their adolescent children pervades parent–child relations in this phase. A UNESCO-sponsored study of reciprocal images between parents and children in the family (Mahler, 1973) found that education drives a wedge between parents and their children (particularly in the 'developing' countries where parents are much more tradition-minded). But in all fast-changing societies, including 'developed' ones, the experiences of respective generations vary, and give rise to differences in prevailing values. Thus, for example, the present cohort of adolescent girls are likely to have many experiences that were unavailable to their mothers, as their mothers' experiences differed from their grandmothers'. These include the growth of the feminist movement, the public discussion of contraception and abortion, and public challenges to sexism in schools and in the workplace. These events provide social forces that affect the young (particularly girls) differently from their parents.

Models of acceptable social roles are altering quite rapidly and, on the whole, adolescents have many more family life options open to them than did their parents. Whereas conventional parents are more likely to be concerned with the family background and occupational prospects of the man their daughter wishes to marry, the young girl whose consciousness has been raised is more likely to be concerned with whether he is a relatively egalitarian-minded companion and shares personal interests. There are many young people at least as conventional-minded as their parents, and the adoption of modern attitudes and aspirations by the young does not necessarily put them into conflict with their parents. However, new styles of life, and new concerns for future family and work interaction, do mean that parents have to cope with changing models of right and wrong.

In families in which daughters aspire to an occupational career *and* marriage, the confrontations that parents find themselves involved in are more likely to have positive outcomes if they understand social trends and accept a value orientation which may allow for new patterns given appropriate supports. Many young couples wish to live together without getting married; others marry while both continue their education or while one supports the other. They may defer or even reject the idea of having children. This may be a source of considerable dismay to conventional parents who dream not only of church weddings but of grandchildren and a way of life in which they see their children 'settled' in a manner they understand.

Parents are faced with changing sex roles in society and so themselves go through changes in expectations of their sons and daughters. Until fairly recently, the way adolescent girls and boys channelled their identity concerns tended to be different and to result in different behaviour patterns. While many differences still exist – partly as a result of earlier and current socialization experiences and partly as a result of channels open to them – in many ways the *adolescent girls' and boys' patterns are becoming more similar.* For instance, there have been considerable changes in female sex mores in the past fifteen years or so; with increasing sex equality for males and females and the widespread use of effective contraceptives, 'the development of the female sex drive may become more and more similar to that of the male' (Chilman, 1968, p. 302). Divergence in interest patterns may also be decreasing. Strong (1931) described adolescent young men's (15–25) interests as characterized by multiple and shifting interests, enjoyment of risk-taking and active sports, gregariousness and restlessness. This research, undertaken over forty years ago, also reported that at age fifteen, the measured interests of boys and girls was further apart at that stage than at any other time during the life span; it also indicated the striking dissimilarity between the interests of fifteen-year-old boys and middle-aged women; such situations have implications for parent–adolescent relationships as well as general family dynamics within which they take place at mid-stage.

These interest patterns may well have altered with increasingly shared activities of male and female groups, and with the decreasing segregation of behaviour and options. Fewer and fewer females at adolescence, for instance, are likely to consider marriage and motherhood their exclusive option. Various patterns of combination are likely to be found, and there is likely to be an increase in non-marriage as a primary choice (rather than through force of circumstances, as in the cohort of women immediately after the Second World War). Jessie Bernard (1975a, p. 70) quotes the following excerpt from *Monthly Vital Statistics Report* in the USA (23 October 1974, p. 1):

During the 12 months ending with August 1974, 2,233,000 marriages were reported. This was 68,000 fewer than the number for the 12 months ending with August 1973, a 3·0 percent decline. The marriage rate for that period was 10·6 per thousand population, a decline of 3·6 percent. Cumulative data for the first 8 months of 1974 show a 2·9 percent decline in the number of marriages and a 3·6 percent decline in the marriage rate from the comparable figures for 1973.

Glick and Norton (1973) also suggest that demographic trends show a lessening of enthusiasm for marriage among women. More young women are seeking fulfilment in channels other than child-bearing and -rearing. In this way, the disjunction between early patterns of parent–child relations (in which the child's needs are paramount) and the expectations that when a girl child becomes an adult she will suddenly give this up and concentrate on her husband's and children's needs, are decreasing.

Jessie Bernard describes the current intergenerational issues (Bernard, 1975a, pp. 70ff). Previously the literature concentrated on the problems stimulated by adolescent boys. During the lifetime of the present generation of adolescents, new life styles have been adopted by mothers as well as the children. If the mothers are between 35-54, over half were in the labour force in 1972 in the USA. They may be more feminist in value orientation than their daughters. They may have cried as well as laughed when their young daughters had said they wanted babies of their own to play with. They are the first young women to be exposed to the feminist movement, to the rebellion against motherhood as it has been recently known, and to the idealization of parenthood more generally; they are attuned to a concept of motherhood which no longer takes up the whole of a woman's lifespace. Bernard (1975a, p. 72) has described how the mother's own socialization for motherhood was counter-productive in their view – and how the modern mother may seek to counteract this culturally pervasive force in which 'the young woman in marriage moved from one dependency to another, that of the parental family to that of her husband'.

This dependency model is felt increasingly to be inadequate for socializing young women for the world they inhabit today, whether as mothers (which also requires strength, cf. Newton, 1955) or as workers.

Another element in the contemporary situation centres on contraception. As a consequence of modern contraception a girl can defend herself against irresponsible motherhood without remaining a virgin. In addition, as Bernard points out, the girl may engage her young men in the responsibility for parenthood more actively. Exactly how this will work out is still unclear. But socialization for a new kind of adolescent – young man and young woman – in a new kind of world for a new kind of parenthood 'calls for a thoughtful new look'.

It also seems likely that the quality and content of parent–adolescent relationships will alter with these changes. It may be that after a transitional period it will be easier to incorporate a fully sexual being, who is also one's child, in the family. Some contemporary problems may thus decrease while others increase (Rapoport and Oakley, 1975).

The point about all this, for the parent–child relations at this phase of the family cycle, is that changes in the socialization of the adolescent generation and changes in the expectations of mothers and fathers in parenting are likely to affect the quality of all these relationships. What is striking about the literature is the lack of research on the parent–child relationship during this period. As Chilman points out, the bulk of research has been on the younger years and even it has great deficiencies, particularly on father–child relations.

Furthermore, Hoffman (1974) points out that the research on the effects of mothers working is mainly concerned with children under three. The little that does exist about adolescents and their parents, is rather superficial and does little to inform us about the quality of the experience of parents in relation to their adolescent children.

On changes in socialization that are being observed, we need to know more about relevant adult intentions and experiences. Through an analysis of these processes, we may begin to consider strategies which might facilitate specific experiences (Brim and Wheeler, 1966).

To end this chapter we reiterate the requirement for research on parent–adolescent relations and summarize some speculations about parent–child relations – that have been made for this period. The most useful publications available on this topic at present are those by Chilman (1968), the GAP report on the *Joys and Sorrows of Parenthood* (1973) and Jessie Bernard's papers in *Women, Wives, Mothers: Values and Options* (1975b).

In general, these deal more focally with mother–daughter relations than the other possibilities. The mother–daughter relationship is affected by the biological changes that take place in both generations about the same time. As the mother's reproductive capacity wanes, her daughter's reaches a peak; both mother and daughter are likely to be subject to mood swings and other psychosomatic phenomena related to hormonal and other changes at this phase of life. The situation has built-in conflicts and potential comforts. The ties between mother and daughter (which may or may not be stronger than those, say, between father and daughter) lead to difficulties and have potential strengths. The stronger the bond, the more difficult for the adolescent child to break away; on the other hand, perhaps there is potential in such a situation for a more satisfactory return at a different level after the break-away. To maintain a positive relationship at this stage seems to involve tight-rope walking: as Chilman puts it, both mother and daughter want to be understood by each other – but not too much. To really understand what goes on, new research must concentrate on experimental processes.

The turbulent processes that occur between mothers and daughters probably have an analogy in father–son relationships. Chilman (1968, pp. 306–7) feels that this

> may be less intensely relational and sex-specific because the father–son identification is not likely to be so strong and personal in these days when fathers are out of the home so much of the time. Then, too, changes in the reproductive cycle are not so dramatic for males nor is a man's sense of sexual adequacy so closely tied to physical appearance, as it is in the case of a woman's. On the other hand, adequate virility is generally a source of extreme concern for father and son alike, and it is apt to be spread over a broader range of roles. Thus, both father and son, at mid-stage of family development,

are likely to be caught up in similar anxieties over many areas, such as: physical strength and agility, economic adequacy and, of course, desirability and prowess with women, both within and outside the family circle.

The son, in his ascendancy to all these spheres of manhood, has not yet reached the plateau of the 'years of culmination' and the father has many intimations that he has begun a gradual descent to increasingly waning powers. Thus, father and son, like mother and daughter, are apt to find themselves coming full circle, simultaneously, to a similar, but different point in human development.

Mother–son and father–daughter relations are even less discussed in the literature, though we do know that close ties with mothers are found amongst sons as well as daughters (Hagestad and Fagan, 1974; Rapoport and Rapoport, 1971). We know from our own field studies, both among dual-career families and in families of adolescents, that mothers who feel they have no way of influencing their husbands – for example, to take a more active part in domestic life – feel they can, at least, influence their sons. We still have to rethink what the important dimensions are for looking at parent–child relationships at adolescence. With change in sex roles, in which men may spend more time at home and women more time out of the home, theories about identification processes between children and their same-sex parents may require revision. New patterns should contribute to improved theories.

Another aspect of changes in sex roles, is that far more of the socialization of children may be shared with people not in the immediate family. This too will alter not only identification processes of the young, but the needs of their parents at this phase, and the potentials available, if these new relationships are seen as alliances, for avoidance of some of the characteristic strains on the marital relationship. It may become less necessary than in the past to await the children's leaving home to create or discover the potential for an 'upswing' in marital satisfaction (Troll, 1975, pp. 88–9).

8

Parenting with adult children and grandparenting

The final parental phase we distinguish is also long and variegated. For most parents it starts before occupational retirement and evolves for the rest of their lives. For some the phase begins when they are only about forty; others may be well into their sixties or perhaps even older. What distinguishes the phase in terms of parenting is that the children are adult and the *active* element of the parenting role recedes. In other words the physical energy and time spent on daily parenting activities decreases, and may stop altogether. Perhaps for this reason numerous social scientists have referred to the phase as 'post-parental'. We prefer not to use this term, because it implies that parenting has no further place in the lives of the individuals. Although the nature of parenting and the issues facing parents differ in this phase from those in earlier phases, and although parents' involvements with their children may lessen in intensity at some stage during this long phase, most parents nevertheless remain involved in some way with their children and/or their grandchildren throughout these years. In many cases the involvement may be a vital one for either or both parties. We prefer, therefore, to speak of 'parenting with adult children' as this allows for some of the variation in content and quality of parent–child relations that may in fact exist. Additionally, 'grandparenting' can become a part of this phase of life with elements of recapitulation, and elements of new experience for the parents in the later years of their lives.

The actual experience of parenting with adult children has received very little systematic study, perhaps because of the relative lack of first-order problems it has presented. Ageing has largely been seen as a gradual process of decline, and old people are expected, in our youth-oriented society, to fade away as unobtrusively as possible. It has long been accepted that old age pensions should provide a basis for material survival in this phase, independently of private or familial supports, and in all advanced industrial societies, even those lacking a national health service (as in the USA) the medical care of the elderly is seen as a societal responsibility. Private, familial involvement has been an optional way of providing extra amenities for those who can afford it, either in the family home or in specialized care facilities. But except where there are several problems of deprivation, isolation, or disability, people in this age group have attracted little attention in research.

Our focus here, as in other chapters, is on the issues that relate to people as parents. There is relatively little in the literature on the later stages of the phase that has direct relevance to this purpose.

As a result of these deficiencies, the portrait that emerges from the literature is one of people declining physiologically, cognitively and psychologically. This gives rise to a stereotype described as 'reversed role', where aged parents become dependent on their adult children and then in the end, withdraw into their nostalgic fantasies and eventually to death, completing a psychobiological cycle of life. These are not the characteristics of this phase that we emphasize. To the extent that this decline and withdrawal may be conspicuous for people in this long and varied phase, it is mainly for a brief period toward the end, when the person is in the seventies to eighties. Also there is growing evidence that even for the older people in the phase this portrait does not adequately take into account the positive potentials for life satisfaction in the later years of parenting, and, whether satisfying or not, the continuing involvement of many parents in the concerns and interests of their children and grandchildren.

The point which one defines as the beginning of children's adulthood, and therefore of this phase of parenting with adult children, is variable, as are most of the other boundaries we have identified. The 'independence' of children is a critical element, but this is a complex of characteristics (legal, demographic, emotional, social, geographical) which develop variously. In some families children may leave school, live at home for several years and then move out permanently; in others there may be an extended period of higher education using the home as a base for intermittent residence. Sometimes only marriage marks the final 'launching'; and in some situations an adult child or a married couple continues to live with their parents for a period of years, perhaps even with *their* children.

The feeling of both parents and children that the latter are 'launched' provides a turning point in the experience of most parents who may then feel less directly responsible for their children. This may occur when the child is legally adult, or when the child leaves school or home, or marries. The actual point is variable, and the experience fluid rather than ritually marked and culturally prescribed. The GAP Committee (1973, p. 117) convey this quality:

In most cases, the active phase of parenthood does not end with a big bang, a final flash. It fades slowly, like the dimming of the houselights in a theater. Whether that dimming proceeds to total darkness or the curtain lifts on a new and brighter scene depends on how husband and wife have weathered the storms of parenthood, how they have matured, and how they take up their new roles.

Besides the term 'post-parental', there are other terms and concepts that have relevance for parental experience in this period of parenting with adult children. One is 'middle generation'. In a strictly structural sense, this refers to an intermediate generation between an older and a younger generation (e.g. Troll, 1975; Chilman, 1968; Hill *et al.*, 1970). 'Keystone generation' has also been used to make a similar reference (e.g. Fogarty, 1975). Middle generation in the sense just defined, is not equated with 'middle age'. In fact, people in the middle generation of a three- and maybe four-generational web are often middle-aged in life span terms. But parenting with adult children can commence before middle age. And it is generic to the length and nature of the later parenting phase that parents will enter and pass through a number of stages, from younger to older age, as they live through the phase. The implication for individuals' own capacities, interests and activities, and for their part in parent–child relations as they move through the ages and stages of the later parenting phase can vary greatly. As he or she proceeds through this phase, each individual's own position in the family and generational cluster will vary enormously.

The average age at which people enter the later parenting phase has been falling, whilst average life spans have increased, so it does not make sense to equate it mechanically with middle age. The extra years of contemporary life expectancy extend into the later parenting phase, enlarging the elastic concept of middle age even more than hitherto,

Table 12 *Life cycle of women born 1880–9 and 1930–9 in the USA*

Stage of Family	Median age, 1880–9	Median age, 1930–9
First marriage	21·6	19·9
Birth of first child	22·9	21·5
Birth of last child	32·9	30–31
First marriage/last child	56·2	51·5–52·5
Death of spouse	57	64·4

and making it still less meaningful. The statistics published by Glick and Parke (1965) indicate the increased span for active life (of women) for parenting with adult children (see Table 12). This should not be taken to imply that active parenting for women inevitably ceases with widowhood. Whilst this is perhaps still true for some women today, there is now evidence suggesting that widowhood can be a liberating transition for women, after which an efflorescence of new activity may follow, including new phases of parenting or stepparenting (Maas and Kuypers, 1974; Troll, 1971). For men, too, new parenting experiences remain a possibility until the end of their lives.

The number and proportion of people in this long phase of life have been increasing. In the United Kingdom the proportion of the population aged 65 + rose from 5·4 per cent in 1911 to 13·2 per cent in 1971 (Annual Abstract of Statistics, 1974). In 1972 there were 11,575,000 people in the UK between age forty-five and the conventional age for retirement – 21 per cent of the whole population, and 35 per cent of the population between school-leaving age and retirement. The proportion is expected to fall to 18 per cent in 1991 and rise again to 21 per cent of the total population in 2011 (Fogarty, 1975, p. 14). Neugarten (1975) observes a similar shift in the make-up of American society: the proportion of total population of the 65 + group is around 10 per cent, and predicted to remain at 10–12 per cent in the next two or three decades. She suggests that at this point (though she stresses there is nothing magical about age 65 as a break point) one may begin to speak of an 'ageing society'.

The period involved is indeed long and complex. Michael Fogarty's (1975) book on 'mature middle age' is called *Forty to Sixty*. The age group of Maas and Kuypers's (1974) Californian sample is from sixty to seventy-five years of age, and most of these, though ageing, are not yet what are stereotypically seen as 'old'. The elderly and old are, however labelled, involved in the later parenting phase over a potentially very long period. They are not, however, the largest proportion of people in the phase, despite the impression given in writings which highlight the decline of the later parental years. In addition to the physiological, cognitive and psychological declines that have been so heavily emphasized, this image is reinforced by the stereotype of 'role-reversal' in old age, whereby aged parents become dependent on their adult children.

But, if one takes a cross-cultural perspective on ageing, it is clear that the position of ageing people, in terms of parental and other spheres of authority, is not universally regarded as a decline and in many pre-industrial societies emphasis has been placed on the positive assets of age in wisdom, experience, detached perspective. In our society, what Doris and David Jonas (1973) have described as the 'cult of youth' has distorted the image of the ageing and impaired the 'movement toward meeting their needs and requirements'.

The reasons that this situation has arisen are clear enough. There have been rapid changes in the sheer amount of knowledge and information available, and in the relevance of trained skills, many of which become obsolescent under the impact of technological changes. Also, many of the material conditions of life which in the past kept younger people dependent on their elders – e.g. in relation to the inheritance of land and other property – no longer have the same relevance. Young people can, with appropriate education and training, often earn more than their elders shortly after leaving school. Furthermore, with secularization and the devaluation of the wisdom that is linked to tradition, older people are less revered than previously.

These considerations are relevant to people in the later parenting phase at the present time. Their prior experiences are very different from those of their children and grandchildren. People now in their sixties and seventies experienced events such as two major world wars and a depression which their grandchildren probably cannot comprehend. The aftermath of these experiences and the new conditions in which their younger children have grown up may have widened the experiential gap. Changing sex-ratios following the wars, different moral codes in relation to sexuality, different norms for marriage and child-rearing, different conceptions of sex-roles and equalization of educational and occupational opportunities for men and women have created new conditions of life which affect parent–adult child–grandchildren relationships.

This cohort effect is especially relevant to understanding the contemporary needs of those in the later parenting phase, and considering what are likely to be the common and different needs of rising cohorts. Troll (1975) treats this phenomenon especially well.

Fogarty (1975, p. 11) also makes this point from the perspective of his focus on *today's* mature middle-aged:

> There is a sense in which the middle-aged as we know them today present a one-off problem. People who are now fifty or over grew up in a very different world from those now aged twenty or twenty-five, and missed a number of experiences and opportunities to learn which today's younger people seem likely to turn to good account when in due course they become middle-aged themselves.
>
> Individual younger and older people may have had very similar experiences. Typically, however, today's older people had less of an opportunity to acquire a basis for further learning through school or further education, less experience of flexibility in careers and social or family relations, and less help in learning to think about themselves and others as people with individual needs, and to express and explore these needs explicitly. If they had had these things they

would have been better able to manage the transitions of their own careers and life cycle in a rapidly changing world. Comments from informants with experience in many fields – in personnel work, in marriage counselling, in voluntary social service – suggest that today's younger people do in fact seem likely to be able to cope more skilfully with the problems and transitions of middle age when they come to them.

So the life styles of parents with adult children may be very different for people who are only now becoming parents as compared to the current experience of people in the late parenting phase today. One indicator of this at present is the experience of young married women employed outside the home. So many more of them than their mothers are in this situation, and in it as a normal part of adult life (rather than a temporary expedient as during the war) that they are bound to be different sorts of parents from their adult children when the time arrives. The significance of the difference between cohorts in their life experience, and its implications for needs and policy, is still only beginning to be understood. The Russell Sage Foundation have compiled a round-up of available information on these issues and point to the need for further research (Riley *et al.*, 1968). Nevertheless, Fogarty (1975, p. 10) cautions:

> the importance of this point should not be exaggerated. The present generation of the middle aged will be with us for many years yet. Whatever new accents of policy may be appropriate when a new generation reaches middle age, we have in the coming years to help with the problems of those who are at that stage here and now.

We would add that this includes not only the forty- to sixty-year-olds Fogarty deals with, but those now over sixty, and indeed seventy years old too.

Grandparenthood usually occurs in this period. The average age of first grandparenting has also been falling. Fogarty (1975, pp. 195–6) highlights the altered demographic situation with respect to grandparenting:

> Thanks to the greater survival rate among the old than in the past and to the fall in the number of children per family, more grandparents or even great-grandparents . . . are today chasing fewer children and grandchildren. The relation between any pair of family members of different generations can be correspondingly more intense.

Leading on from the findings of various researchers (e.g. Streib, 1965; Holman, 1970b) that the descending generations are less desirous of intense emotional investment than their grandparents, Fogarty (1975, p. 197) points out the possibility of diverting grandparental nurturant inclinations into a larger community context:

> To use for a wider circle the 'generativity', in Erikson's sense, of the mature middle-aged, their capacity for taking responsibility for other adults as well as children and the time and resources which they have for doing so, would call for an upsurge in community activity as people reach this age, on a scale of which the data show no evidence.

Grams (1975) has outlined a similar approach. This is not, of course, to ignore that there are many families which can realize enriching three-generational relationships within their bounds. But, as Somerville (1975) indicates, many individuals welcome alternative channels – as in the case of grandparents who have had the experience of a long-awaited active grandparenthood denied them, say by their children's distant migration, or a divorce with custody in favour of the in-laws. Generic grandparenting in the community need not be seen only as an exclusive option. People can grandparent in both contexts, family and community.

While the average age of parenting of adult children, and of grand-parenting, has been falling, so too have the peak years of occupational careers. Roughly speaking, the beginning of parenting with adult children seems to coincide for many parents with what we have called the late establishment phase, extending onwards into the various sub-phases of later life (Rapoport and Rapoport, 1975, pp. 243–4). We distinguish as the late establishment phase the period in which children are out of school. This is one indicator of children's emergent adulthood, and the late establishment period does seem to coincide with the beginning of 'post-parental' life for many people. The main preoccupation of that period appears to be revision. This involves considering the meaningfulness of the commitments that have been made, whether or not there is a psychological 'pay-off' in terms of feeling happy and satisfied, and whether one's life is adding up to a meaningful whole. While this has been going on already, it comes sharply into focus during this phase.

Life revision involves the task of settling for what is possible. This often means discarding unrealistic aspirations and resigning oneself to all the things that might have been but which are now manifestly impossible. Depression – sometimes quite severe – may arise if it is felt that what one has to settle for is not good enough. On the positive side, however, there are potentials for great satisfaction in this period. If one is able to 'settle' for what one has or to make whatever adjustments are necessary to improve life's balance sheets, there is still the

benefit of wide experience of life and a sense of perspective in knowing
what is possible. Though this sort of preoccupation is immediately
recognizable as part and parcel of the more striving middle-class
occupations, it is by no means confined to them. Farmers who have
invested their energies in the land – rather than having opted earlier to
leave it for the industrial labour force in the cities; miners who opted to
follow in their fathers' footsteps rather than having left for greener
pastures; skilled tradesmen who opted to work with their hands rather
than going on for further training; and ordinary workers who settled
for a present-time orientation rather than striving earlier for delayed
rewards – all tend to review their lives at this phase and ask themselves
whether they have done the right thing for their own life satisfactions,
and if not, whether it is too late to do anything about it. Women may
review the same or comparable issues.

The conclusions to the revision process have implications for parenting and the felt needs and interests of parents. When their children are
grown up and more independent some couples arrive at a feeling of
liberation, a 'new lease of life', relief that they have come through the
struggles and accomplished so much against whatever odds and
anxieties they may have envisioned. Many feel that they have come out
better than they would ever have imagined, and they wish to put these
achievements to use for the enjoyment of their lives. While the remaining time to live may be less than what has already been lived, it is
known to be longer now than ever before in history, and material
conditions for living it are now more comfortable than before. It is
therefore possible to think of doing something entirely different,
perhaps something one always wanted to do, and the late establishment
period may consist of a deliberate effort to bring into reality fantasies
that were kept at bay while the challenges of career, home-building and
child-rearing were all so absorbing.

One of the tasks of the present generation is to de-stereotype the
meaning of old age and the ageing process. Fogarty suggests that an
early confrontation with the ageing process, rather than its denial, can
help with this personal destereotyping process. This allows the
individual and marital pair to come to grips with what the substantive
issues of the phase really are. In recognizing the positive potentials of
this phase up to sixty years of age, the perspective is set for greater
receptivity to recognizing positive potentials in the next ten or fifteen
years of life (Maas and Kuypers, 1974).

Fogarty (1975, p. 14) argues that the early part of the 'post-parental'
years are the keystone of the life cycle in that this is 'the group which
looks both backwards and forwards and has responsibilities in both
directions at once'. He observes that it is the mature middle-aged
people who for the most part fill positions of formal authority in

management, trade unions, and community organization, or are likely at least to carry the weight that goes with seniority. Yet at the same time this age group includes those who have reached their limit or passed it, those whose hopes have been disappointed and whose capacities have been left unused or are beginning to fail. It is in people at this stage that one sees the whole range of outcomes to the 'mid-life crises' of the earlier phase – from depression and stagnation to new vigour and creativity. But, Fogarty (1975, p. 18) argues, despite this period encapsulating the extremes, it is a period in which even the worse off tend to be in a better position in many ways that at other times in their own life cycle:

> If they belong to one of the poorer income groups they are likely at least to be doing as well within that group and to be at one of the higher points of the poverty cycle. In terms of income per head, of housing, of marital stability and of the easing and broadening of family responsibilities, they are, in terms of what is usual in their respective social class, visibly on top of the curve.

For these reasons, he calls the mature middle aged 'the comfortable people' (1975, pp. 18–19):

> Workers in their forties and early fifties are likely still to be at or near the top of their earnings curve, and far as yet from the financial strains of retirement. Many married women are likely by this time to have gone back to work and to be adding to the family income. The proportion of all women who are in the work force or studying fell in 1971 to 44 per cent at age 25 to 29, but recovered to 62 per cent at 40 to 44 and 63 per cent at 45 to 49. Though many workers, especially in manual grades and the fee-paid professions, find their earnings potential falling as they move on towards retirement, so too there is a fall in their financial obligations as their children become independent. . . .
> Moreover, by contrast with the people aged under thirty, people in the 45 to 60 age group are established householders. And by contrast both with the under 30s and with those aged 30 to 44, they tend to be householders on particularly favourable terms. . . .
> And though the number of widows is rising in this age group, the great majority of women are still married with husband present. Divorce can still happen, but is less likely than at ages from 35 to 44, and far less likely than from 25 to 34.

Health is far better in the early part of this parental phase than in the later years. Nevertheless, mortality rises sharply, especially for men. Cancer and heart disease are the great killers in this phase of life for men and the risk of widowhood for women rises. These risks increase as individuals proceed into their 70s. Another major risk area in the pre-retirement stage is unemployment. The risk of redundancy for men over forty is about twice as high as for younger men. The threat of prolonged unemployment before official retirement is great because once a job is lost, by and large it is more difficult for an older man to find new employment than a younger man. But, overall the picture of the first stage of later parenting life is favourable; retirement is a pivotal point for most people. The way they manage this affects the subsequent phases of their lives as individuals, as a couple, and as parents.

The couple relationship (if it survives) comes into a new era, and the marital pair are 'alone' once again. Studies of marital satisfaction at this time indicate a favourable picture, though there are differences in the total curves they outline (e.g. Abrams, 1973, compared with the work of Rollins and Feldman, 1970). Some literature conveys the impression that the marriage relationships become paramount at this stage. This overlooks the varied salience of these relationships in people's lives as the later parental phase develops. The salience of marriage interests compared with other family interests, and with work, community and similar interests is central in shaping the patterns of life styles for later years. Maas and Kuypers's empirical study demonstrates this clearly (1974). For those for whom the positive potentials are not felt in any spheres, the problems are all too real. There are many – and no one knows just how large this submerged passive sub-group is – who have no exciting, revitalizing interest. Their acceptance of ageing is acquiescent. They feel 'finished', that they are old and that their chances for advancement in work or for a happy family life have passed them by, and they settle into a more vegetable form of the late establishment period – set in habits, routinized and passive, watching television, sitting at home, unstimulated and unstimulating. If depressed and unhappy, this can be seen as a wasteful pattern, a pattern which needs stirring up, for, unlike adolescents (whom some late establishment people may surprisingly resemble in their new sense of 'freedom' and quest for excitement), the drive outward from the home is less strong and it is easy to sink into a passive and miserable lethargy.

The focal preoccupation that comes to the fore, particularly following retirement, is with achieving a sense of social and personal integration, which entails an effort to bring a sense of integration into one's whole life – a sense of personal meaning and harmony with the world around one. Here again, there are no universal dividing lines between the periods in which different preoccupations gain ascendancy. Nevertheless, the statutory retirement age of 60/65 is an important reference point for many people. Occupational retirement, or the retirement of one's spouse, tends to be the central event in this period (Crawford, 1971).

A satisfying integration can be difficult to attain at the point where people's lives take on the radical change often entailed by cessation of work. Especially if the work channel was a primary sphere of involvement, and involvements in other spheres were at a low level or non-existent, occupational retirement implies disruption and the need for reconstruction in life styles.

Research on the determinants of activity in later years seems to indicate a significant trilogy: education, income and health. Where all three are high, the activity rates are high. If any one drops significantly, the pattern of activity rapidly deteriorates. As Riesman and others have pointed out, this should not be taken to mean that activity is in and of itself a good thing in this or in any other age group. But taken in its most general form, most people want to be active in some way; where they are unable to be so, they feel their lives are empty, that they are unfulfilled and depressed. Taking activity in its broadest sense – to include meditation, reminiscence, conversation, as well as the more physical activities – there are not only variations in patterns, but these variations are associated with different degrees of satisfaction and they are determined by an interplay of earlier experiences and supports via the transition itself. While this general formulation is true for all the phases we have described, the weightings and configurations are different for each phase. Older people have a heavier load of early experience (or lack of it, as with education) to overcome; at the same time they can become more 'present oriented' than at earlier phases as they work out their personal and social patterns of integration.

Several studies have indicated a correlation between earlier levels of interest and activity and the levels of life satisfaction at this late life stage (Guillemard, 1973; Crawford, 1971; Townsend, 1957; Shanas *et al.*, 1968). Basically, active life styles appear to promote satisfaction in both the short and longer term. This seems to be true even allowing for the associated hazards of overload implied by too much activity. Where activity drops below a certain level, satisfaction seems to fall. This has been well described for occupational retirement. It is less familiar in relation to parenting, where there is a kind of parental retirement implied in the autonomy and departure of adult children. Once people move away from the structure implied by active parenting and/or work, many of the channels for sociability and for the pursuit of interests require alteration. People differ in their capacity to do this.

Though the social security systems of advanced societies provide the material basis for personal survival of ageing people, self-actualization is another matter. For many, the idea that any agency outside the family should have a hand in facilitating this self-realization is unacceptable. But lack of facilitations may lead to disastrous consequences, as seen in some of the negative indicators of neglect of the elderly. These include isolation, apathy, depression and general deterioration of capacities as individuals move into relatively undefined, undervalued, powerless and dependent social roles. Looking at the overall picture, it would seem that we may think of the problem of developing meaningful life styles for the later years in terms of four propositions:

1 The task of reconstructing one's life style is likely to be salient in later years, whether the individual formally retires or not, because even without occupational retirement there are changes in parenting patterns.
2 Some people are well equipped to approach this set of tasks, while others are less so, denying it as long as possible or even dreading it.
3 The core challenge is to evolve a life style for the later phase of life that is satisfying and enjoyable, rather than becoming bitter and unhappy.
4 The development of meaningful life interests is critical in this process.

Review of the research literature

The research literature relevant to the later parenting years seems to fall into several 'strands' of data and analysis, relating, for example, to the physiology, psychology, sociology, economics, medicine, psychiatry, social work, etc. of the phase.

Three approaches represent a recognizable set of conceptions. Each has a history and a continuity into the present. The first of the three looks at later life in terms of decline – biological and psychological. This was an approach that was established early, and though its perspective is not now the most modish or the most relevant for our purposes, it is still widely prevalent. The second strand, based on the theory of disengagement has become prominent more recently. Whilst its perspective is not adequate for the issues involved in parents' needs, it has been influential in setting up an influential orientation to the later parenting years. The third strand has a more developmental orientation. It is distinct in that it deals more focally with the phenomenology of life in the later parenting years. The most recent publications in the field seem to fall into this category. We find it most relevant to our own approach towards understanding the needs of parents with adult children and grandparents.

Studies detailing biological decline and associated decrements in psychological functioning

At some time during the years of parenting with adult children and grandparenting people's psychological and physical functioning are likely to be affected by ageing and this may show up in their ways of relating to other people: their level of physical mobility, tolerance of noise levels, ability to concentrate, and so on, may all affect their relationships with other adults as well as children. However, there are many who for most of their grandparenting years will not be so debilitated that they cannot carry on relationships and interactions with their adult children and their grandchildren which may be of interest to all concerned.

The best known works in Great Britain in this field are the studies by A. T. Welford (1958) and in the USA, those by James E. Birren (1960, 1961, 1964, 1968). Welford, in a number of carefully controlled and meticulous laboratory studies, documented the decline of the organism with age. Conceptualizing the human organism as analogous to a communications system, he shows how – like any machine – the human one is subject to gradual wearing-out of functions in areas such as memory, acquisition of new information, attention arousal, verbal learning, and other variables indicating performance skills. Talking about jobs on the production line, Welford expressed the idea that in youth most people work well beneath their capacity, and that as they get older they gradually become fully extended by their work. Then they start to improve the job – by using their experience and wisdom to make judgments or take short-cuts, or by altering their own methods to streamline their actions. But, at a still later stage, these steps may not be enough to compensate for the ageing process; then performance begins to suffer. The impact of this will depend, of course, on the situation in which older people find themselves. If they have more onerous duties thrust upon them (e.g. if they are promoted to more senior jobs) they may begin to feel that they cannot handle them, and they may feel and be seen to be at a disadvantage. This phenomenon was later discussed as a universal process in senior management by Peter and termed 'the Peter principle' (Peter, 1969/71).

Welford (1958) and his colleagues did not indicate the implications of their findings for parenting with adult children or grandchildren which characteristically occurs during the phase of life that they were studying. They concentrated on designing work tasks and organizations that could sustain ageing persons in productive output for industry.

Birren (1960, 1964) also a pioneer in the field of gerontology, studied perception and cognition. Though he was clear about the distinctions that had to be made between chronological, biological, and psychological age, he noted the general tendency toward decline with biological age: loss of acuity in perceptual responses, loss of speed and co-ordination in psychomotor skills, reduction in drives, increase in medical and social problems including suicides, and the increased need for social services. In a later review article (1968), Birren noted the general tendency among psychologists, even holistic psychologists like Buhler (1961), to consider the life cycle in similar tri-partite phases as those outlined by Welford. Buhler spoke of the phases of construction, culmination, and reduction. Even in 1922 G. Stanley Hall, an early pioneer in developmental psychology, wrote in his book on *Senescence* (where he noted that it is superficial to think of ageing as the inverse of development) that older people, like adolescents, have age-specific psychological processes and that they exhibit a wide range of variability.

The effort to reach a conclusion about what the age-specific psychological processes are has been less satisfactorily resolved. As we shall discuss further below under studies of social decline, Cumming and Henry (1961) attempted to tackle this task. They presented the thesis, on the basis of community studies in Kansas City in the 1950s, that a general human tendency in old age is toward 'disengagement'. Society and individuals concur in this, bringing about a mutual withdrawal culminating in 'successful' ageing and demise, without guilt or recrimination.

There is in fact a fair amount of empirical evidence that the usual assumptions of less mental flexibility and agility among, say, sixty-year-olds, as compared with forty- or fifty-year-olds, are not entirely justified (Neugarten, 1968; Fogarty, 1975). For many the decline comes later. Physically, any change in work-relevant capacities is relatively minor as compared to the ideology predominating among employers that middle-aged and older workers are necessarily inferior. In health terms, there is some decline: the British General Household Survey (1971) found the proportion of people over fifteen who reported chronic illness or injury restricting their activities rose from 9·6 per cent (men) and 8·3 per cent (women) in the fifteen to forty-four age group to 25 per cent of those aged forty-five to sixty-four. (The increase is most marked among skilled manual workers.) Both the change in physical/mental capacities and the greater incidence of ill health are more marked for men than for women, suggesting that this is a peak risk period for symptoms in males, as the earlier period of active parenting is for females. For example, general practice consultation rates and hospital admissions rise sharply for men in middle and old age (who are liable to suffer from the 'masculine' illnesses of lung cancer and heart disease) but not for women, who are no longer vulnerable to pregnancy-associated morbidity and mortality.

Modern versions of the psychobiological decline approach are seen in the work of Heron and Chown (1967) and Talland (1968) in which further documentation is produced, from the community as well as the laboratory, that there is an overall reduction in people's competence, skills and efficiency as they age biologically. Schaie and Strother (1968) outline the importance of studying factors other than illness that effect the variation, and Heron and Chown (1967, p. 137) point up the phenomenon of increased variation as worthy of further attention:

> Individuals vary enormously at any given age in respect to almost all human characteristics. In the case of the characteristics studied here (psychological, physical, sensory and physiological variables as tested by such devices as vocabulary tests, auditory acuity tests, perceptual maze tests, design memory tests, etc.) *the variation among individuals increases as the age of the people increases* (emphasis ours).

Studies emphasizing social decline and disengagement

Social science approaches to ageing are more relevant to our attempt to clarify issues of parenting with adult children. Irrespective of whether studies say anything directly about parent–child relationships, the available conceptualizations indicate aspects of the stereotyped thinking, e.g. 'the retired', 'the post-parental parent', 'the dependent parent'. Brehm (1968) has described these labels as 'culturally induced conceptions of aging'. In Britain the label 'old age pensioner' persists into the 1970s, despite the fact that people in the qualified age group may remain active as heads of government and industrial organizations, professionals and leaders of unions, community organizations, small businesses and voluntary groups – let alone as entertainers, sportsmen, friends and family members.

Talmon (1968) in reviewing the sociological literature on ageing, noted that sociologists have tended to view the ageing process as disturbing to individuals in our society because they are stripped of many of their most meaningful social roles which have earlier supported their personal functioning. Because our society emphasizes mobility and the 'independence' of the nuclear household, conventional homemaker women lose their mothering roles when their children leave home and marry. On the men's side, the arbitrary and usually abrupt withdrawal of occupational roles at retirement from those whose life interests were centred around work, means that most conventional men have their meaningful statuses withdrawn at sixty-five.

Kooy (1963, p. 58) sums up the sociological view of this phase of thinking in reviewing the Dutch data on ageing:

> The increased individualism has a degrading effect on the older people in the extended family. The command of the older generation in extended family matters or with particular members has decreased as rapidly as the individualism of the family has grown . . . making old age a burden to many people for whom it was a privilege a few generations ago.

Cavan (1949) and other sociologists writing in the 1940s and 1950s emphasized this phenomenon of role discontinuity as being the prime causal element in producing the malaises of later life; they accordingly emphasized the necessity for continuities of activity.

Against this emphasis on the continuity of roles and relationships as an antidote to the burdensomeness of old age in industrial society there is the emphasis by Cumming and Henry (1961) on 'disengagement', already mentioned. This has provided in recent years one of the two main issues for controversy in relation to social aspects of life in this phase. The other is the issue of appropriate housing for the elderly as represented in the work of Rosow (1961, 1967). Cumming and Henry suggest that 'successful' ageing involves voluntary withdrawal or disengagement by the individual from his social roles. The withdrawal may be initiated either by the individual or by the social system and the individual may withdraw further from some relationships than from others. The theory also postulates that critical social-psychological differences between the middle-aged and the old relate to this factor of social involvement. The middle-aged are socially engaged and the old are relatively disengaged (Cumming, Dean, Newell, and McCaffrey, 1960; Cumming and Henry, 1961). These writers see the disengagement process as adaptive in that it relieves the aged from having to adhere so closely to social norms. Shukin and Neugarten (1964, p. 150) refer to the decrease in normative influences being viewed as contributing to behaviour which would be regarded as deviant in middle-age but as merely eccentric if it occurs in the old. It should be remembered that the sample used by Cumming and Henry consisted of relatively healthy and financially secure Kansas City residents. Other investigators (Taietz and Larsen, 1956; Zborowski and Eyde, 1962; Prasad, 1964; Youmans, 1967) who tested the disengagement theory on a number of different types of samples, did not find corroboration for the voluntary disengagement theory – except amongst those over eighty years old. On the contrary, Townsend (1957) for example, found that among retired East End Londoners, retirement was strongly resisted and when it came about led to much unhappiness. Marion Crawford (1971, p. 256) raises the question as to whether successful ageing by disengagement is possible 'therefore, only and always for the middle class or can voluntary disengagement be found among other groups of the population?'

In Crawford's own study (1971) she examined the frequency with which retirement is actually associated with disengagement in the minds of pre-retirees in a large urban area in south-west England. In her analysis of data from 99 married couples, she describes three patterns of retirement, only one of which approximates the disengagers of Cumming and Henry's study. In Crawford's sample, under half the men and women identified retirement with disengagement. She concludes that although 'disengagement is a viable and useful concept, grounded in reality in the way in which ageing people see their lives', it is not a universal process. This has also been found to be so by other investigators (Maddox, 1963; Rose, 1964; Havighurst *et al.*, 1969). Some ageing men and women have no intention of disengaging; they plan to maintain old relationships and activities and to enjoy new ones. For those who do identify retirement with disengagement, it is an unpleasant prospect rather than a voluntary or mutually desired withdrawal as originally suggested by Cumming and Henry.

In a recent review of research stemming from the original disengagement proposition, Hochschild (1975, p. 567) concludes that the theory is inadequately formulated (it cannot be disproved in the form it takes); that it is really made up of a number of different components, and these may vary independently (for example, the individual's wish to withdraw and society's facilitation of the withdrawal process), and finally that it does not check with the subjective experience of many people – who cannot be dismissed as simply 'failures' at disengagement. The obvious vigour of people like Bertrand Russell, Franco, Casals, Picasso, Rubinstein, etc. into their eighties fly in the face of the theory. Hochschild suggests that disengagement be seen as a variable, and that studies be conducted of the conditions under which old people prefer to disengage as compared to those where remaining socially engaged is preferred and supported.

The disengagement hypothesis – postulated at the beginning of the 1960s – was very much a product of its era. It may have reflected a value position based on rationalizations of an awkward situation for the elderly in relation to small mobile family units and a relatively undeveloped public policy for their age group. The present generation of ageing people is not only in better health and in better economic circumstances, but in comparison with earlier ones there is a greater consciousness of the potentials for self-realization in the use of leisure. It may be quite inappropriate to expect them to withdraw, and they are likely increasingly to want to create ways of continuous engagement and personal development. Crawford (1971, p. 276) believes that 'this retiring generation is perhaps the first to be confronted with this conflict between cultural demands on the one hand, and personal capabilities on the other'.

The preceding discussion underlines once more the necessity to recognize variations amongst sub-groups and for different sub-stages in the phase. After discussing further *stereotypes about ageing people* – and the effect of the stereotypes on parenting – we will return to a consideration of recent social research, particularly that which has concentrated on critical transitions that tend to occur during this phase.

The cult of youth in industrialized societies has as its corollary the devaluation of maturity and old age. When one no longer has children in one's home, and when one is no longer capable of having children, the tendency is to feel and to be seen as socially redundant. This stereotype applies more to women than to men, for the reasons already abundantly documented, and it may feed any difficulties that are experienced in relation to the menopause. Although the existence of a psychological male menopause has been suggested, and certainly male middle age seems to have its own characteristic sexual and psychological problems, there is no exact parallel biological event for men. The menopause is perceived not only as the cessation of menstruation, the end of the ability to have children, but the 'change' of life:

> The popular image of the typical menopausal woman is negative – she is exhausted, haggard, irritable, bitchy, unsexy, impossible to live with, driving her husband to seek other women's company, irrationally depressed, unwillingly suffering a 'change' that marks the end of her active (re)productive life (Boston Women's Health Collective, 1971, p. 229).

Somerville (1975) argues that few women (or men) wish to become parents (again) at the age of forty-five or fifty, so the idea that women should mourn the loss of this potential may be irrelevant. What, then, do women want and need in relation to their approaching middle and old age? Is there anything to mourn or not? How does this compare with the changes that occur in men's lives? And how do these factors affect relationships between parents, adult children and grandchildren?

In the first place, it is estimated in Britain that about two thirds of women experience the menopause without requiring treatment for adverse symptoms. Symptoms due to oestrogen deficiency can be quite severe: for example Llewellyn-Jones (1970, p. 254) reports that 70 per cent of a sample of 500 women who sought medical aid during the menopause reported 'hot flushes'. But these symptoms have for some time been amenable to oestrogen replacement therapy. According to a United States Government report cited by Somerville (1975), 10 per cent of American women have reached the menopause at thirty-eight, 20 per cent at forty-three, 50 per cent at forty-nine, 90 per cent at fifty-four and 100 per cent by fifty-eight. The correlation of these ages with critical events in the cycle of parenthood is high. The coincidence of menopause with children's transition to adulthood may underline the symbolic significance of the menopause as the threatened end of feminity. At the same time, the woman's position in the family is changing and the centrality of her domestic role as homemaker is being partially eroded. Her own parents have probably reached the stage at which she may have to assume some responsibility for them, and

Bernard (1975b, p. 133) describes a characteristic dilemma between 'babysitting for her daughter or chauffering her mother . . . neither of which . . . may appeal to her'. Phyllis Chesler (1974, pp. 40–2) states the case for the social accompaniments of the menopause as the underlying cause of psychological symptoms:

> Women become 'depressed' long before menopausal chemistry becomes the standard explanation for the disease. . . . Perhaps more women *do* get 'depressed' as they grow older – when their already limited opportunities for sexual, emotional and intellectual growth decrease even further. Dr Pauline Bart studied depression in middle-aged women and found that such women had completely accepted their 'feminine' role – and were 'depressed' because that role was no longer possible or needed.

The stereotypes of women which make the 'depression' effect predictable treat the lives of women as dependent variables, endlessly responding to the lives of others but never providing an autonomous force. But as we have indicated, some evidence now suggests that satisfaction with life may increase when responsibility for children is shed (Blood and Wolfe, 1960; Chilman, 1968; Rollins and Feldman, 1970). There is also evidence that women who have opted for a modified form of domestic role earlier in life, usually by taking up some occupational commitment, are less likely to feel such major discontent and the 'loss' of femininity with the alterations in parenting at this phase.

The differences in major *status transitions* experienced by conventional mothers and fathers in this phase are usually critical. The alteration of parental responsibility and retirement from work have different impacts on the two parents. The tendency is for men who derive their major satisfaction from work to feel relatively severe dissatisfaction with loss of occupational status, affecting his marriage negatively. Conversely, for women who have derived major satisfactions from motherhood, there may be negative effects. But a woman's sense of relief at the exit of children may rebound in a more positive orientation toward her husband.

Other studies support the idea that there may be new problems of marital communication in this phase, particularly where a traditional division of sex roles has been maintained. Lotte Bailyn found a difference between dual-career and traditional couples in this regard for an earlier phase. The latter were more likely to have difficulties with communication, presumably because of the divergence of interests that had occurred between husbands and wives already mentioned in the previous chapters. On the other hand, employed wives more often have a critical rather than accepting attitude to marriage (Fogarty, Rapoport and Rapoport, 1971) and this may result in a higher incidence of conflict at this point, when husbands and wives confront one another with their differences rather than being preoccupied with their respective 'jobs' (Landis, 1962). Consequently, for both these causes we may be seeing the advent of a new pattern in which divorce rates among the middle-aged rise to approximate those among the young (Somerville, 1975).

Another relevant area is sexuality. Stereotypes of ageing present the loss of female sexuality as a process which follows automatically from the loss of reproductive ability. One personal account puts it like this:

> What, fat, forty-three, and I dare to think I'm still a person? . . . Everything she reads, every comic strip, every song, every cartoon, every advertisement, every book and movie, tells her that a woman over thirty is ugly and disgusting. She is a bag. She is to be escaped from. She is no longer an object of prestige consumption. For her to have real living sexual desires is obscene.

And yet,

> I think stripped down I look more attractive on some abstract scale . . . than my husband, but I am sexually and socially obsolete and he is not. . . . When I was young, my anxiety about myself and what was to become of me colored all my relationships with men, and I was about as sensual as a clotheshanger. I have a capacity now for taking people as they are, which I lacked at twenty; I reach orgasm in half the time and I know how to please (Moss, 1970, pp. 170–4).

The anger of this description perhaps overstates the case, but it makes some crucial points. The development of sexuality in men and women follows a different pattern (Gagnon and Simon, 1974). Whereas in marriage manuals this difference is assumed to inhere in the generally lower sexual interest displayed by women throughout their lives (Gordon and Shankweiler, 1971) in fact as Kinsey (1953) and, more recently, Masters and Johnson (1966) have observed, women reach their sexual peak later than men and often experience a renewed sexuality in middle and early old age. As Masters and Johnson comment (1966, pp. 243–5) there may well be problems for this age group in reconciling the increased, or at least maintained, sexual interest of the women with a male sexual capacity which tends to fall from middle age onwards. The boredom and waning sexuality of middle-aged marriage from the male point of view is a well-established stereotype, and the cultural recipe for male discontent is the younger woman. While men may become more sexually attractive as they get older, women stereotypically become less so; sexual capacity is deduced directly but erroneously, from superficial attractiveness. Along with the idea of waning sexuality goes an assumption (within the ageing parent stereotype) that people's general competence and effectiveness decline as they get older.

Old, ill and alone are other dimensions of the ageing parent stereo-type. The model assumption in family sociology is that parents in this period are thoroughly incapacitated and a reversal of roles has occurred; the parent becomes the child, the child the parent. Ethal Shanas (1968, p. 18) attacks this notion in a survey of *Old People in Three Industrial Societies*:

> In most western countries old age is associated with illness. The person who is old is thought to be sick. This belief is widely accepted both by those who are active in providing medical care for the elderly and by the public at large. The fact is, however, that although widespread pathology exists among the elderly population, old age and illness are not synonymous. There is no such disease as 'old age'. Some old people function well, others poorly. Some old people are severely restricted in their mobility, others are able to maintain themselves in the ordinary activities of daily living. The variation among the elderly in their physical health and in their degree of impairment is enormous.

Using an index of incapacity derived from Townsend's work on old people, Shanas *et al.*, found that half the population of old people in their study had no incapacity, and a further quarter were only minimally incapacitated (they had a score of one or two on a scale from zero – no incapacity – to twelve).

While the 'problem' of elderly parents is stereotypically one of elderly women, since the longevity of women is greater than that of men (two thirds of pensioners in Britain are women, for instance (Hewitt, 1973)) this is not always and necessarily a 'problem'. A woman of seventy-five is likely to have middle-aged children, grandchildren in their twenties and possibly great-grandchildren as well. She may enjoy visiting them on a constant round and, as American studies now show, many of these widowed women control considerable sums of cash as a result of inheritance and insurance. Even Peter Townsend's (1957, pp. 33, 43, 49) early work in Britain demonstrated that many elderly people enjoyed relationships with their adult children. These were shown to be more common than the stereotype of the sick, isolated old person would suggest. In his Bethnal Green survey of old people, Townsend found that almost half of a sample of 203 old people shared a household with relatives other than a spouse, and between them they had 2,700 relatives living within a mile. Only 4 per cent did not see at least one of their children once a week. A particularly isolated and vulnerable group are old people without children, as children have traditionally been a principal source of emotional, practical and financial support. It is interesting to note that having only male children was found to be almost as isolating as having no children at all. By far the largest part of the help given to elderly parents comes from women.

Townsend argues that childless old people and old people without daughters make up a single category with respect to their isolation. As we have indicated, this situation is associated with a predominantly conventional pattern of family life, where it is the wives and mothers who are expected to perform such nurturant functions.

For the reasons indicated in describing the prevalence of the conventional model, research on middle and old age has reflected the same lack of symmetry as research on early parenthood. The focus has been on the problem of retirement (or early redundancy) for men and on the emotional difficulties of launching children and creating a new set of life interests for women. The meaning of this later parental stage to fathers has been largely ignored, and the inflexibility of the occupational system in accommodating the needs of 'returned married women' have been considered in isolation, rather than as a general issue for middle-aged and older workers. Because of stereotypes, which sustain as well as reflect modal statistical patterns, the occupational system does not, on the whole, allow for flexible and varied patterns of work or for a flexible retiring age. Opportunities for retraining in mid-career, or for switching jobs/careers altogether, have only recently become salient for both men and women, and this under the spur of unemployment. Also, because of the stereotypes, variations between individuals in commitment to work at different stages of the life cycle are not adequately recognized, e.g. the idea that some fathers may prefer to withdraw from playing a major financial provider role at this phase, and may be able to tolerate their wives actually taking on this responsibility. So, there are many changes – social and financial – and many variations in patterning of social life of the elderly which make the older stereotypes of old people's needs increasingly dysfunctional.

Social science literature on parenting with adult children

The point at which children become legally and socially independent of their parents marks the beginning of a twilight area in the family social science literature (Rapoport and Oakley, 1975). There is little material available between reaching adulthood and the so-called 'reversed role' situation of becoming old. This gap in the literature has been emphasized by Chilman (1968). Thus a large segment of the parenting (including grandparenting) life cycle is either omitted in the literature or minimally covered. In earlier phases, the tendency has been not only to see parenting as women's work, but to see it in a fairly static way. Women were seen as active parents until their children were grown. Once the stage of active parenthood is passed they are regarded, in much of the literature referred to in the last section as without meaningful roles. Amongst the social scientists who take a developmental point of view, however, there is awareness that active life may continue and that this may include parenting, albeit in a much altered form.

The concept of the family life cycle is central to the developmental approach. It has been used now for some decades in the literature, but even here the research data and theorizing is much greater in regard to the earlier stages of the family life cycle than the later ones. Troll (1971, p. 263) observes that:

> much more is known about mate selection, early years of marriage, parenting of the young child, or sibling rivalry among children than is known about marital satisfaction in middle and old age, parent–child relations when the child is adult, or sibling relations among the middle aged.

Relationships between parents and adult children are more complex than the simple parents-meet-children's needs model of early dependent childhood. In some ways, they become relationships between equals but in other ways the parent–child axis of differentiation may persist. A revised basis for the relationship may have to be negotiated. Other factors, such as the introduction of sons- or daughters-in-law and grandchildren, may have to be accommodated.

Another imbalance in the literature on parenting with adult children is that while grandparenting is sometimes considered – being viewed as the continuation of the role of mother – grandfathers, like fathers, get almost no attention. We thus know little about the felt needs of grandfathers, let alone grandmothers who may feel pulled between their own desires to become involved in strictly non-parental roles but who may feel obliged to help out with their children's families. The conventional assumption is that grandmothers need to continue to feel needed. There is little empirical work to support this.

Most of the available data relates to variables such as how far children live from their parents, how frequently there is contact, etc., but very little on the quality of their relationships or the phenomenology of the interrelated statuses.

In the USA, Litwak and Sussman argued, with supporting data, that modern married individuals are not as isolated from their parental families as one would suppose in this most mobile of the world's societies. They keep in touch by post, by rail, air, road, telephone and other modern means of transportation and communication – all made possible through highly developed technology and high literacy rate. Litwak's interpretation is that it is precisely the mobility and anomic quality of many American communities that makes it so important that individuals hang on to their original families as reference groups. They, after all, know better than anyone else how far the mobile individuals have travelled socially in spiralling upward (Litwak, 1960).

Gordon Streib (1958, p. 60) in a study of 1,500 families in New York State found that:

> There is a higher degree of family solidarity as measured by our indices [financial aid and assistance] than has been noted by other writers. The data suggests that family solidarity is not adversely affected by social mobility. There is a high degree of congruity between parental expectations for their children and the children's behaviour.

Sussman (1965), in one of the few papers directly on the topic of the relationships of adult children with their parents in the USA, summarizes the findings of numerous empirical studies as follows (see also Figure 2):

1 Help patterns may take many forms, including the exchange of services, gifts, advice and financial assistance. Financial aid patterns may be direct, as in the case of young married couples (Burchinal, 1963) or, through a wide range of indirect and subtle help patterns (Sussman 1965).

2 Such help patterns are probably more widespread in the middle and working class families and are more integral a feature of family relationships than has been appreciated. . . . Very few families included in available studies reported neither giving nor receiving from relatives.

3 The exchange of aid among families flows in several directions: from parents to children and vice versa, among siblings and, less frequently, from more distant relatives. However, financial assistance generally appears to flow from parents to children.

4 While there may be a difference in the absolute amount of financial aid received by families of middle and working class status, there are insignificant differences in the proportions of families in these two strata who report receiving, giving or exchanging economic assistance in some form.

5 Financial aid is received most commonly during the early years of married life. Parents are probably more likely to support financially 'approved' than 'disapproved' marriages, such as elopements, interfaith and interracial marriages. Support can be disguised in the form of substantial sums of money or valuable gifts at Christmas, anniversaries or birthdays.

Events which serve as occasions for kin gatherings provide contacts for non-financial aid and assistance (e.g. shopping, child-minding or care, counselling, service to older persons, etc.). Sussman (1953) earlier noted that the norm of independence is so strong in our society, that parents have to be careful in their giving so as to avoid implying that

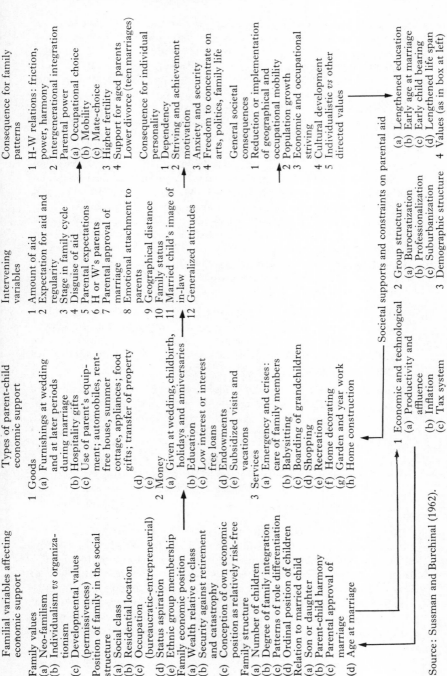

Figure 2 *Functional analysis of parental aid to married children*

the son (or son-in-law) is not a competent provider; and that mothers and daughters had to have secret sessions to 'tell' if there is anything needing assistance – e.g. an unexpected hospitalization – that cannot be mentioned openly lest it be implied that the young couple cannot cope.

Most of these data have British counterparts though the style of research is different. It was the Young and Willmott (1957) study of Bethnal Green that first detailed how unfounded the assumption was that urbanization and industrialization led to complete isolation of the nuclear family. In their study of family and kin in East London, Young and Willmott provided an ethnographic model for what was to become a type of study the world over, documenting the fact that in some settings, for example traditional working-class communities or ethnic communities, as subsequently studied by Gans (1967) and Fried (1973), there is a considerable degree of solidarity among households – what Bott (1957) called 'tight-knit' social networks. Young and Willmott (1957, p. 128) interpreted this in part as being sustained by the insecurities that existed in early industrialization. The women needed to band together in the community – much as the men did in their trade unions – to provide some cushioning against the exigencies of urban industrial life:

> The wife had to cling to the family in which she was born, and in particular to her mother, as the only other means of assuring herself against isolation. . . . The extended family was her trade union, organised in the main by women and for women, its solidarity her protection against being alone.

Similar solidarity relationships between the generations, particularly in the female line, were reported in Ireland (Arensberg and Kimball, 1968), Wales (Rees, 1950), and small English towns such as Banbury (Stacey, 1960).

In a study of 2,000 people in Swansea, Rosser and Harris (1965) found that two thirds of the married men and over three quarters of the married women had at least one parent living in the same city (i.e. the 41 square miles of greater Swansea) and that visiting patterns were similar to those reported in Bethnal Green by Young and Willmott (Table 13).

Stacey (1960) noted in her analysis of the Banbury material, that though people move away from home – from the country into the city, as well as from the tight-knit inner-city neighbourhoods to the new fragmented suburban housing estates – this does not inevitably lead to loss of contact. The most frequent reason given among her Banbury respondents for not knowing about grandparents, for example, was that they were dead. As in London, the women tend to keep closer ties with parents than do men. Stacey reports that her respondents still reiterate

Table 13 *Visiting patterns in Swansea families*

Last seen	Frequency of Contact (%)			
	Mothers		Fathers	
	Married sons	Married daughters	Married sons	Married daughters
Within the last 24 hrs	31	54	29	47
Within last week	40	27	41	30
Week – month ago	14	7	15	9
Less frequently	15	12	15	14

the old saw that 'a son's a son till he gets a wife. A daughter's a daughter all her life.' She recounts many incidents such as the mother of a girl having a baby coming several hundred miles to be on hand to help, 'so strong is the customary obligation'. And as in Bethnal Green she finds that women keep close parental ties even after marriage so that they can 'go home to mother' if their man should die or leave them (Stacey, 1960, p. 125).

Stacey (1960, p. 128) also observes that migration into Banbury does not completely destroy the kin bond: '[some] pioneers recommend that their siblings come along, and there is a small but distinct tendency for parents to retire in the town to be near their migrant children.'

In Banbury, as elsewhere, traditional lineal influences are less closely attended than previously. For example, grandmother's advice about the Church bazaar is given less attention. Similarly in the male line, there is a less compulsive tendency for fathers to press their sons into the family business, though the tendency still exists for families to keep small businesses operating in their own interests. In such situations mothers tend to help with the phone or books, and sons or brothers work together in the shop. Parenting with adult children may be sustained in occupational working relationships. She concludes that the two groups that keep the tightest inter-generational relationships at this phase are the highest status groups (where there is considerable property and status symbols to hang onto) and in the working class (particularly among the women, as in Bethnal Green).

Business, property, jobs and the like seem to be recurrently mentioned as the media through which ties between fathers and their adult male children are sustained. Colin Bell (1969) describes the father–son relationship as important in providing a channel for financial aid to the son even after the latter marries. Mothers are reported as helping in other ways as the mechanisms for sustaining ties – household chores, visiting, birth and child-care assistance, counselling and advice. Yet there are other mechanisms and other events which occasion contact between the generations, which cannot be thought of simply as the continuing provision of supports and services from the elder to the younger generation. Nor can they be thought of as necessarily easier at this stage.

The mother's involuntary 'loss of domestic role' is assumed only to occur primarily if the daughter moves so far away or is very rejecting. But, from a purely structural point of view, the relationship between parents and their adult children is problematic. There is a 'potential conflict between conjugal and filial ties' (Rosser, 1969, p. 192). Or, as Leichter and Mitchell (1967) conclude following a study of New York Jewish families, it is easier to reconcile the mother/wife role in the family of procreation with the sister/daughter one in the family of orientation than it is to reconcile the husband/father role set with the son/brother ones. Our society lacks clearly demarcated age grades and generation transition points. We have few rituals of prescriptions that cushion people from potential conflicts. In primitive societies, a frequently found prescription of this kind is the 'mother-in-law avoidance rule'. This is frequently put in the form of a taboo. If a man looks at his mother-in-law, for example, it is believed that he will become ill. This taboo pre-empts the possibility that the son and the mother-in-law may form an alliance which would interfere with the marital tie. Similarly, if the son's mother is forbidden access to the household of the new conjugal pair, competition between wife and mother is avoided. We have no such rituals or taboos but, as Deutscher (1962) has pointed out, we do have rehearsal-type separations – as at summer camp, or at university or military service for sons. The cultural myth of the mother-in-law relationship as an impossibly difficult one serves to insulate people through a kind of secular prescription to make and keep some distance.

Rosser (1969, p. 194) observes that in both Britain and the US studies show a widespread belief that 'Parents and children should live near, but not too near. Living *not too near* implies living far enough away to be able to control the frequency of contact with parents.' Moroney (1976) finds that most available studies show that parents prefer not to live with their children.

Becoming a *grandparent* is one of the ways in which parents and their adult children evolve a new relationship. Unlike the 'in-law' relationship, it seems to be highly idealized in our society, without being specified and defined. Images of kindly old grannies reading stories to children and wise old grandfathers busy carving toys for them are part of our cultural heritage of family-process myths. They are of the 'happily ever after genre'. Many writers – including Gorer (1955) who takes a cross-cultural perspective, and the GAP Committee

(1975) who take a psychodynamic perspective – have observed that grandparents and grandchildren feel close bonds. Gorer describes this as the principle of 'alternating generations' in the possession and use of authority, and the GAP Committee analyse it in terms of grandparents and grandchildren having a common target of aggression, the parents. Burke (1967) notes that in modern families where mothers work – even when they have young children at home – the grandmothers and children have more time for one another than the working mum has for either (Burke, 1967). Agnello (1973) found that young people and the older members share a sense of powerlessness (not only in the conjugal family, but in relation to the larger community – for example in such matters as voting and politics).

The ideal picture is one of complementarities, dovetailed role cycling, and happy continuity. Just as a conventional mother is faced with the problem of reconciling herself for the departure of her children from home, her daughter marries and has a child – calling on her help with the new family crisis. Christopher Harris (1969, p. 190) notes:

> If the adult children continue to reside in the same dwelling or locality after marriage the mother may still be involved in the raising and rearing of children – in this case her grandchildren. If the post-parental role is defined in this way, the very term 'post-parental' becomes a misnomer – 'grandparental' would be more apposite.

The traditional, benign imagery of grandparenthood creates a situation which Somerville (1975) describes as a deprivation one when some women feel shock and disappointment at not having the opportunity to grandparent. Nevertheless, the assumption on either the parent's side or the adult child's side that the idealized situation of availability and motivation to grandparent will prevail is on the wane. Many grandmothers feel relief at shedding the duties of active motherhood, and once launched into the outside world of work or voluntary activities, domestic concerns may become second-class.

What is less well understood, as might be expected, is the *grandfather's* potentials. His wishes and felt needs may be the obverse in many instances. Having been denied the pleasures of active parenting, he may yearn for a phase of active grandparenting. This merits research.

In any case, the age of becoming a grandparent is falling. Women become grandparents at around 49–51 and men 51–53. Cultural norms legitimate a woman's withdrawal from employment to play an active role as a grandparent (whereas the same is not true of grandfathers) but she may not wish to exchange one set of domestic obligations (parenting) for another (grandparenting). The issues involved here – of new pressures and strains within the mother–daughter relationship in these changed and changing conditions – have not been looked at.

The extent to which grandparents participate in the care of their grandchildren has nowhere been sufficiently documented. Material from countries such as China and the USSR indicate that grandmothers often play a traditional role *vis-à-vis* grandchildren and are in practice an enabling factor in the employment of young married women which is so valued within socialist economies (Geiger, 1968; Davin, 1976). In Britain and the USA a significant part of substitute child-care appears to be carried out by relatives, including grandparents, but a prevailing mystique about the ease with which grandmother may step into mother's shoes overstates the frequency and acceptability of this arrangement (Bernard, 1975b).

Neugarten (1964) distinguishes five different styles of grandparenting: (1) the 'patriarchal', in which the basis of interaction between grandparents and grandchildren is hierarchical and grandparents act as 'reservoirs of family wisdom'; (2) 'substitute parent' where grandmothers actually and routinely care for grandchildren; (3) the 'formal' grandparent who maintains an interest in her/his grandchildren but is careful not to 'interfere'; (4) 'funseekers', grandparents who stress informality and playfulness; and (5) 'distant' grandparents who play a benevolent role towards their grandchildren but with infrequent contact. Neugarten's study shows the last three patterns to be the most common, but we need a great deal more exploration of the different styles of interaction between grandparents and grandchildren before the void in the family sociology literature is adequately filled.

As Somerville (1975) points out, this area can be looked at from three perspectives: those of the grandparents, parents and children. There may be discrepancies between these perspectives – for example, one form of interaction that is satisfactory for grandparent and parent may not be so from the viewpoint of the child. Clark and Summers's (1961) study of the backgrounds of maladjusted children is one of the few attempts to explore this problem. They found that symptoms of maladjustment in children (such as tics, stammering, enuresis and failures at school work) were associated with situations in which the child's household contained an extra adult – most commonly the grandmother – in addition to the child's parents and siblings. The grandmother's presence gave rise to a battle between mother and grandmother for the child's allegiance and was associated with a withdrawal of the father from participation in family activities, particularly those concerning the children. Nevertheless, there is conflicting data on the effects of having an old grandparent in the home. Some data on family violence suggests that it exacerbates conflict. Other data, such as Belson's (1975) study of juvenile theft in London, provides contradictory evidence. Belson reports that in a study of 1,425 London boys between the age of thirteen and sixteen, the presence of a grandparent in the home is negatively correlated with delinquency. Clearly there is a need for clarification of the different circumstances in which the presence and participation of a grandparent in the home of their adult married children is beneficial or not to the various family members.

Thus the involvement of grandparents in their children's and grandchildren's lives may not be an unmixed blessing from the viewpoint of the younger generations, since they frequently have an urgent need for substitute child care. Both popular ideology and the official policy of social work agencies emphasize grandparents as the most appropriate substitute caretakers. In Robert Holman's study of British unsupported mothers (1970b, p. 26) nearly a third of the sample lived with their mothers. Holman observes:

> To many social workers such a finding may make pleasing reading. The Ministry of Health's Circular No. 2866 urges social workers 'wherever possible to persuade the girl to make known her circumstances to her parents and, if the home is likely to be a satisfactory one, to persuade the grandparents to make a home for the little one'.

But Holman goes on to say that despite the popular beliefs and despite the official policies, this is not usually the preferred option of the single parents. Only 3 of the 95 mothers in his sample said they would prefer this form of care. Their reasons were primarily because of the conflict between the generations in child-rearing values and practices, and because of the confused loyalties they felt would result for the children.

Once again the grandfather is conspicuously invisible. David Gutmann (1973) argues on the basis of cross-cultural studies that our society's models of masculinity and femininity apply to (or are derived from) the young adult phase of the life cycle. In middle and particularly old age a wider range of behaviour is tolerated and displayed: 'Grandpa becomes sweet, affable but rather vague, Grandma becomes tough-minded and intrusive.' The active involvement of older men in child-care may be felt to be less dissonant with sex-role conceptions at the grandparental stage, but the reappraisal of potential new parenting patterns has not so far been extended to grandfathers. Even in George and Wilding's (1972) pioneering study of motherless families, the aid to these fathers and their dependent children is assumed to come from female relatives, and this is not focally examined as an issue.

Actual research on grandparenting, and the effects of different patterns of residence and interaction on the people concerned is scarce. The study by Hill *et al.* (1970) of the three-generational family is one of the few major empirical studies. Though the study concentrates on consumer behaviour and how it changes from one generation to the next, it is relevant to a variety of concerns in the area of intergenerational relationships among adults. Their study is based on 120 sets of three generational families (360 nuclear families) drawn from a universe of 3,000 such sets in Minneapolis. As in the British studies of Young and Willmott (1957) and Firth *et al.* (1969), women were the main figures to maintain contacts – they are the 'kin-keepers'. The pivotal middle generation are found to be the most effective planners and decision-makers – the most sensitive to the needs of the other generations. However, 'planful' and 'unplanful' families are found at each generation, and kin-keepers are often elders. Hill and his colleagues suggest that the most effective management of life-cycle events is achieved if the relations between work and family involvements are planned. Career decisions which include family considerations have the best chances for a satisfactory outcome. Normal, expectable events such as birth, marriage, entry or exit (of the wife particularly) from the workforce are examples of such interactive events which affect parents' felt needs and interests as well as their actual requirements. If a move to the country, which the father may have desired for several years before retirement, precedes mother's efforts to train for re-entry into the labour force or a community activity, both transitions may be felt to be harmonious. If, on the other hand, she re-enters work and has developed new enthusiasm and commitments and then he decides to move to a place where she cannot find outlets for her new interests, discord is more likely. These are only illustrative of the dilemmas that arise at this stage, and it is not uncommon to find that the adult children become involved in the new family dramas that develop. If father moves to a place too far for his wife to visit their children and grand-children *or* to engage in her interests or occupations, he may find himself with an empty nest, and their daughter may find herself with a resident granny for her new baby.

There are a number of pieces of research that illustrate aspects of these scenarios. One set of studies deals with the whole issue of *occupational retirement*. Most of this literature is couched in terms most meaningful to men – and it covers a range of facets associated with retirement, including financial, legal, housing, personal interests, marital relationships, etc. Crawford (1971) attempted to look at wives' feelings about husbands' retirement. We know of no study of women's feelings about their own retirement from occupational employment. There is some evidence to suggest that just as many marriages improve in quality following the launching of children into their own independent orbits of work and family life, so with retirement. Townsend (1957) notes, in one of his earlier studies of 'the family life of old people' that men did come closer to their wives in Bethnal Green following retirement – because they saw more of one another and because 'when people get older, they cling together more'.

Occupational retirement, however, has more often been seen as a shock for many men, and is frequently followed precipitously by death or disability – not so much because the organism is depleted, so the theory goes, but because the men's significant roles and commitments have been withdrawn and they are unprepared to learn new ones. The work of The Pre-retirement Association and kindred bodies is to prepare people for this event. The rising level of education and general improvement in anticipatory preparation now built into our culture are moving in the same direction. Nevertheless, many aspects of retirement still come as a shock to many individuals and to their families. This partly relates to the drop in financial resources that occurs when the individual ceases earning. Hoggart (1967) suggests that this is like a mild form of unemployment, and notes for working-class men that:

> when a man had no money in his pocket he would . . . feel less than a man; for beer, cigarettes, or pools [require money] and he must not be tied to his wife and thus inferior to her; such a situation [is felt to be] against nature.

Townsend (1957) notes that the loss of job and income often affects a man's authority within the home: 'for his position has relied mainly on his traditional authority in the home derived from his role as bread-winner, and he was now bringing less money into the home.'

But other studies have documented the fact that the changes involved with retirement are more than economic in character. Gorer (1965) has suggested that the shock of retirement is less catastrophic for many middle-class families because they have planned for it, have cultivated other interests, and have sustained a closer domestic sharing pattern. Middle-class parents are less likely to be living near their married children and so the strains that may arise from the 'too near' situation are avoided. Also, there tend to be a wider range of ideas and models for sustaining the relationship between the adult generations as compared to the simple conception of the mother continuing to provide services for her married daughter which so dominated the life of Bethnal Greeners.

Other major events that are near-universal to this phase are illness and death. A less frequent one (but perhaps increasing in frequency) is the *shift from being a married couple to being a single-parent family* with adult children. There are different views as to how this situation is or should be handled, as it is an even less prescribed-for situation than grandparenting generally.

Loss of the spouse is likely to occur in parents' lives at this phase – more often than not it is the male who goes first. This raises some practical problems of living and some social-psychological problems. An example of the first is seen in situations where the couple retire to a cottage by the sea or in the country. They may be able to cope with making this transition while the husband lives, but as Karn (1974) found in her study of retirement to the seaside, coping with a home on one's own after the death of the spouse is often more than an elderly widow can handle.

The literature on the social-psychological issues of bereavement has proliferated recently, with major works by Hinde (1974), Cartwright *et al.* (1973), Parkes (1972), Marris (1974), and Pincus (1974/6). Also associated with this literature is the controversy on the disengagement hypothesis (mentioned earlier as having emerged from the studies of Cumming and Henry) and the literature on illness and care of the ailing elderly. The literature deals primarily with personal problems of bereavement.

In the past, family aid for ailing and dependent relatives concentrated on the question of the family's ability to prepare for and support relatives in their old age, when the parents become financially dependent on their children. Widows and widowers were found to be desolate not only because they had not been sufficiently skilled and rehearsed in the dynamics of grief and mourning, but because they had become too habituated to dependence on a single other person:

> Once a spouse is lost, the support given by the rest of the family depends partly upon the lifetime pattern of relationships with siblings, who are themselves ageing anyway, and partly on the stage of the family life cycle reached by the persons' children (if any) (Hadley *et al.*, 1975, p. 98).

Some blend of family help and participation, and state provision in housing and domiciliary services seems most prevalent in industrial societies; studies show that older persons themselves prefer it this way. One American study by Sidney Croog and his colleagues (1972) of help patterns in relation to coronary illness, for example, found that close friends were preferred to family members as resources in the event of a heart attack. In another American study by Gibson (1972) clergymen and doctors were found to be more important sources of emotional support than either siblings or parents in such events.

The necessity for further research on variation, made throughout this book, is again seen in relation to this phase of parenting. It is not only because the lack of structure for social roles in this age range has made for more-than-usual ranges of behavioural and attitudinal variation, but because there are such conflicting ideas as to what difference it makes for the fulfilment of felt needs of the people concerned if one or another pattern is adopted. One point that seems to be emerging in contemporary research is the conviction that this is a period of potential growth for individuals, rather than necessary stagnation or decline. This idea in itself is likely to give rise to experimentation by individuals in this life phase – trying different arrangements, creating pressure and interest groups, and recording their experience, with or without social research collaboration.

There have recently been some studies emphasizing variation of optional life styles and the possibility of continuous growth. While this idea has been mentioned for a number of years – e.g. in the World Federation of Mental Health Organization seminars, edited by Kenneth Soddy (1967) and with the participation of Margaret Mead and others – it is only recently that many of the ideas are being tested empirically in research. One major stream of such research emanates from the University of Chicago's Committee of Human Development. The Chicago sociologist Ernest Burgess wrote: 'Old age is not a retreat but an opportunity' – but it needs to be activated (cited in Williams *et al.*, 1964, p. 182). This tradition – followed by Havighurst and his colleagues, Neugarten and her colleagues (1964) and then extended to the West Coast of the USA in the work, for example, of Maas and Kuypers (1974) – is also seen in Britain in the work of Rapoport *et al.* (1975) and in the work of Fogarty (1975). Peter Townsend's work (1957), though differently conceptualized, has elements of compatibility with this in the extent to which he urges that old people be given options about their own development throughout their lives – rather than being put away for the convenience of others.

The work of Maas and Kuypers illustrates the variety of life styles that people over sixty years of age actually enact and enjoy. Some of the details of the life styles they have delineated are more characteristic of their well-to-do Californian sample than to people in this phase elsewhere, but there are generic types. Maas and Kuypers (1974) empirically derived clusters of life styles in the later years include characteristic patterns of parenting and grandparenting. Examples are:

The *disabled disengaging mother*, is often dissatisfied with her neighbours, and often the company her children keep if they are not sufficiently socially acceptable. Disappointed in her husband's level of achievement, she may feel a cut above her neighbours, and when disappointed with her children's matches she may disengage from grandparenting, often pleading illness (pp. 67, 69).

Family-centred fathers are very high on marital adjustment, very child-centred, and tend to have their children living nearby. They have stable occupations and enjoy grandparenting, seeing their grandchildren often (pp. 18, 20, 102).

The *employed mothers* are of at least two types – those who are of low economic status and have to work, perhaps reluctantly, to make ends meet; and those who have higher education. Most of these are widows at this stage, and they tend if they have at least one of their children living nearby to see their grandchildren often. Group-centred mothers, heavily engaged in voluntary associations, church groups and the like tend to be optimistic and satisfied with their life styles, but there is no clear relationship between this and grand-parenting. They may see a good deal of their grandchildren or not, depending on the situation (pp. 72, 74).

Hobbyist fathers tend to be heavily involved in their hobbies. Whether through cause or effect, this group of fathers tends to have their children living very far away and to have fewer of them, so they do not see them as often (pp. 26, 103).

Husband-centred wives also have children living far away, and their siblings too live at a distance. Their intense involvement with their spouses seems related to this – somewhat similarly as in the case of hobbyist husbands (pp. 47, 48, 86).

Uncentred mothers, who do not have any particular idea of involve-ment, tend to be notably dissatisfied with their health and with the state of their finances. They do see their grandchildren often, though it is not immediately clear what the dynamics are underlying this pattern (pp. 54, 56).

Visiting mothers are highly sociable, act as hostesses a great deal, have many involvements which are of a reciprocal nature, and favour relationships which have a balanced mutuality about them (pp. 57, 58, 94).

Though Maas and Kuypers's work is influenced by the Chicago school and they are sophisticated psychodynamically and sociologically, their computer-based typologies are not immediately revealing in terms of the underlying dynamics presented by these cases. Another California study presents a similar blend of insights and difficulties. Lowenthal and her colleagues (1975) have produced a series of loosely linked papers on facets of experience through four life-cycle stages – for example, in relation to style of life, friendship, concept of self, responses to stress and the management of continuities and discontinuities. They note the contrasts between men and women in this life cycle stage, with women experiencing greater anticipation of doing some good in the outside world, while men anticipate a higher valuation to be placed on interpersonal-expressive goals (p. 233). This represents, for men, the kind of major discontinuity that comes with an adaptive response to occupational retirement. Accordingly, Lowenthal notes that women seemed to feel the need for increased self-assertion – but many variations are noted, both in behavioural patterns and in their consequences.

On the basis of these studies, there are some key issues apparent in this phase which provide the basis for the perceived needs of parents in relation to their grown children. On the parents' side, there is the felt need to decide on issues like whether to live with their children or not; whether to try to encourage them to go away if their personal development or success lies in that direction or not; whether to continue with work oneself and what kind of work; whether to locate oneself in postretirement years close to friends or to family or in one's own preferred milieu if different. There are reciprocal concerns on the children's side and the various life styles observed indicate how diverse the solutions are. What for one set of parents in one set of circumstances constitutes a rewarding situation, for another, constitutes a strain. We seem to need now to go beyond the accumulation of statistics and try to understand what the meaning of given patterns is in people's lives – for only then can statistical findings that are puzzling or contradictory become sensible.

Critical issues in the literature

Having reviewed the various strands of literature that deal with the years in which parenting with adult children takes place, we are struck by a paradoxical aspect of the situation. We have argued throughout the book that parents are people too. Parents have life interests other than parenting and they may well suffer if they do not express them. Until this point the book has in effect said: parenting can be very gratifying but one may not wish to try to find total personal fulfilment in it. Another of our central themes has been that work is a major source of personal satisfaction in our society, and that it requires sharing out in families: less parenting and perhaps more occupational involvement for mothers; less occupational work and more parenting for fathers.

In the earlier years of marriage and adulthood there is a vast literature on parenting, how to do it, what to expect in children's development, etc. In contrast, we find that in the later parenting phase, the literature deals with the other spheres of life, but gives little attention to parenting or grandparenting. We dealt with three 'wedges' of literature. The first, emphasizing psychobiological decline, deals with 'bodies' rather than with people. In so far as increasing physiological decline in this phase has implications for parent–child relationships, these tend to be overlooked.

The second wedge, which focuses on social roles, has little to say about the experience of parenting with adult children, or grandparenting, except to emphasize the withdrawal of adult roles from the elderly, and the often humiliating reversal of roles. This emphasizes dependent elements of older people, which we know to be inaccurate for many and inappropriate for the first two decades or so after active parenting recedes.

The third wedge emphasizes status transitions. These include occupational retirement, widowhood, women's re-entry to work, and perhaps increasingly, divorce. Finally there is death, first of one's spouse, then of oneself. It is a mistake to assume that one does not participate in one's own death. Contemporary emphasis on 'thanatology' – and the associated art of dying gracefully and providing for the emotional as well as fiscal well-being of those left behind, is a growing emphasis. These are all transitions which, while having important implications for parent–child relationships, are not focal to parenting or grandparenting. This led on to research with a developmental approach which comes closest to our own orientation. It tends to emphasize self-actualization in later life, and it is not tightly or inevitably linked with parent–child relationships, though it may be.

One reason for the scant attention given to parents of adult children who are not yet problems, is a widespread ethos that adult children should be left to lead their own lives. Parents should not interfere with them. Therefore the literature oriented to parents in the younger phases drops away. The children will now look after themselves, and their own children.

Adult children are usually married and relationships between parents- and children-in-law are not clearly regulated in our society and are often tense. Avoidance of parents-in-law is popularly recognized as a chief means of averting strained and troubled relationships. Parents may experience strong expectations that they should leave their adult children to their own destiny, except for maintaining a reasonable sociable contact, and giving help and support when the children require it. In fact, parents may be so influenced by the dictum not to interfere that they keep themselves out more than either they or their children might prefer. This is not to imply that avoidance is always practised. Many parent–adult child relationships are active and intense, and some are highly stressed, but others are not so. The point underscored here is that the expectation of leaving adult children to lead their own lives, has a corollary: that parents of adult children must seek their gratification elsewhere. Their ability to do that depends on their having viable alternative channels of involvement.

Another reason for the inattention given to parents and their needs in this phase may be that our society equates marriage and family life with the production of children (Busfield, 1974; MacIntyre, 1974). Phases in the lives of parents and children which follow after dependent childhood do not seem to be worthy of serious consideration. Young and adolescent children encourage an orientation to family life for both parents, through the demands they create for daily care, emotional involvement, and the provision of income to meet material needs. When children become adult, this ceases, and the pressures towards parents' material and emotional investment in family life are in principle lessened.

Pauline Bart's (1970) study of depression in middle-aged women indicated that depression is a likely correlate of parental redundancy. But the apparent 'phenomenon' of the depressed menopausal woman is now being studied in relation to a complex of variables. Several phenomena are tied up in a package at this point in time. The chemistry of the menopause itself may not in fact be so determining as has conventionally been thought. The void in the lives of men created by loss of their main source of identity, occupational employment, has been recognized for rather longer. For men, apprehension about enforced retirement, or worse still, the increased risk of early long-term redundancy, is widespread in this phase, as Fogarty (1975) has documented. And the prevalence of depressive phenomena of males in this phase is less directly relevant to reproductive biology, suggesting the importance of social-psychological considerations applicable to both sexes. If the meaning of parenthood to fathers is overlooked in the active parenting years, it is not surprising that the potentials for fathering in the later years have been ignored. Suggestions for potential involvements for those who have 'empty lives' in this phase, tend to follow the lines of a second chance at the same sort of things they have done up until this point. For women it is helping with their daughters' mothering: 'Grandmothers frequently care for the new mother, her baby and her family during the immediate postnatal period . . . grandmotherhood often is a major part of the middle-aged woman's solution to the loss of her children through marriage' (Leslie, 1967, p. 684). This tends to centre on practical ways of helping like babysitting. For men the central issue seems to be occupational retirement, when it will be, how to plan for it, and how to adjust to it usually by developing continuities of one kind or another.

There is another perspective in the literature which is 'reconstructionist' in nature (cf. Neugarten, 1968). This is the view that asserts the potentials for development of people's selfhood independently of their parenthood. Channels for continuing self-development are emphasized: occupational work; voluntary work; marriage; hobbies; leisure interests; community activities; health. Our own approach lies within this reconstructionist perspective. We argue that people who can realize it in their lives, are potentially able to achieve greater satisfactions in the later parts of this phase. There is conflicting and incomplete research evidence on the actual capacities of older people to develop new interests (Belbin, 1969). This is a critical element in the realization of a reconstructive approach given our society's emphasis on occupational and familistic involvements in the earlier phases. Men and women who had a spread of commitments earlier in life, have a wider range of channels for involvements and gratification potentially available to them at this stage. For those who require re-orientation, new areas of learning and cultivation of interests and relationships, we suggest there is still a good deal to be explored. There is some recognition that many people in fact flourish, rather than crumble, when relieved of active parenting roles and other domestic responsibilities and even of their spouses (through divorce or widowhood) at this stage. This seems especially true for women (Somerville, 1975). In a recent study in Chicago Gunhild Hagestad (1976) found that women in their forties and fifties in contemporary America are involved in an astonishing range of new activities and interests – set aside, but not buried during their years of active parenting. Many are glad to have reached this stage, and feel legitimately entitled to the rewards of self-development – which takes the form of everything from scuba-diving to belly-dancing.

Hagestad believes that this situation is not only potentially reconstructive for the hitherto overburdened and perhaps depressed women, but that it provides a lever for the reconstruction of their marriages. Their husbands, having devoted their main energies to occupational work, may not only have missed out on having developed relationships with their children, but on developing personal leisure and recreational interests. She can explore these now and encourage her husband. In helping to overcome the inhibitions which have been built up they may develop a new basis for their marital relationship in the later years.

The reconstructionist perspective should not be taken to exclude the potentials in the parenting and grandparenting channels because it emphasizes new learning and development. This is not intrinsic to the perspective. Perhaps the conventional emphasis on finding solutions for personal issues of later life via the family is a time-bound phenomenon that is being expressed in this way at this time, e.g. by social scientists and by their research subjects, reacting against the potential void in lives that results when all emotional eggs have been placed in the parental basket.

Another possibly time-bound issue is in relation to gender-differences. Lowenthal and her colleagues (1975, pp. 223 ff) found that in their sample of over 200 Californians at different life-cycle stages, sex-differences on a number of counts transcended life-cycle stage. Marital dissatisfaction was highest among middle-aged women (p. 226); they were more concerned with friends, emphasizing feelings and reciprocity (rather than shared interests or activities, as the men did), and had more conflicted and negative self-images, particularly in the 'empty nest' stage. Lowenthal also notes (p. 23) that while many women often show a desire for personal growth at this stage (while men tend to seek a stable work situation running up to retirement), they are often discouraged by their slim chances in a youth-centred society, and where anything goes wrong with their own children (including choice of job or mate or location that are incompatible with parental values) the mother may feel a sense of desperation and futility.

Many women whose children leave home and who do not re-enter employment are found (p. 236) to turn their nurturant attentions to their husbands, another factor possibly making for an upturn in the marital relationship's positive quality at this stage. While this may restore a level of satisfaction in the marriage, Lowenthal questions whether this is not sometimes attained at the cost of the wife's further personal development.

It may be that as more people maintain a spread of interests in the early and middle parenting years, they will wish to retain involvements in parenting and grandparenting as well as their other interests after their children are adult. And their children, less striving to cast off the weight of parental over-involvement, may allow this more easily to happen.

It is quite possible that this situation is emerging already. From the literature, however, we know little about the substantive content of ongoing parent–adult child relationships. The lights on active parenting do not go out in a flash, but there is very little written on the feelings involved in what is doubtless a salient, if drawn-out transition. This is quite opposite from the welter of attention in the literature to the feelings parents experience when children – especially the first child – enter the family. Yet the amount of contact that is known between parents and their adult children and grandchildren would seem to indicate more than a simple fulfilling of formal duties and obligations. The satisfactions of wishes and felt needs, the experience of love and respect, of wonder and curiosity – these have fallen between the stools of the scientists and the novelists, and they have scarcely caught the eye of the clinicians and social workers. Yet, they are the stuff of life for a large proportion of people in this late stage of parenting – pursued awkwardly, without guidelines or prescriptions, but important and worthy of cultivation.

For the variant groups who do not fit the picture described – the elderly who are ill or disabled, or whose children are chronically dependent and handicapped – we have special situations that require special understanding and special supports. The specialist literature on illness and handicap, on residential and medical care facilities, and on psychiatric, financial and legal aspects of this phase are only mentioned here. They become concerns of the state, or professional care-givers, and of the children or other relatives of elderly people with special needs. Their requirements are variations, we believe, on the themes presented.

9

New directions in parenting

We set out to review the literature on parents' needs, with a mandate to chart the state of the field and point to new directions in the changing roles of men and women as parents, so that their unfolding needs could better be understood. We expected the task to be very difficult as it had no guidelines and involved cutting across so many disciplines concerned with the family – sociology, psychology, anthropology, paediatrics, psychiatry, gynaecology, education, social work, architecture, planning and so on.

In many ways the task has been very difficult – often confusing and involving controversy in making choices. But there emerged an ameliorating factor when it became clear that the different fields all operated according to a model of family life with many common elements, but at the same time were at variance with new developments in the experiential world of parents as people. We are at what seems to us to be a pivotal point in history, in which new models of family life itself and the relationship between family and society are required. These are being worked out by parents themselves, with or without the 'experts'. From that point, our efforts have been directed toward searching for clues as to what the new paradigms might be, and what their properties are in terms of satisfying or frustrating the needs of parents.

We shall review the characteristics of the conventional paradigm, prevalent in the decades immediately following the Second World War (though with much deeper historical roots). Following the course of the presentation in the book, we shall summarize contemporary pre-occupations, perceived needs, interests and requirements of parents in different family life-cycle phases. Finally, we shall present our conceptions of the new directions in which parenthood is developing. To anticipate this last section of the chapter, we can state that the key element in the new directions, paradoxically, is that of new alliances: alliances between fathers and mothers; between parents and children; between families and experts; and between families and society.

Paradoxically because this is an era in which there is considerable anxiety about the family as a social institution, and many of the trends are toward individualistic rather than co-operative solutions.

This does not mean that we suggest a single trend. There are trends of different kinds: individualistic ones (e.g. in divorce, infidelity, single-parent families of choice, non-marriage and non-parenting) as well as cooperative ones (e.g. communes, group relationships of various kinds, public interest in the family). And there are variant patterns within each.

The elements of the previously dominant paradigm (which we call the *conventional model* of the conjugal family) are as follows:

1 The male head of the household, the father, is the sole economic provider.
2 The female head of the household, the mother, is the home-maker, and is responsible for domestic care and the socialization of the children. She is a helpmeet to the husband, providing support for him in his struggle for the family's survival.
3 The children are helpless and dependent, vulnerable and malleable. They must be nurtured full-time by the mother (or mother-surrogate) only, as emotional stability is essential.
4 The family is a private institution and within it individuals can fulfil their most important needs. This fulfilment is based on the foundation of the economic income provided by the husband (where necessary, supplemented by the state). Only when economic and material needs have been met do expressions of psychological and social needs for love, esteem, self-expression and fulfilment emerge within the family.
5 Healthy families produce healthy individuals, who adjust to social roles.

The conventional model assumed a Darwinian 'fitness' of all of the elements to one another and to the environment. Men were assumed to be fitted to the masculine role models because they were bigger, stronger, more aggressive, more competent and more capable of forming bonds with other men to defend their families and social groups. Women were assumed to be more fitted to the domestic/maternal role because they were assumed to be nurturant, patient and caring, intuitive of the needs of children, and naturally more concerned with their small family groups rather than with forming bonds with others to pursue extraneous goals. The conjugal family as a unit was assumed to be more fitted to the kind of social environment that industrial society provided because it was small, mobile, flexible and had complementary internal structures, so that the head of the household could respond to market forces without constraints from his spouse. The child-centred attitude was considered fitted to the needs of children, who are so vulnerable for so long – mentally as well as physically – and who require the focused and intense emotional inputs provided in small families to develop optimally. The ideology surrounding the conventional model even suggested, in the 1950s and 1960s in the USA, that this model was fitted for parents in that they could realize the fullest joy and 'fun' through having their own homes, their own children and playing a creative role in relation to them.

Research in the 1950s and early 1960s tended to support the conventional paradigm. More males than females were found, statistically, to be aggressive, for example. And this was found throughout the mammalian species and in lower animal forms. More females were found to be nurturant, unambitious and child-centred in their values. More nuclear families with single earning heads were found to be responsive to job opportunities in other locations, and more children were found to suffer if deprived of their mother's care through precipitous institutionalization. Research of that era was addressed primarily to women; data was drawn primarily from women, and researchers asked the kinds of questions which were limited in scope to the conventional framework of assumptions.

Recently this has been overlaid with two additional types of research findings. The first queries the validity of the earlier data or conclusions – or its applicability to current situations. Skolnick, 1973; Hoffman and Nye, 1974; Maccoby and Jacklin, 1974; Yudkin and Holme, 1963; Rutter, 1974, etc., indicate how each of the fundamental points is open to query. The second type of research showed that the conventional model was not working as well as it had been assumed to do in its own terms. Many children cared for by full time mothers get into difficulties or create difficulties for others; many home-making mothers are distressed; many households have dual-workers and this is demonstrably not inevitably associated with malfunctioning of the family or of individuals in it. Divorce occurs in conventional families, and for reasons associated with the conventional pattern (e.g. that the wife does not 'grow' in a way co-ordinated with the husband). Responsiveness to occupational demands makes for marital stresses.

In fact, the nuclear conjugal family of the conventional model is no longer the mode statistically. It is a variant pattern, with its own problems and advantages – like the others. One element in the new direction implied then is to accept the idea of variation as the norm. But variation is not necessarily a good in itself. Some variants are satisfying for some people, not for others. Take the single parent situation for example. Some single-parent families are associated with negative characteristics – for example, poverty, abandonment, marital violence, child abuse and neglect, psychological depression, sexual exploitation and personal dissatisfaction. Other single-parent families are so by choice and enjoy a low level of parental conflict, and often a sense of family solidarity and co-operation.

One approach to an appreciation of how patterns of preoccupations, needs and requirements emerge and become established is the life-cycle framework. We have treated the family cycle in four phases – but it should be recognized that to some extent these are arbitrary. They are overlapping and may be variously experienced in different circumstances.

In Chapter 4, 'Parenting begins before birth', we began with a discussion of the decision to parent. Given the modern medical and technological resources available to young adults, the decision of whether to parent, when to parent, and with whom to parent has become increasingly, though still not entirely, a matter of personal choice. Considerations which formerly dominated this decision, such as expectations of one's own parents, of people generally, ideas of normality, etc., are now part of a larger array of considerations which include information about risks of parenting at different ages, methods of contraception and insemination. New definitions of parenting centre on consideration of the relevant tasks, costs and benefits, from an emotional as well as a financial point of view. A realistic appraisal in advance of undertaking the role is called for, and there is no assumption that one solution is the only or the universally preferred one. Though there are accidental pregnancies and pregnancies which are unplanned on principle or religious scruple, there is a tendency among young couples to be preoccupied with the decision to parent at this early stage of their marriage or intimate relationship, even if only to defer the decision. The perceived needs of specific individuals – to plan or not to plan, to parent within a conventional family structure or outside it – are increasingly recognized as legitimate alternative options, provided the individuals are competent and caring.

Beyond this, parenting begins before birth in that the pregnancy stage allows not only for biological growth and its associated psychological and social adjustments, but for anticipatory experience. Individuals during pregnancy experience a flood of feelings from within, whatever the source, which can be disturbing and which also have the potential for a reassessment of personal life values that may allow for growth and for changes in important relationships. There are many value elements and 'meanings' attached to having a child; in reviewing them, implicitly or explicitly, individuals come to have a new conception of themselves, their motivations and values. While it is possible to just let childbirth 'happen', there are indications that psychological rehearsal of the experience is helpful as a preparation for parenthood. It may dispel over-idealization of the experience which can divert individual parents from confronting some of the more demanding and frustrating elements of the transition to parenthood. It can also be useful in preparing for the practical tasks that must be accomplished if a place is to be made in the home for the new baby. Finally, it can be useful in planning for the impact of the baby on the family's pattern of work and marital relations.

The father's participation in the experience, both during pregnancy and in the course of the delivery and early infancy, is increasingly being recognized, at least as a potential element of value in the situation. Part of the reason that the father's involvement has been neglected in our society is the assumption that birth is purely a female experience following conception, and partly because of the medical mystique, making the experience one that has to be handled on a technical level by physicians and hospital staff. It is their birth. With increased recognition of the psychological meanings of the experience for the mother and child there is also an increased recognition of the father's concerns and his potential rewards in being involved and tied into the experience.

There are suggestions in recent research that preparation for parenthood by both mother and father will increase their own satisfactions in the experience and improve their relationship with the child, with potential long term benefits for all involved. The tendency in our society to shield parents from such experiences – the sight of birth process, of newborn babies, etc. – makes the shock of the transition a potentially overpowering experience. Or it may create or crystallize a feeling of being excluded. To the extent that participation in the whole process can be encouraged, felt needs other than those associated with recovering from the shock of the experience can be met – to enjoy it, to share it, to get involved in it, even to suffer with it and to feel that it was the parents' (not only the doctors or the hospital's) achievement; to feel that there has been a productive alliance in which parents, baby and technical experts all had a share.

In Chapter 5 we discussed some of the main *development issues that children experience in the long span of growth from toddlerhood to puberty*. The reason for considering these issues separately was that this is the topic and phase of life that has received the greatest attention in the literature; this reflects both the paramount expressed interest in children in our society and also the intrinsic drama and complexity of children's development through these years. The constant challenge and stimulation of the child's growth as a person in the household – in language, in motor skills, in thinking and reasoning, in expressions of feelings of love and anger, in problems of dealing with the demands of life in society – controlling appetites and instincts, channelling wishes and desires, handling competitive and rivalrous feelings and so on – are the ordinary stuff of child development. They also are of the essence in parenting, and therefore require to be incorporated into the lives of parents, who as people, are simultaneously experiencing developmental problems and issues other than procreation and child rearing.

Six child-developmental issues which parents confront were discussed; separation and the child's development of autonomy; aggression and discipline; early sex-role identity formation; social and moral development; performance and achievement motivation; and the consolidation of gender identity.

In relation to each of these issues, the experts and authorities in different fields have developed various theoretical formulations to understand the observed behaviour, underlying psychological dynamics, and social influences of the growing child. Parents, too, are guided by such formulations – not always explicitly. Relatively little is known about how parents integrate the theories and recommended practices of authorities into their own conceptions and perceptions of the situations presented by their growing children. Educators have tended to favour Piaget's theories, and social workers Freud's. But parents seem to show variations by social class, by type of occupational setting (bureaucratic *vs* entrepreneurial), and ethnic group in terms of how they interpret children's behaviour, and do not seem to fall easily into the moulds of the different theoretical schools. Middle-class tendencies to be permissive and to encourage interpretive discussions and explanations of thoughts and feelings may be seen as akin to the psychoanalytic approach. Working-class tendencies to respond to overt behaviour and to place limits by physical punishment if necessary, may be seen as akin in some ways to Skinnerian, behaviourist approaches. The relatively lower expectation that working class parents hold that they can mould the child's development (as compared with the middle-class view) is similar, to some extent, to the Piagetian approach. These resemblances are speculative and not integral to our analysis which centres on an attempt to understand how the children's issues bear on the parents' *own* preoccupations at this stage of their lives. This forms the basis of the discussion in Chapter 6.

In Chapter 6 we note that *parents of children in the stage from toddlerhood to puberty are in the early and mid-establishment phases of their own family and work careers.* In these phases they tend to be preoccupied with being productive and performing well in areas of personal investment. The conventional gender-based division of labour in the family has directed women toward satisfying their preoccupations with productivity in home-making and being *re*-productive within the family setting. They are expected to feel a natural need to create a stable and satisfying environment for their husbands and a healthy atmosphere within which their children can develop. In doing so, it has

been expected that they should satisfy their own needs. Complemen-
tarily, husbands have been expected naturally to feel the need to direct
their productive energies into the occupational world outside the home,
to make their investments of energy in the economy and in so doing to
provide for their families and simultaneously satisfy their own needs.

Contemporary research, as distinct from earlier work conducted in
a framework of conventional assumptions and value orientations, has
emphasized the ways in which this overall picture has become blurred.
While many women fit the classical picture, others feel that their needs
are not fulfilled by being homemakers. Similarly, many men are
rejecting the idea of an all-out commitment to work, feeling that it
robs them of the possibility of developing other facets of themselves.
Some women do not wish to have children, and some men would like
to be more with their children. People have needs which are more
diversified than can usually be encompassed by sorting them into
sharply differentiated roles by gender; the housewife role on the one
side and the occupational role on the other. These needs are legitimate
and 'natural' and may conflict with the demands of child-rearing,
particularly if it is conceived of as a full-time, totally demanding,
one-person job. A woman who is trained in a skill, for example, may
feel the need to exercise her skill, to interact with others who share her
interests, and to develop herself as a person partly through the expression of this skill. In this she is no different from her husband and
they may both be highly responsible and conscientious parents
with a deep interest in their child's development.

Much of the available literature documents the difficulties that such
individuals experience in altering their life circumstances to accommodate these diverse, equally valid sets of felt needs. High rates of
depression and attempted suicide among lonely, captive wives; increasing levels of marital tension as the phase progresses; accumulating
alienation in the husbands – not only from their families but from their
jobs, with their principal toll delayed and paid in later phases through
stress-induced disease and lower life expectation.

Aside from the difficulties that parents experience in reconciling role
expectations with personal needs, there are difficulties induced by the
conventional division of labour in relation to parenting. The whole
separation issue (of mother and child) might be less emotionally
charged were individual mothers less totally assigned the responsibility – and with such terrible potential consequences held out for
defection. The whole issue of discipline and the management of aggression might be less exhausting for wives were fathers acknowledged as
having a regular responsibility.

Sex-role identification and gender identity too, might be less distressing as an issue if parents did not feel constrained to press each

child into culturally defined roles – little girls like mother; little boys like father. Children, in fact, embody facets of each and might be facilitated to have an easier and richer developmental experience if it were recognized rather than creating confusions and a sense of mismatch if the two sets of roles are considered as discrete.

The linked issues of moral development and achievement are also tied in with parents' conceptions of their own lives. If parents feel that there is equity in their relationship and that the satisfactions that they accumulate with their pattern of emotional investments are acceptable, they are not only more likely to produce children who will have a well developed moral sense, but this is likely to reinforce their own sense of having done the right thing.

A mother who feels lonely and isolated, unfairly treated and wasted is hardly likely to provide a satisfactory role model *even* for her growing daughter; and she is unlikely to be an effective disciplinarian for her children. Neither mother nor father are likely to present a firm moral basis for their children's formation of values if they have mixed feelings about what they are doing. The father who feels trapped 'in a rut' or caught up in a 'rat race' is hardly likely to encourage his child with any conviction to follow in his footsteps. A mother who is angry with father's inaccessibility is hardly likely to provide a convincing argument to her children that they should emulate him, or more generally accept the parents' life style and values. These are only illustrations of how parents' own concerns with their life predicaments rebound on their performance as parents, and thereby their life experience as developing individuals.

It should not be implied from this that there are easy or unitary solutions. Parents who argue, for example, for a dual-worker pattern and who practise it themselves but with heavy emotional costs in terms of overloads and tensions, may also create an atmosphere in which their children say 'not for us'; but there may be less of a sense of hypocrisy than in some other situations where parents say, in effect 'do as I say, not as I do'.

In attempting to assess the lines along which these structural dilemmas are likely to be resolved, we have indicated that contemporary research and action suggest a range of new alliances and supports for the family which foreshadow the directions along which parents are likely to seek future resolutions. These new patterns include the increased recognition that fathers have talents, interests and potentials as sharers of the active parenting required at this phase. This is for themselves as well as their children. There is a domestic work-sharing morality that centres on the idea of *equity*, and the potential benefits and satisfactions that a sense of equity can bring. The growth of family supports in the community – child-minders, playgroups, neighbourhood networks, pre-school groups, crêches associated with the work-place, and so on, is a very significant aid to the development of new parenting patterns. These are felt by many parents to be supportive of family life in the contemporary situation rather than seen as threats to the family, as some opponents of such programmes have argued. There are problems of economic cost and of quality control, and of compatibility with the specific families concerned. But these represent tasks and challenges rather than insuperable barriers.

There are risks of casualties which must be anticipated and guarded against. But it is fallacious to presume that there are no risks and no casualties in the conventional pattern. Many are simply less visible.

At a more ambitious level, the re-structuring of the workplace and pressure on government to assign greater priority to the needs of families is an issue that is increasingly to the fore. Here we are only beginning to consider the real, as contrasted with the presumed, impact on economic production of a re-structured social organization of work – allowing for more part-time jobs, flexible working arrangements, and job sharing.

We return to these issues below, but note them here because it is in this phase of the family cycle that the whole question of supports and changes for the family arises and requires action. It is important in the context of the present book to note that the inputs to support parents at this stage of life are crucial not only in the interests of the children who are vulnerable and whose personalities are being formed, but for developing parents themselves. They are in the prime of their lives and seek meaning for their lives at this stage. Many fear (and some research supports their anxiety) that if they do not develop themselves as well as their children at this stage, they never will.

In Chapter 7 we consider another range of problems and issues as they are presented to parents by *adolescent children*. Characteristically, the issues posed by adolescents impinge on parental lives at a point when the latter are at a late establishment phase. Parents at this stage are preoccupied with making a critical evaluation of how the life investments they have been making are paying off. Has it all been worthwhile? What has it added up to? Could I have done better? These are the sorts of questions that parents feel the need to answer for themselves at this stage of their lives. Contrary to popular images, children at this stage not only do not always accommodate their parents' needs by being model products of the parental investment in child rearing, but they often raise new problems which complicate the parents' lives.

We noted the resemblance between the emotional turbulence experienced by the adult at midlife (when a revision of life values is salient) and that of adolescence (when the task of crystallization of personal values in order to form an identity separate from that of the parents is salient). The two may form a reverberating chain of interactions affecting the experience and life resolutions of both.

If the parent is depressed about the life investments, his child may be influenced, for example, to reject the occupational or other value choices the parent has made, only further depressing the parent. If the child is heterosexually adventurous, this may influence one or both of the parents whose relationship has become sterile to 'open' their marriage, overtly or covertly, with potentially far-reaching consequences. The overpowering urge to 'take off' and strike out in a new direction may originate at either generational level and affect the other. Competitiveness, struggles over setting limits to behaviour, conflicts over life goals and values, may all be personal issues which take on a heightened character because of the interactive quality of the relations between parents and their children at this phase.

For the most part, however, parenting with adolescent children involves a more mundane range of tasks and problems, which continue to absorb parents' time and energies. Though young people mature biologically and socially at an earlier age than previously, this may only exacerbate the problems created by their feeling 'ready to fly' before their parents consider they have the wherewithal to do so. Young people's manners, dress, hours, associations, habits, choices of job, leisure activities, travel plans – all may stimulate parents to become involved. Children may make false starts, get into difficulties, and quite suddenly feel the need of care and help. Or, if it is an unruly child or one under the influences of delinquent peer groups, parents may feel unable to control the child any longer, and want to call in external help or to eject the child.

The financial costs of having an adolescent child may also be greater, particularly if the child continues with higher education. It may be a close match between these rising costs and the rising income of the father, and this may precipitate the mother's choice to re-enter work.

Parents at this phase of their lives may also confront the fact that *their* parents are now very old and may need active help for the first time. This gives many parents a feeling of being caught in the middle, between the demands of the rising generation and those of the declining one – with less chance than they would have liked at this stage to attend to their own needs without considerable conflict or guilt.

This does not imply that there are no joys of parenting with adolescent children. They can be delightful. They are no longer children. They have interesting ideas and interests. They may be sexually attractive, sometimes disturbingly so. And they may have charming and attractive friends – as well as friends who worry parents.

In the autonomous achievements of the adolescent child – at school or college, at work or in the community – parents may feel the kind of pride at having come through an arduous set of hurdles not only intact themselves, but with a tangible product for their work in the well-being of their child.

In Chapter 8 we consider the *later years, parenting with adult children and grandparenting, in which there is a preoccupation with personal integrity.* In most textbooks and research treatises, these years are considered 'post-parental', and a common picture portrayed is that as the need for active parenting recedes, the individual parent declines physically, psychologically and socially, perhaps reversing their roles with their children in a 'second childhood'. For a complex of reasons, this formulation is not accepted as adequate. Changes in health care and life expectancy, changes in levels of affluence and economic provision for the older years, improved housing and other provision for elderly people make possible a long and potentially active period of life when people are parents of adult children. Physical impairment may eventually require withdrawn or dependent patterns of relating to one's children, but for many this contingency never arises. During the long period following the child's reaching adulthood parents may evolve a new relationship with the children over a span of 20 or 30 years. Preoccupied at this stage of their lives with realizing a sense of integrity, and a capacity to take a mature and balanced perspective on their life experiences, parents may be a family resource. They may relate to their children in this phase as advisers and as friends, and to their grand-children as people who have 'time to stop and stare', to play and listen and struggle to master and discover (again) the wondrous things of life and experience. This kind of relationship was described by Young and Willmott between young mothers and their mothers in the conventional setting of old Bethnal Green. It is less well described in other settings, and there are some indications that this is an idealized picture which, like the conventional family structure, may work well for many but is far from a universally acceptable prescription. The modern grand-mother may herself be part of a dual-worker family, perhaps even more actively engaged than her husband, having returned with a zest to employment outside the home after remaining at home for many years. Her availability for child-minding may be much more limited than she would earlier have envisioned. Or there may be asymmetries, with the grandparents' desired inputs to their children's family life and parental activities being perceived as problematic.

In general, parents of adult children are confronted by the need to reorganize their relationships and commitments. Husbands and wives have another chance to re-generate some of the old interest in one another now that the daily distractions of child-rearing have abated.

They may feel the need to do something active to make the rest of their lives together enjoyable when they are no longer oriented for so much of the time to the children's daily needs. They may remain on call from the children, for material aid on occasion, or for baby-sitting, advice or help in times of distress (a child's divorce is likely to be an increasingly common late-life crisis). To some extent they may welcome these demands as a sign that they are still needed. Alternatively, the older parents' interests may diverge as the older wife unleashes her pent-up wishes to be out and involved with new experiences at a time when her husband is seeking a quieter life. There are potential problems of being out of phase with one another at this stage, and there is a discernible sub-group opting for divorce at this stage, when 'the children' are no longer a daily pressure to deter them. But overall the picture obtained by surveys of the cycle of marital happiness shows a tendency for an upturn of satisfactions in marital relationships at this phase.

The occupational retirement of the husband provides one of the most characteristic critical transitions for elderly parents. According to the husband's occupational situation and his other interests, his retirement may be a smooth one allowing a new phase of personal development and enjoyment, or it may be a shock and produce a sense of emptiness, goallessness, and demoralization. If the wife has remained a full-time homemaker, she may feel the unaccustomed presence of a demoralized husband around the house so much of the time as disruptive. In any case, the new routines are likely to require adjustments. If she is involved in an occupation outside the home and is not yet ready to retire, there may be conflicts, for example, about where they should live. In this there are elements comparable to the earlier conflicts when the husband was presented with a desirable job opportunity which required moving while the wife wished to remain where she was. Nevertheless, while many couples continue in an alienated, or even conflict-habituated rut in this period, others are able to alter their relationship toward a more satisfying one.

The course of parents' lives as people in this later life phase is affected by an additional event that is likely: bereavement. One of the spouses has to die first, and this has tended in our society to be the male (given the practice of older males marrying younger females, and males reaching old age after a protracted period of high stress of occupational commitments over a forty-year span). Bereavement is a process that is often not satisfactorily managed. Many patterns are observed, from the pathological mourner who does not disengage from the emotional involvement with the dead person, to the 'merry widow' who is happy to be released. Housing is a major issue here. Elderly people, and often their adult children as well, prefer something between living alone and actually living in their children's homes. Our society, with its emphasis on the independence of individual and conjugal households, has not provided viable cultural patterns, rituals or social structures to handle many people's requirements at this time.

If alliances of a regular and mutually rewarding kind cannot be sustained with one's own children, elderly parents require other kinds of alliances; with their peers, with groups of varied age sharing an interest, with local groups and in different activities, including care for other people's children. The continuing felt need of many elderly people to be able to give and to feel useful is only partly tapped in our society, for example, through voluntary work. Correspondingly elderly people's capacities for continuing self-development are only partly realized.

Research and policy issues

Research on the family, as in other branches of social science, has suffered not only from the expectable immaturities that are natural accompaniments of new disciplines, but also, and most poignantly, from the schismatic tendencies between different scientific approaches. Those favouring experimental and quantitative approaches require preformulated questions that can be answered within a feasible controlled design framework. They do not regard other types of investigation as scientific. The more naturalistic approach that seeks inductively to understand people through immersion in their experience (rather than observation of their behaviour) is more tentative in its conclusions, more applicable to the formulation of new questions or the development of new concepts. Of course the two are complementary and should be in perpetual alliance, as Medawar (1965) has pointed out.

In practice, the conception has developed, following Popper (1963) and others, that the most productive sequence of scientific investigation is to discover or invent a formulation, a conjecture, and then proceed to the business of verifying it. A conceptual model or paradigm is developed that serves as a framework within which systematic tests are applied for confirmation or refutation. But this approach may not only fail to exhaust the potential for scientific development if constrained by a dominating conceptual model or frame, but it may actually provide an impediment to advancing knowledge. The insistence on objective tests may become what Liam Hudson (1972) has described as 'Cult of the Fact.' This occurs when the paradigm within which the facts are relevant has become obsolescent, however 'right' it may have been at the time of its early establishment.

We feel that we are at such a point now in relation to understanding family life, of fathers, mothers and their relationships to their children, one another and society. Social changes in occupations, in domestic life, in the conceptions and values we have about men and women and their developmental experiences have brought about a situation where a new formulation is required about the nature of men and women and of the family as a social institution. The new formulation should be a dynamic, ecological one (Emery and Trist (1973); Bronfenbrenner (1976)). At the heart of the new formulation we propose is the emphasis on family linkages and alliances in the social environment rather than, as in the past, family isolation and privacy.

It is in this context that the suggestions that follow are formulated. We hope that the issues proposed will serve as springboards for research and social policy. As we have indicated, research formulations relate not only to the state of scientific knowledge but to prevailing social conditions and personal value orientations. Accordingly we present a selection of salient topical areas which reflect the pluralistic value orientation which we and others hold and discern as coming into prominence. They are stated as zones or wedges of interest for potential research and social policy.

1. *Sharing of parenting within the family*

This indicates the importance of assessing the experience of different patterns of parental division of labour. What, for example, are the conditions under which fathers experience satisfactions by increasing their share of parenting? What are the impediments? What are the implications for mothers? What are the potential losses as well as gains for mothers and fathers in a restructuring of parenting within the family?

2. *Broadening the concept of parenting to include supplementary figures other than mothers and fathers*

This implies a recognition of the potentials for parenting by people other than fathers and mothers – inside and outside the family. Children, kin, neighbours, professional helpers, and friends may contribute to parenting. What are the potentials of these other parent-figures (in terms of their motivation, their competence, their compatibility) and what are the drawbacks? There are likely to be advantages and pitfalls of 'opening' families more than has been customary hitherto. In our society, this 'opening' has tended to relate to deficiency or inadequacy of family functioning. Potentially it could relate also to a desirable strengthening or expanding of family functions, linking them in various alliances with other persons and agencies.

3. *Alternative parenting arrangements*

New parenting arrangements are occurring outside the conventional family structure altogether – for example, in communes, intimate networks and informal fostering. The experiences of parental figures and of children within such contexts are important to assess so that a better understanding may emerge as to conditions under which alternative arrangements deal constructively with deficiencies of the conventional family pattern, and those where the new problems raised are as troublesome or more so than those they seek to avoid.

4. *Gender identity*

Under what conditions does an alteration in the patterns of parenting result in a situation that is confusing, both to parents and children, in relation to their sexual identity? Do confusions of sex role and identity arise with departures of fathers and/or mothers from their conventional parenting roles? Who is confused? Why and with what consequences? Are there new positive effects? Do these cancel or balance any confusions that may arise?

5. *The management of separations and attachments*

The processes of separation and attachment for both parents and children is crucial in forging new parenting alliances. But, it is crucial in a different way from that emphasized in simplistic theories of separation. Managing separation is likely to be seen as neither an innate instinctual process nor as an easily acquirable management skill, but as something with elements of both. It is likely to be an increasingly important requirement of modern living generally. Past research, focusing on unfavourable conditions, has provided information on hazards and limits. New research is now required to study the cultivation of latent potentials for dealing with these processes constructively.

6. *Parental values*

There are various value conflicts necessarily involved in parenting within the new framework proposed. Values of self-actualization must at some points be recognized to conflict with those of care-giving. At a societal level, there are recurrent value conflicts between groups, for example, that see abortion as a right and those that see it as a sin; groups that see the provision of day-care facilities as a threat to the family and those who see it as a support; groups that see mothers' work as a boon and those that see it as a menace. Research is needed on the various value positions that exist in relation to family and parenting issues, and how they get resolved at personal, interpersonal and societal levels. How, in a pluralistic society and a time of changing values do parents develop a sense of how they should behave from among the value options in their environment? How do industries, local communities and government departments confront and reconcile these potential conflicts when they arise?

7. *Information for parenting*

There is a sense, of course, in which parenting cannot be taught. But, it would be fallacious to assume from this part-truth that there is nothing that can be taught about parenting, or that there is no one who requires such teaching to become effective as a parent. A great deal of information is provided for parents by experts, by parent advice agencies, by friends, neighbours and relatives, on the assumption that there is some knowledge that can be usefully applied; and, indeed that some knowledge is important in parenting, as in other areas of living. But little is known about how parents and others engaged in the parenting enterprise obtain, apply and modify through experience the information available to them in ways that retain the specifically humanistic caring components required for healthy parenting. In an area where expert authoritative prescription is likely to be put in a different perspective from the recent past, it is perhaps more important than ever to understand how parents use information and with what effect.

Underlying all these points, it is important to keep alive a consideration of human variability and potential for new patterns of parenting. The tendency has been to see people's fitness for parenting in terms of their having or not having particular stereotyped traits – such as nurturance, or a maternal instinct. But people have different personality constellations, skills and interests. This implies that they are potentially capable of contributing to parental love and care in *various* ways while meeting both their children's and their own needs. This is the basis for the suggestion of new alliances based on the different and complementary inclinations and capacities people have.

The issues suggested require specification and follow through on various levels – for example as they reflect cultural patterns and contradictions in our society as a whole (Bell, 1975); as they affect and are affected by different conceptions of the state's relation to the family (Moroney, 1976); as they relate to specific social policies (Rein, 1976; Kahn and Kamerman, 1975; Land, forthcoming); as they relate to changing sex roles (Safilios-Rothschild, 1974); as they relate to values in having and rearing children (Bronfenbrenner, 1971); and as they relate to specific partnerships that may be developed between parents and professionals (Brimblecombe, 1976).

The kinds of issues that become salient as threats to the family, or as unmet policy needs for families, vary through time. In early industrialization, for example, the problems of exploitation of women and children in sweatshop factory conditions and mines, the toll of infant mortality and unhygienic living conditions, and the lack of educational and health facilities were salient. With advances in medicine and technology, new conditions of domestic and occupational life and new orders of organizational provision these problems are no longer so salient but new issues and problems have arisen. We do not of course examine all of them here, because many relate to the topic of parents' needs only peripherally; for example, the problems of forging a multi-racial society. However, for a complex of reasons indicated above, we feel that it is now both possible and important to make policies that will take into account the predicament of ordinary families, not just deprived or pathological ones. As Kahn and Kamerman have written, social policy is 'not for the poor alone'.

This does not mean that those in dire need should not be helped: nor does it mean that the state should have a guiding hand in everyone's private life. But the reality of contemporary life points to the impression that many ordinary families are in trouble. They are in trouble not so much because of the older problems of poverty, poor housing and sanitation, but because they have inherited conceptions of family life that are inadequate to cope with the requirements of modern living. This is not merely a matter of over-idealization of marriage and the family, though this is certainly part of the inadequacy of our inherited pattern. Nor is it only a question of coping with the problems posed by mass society, the problems of traffic, pollution, noise, impersonality and other noxious elements of the urban environment. It includes these elements, and more.

From the perspective of parents as people, a central issue confronting them is how to function in a society such as ours, with its conflicting and rapidly changing directives. Authoritative standards on parenting are lacking or incompatible, and neither traditional sources nor the experts provide satisfactory guides. Neither is it acceptable that parents should simply do as they feel; the vulnerabilities and difficulties of such a course are too great. What is required, though, is not an attitude of indifference, however benign, but a recognition of the complexity of contemporary issues, a readiness to accept that there are likely to be different ways of dealing with them, and a cultivation of the capacity to work with and resolve problems of living as parents in today's society. This is likely to take time; it is likely to involve non-rational, instinctual, even genetically determined elements as well as those accessible to intellectual mastery. Nevertheless, it is likely to be facilitated, not impaired, by the development (not necessarily provision) of social supports and alliances. There is the need for an acceptance of new linkages between the family and its environment. This is required as a potential channel for correcting inequities hidden in the excessive privatization of the form of family life we have received from the past. But return to a nostalgic form of idealized family life is not the solution. We live in a pluralistic society, requiring tolerance of variation and acceptance of a multiplicity of models for living. We desire a responsible and caring society, requiring a high degree of human involvement. The challenge facing parents and society today is how to forge new alliances, both within the family and between the family and society that will accomplish these diverse requirements.

Bibliography

Abrams, M. A. (1963), 'How and why we spend our money', *Twentieth Century*, 134-8.

Abrams, M. A. (1973), 'Subjective social indicators', *Social Trends No. 4*, London, HMSO, 35-50.

Abrams, M. A. (1974), 'This Britain: 1. A contented nation', *New Society*, 21 February.

Abrams, P. and McCulloch, A. (1976), *Communes, Sociology and Society*, Cambridge University Press.

Ackerman, N. W. (1958), *The Psychodynamics of Family Life*, New York, Basic Books.

Adams, M. (1960), *The Mentally Subnormal, a Social Casework Approach*, London, Heinemann.

Adams, M. (1967), 'Siblings of the retarded – their problems and treatment', *Child Welfare*, 46, 310-16.

Agnello, T. J. Jr (1973), 'Aging and the sense of political powerlessness', *Public Opinion Quarterly*, summer, 37, 2, 251-9.

Ainsworth, M. D. S. (1962), 'Object relations, dependency and attachment: a theoretical review of the infant-mother relationship', *Child Development*, 40, 969-1027.

Ainsworth, M. D. S. (1972), 'Further research into the adverse effects of material deprivation', pt III of 2nd edn of Bowlby, J. *Child Care and the Growth of Love*, Harmondsworth, Penguin.

Aldous, J. (1969a), 'Wives' employment status and lower-class men as husband-fathers: support for the Moynihan thesis', *Journal of Marriage and the Family*, 31, 3, 469-76.

Aldous, J. (1969b), 'Occupational characteristics and males: role performance in the family', *Journal of Marriage and the Family*, 31, 4.

Anderson, R. E. (1968), 'Where's dad? Paternal deprivation and delinquency', *Archives of General Psychiatry*, 18, 641-9.

Andry, R. (1960), *Delinquency and Parental Pathology*, London, Methuen.

Andry, R. (1962), 'Paternal and maternal roles and delinquency', *Deprivation of Maternal Care*, Geneva, WHO Public Health Papers, no. 14.

Anthony, J. and Benedek, T. (eds) (1970), *Parenthood: Its Psychology and Psychopathology*, Boston, Little, Brown.

Arensberg, C. M. and Kimball, S. T. (1968), *Family and Community in Ireland*, 2nd edn, Cambridge, Mass., Harvard University Press.

Aries, P. (1962), *Centuries of Childhood: a Social History of Family Life*, Robert Baldick (trans.), New York, Knopf.

Ashdown-Sharp, P. (1975), *The Single Woman's Guide to Pregnancy and Parenthood*, Harmondsworth, Penguin.

Atkin, M. (1974), 'The doomed family – observations on the lives of parents and children facing repeated child mortality', in Burton, L. (ed.), *Care of the Child Facing Death*, London, Routledge & Kegan Paul.

Aves, G. (1976), 'Pivot: Report of a working party on the National Association of Voluntary Help Organisers', Berkhamsted, Volunteer Centre.

Bailyn, L. (1970), 'Career and family orientations of husbands and wives in relation to marital happiness', *Human Relations*, 23, 12, 97–113.

Bailyn, L. (1974), *Accommodation as a Career Strategy: Implications for the Realm of Work*, Sloan School of Management, MIT.

Bailyn, L. (1976), 'Involvement and accommodation in technical careers: an enquiry into the relation to work at mid-career' in Van Maanen, J. (ed.), *New Perspectives in Organizational Careers*, New York, Wiley.

Bales, R. F. (1950), *Interaction Process Analysis: a Method for the Study of Small Groups*, Cambridge, Mass., Addison-Wesley.

Bandura, A. (1965), 'Influence of model's reinforcement contingencies on the acquisition of imitative responses', *Journal of Personality and Social Psychology*, 1, 589–95.

Bandura, A. and Walters, R. H. (1959), *Adolescent Aggression*, New York, Ronald.

Bandura, A. and Walters, R. H. (1963), *Social Learning and Personality Development*, New York, Holt, Rinehart & Winston.

Barber, D. (1975), *Unmarried Fathers*, London, Hutchinson.

Bart, P. (1970), 'Mother Portnoy's complaint', *Transaction*, 8, 69–74.

Bart, P. (1971), 'The myth of a value-free psychotherapy', in Bell, W. and Man, J. (eds), *The Sociology of the Future*, New York, Russell Sage.

Beck, J. (1968), *How to Raise a Brighter Child*, London, Allen & Unwin.

Belbin, R. M. (1969), *The Discovery Method: an International Experiment in Retraining*, Paris, OECD (Employment of Older Workers, no. 6).

Bell, C. (1969), *Middle Class Families*, London, Routledge & Kegan Paul.

Bell, C. and Healey, P. (1973), 'The family and leisure', in *Leisure and Society in Britain*, Smith, M., Parker, S. and Smith, C. (eds), London, Allen Lane, ch. 11, 159–70.

Bell, D. (1975), *Contradictions of Capitalism*, New York, Basic Books.

Bell, R. Q. (1968), 'A reinterpretation of the direction of effects in studies of socialization', *Psychological Review*, 75, 2, 81–95, March.

Belson, W. A. (1975), *Juvenile Theft: the Causal Factors*, London and New York, Harper & Row.

Benedek, T. (1959), 'Parenthood as a developmental phase', *Journal of the American Psychological Association*, 7, 389–417.

Benedek, T. (1970a), 'The psychobiology of pregnancy', in Anthony, E. J. and Benedek, T. (eds), *Parenthood: its Psychology and Psychopathology*, 137–51, Boston, Little, Brown.

Benedek, T. (1970b), 'Fatherhood and providing', in Anthony, E. J. and Benedek, T. (eds), *Parenthood: its Psychology and Psychopathology*, 167–83, Boston, Little, Brown.

Berelson, B. (1974), 'The value of children', in Talbot, N. (ed.), *Raising Children in Modern America*, Boston, Little, Brown.

Berger, B., Hackett, B. and Millar, R. M. (eds) (1972), 'A Communal Family', in Sussman, M. B. (ed.), *Non-traditional Family Forms in the 1970s*, Minneapolis, National Council of Family Relations.

Bernal, J. (1973), 'Night waking in infants during the first 14 months', *Developmental Medicine and Child Neurology*, 15, 760–9.

Bernard, J. (1956), *Remarriage: a Study of Marriage*, New York, Dryden.

Bernard, J. (1972), *The Future of the Family*, New York, World.

Bernard, J. (1975a), *The Future of Motherhood*, Baltimore, Penguin.

Bernard, J. (1975b), *Women, Wives, Mothers: Values and Options*, Chicago, Aldine.

Bernstein, B. (1961), 'Social structure, language and learning', *Educational Research*, 3, 2, 163–76.

Bernstein, B. (1963), 'Social class and linguistic development: a theory of social learning', in Halsey, A. H., Floud, J., and Anderson, C. A. (eds), *Education, Economy and Society*, New York, Free Press.

Bernstein, B. (1965), 'A sociolinguistic approach to social learning', in Gould, J. (ed.), *Penguin Survey of the Social Sciences*, Harmondsworth, Penguin.

Bernstein, B. (1971), *Class, Codes and Control*, vol. 1, London, Routledge & Kegan Paul.

Beveridge, W. (1944), *Social Insurance and Allied Services: the Beveridge Report*, London, HMSO.

Bibring, G. L. (1959), 'Some considerations of the psychological processes in pregnancy', in Eissler, R. S., Freud, A., *et al.* (eds), *The Psychoanalytic Study of the Child*, vol. 16, New York, International Universities Press; London, Imago.

Bibring, G. L. (1961), 'A study of the psychological processes in pregnancy of the earliest mother-child relationship', in Eissler, R. S., Freud, A., *et al.* (eds), *The Psychoanalytic Study of the Child*, vol. 16, New York, International Universities Press; London, Imago.

Bigner, J. (1970), 'Fathering: research and practice implications', *Family Coordinator*, October, 357–62.

Biller, H. (1970), 'Father absence and the personality development of the young child', *Developmental Psychology*, 2, 181–201.

Biller, H. B. (1971), *Father, Child and Sex Role*, Lexington, Mass., Heath.

Biller, H. and Meredith, D. (1974), *Father Power*, New York, David McKay.

Birren, J. E. (ed.) (1960), *Handbook of Aging and the Individual: Psychological and Biological Aspects*, New York, Crowell Collier & Macmillan.

Birren, J. E. (1961), 'A brief history of the psychology of aging', *Gerontologist*, 1, 66–7.

Birren, J. E. (1964), *The Psychology of Aging*, Englewood Cliffs, Prentice-Hall.

Birren, J. E. (1968), 'Aging: psychological aspects', in Sills, D. (ed.), *International Encyclopedia of the Social Sciences*, New York, Macmillan and Free Press.

Birren, J. E. (ed.), (1976), *Handbook of Aging and the Social Sciences*, New York, Van Nostrand Reinholt.

Blackstone, T. (1973), *Education and Day Care for Young Children in Need: The American Experience*, London, Bedford Square Press.

Block, J. (1973), 'Conceptions of sex-role: some cross-cultural and longitudinal perspectives', *American Psychologist*, 28, 512–26.

Blood, R. O. (1969), *Marriage*, New York, Free Press (2nd edn).

Blood, R. O. and Wolfe, O. M. (1960), *Husbands and Wives*, Chicago, Free Press.

Blos, P. (1962), *On Adolescence: a Psychoanalytic Interpretation*, New York, Free Press.

Blumberg, R. L. and Winch, R. F. (1972), 'Societal complexity and familial complexity: evidence for the curvilinear hypothesis', *American Journal of Sociology*, 77, 5, 898–920.

Blurton-Jones, N. G. (1974), 'Biological perspectives on parenthood', *The Family in Society: Dimensions of Parenthood*, London, DHSS, HMSO.

Blurton-Jones, N. G. and Konner, M. J. (1973), 'Sex differences in behaviour of London and Bushmen children', in R. P. Michael and J. H. Crook (eds), *Comparative Ecology and Behaviour of Primates*, London, Academic Press.

Bohannan, P. (ed.), (1970), *Divorce and After*, New York, Doubleday.

Bone, M. (1973), *Family Planning Services in England and Wales*, London, DHSS, HMSO.

Bone, M. (1975), *Day Care for Pre-school Children: Use and Preferences*, London, OPCS Report.

Booth, C. (1902), *Life and Labour of the People in London*, London, Macmillan.

Boston Women's Health Collective (1971), *Our Bodies Ourselves*, New York, Simon & Schuster.

Bott, E. (1957), *Family and Social Network*, London, Tavistock Publications.

Bowlby, J. (1951), *Maternal Care and Mental Health*, Geneva, World Health Organisation.

Bowlby, J. (1969/1971), *Attachment and Loss*, vol. 1, *Attachment*, London, Hogarth Press, Harmondsworth, Penguin.

Bowlby, J. (1972 edn.), *Child Care and the Growth of Love*, Harmondsworth, Penguin.

Bowlby, J. (1973), *Attachment and Loss*, vol. 2, *Separation*, London, Hogarth Press.

Bozemann, M. F., Orbach, C. E., and Sutherland, A. M. (1955), 'The adaptation of mothers to the threatened loss of their children through leukemia', *Cancer*, 8, 1–19.

Brannen, P. (ed.), (1975), *Entering the World of Work: Some Sociological Perspectives*, London, HMSO.

Brazelton, T. (1974), *Toddlers and Parents*, New York, Delacourt.

Breen, D. (1975), *The Birth of a First Child*, London, Tavistock Publications.

Brehm, H. P. (1968), 'Sociology and aging: orientation and research', *Gerontologist*, 8, 24–31.

Briggs, A. (1965), *Victorian Lives*, Harmondsworth, Penguin.

Brim, O. G. (1976), 'Theories of the male mid-life crisis', in *The Counseling Psychologist*, New York, American Psychological Association.

Brim, O. and Wheeler, S. (1966), *Socialization after Childhood: Two Essays*, New York, John Wiley.

Brimblecombe, F. S. W. (1976), *When the Bough Breaks: The Honeylands Project for Handicapped Children*, (in prep.)

British Institute of Management (1973), *The Management Threshold*.

Broderick, C. B. (1971), 'Beyond the five conceptual frameworks: a decade of development in family theory', *Journal of Marriage and the Family*, 33, 1, 139–59.

Bronfenbrenner, U. (1961), 'Some familial antecedents of responsibility and leadership in adolescents', in Petrullo, L. and Bass, B. M. (eds), *Leadership and Interpersonal Behavior*, 239–71, New York, Holt Rinehart & Winston.

Bronfenbrenner, U. (1962), 'Soviet methods of character education: some implications for research', *American Psychologist*, 17, 550–65.

Bronfenbrenner, U. (1971), *Two Worlds of Childhood: U.S. and U.S.S.R.*, London, Allen & Unwin.

Bronfenbrenner, U. (1974), 'Children, families and social policy: an American perspective', *The Family in Society, Dimensions of Parenthood*, 89–104, London, DHSS, HMSO.

Bronfenbrenner, U. (1974/76), 'The roots of alienation', in N. Talbot (ed.), *Raising Children in Modern America*, Boston, Little, Brown.

Bronfenbrenner, U. (1977), *The Experimental Ecology of Human Development*, Cambridge, Mass., Harvard University Press.

Brown, G. *et al.* (1975), 'Social class and psychiatric disturbances among women in an urban population', *Sociology*, 9, 225–54.

Brown, G. W. (1974), 'Meaning, measurement and stress of life events', in Dohrenwend, B. S. and B. P. (eds), *Proceedings of Conference on Stressfulness of Life Events: Their Nature and Effects*, New York, Wiley.

Brown, G. W., Harris, T. O. and Peto, S. (1973), 'Life events and psychiatric disorders. Part 2. Nature of causal link', *Psychological Medicine*, 3, 159.

Brown, G. W., Sklair, F. Harris, T. O., and Birley, J. L. T. (1973), 'Life events and psychiatric disorders, Part 1', *Psychological Medicine*, 3, 2, 159–70; and 'Part II' (1973), *Psychological Medicine*, 3, 2.

Brown, R. (1965), *Social Psychology*, New York, Free Press; London, Collier-Macmillan.

Buhler, C. (1961), 'Meaningful living in the mature years', in Kleemeier, R. W. (ed.), *Aging and Leisure*, 345–87, New York, McGraw Hill.

Burchinal, L. G. (1963), 'Research on young marriage: implications for family life education', in Sussman, M. B. (ed.), *Sourcebook of Marriage and the Family*, Boston, Houghton-Mifflin.

Burgess, E. W. and Wallin, P. (1953), *Engagement and Marriage*, New York, Lippincott.

Burke, H. (1967), 'A family over three generations: the transmission of inter-active and relative patterns', *Journal of Marriage and the Family*, November.

Burlingham, D. (1973), 'The pre-oedipal infant-father relationship', in Freud, A. *et al.* (ed.), *The Psychoanalytic Study of the Child*, vol. 28, 23–47, New York, International Universities Press; London, Imago.

Burton, L. (1972), 'An investigation into the problems occasioned for the child with cystic fibrosis', paper, 84th AGM of the ICAA, London.

Burton, L. (ed.), (1974), *Care of the Child Facing Death*, London, Routledge & Kegan Paul.

Burton, L. (1975), *The Family Life of Sick Children. A Study of Families coping with Chronic Childhood Disease*, London, Routledge & Kegan Paul.

Busfield, J. (1974), 'Ideologies and reproduction', in Richards, M. P. M. (ed.), *The Integration of a Child into a Social World*, Cambridge University Press.

Byng-Hall, J. and Miller, M. J. (1975), 'Adolescence and the family', in Meyerson, S. (ed.), *Adolescence*, London, Allen & Unwin.

Campbell, D. (1972), 'Activity and attachment in early life', *Proceedings of the British Psychological Society*, London Conference.

Caplan, G. (1959), *Concepts of Mental Health and Consultation: their Application in Public Health and Social Work*, Washington, US Department of Health, Education and Welfare.

Caplan, G. (1960), 'Patterns of Parental Response to the Crisis of Premature Birth', *Psychiatry: Journal for the Study of Interpersonal Processes*, 23, 4, 365–74.

Caplan, G. (1961), *An Approach to Community Mental Health*, New York, Grune & Stratton.

Caplan, G. (1974), *Support Systems and Community Mental Health*, New York, Behavioral Publications.

Carter, H. and Glick, P. C. (1976), *Marriage and Divorce*, Cambridge, Mass., Harvard University Press.

Cartwright, A. (1970), *Parents and Family Planning Services*, London, Routledge & Kegan Paul.

Cartwright, A. (1976), *How Many Children?*, London, Routledge & Kegan Paul.

Cartwright, A., Hockey, L. and Anderson, J. (1973), *Life Before Death*, London, Routledge & Kegan Paul.

Cartwright, A. and Moffett, J. (1974), 'A comparison of results obtained by men and women interviewers in a fertility survey', *Journal of Biosocial Science*, 7, 207–31.

Casler, L. (1961), 'Maternal deprivation: a critical review of the literature', *Monograph of Social Research and Child Development*, 26, 1–64.

Casler, L. (1968), 'Perceptual deprivation in institutional settings', in Newton, G. and Levine, S. (eds), *Early Experience and Behavior*, Springfield, Ill., C. C. Thomas.

Cavan, R. S. (1949), *Personal Adjustment in Old Age*, Chicago, Science Research Associates.

Central Advisory Council for Education (England) (1967), *Children and Their Primary Schools (Plowden Report)*, London, HMSO.

Central Statistical Office, Social Survey Division (1973), *The General Household Survey*, London, HMSO.

Central Statistical Office (1974), Nissel, M. (ed.), *Social Trends*, no. 5, HMSO.

Chatelaine (1974), 'Baby Talk' (advertisement), November 18.

Chesler, P. (1974), *Women and Madness*, London, Allen Lane.

Chester, R. (1972), 'Current incidence and trends in marital breakdown', *Postgraduate Medical Journal*, 48, 529–41.

Chester, R. (1973), 'Divorce and the family life cycle in Great Britain', paper presented to the 13th Annual Seminar of the Committee on Family Research of the International Sociological Association, Paris.

Chester, R. (1977), *Divorce in Europe* (forthcoming).

Children's Community Centre (1974), *Our Experiences of Collective Child-care*, London.

Chilman, C. S. (1968), 'Families in development at mid-stage of the family life cycle', *Family Coordinator*, 17, 4, 306.

Chilman, C. S. and Meyer, H. (1966), 'Married undergraduates: a study of their educational–vocational goals and attitudes and other associated variables', unpublished MS.

Chodoff, P., Standford, B., Friedman, B. and Hamburg, D. A. (1964), 'Stress, defenses, and coping behavior: observations in parents with malignant diseases', *American Journal of Psychiatry*, 120, 743–9.

Chomsky, N. (1968), *Language and Mind*, New York, Harcourt Brace & World.

Clark, A. W. and Summers, P. (1961), 'Contradictory demands in family relations and adjustment to school and home', *Human Relations*, 14, 97–111.

Clausen, J. S. and Suzanne, R. (1973), 'The effects of family size on parents and children', in Fawcett, J. T. (ed.), *Psychological Perspectives on Population*, 185–208, New York, Basic Books.

Cloward, R. and Ohlin, L. (1964), *Delinquents and Opportunity*, London, Routledge & Kegan Paul.

Cogswell, B. E. (1969), 'Uni-directional socialization: a sociological and popular myth', paper given at the Merrill-Palmer Institute Family and Society conference.

Cogswell, B. E. (1975), 'Variant family forms and life styles: rejection of the traditional nuclear family', *Family Coordinator*, October, 391–406.

Cogswell, B. E. and Sussman, M. B. (1972), 'Changing family marriage forms: complications for human service systems', in M. Sussman (ed.), *Non-Traditional Family Forms in the 1970s*, Minneapolis, National Council on Family Relations.

Cohen, A. K. (1965), 'The sociology of the deviant act: anomic theory and beyond', *American Sociological Review*, 30, February, 5–14.

Cohen, G. (1976), 'Absentee Husbands in Spiralist Families: the Myth of the Symmetrical Family', London, Civil Service College; *Journal of Marriage and the Family* (forthcoming).

Coleman, J. S. (1961), *The Adolescent Society*, New York, Free Press.

Coleman, J. S. (1972), 'The children have outgrown the schools', *Psychology Today*, 5, 9, 72–5, 82.

Coleman, J. S. *et al.* (1966), *Equality of Educational Opportunity*, Washington DC, US Government Printing Office.

Comfort, A. (1973), *The Joy of Sex*, New York, Simon & Schuster.

Condry, J. D. and Siman, M. A. (1974), 'Characteristics of poor- and adult-oriented children', *Journal of Marriage and the Family*, 36, 543–54.

Conran, S. (1975), *Superwoman*, London, Sidgwick & Jackson.

Constantine, L. and Constantine, J. (1971), 'Groups and multilateral marriage: definitional notes, glossary and annotated bibliography', *Family Process*, 10, 157–76.

Constantine, L. and Constantine, J. (1972), 'Dissolution of marriage in a non-conventional context', *Family Life Coordinator*, 21, 4, 457–62.

Constantine, L. and Constantine, J. (1973), *Group Marriage: A Study of Contemporary Multilateral Marriage*, New York, Macmillan.

Constantine, L. and Constantine, J. (1976), 'Marital alternatives: extended groups in modern society', in Grunebaum, H. and Christ, J. (eds), *Contemporary Marriage*, Boston, Little, Brown.

Cook, A. H. (1975), *The Working Mother*, New York State School of Industrial and Labor Relations; Cornell University.

Cook-Gumperz, J. (1973), *Social Control and Socialization*, London, Routledge & Kegan Paul.

Cooper, D. G. (1970), *The Death of the Family*, New York, Pantheon.

Cooper, J. (1974), 'Dimensions of parenthood', *The Family in Society, Dimensions of Parenthood*, 9–13, London, DHSS, HMSO.

Coote, A. and Gill, T. (1972), *Women's Rights*, Harmondsworth, Penguin.

Cottle, T. (1973), 'Parent and child: The hazards of equality', in Gottlieb, D. (ed.), *Children's Liberation*, Englewood Cliffs, Prentice-Hall.

Court, J. (1970), 'Psychosocial factors in child battering', *Journal of the Medical Women's Federation*, 99–104, April.

Court, J. and Robinson, W. (1970), 'The battered child syndrome', *Midwives Chronicle and Nursing Notes*, 213–14, July.

Crabtree, T. (1976), 'Father away – and a family without faces', *Guardian*, 22 January.

Craft, M. *et al.* (1967), *Linking Home and School*, London, Longmans.

Crawford, M. P. (1971), 'Retirement and disengagement', *Human Relations*, 24, 3, 255–78.

Croog, S., Lipsom, A., Levine, S. (1972), 'Help patterns in severe illness: the roles of kin network, non-family resources, and institutions', *Journal of Marriage and the Family*, 1, 32–41.

Crow, D. (1971), *The Victorian Woman*, London, Allen & Unwin.

Crowe, B. (1975), *The Playgroup Movement*, London, Allen & Unwin.

Cuber, J. and Harroff, P. (1965), *The Significant Americans: A Study of Sexual Behavior among the Affluent*, N.Y., Appleton-Century-Crofts.

Culbert, S. A. and Renshaw, J. R. (1972), 'Coping with the stresses of travel as an opportunity for improving the quality of work and family life', *Family Process*, 11, 3, 321–37.

Cumming, E. *et al.* (1960), 'Disengagement: a tentative theory of aging', *Sociometry*, 23, 23–5.

Cumming, E. and Henry, W. E. (1961), *Growing Old*, New York, Basic Books.

Dahrendorf, R. (1958), 'Out of Utopia: toward a reorientation of sociological analysis', *American Journal of Sociology*, 64, 2, 115–27.

D'Andrade, R. (1966), 'Sex differences and cultural institutions', in Maccoby, E. (ed.), *The Development of Sex differences*, Stanford, Stanford University Press.

Dare, C. (1969), *Your 6-year-old*, London, Corgi.

Davie, R., Butler, N. and Goldstein, H. (1972), *From Birth to Seven: Second Report of the National Child Development Study (1958 cohort)*, London, Longman, for National Children's Bureau.

Davin, D. (1976), 'Women in China', in Mitchell, J. and Oakley, A. (eds), *Essays on Women*, London, Allen Lane.

Davis, F. (1963), *Passage through Crisis*, Indianapolis, Bobbs-Merrill.

Davis, F. (1972), *On Youth Subculture: The Hippie Variant*, Morristown, N.J., General Learning Press.

Davis, K. (1940), 'The sociology of parent-youth conflict', *American Sociological Review*, 5, 523–35.

De Frain, J. D. (1974), 'A father's guide to parent guides: review and assessment of the paternal role as conceived in the popular literature', paper to National Council on Family Relations/American Association of Marriage and Family Counselors Annual Meeting, Missouri.

Demos, J. (1976), 'Myths and realities in the history of American family life', in Grunebaum, H. and Christ, J. (eds), *Contemporary Marriage*, Boston, Little, Brown.

Densen-Gerber, J. and Bader, T. (1972), *Drugs, Sex, Parents and You*, Philadelphia, Lippincott.

Department of Employment (1975), *Women and Work: Overseas Practice*, Manpower paper, no. 12, London, HMSO.

Department of Health and Social Security (1972), *Report of the Committee on Nursing*, London, HMSO.

Department of Health and Social Security (1974), *Report of the Committee on One-parent Families (The Finer Committee)*, Command 5629, London, HMSO.

Department of Health and Social Security (1974), *The Family in Society: Preparation for Parenthood*, London, HMSO.

Deutscher, I. (1959), *Married Life in the Middle Years*, Kansas City, Community Studies.

Deutscher, I. (1962), 'Socialization for postparental life', in Rose, A. M. (ed.), *Behavior and Social Processes*, Boston, Houghton Mifflin.

Deykins, E. Y., Jacobson, S., Klerman, G. and Solomon, M. (1966), 'The empty nest: psychosocial aspects of conflict between depressed women and their grown children', *American Journal of Psychiatry*, 122, 1422–4.

Dickinson, S. (1972), *Mother's Help (For Busy Mothers and Playgroup Leaders)*, London, Collins.

Dicks, H. V. (1967), *Marital Tensions*, London, Routledge & Kegan Paul.

Dix, C. (1974), *Guardian*, 6 November.

Dodson, F. (1970), *How to Parent*, New York, New American Library.

Dodson, F. (1974), *How to Father*, London, W. H. Allen.

Dohrenwend, B. S. and Dohrenwend, B. P. (eds) (1974), *Proceedings of Conference on Stressfulness of Life Events: Their Nature and Effects*, New York, John Wiley.

Dominian, J. (1969), *Marital Breakdown*, Harmondsworth, Penguin.

Douglas, J. W. B. (1964), *The Home and the School*, London, MacGibbon & Kee.

Douglas, J. W. B. and Blomfield, J. G. (1958), *Children Under Five*, London, Allen & Unwin.

Douglas, J. W. B., Ross, J. M. and Simpson, H. R. (1968), *All Our Future*, London, Peter Davies.

Downes, D. M. (1966), *The Delinquent Solution*, London, Routledge & Kegan Paul.

Downing, P. and Dower, M. (1972), *Second Homes in England and Wales*, DART publication no. 7.

Droppleman, L. and Schaefer, E. S. (1963), 'Boys' and girls' reports of maternal and paternal behaviour', *Journal of Abnormal and Social Psychology*, 67, 648–54.

Durkheim, E. (1893/1960), *The Division of Labor in Society (De la division du travail social)*, Chicago, Free Press.

Duvall, E. M. (1957), *Family Development*, Philadelphia, Lippincott (revised edition 1962).

Duvall, E. M. and Hill, R. (eds) (1948), *Dynamics of Family Interaction*, New York, National Conference on Family Life.

Education Act (1944), *It is the duty of parents to secure the education of their children*, Section 36, London, HMSO.

Eisenstadt, S. N. (1956), *From Generation to Generation: Age Groups and Social Structure*, Chicago, Free Press.

Elmer, E. *et al.* (1967), *Children in Jeopardy: a Study of Abused Minors and their Families*, University of Pittsburgh Press.

Emery, F. and Trist, E. L. (1973), *Towards a Social Ecology: Contextual Appreciation of the Future in the Present*, London, Plenum Press.

Emlen, A. C. (1970), 'Neighborhood family day care as a child-rearing environment', paper to Annual Meeting of National Association for the Education of Young Children, Boston, Mass.

Emlen, A. C., Donoghue, B. A. and La Forge, R. (1971), *Child Care by Kith: A Study of Family Day Care Relationships of Working Mothers and Neighborhood Caregivers*, Corvallis, DCE Books.

Emlen, A. C. and Watson, E. L. (1971), *Matchmaking in Neighborhood Day Care: A Descriptive Study of the Day Care Neighbor Service*, Corvallis, DCE Books.

Emlen, A. C. and Perry, J. B. (1974), 'Child care arrangements', in Hoffman, L. W. and Nye, F. I. (eds), *Working Mothers*, San Francisco, Jossey-Bass.

Engel, M. (1968), 'Orientation to work in children', *American Journal of Orthopsychiatry*, 38, 137–43.

Engel, M., Marsden, G. B. and Woodman, S. (1967), 'Children who work and the concept of work style', *Psychiatry*, 30, 392–404.

Engel, M., Marsden, G. and Pollock, S. W. (1971), 'Child work and social class', *Psychiatry*, 34, 2, 140–55.

Epstein, C. F. (1971), *Woman's Place: Options and Limits in Professional Careers*, Berkeley, University of California Press.

Erikson, E. (1950), *Childhood and Society*, New York, Norton.

Erikson, E. (1959), 'Identity and the life cycle', *Psychological Issues*, 1, 1, 1–171 (special issue).

Erikson, E. (1968), *Identity, Youth and Crisis*, New York, Norton.

Evan, W. M. (1961), 'Organization man and the due process of law', *American Sociological Review*, 26, 540–7.

Family Discussion Bureau (1955), *Social Casework in Marital Problems*, Bannister, K. *et al.* (ed.), London, Tavistock.

Family Welfare Association (1961), *The Family*, London, Faith.

Farber, B. (1960), *Family Organisation and Crises: Maintenance of Integration in Families with a Severely Mentally Retarded Child*, monograph of the Society for Research into Child Development, 25 (whole no. 75).

Farber, B. (1968), *Mental Retardation – its Social Context and Social Consequences*, New York, Houghton Mifflin.

Farrell, W. (1974), *Beyond Masculinity*, New York, Random House.

Fasteau, M. F. (1974), *The Male Machine*, New York, McGraw-Hill.

Fein, R. A. (1974a), 'Men's experiences before and after the birth of a first child', unpublished summary of Ph.D. thesis, Cambridge, Mass.

Fein, R. (1974b), 'Men and young children', in Pleck, J. and Sawyer, J. (eds), *Men and Masculinity*, Englewood Cliffs, Prentice-Hall.

Feldman, H. (1964), *The Development of the Husband-Wife Relationship*, Ithaca, Cornell University Press.

Feldman, H. (1971), 'The effects of children on the family', in Michel, A. (ed.), *Family Issues of Employed Women in Europe and America*, Leiden, Brill.

Feldman, H. and Feldman, M. (1975), 'The family life cycle: some suggestions for recycling', *Journal of Marriage and the Family*, 37, 2, 277–84.

Ferri, E. (1976), *Growing Up in a One Parent Family*, A National Children's Bureau Report, National Foundation for Educational Research.

Ferri, E. and Robinson, H. (1976), *Coping Alone: A National Children's Bureau Report*, Berkshire, NFER.

Ferriss, A. L. (1971), *Indicators of Trends in the Status of American Women*, New York, Russell Sage.

Finney, J. C. (1961), 'Some maternal influences on children's personality and character', Genetic Psychology Monographs, 63.

Firth, R. (ed.) (1956), *Two Studies of Kinship in London*, London, Athlone Press.
Firth, R., Hubert, J. and Forge, A. (1969), *Families and their Relatives*, London, Routledge & Kegan Paul.
Fisher, J. H. and Le Gros Clark, F. (1960), *Middle-aged Women in Training and Employment*, Industrial Training Research Unit.
Flacks, R. (1973), 'Growing up confused', in Skolnick, A. and Skolnick, J. H., *The Intimate Environment*, Boston, Little, Brown.
Fletcher, R. (1962), *The Family and Marriage*, Harmondsworth, Penguin.
Floud, J., Halsey, A. H. and Martin, F. (1956), *Social Class and Educational Opportunity*, London, Heinemann.
Fogarty, M. (1975), *40 to 60: How we Waste the Middle Aged*, London, Bedford Square Press, for the CSSP.
Fogarty, M., Rapoport, R. and Rapoport, R. N. (1971), *Sex, Career and Family*, London, PEP/Allen & Unwin.
Fogelman, K. (1976), *Britain's Sixteen-year-olds*, London, National Children's Bureau.
Foss, B. M. (1972/74), editorial foreword in Rutter, M., *Maternal Deprivation Reassessed*, Harmondsworth, Penguin.
Fox, R. (1970), 'Comparative family patterns', in Elliott, K. (ed.), *The Family and its Future*, London, J. A. Churchill for the CIBA Foundation.
Fraiberg, S. (1974), 'Blind infants and their mothers: an examination of the sign system', in Lewis, M. and Rosenblum, L. A. (eds), *The Effect of the Infant on its Caregiver*, New York, John Wiley.
Francoeur, R. T. and Francoeur, A. (1974), *Hot and Cool Sex*, New York, Harcourt, Brace, Jovanovich.
Frankenberg, R. (1957), *Village on the Border*, London, Cohen & West.
Frankenberg, R. (1966), *Communities in Britain*, Harmondsworth, Penguin.
Franzblau, R. N. (1971), *The Middle Generation*, New York, Holt, Rinehart & Winston.
Fraser, R. (1968), *Work: Twenty Personal Accounts*, Harmondsworth, Penguin.
Freud, A. (1958), 'Adolescence', in Freud, A. *et al.* (eds), *Psychoanalytical Study of the Child*, vol. 13, 255–78, New York, International Universities Press; London, Imago.
Freud, S. (1905/53), *Complete Works of Sigmund Freud*, standard edition, vol. VII, London, Hogarth Press.
Fried, M. (1962), 'Grieving for a lost home', in Duhl, L. (ed.), *The Environment of the Metropolis*, New York, Basic Books.
Fried, M. (1973), *The World of the Urban Working Class*, Cambridge, Mass., Harvard University Press.
Friedlander, B. Z., Jacobs, A. C., Davis, B. B. and Wetstone, H. S. (1972), 'Time sampling analysis of infants' natural language environments in the home', *Child Development*, 43, 730–40.
Gadpaille, W. J. (1976), 'Research on the physiology of maleness and femaleness', in Grunebaum, H. and Christ, J. (eds), *Contemporary Marriage: Structure, Dynamics, and Therapy*, Boston, Little, Brown.

Gagnon, J. H. and Simon, W. (1974), *Sexual Conduct*, London, Hutchinson.

Gail, S. (1968), 'The housewife', in Fraser, R. (ed.), *Work*, Harmondsworth, Penguin.

Gans, H. (1967), *The Levittowners*, New York, Pantheon.

Gath, A. (1972), 'The mental health of siblings of congenitally abnormal children', *Journal of Child Psychology and Psychiatry*, 13, 211–18.

Gavron, H. (1966), *The Captive Wife*, London, Routledge & Kegan Paul.

Geiger, H. K. (1968), *The Family in Soviet Russia*, Cambridge, Mass., Harvard University Press.

Gelles, R. J. (1972), *The Violent Home*, Beverly Hills, Sage.

George, V. and Wilding, P. (1972), *Motherless Families*, London, Routledge & Kegan Paul.

Gesell, A., Ilg, F. L. and Ames, L. B. (1956), *Youth: The Years from Ten to Sixteen*, New York, Harper.

Gibson, G. (1972), 'Kin family networks: over-heralded structure in past conceptualisations of family functioning', *Journal of Marriage and the Family*, February, 13–23.

Gil, D. G. (1973), 'Violence against children', in Dreitzel, H. P. (ed.), *Childhood and Socialization*, Recent Sociology, no. 5, New York, Macmillan.

Ginnott, H. G. (1965), *Between Parent and Child*, New York, Macmillan.

Glaser, B. G. and Strauss, A. L. (1965), *Awareness of Dying*, London, Weidenfeld & Nicolson.

Glasser, P. H. and Glasser, L. N. (1962), 'Role reversal and conflict between aged parents and their children', *Journal of Marriage and the Family*, 29, 267–76.

Glaxo Mother and Baby Book (1960).

Glazer-Malbin, N. (1975), 'The husband-wife relationship: the division of labour', Conference on Family and Sex Roles, Merrill-Palmer Institute, Detroit.

Glick, I. O., Weiss, R. S. and Parkes, C. M. (1974), *The First Year of Bereavement*, New York, John Wiley.

Glick, P. C. (1957), *American Families*, New York, John Wiley.

Glick, P. C. and Norton, A. J. (1973), 'Perspectives on the recent upturn in divorce and remarriage', *Demography*, 10, 301–14.

Glick, P. C. and Parke, R. Jr (1965), 'New approaches in studying the life cycle of the family', *Demography*, 2, 187–202.

Gluckman, M. (1962), *Essays on the Ritual of Social Relations*, Manchester University Press.

Glueck, S. and Glueck, E. (1950), *Unravelling Juvenile Delinquency*, New York, Commonwealth.

Goffman, E. (1959), *The Presentation of Self in Everyday Life*, Garden City, New York, Doubleday.

Goldberg, E. M. (1959), 'The normal family – myth and reality', *Social Work*, 16, 23–8.

Golden, S. G. (1975), 'Pre-school families and work', Ph.D. dissertation, Clinical psychology, University of Michigan, Ann Arbor.

Goldfarb, A. I. (1965), 'Psychodynamics and the three generation family', in Shanas, E. and Streib, G. F. (eds), *Social Structure and the Family*, New York, Prentice-Hall.

Goldstein, J., Freud, A. and Solnit, A. J. (1973), *Beyond the Best Interests of the Child*, New York, Free Press.

Goldthorpe, J. H. *et al.* (1968), *The Affluent Worker: Political Attitudes and Behaviour*, London, Cambridge University Press.

Goldthorpe, J. H. *et al.* (1969), *The Affluent Worker and the Class Structure*, Cambridge University Press.

Goode, W. J. (1956), *After Divorce*, Chicago, Free Press.

Goode, W. J. (1963), *World Revolution and Family Patterns*, New York, Free Press.

Goode, W. J. (1964), 'The theoretical importance of love', in Coser, R. (ed.), *The Family: its Structure and Functions*, New York, St Martins Press.

Goode, W. J., Hopkins, E. and McClure, H. M. (1971), *Social Systems and Family Patterns*, Indianapolis and New York, Bobbs-Merrill.

Goodman, M. E. (1970), *The Culture of Childhood: Child's Eye Views of Society and Culture*, New York, Teachers College Press.

Goody, E. N. (1974), 'Parental roles in anthropological perspective', in *The Family in Society, Dimensions of Parenthood*, 26-35, London, DHSS, HMSO.

Goody, E. (1975), 'Delegation of parental roles in West Africa and the West Indies', in Williams, T. R. (ed.), *Socialization and Communication in Primary Groups*, The Hague, Mouton.

Gordon, B. (1974), 'An interdisciplinary approach to the dying child', in Burton, L. (ed.), *Care of the Child Facing Death*, London, Routledge & Kegan Paul.

Gordon, M. and Shankweiler, P. J. (1971), 'Different equals less: female sexuality in recent marriage manuals', *Journal of Marriage and the Family*, 33, 3, 459, 466.

Gorer, G. (1955), *Exploring English Character*, London, Cresset.

Gorer, G. (1965), *Death, Grief and Mourning*, London, Cresset.

Gorer, G. (1973), *Sex and Marriage in England Today*, St Albans, Panther.

Gorer, G. and Rickman, J. (1950/62), *The People of Great Russia: a Psychological Study*, New York, Norton.

Gorman, C. (1972), *Making Communes*, Cambo, Whole Earth Tools.

Goslin, D. A. (ed.) (1969), *Handbook of Socialization Theory and Research*, Chicago, Rand McNally.

Gove, W. R. and Tudor, J. F. (1973), 'Adult sex roles and mental illness', *American Journal of Sociology*, 78, 4, 812-35.

Grams, A. (1975), 'Parenting: concept and process', paper given at 10th Anniversary of the International Federation for Parents' Education, Menton.

Graveson, R. H. and Crane, F. R. (eds) (1957), *A Century of Family Law, 1857-1957*, London, Sweet & Maxwell.

Green, M. (1976), *Goodbye Father*, London, Routledge & Kegan Paul.

Green, M. and Solnit, A. J. (1964), 'Reactions to the threatened loss of a child: a vulnerable child syndrome', Pediatrics, July, 58–66.

Greenacre, P. (1966), 'Problems of overidealization of the analyst and of analysis', in Freud, A. et al. (eds), The Psychoanalytic Study of the Child, vol. 21, New York, International Universities Press; London, Imago, 193–212.

Greenberg, M. and Morris, N. (1974), 'Engrossment: the newborn's impact upon the father', American Journal of Orthopsychiatry, 44, 4, 520–31.

Grönseth, E. (1957), 'The impact of father absence in sailor families upon the personality structure and social adjustment of adult sailor sons', in Anderson, N. (ed.), Studies on the Family, vol. 2, Göttingen.

Grönseth, E. (1975), 'Work-sharing families: adaptations of pioneering families with husband and wife in part-time employment', paper for the Third Biennial ISSBD Conference, Guildford.

Group for the Advancement of Psychiatry (1973), Joys and Sorrows of Parenthood, New York, Scribner.

Group for the Advancement of Psychiatry (1975), The Educated Woman: Prospects and Problems, vol. 9, report no. 92, New York, GAP.

Guillemard, A. (1973), La Retraite – une mort sociale, Paris, Mouton-La Haye.

Gurin, G., Veroff, J. and Feld, S. (1960), Americans View their Mental Health, New York, Basic Books.

Gutmann, D. (1973), 'Men, women and the parental imperative', Commentary, 6, 56, December, 59–64.

Guttentag, M. and Salasin, S. (1975), 'Women, men and mental health', in Cater, L. A. and Scott, A. F. (eds), Women and Men: Changing Roles and Perceptions, Stanford, Aspen Institute.

Haavio-Mannila, E. (1971), 'Satisfaction with family, work, leisure and life among men and women', Human Relations, 585–601.

Haavio-Mannila, E. (1972), 'Convergences between East and West; tradition and modernity in sex roles in Sweden, Finland and the Soviet Union', paper given at 12th International Family Research Seminar, Moscow.

Hadley, R. et al. (1975), Across the Generations: Old People and Young Volunteers, National Institute of Social Service, no. 28.

Hagestad, G. O. (1976), 'The middle-aged superwoman', cited in article in Daily Mail, London, 30 March.

Hagestad, G. O. and Fagan, M. A. (1974), 'Patterns of fathering in the middle years', paper presented at the Annual Meeting of the National Council on Family Relations, St Louis, Missouri.

Hall, G. S. (1904), Adolescence. Its Psychology and its Relations to Physiology, Anthropology, Sociology, Sex, Crime, Religion and Education, New York, Appleton.

Halsey, A. H. (1972), Educational Priority, London, HMSO.

Halsey, A. H., Floud, J. and Anderson, C. A. (eds) (1961), Education, Economy and Society: A Reader in the Sociology of Education, New York, Free Press.

Hammond, P. (1973), in Stroud, J. (ed.), *Services for Children and their Families*, 31–43, Oxford, Pergamon.

Hansberg, H. G. (1972), *Adolescent Separation Anxiety*, Springfield, Ill., C. C. Thomas.

Hareven, T. R. (1974), 'The family as process: the historical study of the family cycle', *Journal of Social History*, 7, 322–9.

Harré, R. (1975), 'The origins of social competence in a pluralistic society', *Oxford Review of Education*, 1, 2, 151–8.

Harris, A. (1974), 'What does sex education mean?', in Rogers, R. S. (ed.), *Sex Education Rationale and Reaction*, Cambridge University Press.

Harris, C. (1969), *The Family*, London, Allen & Unwin.

Harris, C. C. (1974), 'Parenthood: A theoretical view from the standpoint of a sociologist', in DHSS, *The Family in Society, Dimensions of Parenthood*, London, HMSO, 36–43.

Havighurst, R. J., Munnichs, J. M. A., Neugarten, B. and Thomas, H. (1969), *Adjustment to Retirement*, New York, Humanities Press.

Haward, L. R. C. (1973), 'Effects of domestic stress upon flying profiency', *Revue de medecine aeronotique et spatiale*, 49, 29–31.

Hawkes, G. R. and Pease, D. (1962), *Behaviour and Development from 5 to 12*, New York, Harper & Row.

Health Visitors Association (1973), *New Baby*, London.

Heinicke, C., and Westheimer, I., (1966), *Brief Separations*, New York, International Universities Press; London, Longmans.

Heinville, C. and Westheiner, I. (1965), *Brief Separations*, London, Longmans.

Hemming, J. (1969), *Individual Morality*, London, Nelson.

Henderson, E. and Rustin, M. (1975), 'Work, the child and the family', paper delivered at a scientific meeting of the Tavistock Institute of Human Relations.

Hermelin, B. and O'Connor, N. (1970), *Psychological Experiments with Autistic Children*, New York, Pergamon.

Heron, A. and Chown, S. (1967), *Age and Function*, London, Churchill.

Herzog, E. and Sudia, C. (1968), 'Fatherless homes: a review of research', *Children*, 15, 5.

Herzog, E. and Sudia, C. (1970), *Boys in Fatherless Families*, Washington DC, US Department of Health, Education and Welfare.

Hess, R. and Handel, G. (1959), *The Psycho-social Interior of the Family*, Chicago, Aldine Press.

Hewett, S. (1970), *The Family and the Handicapped Child*, London, Allen & Unwin.

Hewitt, P. (1973), 'Age concern: women's concern', *Women Speaking*, July–September.

Hicks, M. W. and Platt, M. (1970), 'Marital happiness and stability: A review of research in the sixties', *Journal of Marriage and the Family*, 32, 553–74.

Hill, R. (1949), *Families Under Stress*, New York, Harper.

Hill, R. *et al.* (1970), *Family Development in Three Generations: a Longi-tudinal Study of Changing Family Patterns of Planning and Achievement,* Cambridge, Mass., Schenkman.

Hill, R. and Aldous, J. (1969), 'Socialization for marriage and parent-hood', in Goslin, D. (ed.), *Handbook of Socialization Theory and Research,* Chicago, Rand McNally.

Hill, R. and Becker, H. (eds) (1955), *Family, Marriage and Parenthood,* Lexington, Mass., Heath.

Hill, R. and Rodgers, R. H. (1964), 'The developmental approach', in Christensen, H. T. (ed.), *Handbook of Marriage and the Family,* Chicago, Rand McNally.

Hinde, R. A. (1974), *Biological Bases of Human Social Behaviour,* New York, McGraw-Hill.

Hochschild, A. (1975), 'Disengagement theory: a critique and proposal', *American Sociological Review,* 40, 5, 553–9.

Hoffman, L. (1974), 'The effects of maternal employment on the child – a review of the research', *Developmental Psychology,* 10, 2, 204–28.

Hoffman, M. L. and Hoffman, L. W. (eds) (1964), *Review of Child Development Research,* New York, Russell Sage.

Hoffman, L. W. and Hoffman, M. (1973), 'The value of children to parents', in Fawcett, J. T. (ed.), *Psychological Perspectives on Population,* New York, Basic Books.

Hoffman, L. and Nye, F. E. (eds) (1974), *Working Mothers,* New York, Jossey-Bass.

Hoggart, R. (1967), 'A separate culture?', review of Dumazedier, J., *Towards a Society of Leisure, New Society,* 24 August.

Holman, R. (1970a), *Unsupported Mothers and the Care of their Children,* London, Mothers in Action.

Holman, R. (ed.) (1970b), *Socially Deprived Families in Britain,* National Council of Social Services.

Holman, R. (1973a), 'Poverty: consensus and alternatives', *British Journal of Social Work,* 3, 4, 431–46.

Holman, R. (1973b), 'Supportive services to the family', in Stroud, J. (ed.), *Services for Children and their Families,* Oxford, Pergamon Press.

Holmstrom, L. (1972), *The Two-career Family,* Cambridge, Mass., Schenkman.

Holt, K. S. (1958), 'The influence of a retarded child upon family limita-tion', *Journal of Mental Deficiency Research.*

Hooper, D., Gill, R., Powesland, P. and Ineichen, B. (1972), 'The health of young families in new housing estates', *Journal of Psychosomatic Research,* 16, 367.

Howe, L. K. (1972), *The Future of the Family,* New York, Simon & Schuster, section on 'Fathers', 85–138.

Howell, M. C. (1974), 'Can fathers be parents?', *Justice?,* 2, 1.

Howells, J. G. (1969), 'Fathering', in Howells, J. G. (ed.), *Modern Perspectives in International Child Psychiatry,* Edinburgh, Oliver & Boyd; New York, Brunner/Mazel.

Howells, J. G. (1970), 'Fallacies in child care: that fathering is unimportant', *Acta Paedopsychiatrica*, 37, 2–3, 46–55.

Huber, J. (ed.) (1973), *Changing Women in a Changing Society*, University of Chicago Press.

Hubert, J. (1974), 'Social factors in pregnancy and childbirth', in Richards, M. (ed.), *The Integration of a Child into the Social World*, Cambridge University Press.

Hudson, L. (1972), *The Cult of the Fact*, London, Jonathan Cape.

Hunt, A. (1968), *Survey of Women's Employment*, London, Government Social Survey, 55, 379.

Hutt, C. (1972), *Males and Females*, Harmondsworth, Penguin.

Hutt, S. J. and Hutt, C. (1973), *Early Human Development*, London, Oxford University Press.

Hyman, C. A. and Mitchell, R. (1975), 'A psychological study of child battering', *Health Visitor*, 48, 294–6.

Illich, I. D. (1971), *De-schooling Society*, New York, Harper & Row.

Inhelder, B. and Piaget, J. (1958) (first published 1952), *The Growth of Logical Thinking from Childhood to Adolescence*, New York, Basic Books.

Inkeles, A. and Levinson, D. J. (1954), 'National character: the study of modal personality and sociocultural systems', 2, 977–1020, reprinted in Lindzey, C. (ed.), *Handbook of Social Psychology*, Cambridge, Mass., Addison-Wesley.

Inkeles, A. and Smith, D. H. (1974), *Becoming Modern*, Cambridge, Mass., Harvard University Press; London, Heinemann.

Irvine, E. (1954), 'Research into problem families', *British Journal of Psychiatric Social Work*, 9, 24–33.

Jackson, B. (1973), 'The childminder', *New Society*, 29 November.

Jackson, B. and Jones, J. (1971), *One Thousand Children*, Cambridge, ACE.

Jackson, B. and Marsden, D. (1962), *Education and the Working Class*, London, Routledge & Kegan Paul.

Jaehnig, W. B. and Townsend, P. (1973), *The Mentally Handicapped and their Families*, final report to Department of Health and Social Security (not published), Department of Sociology, University of Essex.

Jaffe, D. T. and Kanter, R. M. (1976), 'Couple strain in communal households: a four-factor model of the separation process', *Journal of Social Issues*, 32, 161–92.

James, E. (1973), *The Bounty Baby Book: Baby's First Year*, Diss, Norfolk, Bounty Services.

Janis, M. G. (1964), *A Two-year-old Goes to Nursery School: a Case Study of Separation Reactions*, London, Tavistock.

Jaques, E. (1965), 'Death and the midlife crisis', *International Journal of Psychoanalysis*, 46, pt 4, 203–514.

Jenkins, D. (1974), 'Je suis un papa-maman . . .', *Paris Match*, 24 August, no. 1320, 59–63.

Jessner, L., Weigert, E., Foy, J. L. (1970), 'The development of parental attitudes during pregnancy', in Anthony, E. J. and Benedek, T. (eds),

Parenthood, 209–43, Boston, Little, Brown.

Jolly, H. (1975a), 'Recognising and breaking the cycle of deprivation', *The Times*, 10 January.

Jolly, H. (1975b), *Book of Child Care*, London, Allen & Unwin.

Jonas, D. and Janas, D. (1973), *Young till We Die*, London, Hodder & Stoughton.

Jordan, T. (1961), *The Mentally Retarded*, Ohio, Merrill Books.

Jordan, W. (1972), *The Social Worker in Family Situations*, London, Routledge & Kegan Paul.

Josselyn, I. M. (1962), 'The family as a psychological unit', in Kasius, B. (ed.), *Social Casework in the Fifties*, 106–18, New York, Family Service Association of America.

Kagan, J. (1956), 'The child's perception of the parent', *Journal of Abnormal and Social Psychology*, 53, 257–8.

Kagan, J. (1964), 'Acquisition and significance of sex-typing and sex-role identity', in Hoffman, L. W. and Hoffman, M. L. (eds), *Review of Child Development Research*, 137–68, New York, Russell Sage.

Kagan, J. (1971), *Understanding Children: Behaviour, Motives and Thought*, New York, Harcourt Brace Jovanovich.

Kahl, J. A. (1965), 'Some measurements of achievement orientation', *American Journal of Sociology*, 70, 669–70.

Kahn, A. and Kamerman, S. B. (1975), *Not for the Poor Alone – European Social Services*, Philadelphia, Temple University Press.

Kanter, R. (1973), *Communes: Creating and Managing the Collective Life*, New York, Harper & Row.

Kanter, R. M. *et al.* (1975), 'Coupling, parenting, and the presence of others: intimate relationships in communal households', *Family Coordinator*, 24 October, 435–52.

Kardiner, A. (1945), *The Psychological Frontiers of Society*, New York, Columbia University Press.

Karn, V. (1974), *Retiring to the Seaside*, Mitcham, Age Concern.

Kasius, C. (ed.) (1962), *Social Casework in the Fifties*, New York, Family Service Association of America.

Keller, S. (1974), 'Does the family have a future?', in Coser, R. L. (ed.), *The Family: Its Structure and Functions*, 2nd edn, New York, St Martins Press.

Kellmer Pringle, M. (1974), *The Needs of Children*, London, Hutchinson.

Kellmer Pringle, M., Butler, N. and Davie, R. (1966), *11,000 Seven-year-olds*, London, Longmans.

Kelly, F. J. and Baer, D. J. (1969), 'Age of male delinquents when father left home and recidivism', *Psychological Reports*, 25, 1010.

Kempe, H. and Helfer, R. (eds) (1972), *Helping the Battered Child and His Family*, Blackwell/Lippincott.

Keniston, K. (1971), *Youth and Dissent*, New York, Harcourt.

Kew, S. (1974), 'Handicap and marital crisis', *Marriage Guidance*, 15, 6, Journal of the National Marriage Guidance Council.

Kew, S. (1975), *Handicap and Family Crisis*, London, Pitman.

Kitzinger, S. (1973), *Giving Birth: the Parents' Emotions in Childbirth*, London, Sphere.

Kinsey, A. C. *et al.* (1953), *Sexual Behaviour in the Human Female*, Philadelphia, W. B. Saunders.

Klein, J. (1965, 1967, 1970), *Samples from English Cultures*, vols 1 and 2, London, Routledge & Kegan Paul.

Koch, S. (1959), *Psychology—a Study of a Science*, New York, McGraw Hill.

Koch, S. and Dobson, J. C. (eds) (1966), *The Mentally Retarded Child and his Family: a Multi-disciplinary Approach to a Clinical Condition*, New York, Basic Books.

Kohlberg, L. (1964), 'Development of moral character and moral ideology', in Hoffman, L. W. and Hoffman, M. (eds), *Review of Child Development Research*, 383–436, New York, Russell Sage.

Kohlberg, L. (1966), 'A cognitive-developmental analysis of children's sex-role concepts and attitudes', in Maccoby, E. (ed.), *The Development of Sex Differences*, 82–172, Stanford University Press.

Kohlberg, L. (1968), 'Moral development', *International Encyclopedia of the Social Sciences*, New York, Macmillan and Free Press.

Kooy, G. A. (1963), 'Urbanization and nuclear family individualization: a causal connection?', *Current Sociology*, 12, 1, 13–24.

Kuhn, T. (1962), *The Structure of Scientific Revolutions*, University of Chicago Press.

Laing, R. D. (1973), *The Politics of the Family and Other Essays*, London, Tavistock Publications; New York, Random House.

Laing, R. D. and Esterson, A. (1970), *Sanity, Madness and the Family*, Harmondsworth, Penguin.

Lambert, W. W., Triandis, L. M. and Wolf, M. (1958), 'Some correlates of beliefs in the malevolence and benevolence of supernatural beings: a cross-cultural study', *Journal of Abnormal and Social Psychology*, 58, 162–9.

Lambert, W. E., Yackley, A. and Hein, R. N. (1971), 'Child training values of English Canadian and French Canadian parents', *Canadian Journal of Behavioural Science*, 3, 217–36.

Land, H. (1975), 'The myth of the male breadwinner', *New Society*, 34, 79, October, 71–3.

Land, H. (forthcoming), 'Social security and income tax systems: methods of sex-role stereotyping', in Chetwynd, J. and Hartnett, O. (eds), *Sex Role Stereotyping*, London, Routledge & Kegan Paul.

Landis, J. T. (1962), 'A comparison of children from divorced and non-divorced unhappy marriages', *Family Life Coordinator*, 21, July, 61–5.

Landis, P. (1950), 'Sequential marriage', *Journal of Home Economics*, 42, 625–8.

Lasch, C. (1975), 'The family and history', *New York Review of Books*, pt 1, 13 November, pt 2, 27 November, pt 3, 11 December.

Laslett, B. (1973), 'The family as a public and private institution: a historical perspective', *Journal of Marriage and the Family*, August, 480–92.

Laslett, P. (1972), *Family and Household in Past Time*, Harmondsworth, Penguin.

Laufer, M. (1969), 'Stages in mental development during adolescence', *Adolescence* (second Brent conference) 28–49, London.

Leach, E. (1967), *A Runaway World*, BBC, Reith Lectures, and Oxford University Press (1968).

Leach, E. (1973), Review of Tiger and Fox, *New Society*.

Leach, P. (1975), *Babyhood*, Harmondsworth, Penguin.

Le Gros Clark, F. (1960), *Growing Old in a Mechanized World*, London, Nuffield Foundation.

Le Gros Clark, F. (1966), *Work, Age and Leisure: Causes and Consequences of the Shortened Working Life*, London, Michael Joseph.

Leichter, H. (1974), *The Family as Educator*, Columbia University Teacher's College. Press.

Leichter, H. and Mitchell, W. (1967), *Kinship and Casework*, New York, Russell Sage.

Leighton, D.C. *et al.* (1963), *The Character of Danger*, New York, Basic Books.

Lein, L., Durham, M., Pratt, M., Schudson, M., Thomas, R., and Weiss, H. (1974), *Final Report: Work and Family Life*, National Institute of Education Project No. 3-3-94, Cambridge, Mass., Center for the Study of Public Policy.

Lein, L. *et al.* (1975), 'Tasks and roles in dual-worker families', Cambridge, Mass., Center for the Study of Public Policy.

Le Masters, E. E. (1957), 'Parenthood as crisis', *Marriage and Family Living*, 19, 352–5; also reprinted in Sussman, M. (ed.), *Sourcebook on Marriage and the Family*, Boston, Houghton Mifflin, 1968.

Le Masters, E. E. (1970), *Parents in Modern America: A Sociological Analysis*, Homewood, Ill., Dorsey (revised edition 1974).

Leslie, G. R. (1967), *The Family in Social Context*, New York, Oxford University Press.

Levi, L. D., Stierlin, H. and Savard, R. J. (1972), 'Fathers and sons: the interlocking crises of integrity and identity', *Psychiatry*, 35, 48.

Levine, J. (1976), *Who will raise the Children? New Options for Fathers (and Mothers)*, Philadelphia, Lippincott.

LeVine, R. A. (1973), *Culture, Behavior and Personality*, Chicago, Aldine.

LeVine, R. A. (1974), 'Parental goals: A cross-cultural view', in Leichter, H. J. (ed.), *The Family as Educator*, New York, Columbia Teachers College Press.

Levinger, G. (1964), 'Task and social behavior in marriage', *Sociometry*, 27, 4, December, 433–48.

Levinger, G. (1965), 'Marital cohesiveness and dissolution: an integrative review', *Journal of Marriage and the Family*, 27, 1, 19–28.

Levinson, A. (1967), *The Mentally Retarded Child*, London, Allen & Unwin (first published 1952).

Levinson, D. J. (1976), 'Middle adulthood in modern society: A socio-psychological view', in DiRenzo, G. (ed.), *Social Character and Social Change*, Westport, Greenwood.

Levinson, D. J., Darrow, C. M., Klein, E. B., Levinson, M. and McKee, B. (1974), 'The psychological development of men in early adulthood and the mid-life transition', in Ricks, D. F. *et al.*, *Life History Research in Psychopathology*, vol. 3, Minneapolis, University of Minnesota Press.

Levy, D. (1943), *Maternal Overprotection*, New York, Columbia University Press.

Lewis, M. and Rosenblum, L. (1974), *The Effect of the Infant on its Caregiver*, New York, John Wiley.

Lewis, O. (1960), *Tepotzlan: Village in Mexico*, New York, Holt.

Lidz, T. (1968), *The Person*, New York, Basic Books.

Lidz, T. *et al.* (1957), 'Intra familial environment of the schizophrenic patient', *Psychiatry*, 20, 329–42.

Linner, B. (1967), *Sex and Society in Sweden*, London, Jonathan Cape.

Lipman-Blumen, J. and Tickamyer, A. R. (1976), 'Sex roles in transition: a ten-year perspective', *Annual Review of Sociology*, vol. 1.

Lister, I. (ed.) (1974), *Deschooling*, Cambridge University Press.

Litwak, E. (1960), 'Geographic mobility and extended family cohesion', *American Sociological Review*, 25, 385–94.

Litwak, E. and Meyer, M. J. (1967), *School, Family and Neighborhood*, New York and London, Columbia University Press.

Llewellyn-Jones, D. (1970), 'Fundamentals of obstetrics and gynaecology', vol. 2, *Gynaecology*, London, Faber & Faber.

Lockwood, D. (1958), *The Black-Coated Worker*, London, Allen & Unwin.

Loeser, H. (1974), *Women, Work and Volunteering*, Boston, Beacon.

Lomas, P. (1967), 'The significance of post-partum breakdown', in Lomas, P. (ed.), *The Predicament of the Family*, London, Hogarth Press and Institute of Psycho-analysis.

Lopata, H. L. (1971), *Occupation Housewife*, New York, Oxford University Press.

Lovshin, L. L. (1959), 'The tired mother syndrome', *Postgraduate Medicine*, 26, 48–54.

Low, S. and Spindler, P. G. (1968), *Child Care Arrangements of Working Mothers in the US*, Washington DC, US Government Printing Office.

Lowenthal, M. F., Thurnher, M. and Chiriboga, D. (1975), *Four Stages of Life*, San Francisco, Jossey-Bass.

Lowry, S. (1975), 'Barren pains', *Guardian*, 19 February, 11.

Luker, K. (1976), *Decision-making and Therapeutic Abortion*, Berkeley, University of California Press.

Lynn, D. B. (1974), *The Father: His Role in Child Development*, California, Brooks/Cole.

Maas, H. S. and Kuypers, J. A. (1974), *From Thirty to Seventy*, San Francisco and London, Jossey-Bass.

McClelland, D. C. (1951), *Personality*, New York, Holt.

McClelland, D. C. (1953), *The Achievement Motive*, New York, Appleton-Century-Crofts.

Maccoby, E. (ed.) (1966), *The Development of Sex Differences*, Stanford University Press.

Maccoby, E. and Jacklin, C. N. (1974), 'Sex differences revisited: myth and reality', paper presented at Annual Meeting of American Education Research Association, Chicago, Ill.

Maccoby, E. *et al.* (1962), 'Critical periods in seeking and accepting information', *Studies in Communication*, Paris, Stanford.

McCord, J. and McCord, W. with I. Zola (1969), *Origins of Crime*, New York, Columbia University Press.

McCord, J., McCord, W. and Thurber, E. (1962), 'Some effects of paternal absence on male children', *Journal of Abnormal and Social Psychology*, 64, 361–9.

McGeeney, P. (1969), *Parents are Welcome*, London, Longmans.

McGregor, O. R. (1955), 'The social position of women in England, 1850–1914', *British Journal of Sociology*, 6, 1.

MacIntyre, S. (1974), 'Who wants babies? The social construction of instincts', paper given to the British Sociological Association Annual Conference, *Sexual Divisions in Society*, Aberdeen, April.

Mackay, R. (1973), 'Conceptions of children and models of socialisation', in Dreitzel, H. P. (ed.), *Childhood and Socialisation*, Recent Sociology no. 5, London, Macmillan.

McMichael, J. (1971), *Handicap: A Study of Physically Handicapped Children and their Families*, London, Staples Press.

Maddox, B. (1975), *The Halfparent*, London, André Deutsch.

Maddox, G. L. (1963), 'Activity and morale: a longitudinal study of selected elderly subjects', *Social Forces*, 42, 2, 195–204.

Maddox, J. R. (1972), *The Doomsday Syndrome*, New York, McGraw Hill.

Mahler, F. (1973), *L'Image réciproque des parents et enfants dans la famille*, Centre de recherches sur les problémes de la jeunesse, Bucarest.

Mahler, M. S., Pine, F. and Bergman, A. (1970), 'The mother's reaction to her toddler's drive for individuation', in Anthony, E. J. and Benedek, T. (eds), *Parenthood: its Psychology and Psychopathology*, Boston, Little, Brown.

Maizels, J. (1970), *Adolescent Needs and the Transition from School to Work*, London, Athlone Press.

Malinowski, B. (1964), 'The principle of legitimacy: parenthood, the basis of social structure', in Coser, R. L. (ed.), *The Family: Its Structures and Functions*, New York, St Martin's Press.

Mandelbaum, A. (1967), 'Groups for parents of retarded children', *Children*, 14, 6, 227–32.

Marris, P. (1974), *Loss and Change*, London, Routledge & Kegan Paul.

Marsden, D. (1967), 'Education and the working class', in Craft, M., Raynor, J. and Cohen, L. (eds), *Linking Home and School*, London, Longman, 48–61.

Marsden, D. (1969), *Mothers Alone – Poverty and the Fatherless Family*, Harmondsworth, Penguin.

Marx, K. (1867–79) (1925–26), *Capital: A Critique of Political Economy*, 3 vols (trans.), Chicago, Kerr.

Maslow, A. H. (1954), *Motivation and Personality*, New York, Harper & Row.

Maslow, A. H. (1962), *Toward a Psychology of Being*, Princeton, N.J., Van Nostrand.

Masters, W. H. and Johnson, V. E. (1966), *Human Sexual Response*, Boston, Little, Brown.

Masters, W. H. and Johnson, V. E. (1975), *The Pleasure Bond: A New Look at Sexuality*, Boston, Little, Brown.

Mead, M. (1939), *From the South Seas: Studies of Adolescence and Sex in Primitive Societies*, New York, Morrow.

Mead, M. (1949), *Male and Female: A Study of the Sexes in a Changing World*, New York, Morrow.

Mead, M. (1953), 'National character', in Kroeber, A. L. (ed.), *Anthropology Today*, 642–67, University of Chicago Press.

Mead, M. (1971), 'Anomalies in American post-divorce relationships', in Bohannan, P. (ed.), *Divorce and After*, New York, Anchor (Doubleday).

Medawar, J. and Pyke, D. (1971), *Family Planning*, Harmondsworth, Penguin.

Medawar, P. (1957), *The Art of the Soluble*, London, Methuen.

Meissner, W. W. (1965), 'Parental interaction of the adolescent boy', *Journal of Genetic Psychology*, 107, 225–33.

Menolascino, F. J. (1968), 'Parents of the mentally retarded', *Journal of American Academy of Child Psychology*, October, 589–601.

Merton, R. K. (1957), *Social Theory and Social Structure*, rev. edn, Chicago, Free Press.

Meyerowitz, J. H. and Feldman, H. (1966), 'Transition to Parenthood', *Psychiatric Research Reports*, 20, 78–94.

Michael, D. N. (1973), *On Learning to Plan – and Planning to Learn*, San Francisco, Jossey-Bass.

Middleton, N. (1971), *When Family Failed*, London, Gollancz.

Mihovilovič, M. (1976), *Relations between Generations in the Family*, Zagreb, Institute for Social Research.

Millar, T. P. (1975), 'How to get father to help discipline the kids', *Chatelaine*, August, 86–7.

Miller, D. (1974), *Adolescence*, New York, Jason Aronson.

Miller, D. and Swanson, G. (1958), *The Changing American Parent*, New York, Wiley.

Miller, J. B. (ed.) (1973), *Psychoanalysis and Women*, Harmondsworth, Penguin.

Miller, J. B. (1976), *Towards a New Psychology of Women*, Boston, Beacon.

Miller, N. *Battered Spouses*, Occasional Papers in Social Administration, no. 7, London, Bell.

Miller, S. M. (1972), 'The making of a confused middle-aged husband' in Safilios-Rothschild, C. (ed.), *Towards a Sociology of Women*, Lexington, Xerox, 245–53; originally published in *Social Policy*, 2, 2, 1971.

Miller, W. B. (1958), 'Lower class culture as a generating milieu of gang delinquency', *Journal of Social Issues*, 14, 5–19.

Miller, W. B. (1969), 'White gangs', *Transaction*, September.
Mishler, E. and Waxler, N. (1968), *Interaction in Families*, New York, John Wiley.
Mitchell, J. and Oakley, A. (eds) (1976), *The Rights and Wrongs of Women*, Harmondsworth, Penguin.
Mitscherlich, A. (1969), *Society without the Father: A Contribution to Social Psychology*, London, Tavistock Publications.
Mogey, J. (1956), *Family and Neighbourhood*, London, Oxford University Press.
Money, J., Hampson, J. G. and Hampson, J. L. (1955), 'Hermaphroditism: recommendations concerning assignment of sex, change of sex, and psychological management', *Bulletin*, Johns Hopkins Hospital, 97, 284-300.
Money, J., Hampson, J. G. and Hampson, J. L. (1957), 'Imprinting and the establishment of gender role', *Archive Neurological Psychiatry*, 77, 333-6.
Moore, T. W. (1964), 'Children of full-time and part-time mothers', *International Journal of Social Psychiatry*.
Moorsom, S. (1975), 'Children and a job – how women manage both: do we need a Family Contract?', *Where?*, 101, 44-8.
Morgan, D. (1965), *Social Theory and the Family*, London, Routledge & Kegan Paul.
Morgan, P. (1975), *Childcare: Sense and Fable*, London, Maurice Temple Smith.
Moroney, R. M. (1976), *The Family and the State: Considerations for Social Policy*, London, Longmans.
Morrell Publications (1973), 'The battle for the leisure £', Arthur Sandles Report on the Leisure Industries; London, *Financial Times* Report, 30 April.
Morris, N. F. (1973), *The Baby Book*, London, Newbourne Publications.
Morris, P. (1965), *Prisoners and their Families*, London, Allen & Unwin for PEP.
Morrow, C. and Morrow, F. (1962), *Teenage Tyranny*, New York, Hechinger.
Moss, H. A. and Kagan, J. (1961), 'Stability of achievement and recognition–seeking behaviour from early childhood through adulthood', *Journal of Abnormal and Social Psychology*, 63, 504-13.
Moss, Z. (1970), 'It hurts to be alive and obsolete: the ageing woman', in Morgan, R. (ed.), *Sisterhood is Powerful*, New York, Vintage Books.
Mowrer, C. H. (1950), *Learning Theory and Personality Dynamics*, New York, Ronald.
Moynihan, D. (1965), *The Negro Family: the Case for National Action*, Washington, DC, US Government Printing Office.
Moynihan D. (ed.) (1969), *On Understanding Poverty*, New York, Basic Books.
Murphy, L. B. (1962), *The Widening World of Childhood: Paths Towards Mastery*, New York, Basic Books.

Murray, H. A. (1938), *Explorations in Personality*, New York, Oxford University Press.

Musgrove, F. (1964), *Youth and the Social Order*, London, Routledge & Kegan Paul.

Mussen, P. H. (ed.) (1960), *Handbook of Research Methods in Child Development*, New York, John Wiley.

Mussen, P. H., Conger, J. J. and Kagan, J. (1969) (first published in 1956), *Child Development and Personality*, New York, Harper & Row.

Myrdal, A. and Klein, J. (1968), *Women's Two Roles*, London, Routledge & Kegan Paul.

Nandy, L. and Nandy D. (1975), 'Education for equal parenthood', *Family Planning*, October.

Nash, J. (1965), 'The father in contemporary culture and current psychological literature', *Child Development*, 3, 6.

National Society for the Prevention of Cruelty to Children (1973), *Yo Yo Children: A Study of 23 violent Matrimonial Cases*, London, NSPCC School of Social Work.

Neugarten, B. L. (ed.) (1968), *Middle-age and Aging*, University of Chicago Press.

Neugarten, B. L. (1975), 'The young-old: things you may not know about this emerging population', *University of Chicago Magazine*, Autumn, 22-3.

Neugarten, B. L. *et al.* (1964), *Personality in Middle and Late Life: Empirical Studies*, New York, Atherton Press.

Neugarten, B. L. and Weinstein, K. K. (1964), 'The changing American grandparent', *Journal of Marriage and the Family*, 26, 199-204.

Newill, R. (1974), *Infertile Marriage*, Harmondsworth, Penguin.

Newson, E. (1972), 'Towards an understanding of the parental role', National Children's Bureau's Annual Conference, Sheffield, 20-23 September.

Newson, J. and Newson, E. (1963/72), *Infant Care in an Urban Community*, London, Allen & Unwin (1963); Harmondsworth, Penguin (1972).

Newson, J. and Newson, E. (1970), *Four Years Old in an Urban Community*, Harmondsworth, Penguin; London, Allen & Unwin (1968).

Newson, J. and Newson, E. (1975), *Seven Years Old in the Home Environment*, Child Development Research Unit, University of Nottingham.

Newson, J. and Newson, E. (1976), 'Parental roles and social contexts', in Shipman, M. (ed.), *The Organisation and Impact of Social Research*, London, Routledge & Kegan Paul.

Newson, J. and Shotter, J. (1974), 'How babies communicate', *New Society*, 8 August.

Newton, N. (1955), *Maternal Emotions*, New York, Paul B. Hoeber.

Newton, N. and Newton, M. (1962), 'Mothers' reaction to their newborn babies', *Journal of the American Medical Association*, 181, 206.

Nimkoff, M. F. and Middleton, R. (1960), 'The study of social problems', in Merton, R. K. and Nisbet, R. A. (eds), *Contemporary Social Problems*, New York, Harcourt, Brace & World.

Nisbet, J. (1968), 'Family environment and intelligence', in Halsey, A. H., Floud, J. and Anderson, C. A., *Education, Economy and Society*, New York, Free Press.

Noland, R. (ed.) (1970), *Counselling Parents of the Mentally Retarded*, Illinois, C. C. Thomas.

Norris, A. S. (1964), 'The tired mother', *Journal of Iowa Medical Society*, 54, 8, 478–81.

Oakley, A. (1972), *Sex, Gender and Society*, London, Maurice Temple Smith.

Oakley, A. (1974a), *The Sociology of Housework*, London, Martin Robertson.

Oakley, A. (1974b), *Housewife*, London, Allen Lane. *Woman's Work*, New York, Pantheon.

Obsatz, M. (1967), 'Reaching and teaching the ghetto child', *Main Currents in Modern Thought*, 24, 4, 102–4.

Odegaard, U. (1936), 'Emigration and Mental Health', *Mental Hygiene*, 20, 4.

Office of Population and Census Statistics (1973), *Annual Abstract of Statistics*, no. 110, London, HMSO.

Office of Population and Census Statistics (1974), *Annual Abstract of Statistics*, Table 7, London, HMSO.

Olshansky, S. (1962), 'Chronic sorrow: a response to having a mentally defective child', *Social Casework*, 43, 4, April, 190–3.

O'Neill, N. and O'Neill, G. (1972), *Open Marriage: A New Style for Couples*, New York, Evans.

Opie, I. and Opie, P. (1959), *The Lore and Language of Schoolchildren*, Oxford, Clarendon Press.

Orden, S. R. and Bradburn, N. M. (1968), 'Dimensions of marriage happiness', *American Journal of Sociology*, 74, 6, 715–31.

Osborne, E. L. (1969), *Your 4-year-old*, London, Corgi.

Osborne, E. L. (1969), *Your 5-year-old*, London, Corgi.

Osborne, E. L. (1969), *Your 7-year-old*, London, Corgi.

O'Shaughnessy, E. (1969), *Your 8-year-old*, London, Corgi.

O'Shaughnessy, E. (1969), *Your 9-year-old*, London, Corgi.

Osofsky, J. and Osofsky, H. (1972), 'Androgyny as a life style', *Family Coordinator*, 21, 411–19.

Pahl, J. M. and Pahl, R. E. (1971), *Managers and their Wives*, London, Allen Lane.

Paloma, M. (1972), 'Role conflict and the married professional woman', in Safilios-Rothschild, C. (ed.), *Toward a Sociology of Women*, Lexington, Mass., Xerox.

Parke, R. and O'Leary, S. (1975), 'Father-mother-infant interaction in the newborn period: some findings, some observations, some unresolved issues', in Riegel, K. and Meacham, J. (eds), *The Developing Individual in a Changing World*, vol. II, *Social and Environmental Issues*, The Hague, Mouton.

Parker, S. and Kleiner, R. J. (1966), 'Characteristics of negro mothers in single-headed households', *Journal of Marriage and the Family*, 28, 507-13.

Parkes, C. M. (1972), *Bereavement: Studies of Grief in Adult Life*, London, Tavistock.

Parnes, H. S. *et al.* (1970), *Dual Careers: a Longitudinal Study of Labour Market Experience of Women*, vol. 1, Manpower Research Monograph no. 21, Washington, US Dept of Labor.

Parsons, T. (1942), 'Age and sex in the social structure of the United States', *American Sociological Review*, October.

Parsons, T. (1949), 'The social structure of the family', in Anshen, R. N. (ed.), *The Family: Its Function and Destiny*, New York, Harper & Row.

Parsons, T. (1964), *Social Structure and Personality*, New York, Free Press.

Parsons, T. and Bales, R. F. (1955), *Family, Socialization and Interaction Process*, Chicago, Free Press.

Patten, M. (1974), 'Parents' groups and associations', in Burton, L. (ed.), *Care of the Child Facing Death*, London, Routledge & Kegan Paul.

Paul, N. (1970), 'Parent empathy', in James, E., Anthony, F. and Benedek, T., *Parenthood*, Boston, Little, Brown.

Pawley, M. (1971), 'Garbage housing', *Architectural Design*, February.

Pearse, I. H. and Crocker, L. H. (1943), *The Peckham Experiment: A Study in the Living Structure of Society*, London, Allen & Unwin.

Peck, E. (1975), *The Baby Trap*, New York, Bernard Geis.

Pederson, F. A. and Robson, K. S. (1969), 'Father participation in infancy', *American Journal of Orthopsychiatry*, 39, 466.

Peter, L. J. and Hull, R. (1969), *Peter Principle: Why Things always Go Wrong*, London, Souvenir Press, Pan Books (1971).

Philip, A. F. (1963), *Family Failure*, London, Faber & Faber.

Piaget, J. (1932/48), *The Moral Judgment of the Child*, Chicago, Free Press.

Pinchbeck, I. and Hewitt, M. (1974), *Children in English Society*, vol. 2, London, Routledge & Kegan Paul.

Pincus, L. (1960), *Marriage: Studies in Emotional Conflict and Growth*, London, Methuen.

Pincus, L. (1974/76), *Death and the Family*, New York, Pantheon; London, Faber.

Pineo, P. C. (1961), 'Disenchantment in the later years of marriage', *Marriage and Family Living*, 23, 3-11.

Pines, D. (1969), 'The effect on the adolescent of family breakdown', London, Brent Centre for the Study of Adolescence, Monograph No. 2.

Pines, D. (1972), 'Pregnancy and motherhood: interaction between fantasy and reality', *British Journal of Medical Psychology*, 45, 333-43.

Pines, M. (1969), *Revolution in Learning*, London, Allen Lane.

Pitcairn, L. (1968), *Parents of the Future*, Cambridge University Press.

Pitts, J. (1964), 'The structural-functional approach', in Christensen, H. T. (ed.), *Handbook of Marriage and the Family*, Chicago, Rand McNally.

Plateris, A. A. (1967), *Divorce Statistics Analysis* (United States, 1963), Vital and Health Statistics, Series 32, No. 13 US Department of Health Education and Welfare, Washington DC, Government Printing Office.

Pleck, J. H. (1975), 'Men's roles in the family: A new look', Paper for *Sex Roles in Sociology* Conference, Merrill–Palmer Institute, Detroit, 10–12 November.

Pleck, J. H. (1976), 'The psychology of sex roles: traditional and new views', in Cater, L. A. and Scott, A. F. (eds), *Women and Men: Changing Roles and Perceptions*, Stanford, Aspen Institute.

Pohlman, E. H. (1969), *Psychology of Birth Planning*, Cambridge, Mass., Schenkman.

Polanyi, K. (1944), *The Great Transformation*, New York, Rinehart.

Polanyi, M. (1967), *The Tacit Dimension*, London, Routledge & Kegan Paul.

Political and Economic Planning (1961), *Family Needs and the Social Services*, London, PEP.

Poloma, M. and Garland, T. (1971), 'The married professional woman: A study in the tolerance of domestication', *Journal of Marriage and the Family*, 33, 3, 531–40.

Poor, R. (1972), *4 Days, 40 Hours*, Pan Books, London.

Popper, K. R. (1963), *Conjectures and Refutations: the Growth of Scientific Knowledge*, London, Routledge & Kegan Paul.

Porter, J. F. (1974), 'Dimensions of parenthood and views of society', in *The Family in Society, Dimensions of Parenthood*, 44–55, London, DHSS, HMSO.

Prasad, S. B. (1964), 'The retirement postulate of the disengagement theory', *Gerontologist*, 4, 20–3.

Prechtl, H. F. R. (1963), 'The mother-child interaction in babies with minimal brain damage', in Foss, B. (ed.), *Determinants of Infant Behaviour*, vol. II, London, Methuen.

Pre-School Playgroup Association (1973), *Focus on the Future of Playgroups*, London, PPA.

Provence, S. and Lipton, R. C. (1963), *Infants in Institutions*, London, Bailey Bros & Swinfen; New York, International Universities Press (1963).

Puxon, M. (1972), *Family Law*, Harmondsworth, Penguin.

Rabban, M. (1950), 'Sex-role identification in young children in two diverse social groups', *Genetic Psychology* monographs, 42, 81–158.

Rainwater, L. (1970), *Behind Ghetto Walls*, London, Allen Lane.

Ramey, J. (1972), 'Emerging patterns of innovative behaviour in marriage', *Family Coordinator*, October, 62–88.

Ramey, J. (1975), 'Intimate groups and networks: frequent consequences of sexually open marriages', in *Family Coordinator*, October, 515–30.

Rapoport, A. (1971), *Science and the Goals of Man: A Study in Semantic Orientation*, London, Greenwood.

Rapoport, R. (1963), 'Normal crises, family structure and mental health', *Family Process*, 2, 1, March.

Rapoport, R. (1964), 'The transition from engagement to marriage', *Acta Sociologica*, 8, 36–55.

Rapoport, R. (1967), 'The study of marriage as a critical transition for personality and family development', in Lomas, P. (ed.), *The Predicament of the Family*, London, Hogarth Press.

Rapoport, R. and Oakley, A. (1975), 'Towards a review of parent–child relationships in social science', paper given at Ford Foundation Conference on *Sex Roles in Sociology*, Merrill–Palmer Institute, 10–12 November, convened by C. Safilios–Rothschild.

Rapoport, R. and Rapoport, R. N. (1964), 'New light on the honeymoon', *Human Relations*, 17, 33–56.

Rapoport, R. and Rapoport, R. N. (1965), 'Work and family in contemporary society', *American Sociological Review*, 30, 381–94.

Rapoport, R. and Rapoport, R. N. (1976), *Dual Career Families Reexamined*, London, Martin Robertson; New York, Harper & Row (an earlier edition published by Penguin Books, 1971).

Rapoport, R. and Rosow, I. (1957), 'An approach to family relationships and role performance', *Human Relations*, 10, 209–21.

Rapoport, R. N. (1970), *Mid-career Development*, London, Tavistock Publications; New York, Harper & Row.

Rapoport, R. N. (1975), 'Home and school at the launch: some preliminary observations', *Oxford Review of Education*, 1, 3, 277–86.

Rapoport, R. N., Henderson, E., and Hofton, G. (1976), *Transmission of Maladaptive Coping Mechanisms*, London, Report to the SSRC/DHSS Committee on Transmitted Deprivation.

Rapoport, R. N., Rapoport, R. and Hofton, G. (1975), *Family Enabling Influences and the School Leaver*, London, report to the SSRC.

Rapoport, R. N., Rapoport, R. and Thiessen, V. (1974), 'Couple symmetry and enjoyment', *Journal of Marriage and the Family*, 36, 588–91.

Rapoport, R., Rapoport, R. N. with Strelitz, Z. (1975), *Leisure and the Family Life Cycle*, London, Routledge & Kegan Paul.

Rawls, J. (1972), *A Theory of Social Justice*, Oxford, Clarendon Press.

Read, S. (1974), 'Living without children', *Sunday Times*, 10 November.

Redfield, R. (1941), *The Folk Culture of Yucatan*, University of Chicago Press.

Redfield, R. (1953), *The Primitive World and its Transformations*, Ithaca, Cornell University Press.

Rees, A. D. (1950), *Life in a Welsh Countryside*, Cardiff, University of Wales Press.

Registrar General (1969), *Statistical Review of England and Wales 1967*, Part II, London, HMSO.

Rein, M. (1976), *Social Policy and the Social Sciences*, Harmondsworth, Penguin.

Rein, M., Nutt, T. E. and Weiss, H. (1975), 'Foster family care: myth and reality', in Schorr, A. (ed.), *Children and Decent People*, New York, Basic Books (1974); London, Allen & Unwin.

Reiss, I. L. (1967), *The Social Context of Sexual Permissiveness*, New York, Holt, Rinehart & Winston.

Renshaw, J. (1976), 'An exploration of the dynamics of the overlapping worlds of work and family', *Family Process*, 15, 143–65.

Rheingold, J. C. (1964), *The Fear of Being a Woman: A Theory of Maternal Destructiveness*, New York, Grune & Stratton.

Rheingold, R. L. and Eckerman, C. O. (1971), 'Departures from the mother', in Schaffer, H. R. (ed.), *The Origins of Human Relations*, 73–8, London, Academic Press.

Richards, M. P. M. (1971a), 'Social interaction in the first weeks of human life', *Psychiatria Neurologia*.

Richards, M. P. M. (1971b), 'A comment on the social context of mother-infant interaction', in Schaffer, H. R. (ed.), *The Origin of Human Social Relations*, London, Academic Press.

Richards, M. P. M. (1974), 'First steps in becoming social', in Richards, M. P. M. (ed.), *The Integration of a Child into a Social World*, London, Cambridge University Press.

Richards, M. P. M. and Bernal, J. H. (1971), 'Social interaction in the first days of life', in Schaffer, H. R. (ed.), *The Origins of Human Social Relations*, New York and London, Academic Press.

Richards, M. P. M. *et al.* (1975), 'Caretaking in the first year of life – the role of fathers, and mothers' social isolation', Unit for Research on the Medical Applications of Psychology, London, Cambridge University Press.

Richman, J. *et al.* (1975), 'Fathers in labour', *New Society*, 16 October.

Richman, N. (1975), 'Behaviour problems in pre-school children: family and social factors', Institute of Child Health, University of London.

Rigby, A. (1974), *Alternative Realities*, London, Routledge & Kegan Paul.

Riley, M. W. and Foner, A. (1968), *Aging and Society*, vol. 1, *An Inventory of Research Findings*, New York, Russell Sage.

Riley, M. W., Foner, A., Hess, B. and Toby, M. L. (1969), 'Socialization for the middle and later years', in Goslin, D. A. (ed.), *Handbook of Socialization Theory and Research*, New York, Russell Sage Foundation/Chicago, Rand McNally.

Riley, M. W., Johnson, M. and Foner, A. (1972), *Aging and Society: A Sociology of Age Stratification*, vol. 3, New York, Russell Sage.

Roberts, R. E. (1971), *The New Communes: Coming Together in America*, New Jersey, Prentice Hall.

Roberts, R. W. and Nee, R. H. (eds) (1970), *Theories of Social Casework*, University of Chicago Press.

Robertson, J. (ed.) (1962), *Hospitals and Children: A Parent's Eye View*, London, Gollancz; New York, International Universities Press (1963).

Rodda, M. (1967), *Noise and Society*, London, Oliver & Boyd.

Rodda, M. (1970), *The Hearing Impaired School Leaver*, University of London Press.

Rollins, B. C. and Feldman, H. (1970), 'Marital satisfaction over the family life cycle', *Journal of Marriage and the Family*, 32, 20–8.

Rose, A. (1964), 'A current theoretical issue in social gerontology', *Gerontologist*, 4, 46–50.

Rosen, B. C. (1956), 'The achievement syndrome: A psycho-cultural dimension of social stratification', *American Sociological Review*, April, 203–11.

Rosen, B. C. (1961), 'Family structure and achievement motivation', *American Sociological Review*, 261, 574–84.

Rosenberg, M. (1965), *Society and the Adolescent Self Image*, Princeton University Press.

Rosenbluth, D. (1969a), *Your 2-year-old*, London, Corgi.

Rosenbluth, D. (1969b), *Your 3-year-old*, London, Corgi.

Rosenthal, M. (1972), *Drugs, Parents and Children*, New York, Houghton Mifflin.

Rosow, I. (1961), 'Retirement housing and social integration', *Gerontologist*, 1, 85–91.

Rosow, I. (1967), *Social Integration of the Aged*, New York, Free Press.

Rosser, C. and Harris, C. (1965), *The Family and Social Change*, London, Routledge & Kegan Paul.

Rossi, A. (1964a), 'Equality between the sexes: an immodest proposal', *Daedalus*, 93, Spring, 638–46.

Rossi, A. (1964b), 'A good woman is hard to find', *Transaction*, 2, 1, 20–3.

Rossi, A. (1968/74), 'Transition to parenthood', in Greenblat, C. *et al.* (eds), *The Marriage Game*, New York, Random House, 1974; *Journal of Marriage and the Family*, 30, 26–39, 1968.

Rowe, M. (1974), 'That parents may work and love and children may thrive', in Talbot, N. (ed.), *Raising Children in Modern America*, Boston and Toronto, Little, Brown.

Rutter, M. (1968), 'Concepts of autism: A review of research', *Journal of Child Psychology and Psychiatry*, 9, 1–25.

Rutter, M. (1972) (reprinted 1974), *Maternal Deprivation Reassessed*, Harmondsworth, Penguin.

Rutter, M. (1974), 'Dimensions of parenthood: Some myths and some suggestions', in *The Family in Society: Dimensions of Parenthood*, Seminar held by Department of Health and Social Security, London, HMSO.

Rutter, M. and Madge, N. (1976), *Cycles of Disadvantage: a Review of Research*, London, Heinemann.

Rutter, M., Tizard, J. and Whitmore, K. (eds) (1970), *Education Health and Behaviour*, London, Longman.

Ryder, R. G. (1970), 'A topography of early marriage', *Family Process*, 9, 385–402.

Ryle, A. (1967), *Neurosis in the Ordinary Family: A Psychiatric Survey*, London, Tavistock Publications.

Safilios-Rothschild, C. (1973), 'The mother's needs for child care', in Roby, P. (ed.), *Child Care – Who Cares?*, New York, Basic Books.

Safilios-Rothschild, C. (1974), *Women and Social Policy*, Englewood Cliffs, Prentice–Hall.

Safilios-Rothschild, C. (1975a), 'A macro- and micro-examination of family power and love: an exchange model', paper presented at the Dynamics of Family Ecology Session of the ISSBD Symposium, Surrey.

Safilios-Rothschild, C. (1975b), 'Dual linkages between the occupational and family system: A macrosociological analysis', *Signs: Journal of Women in Culture and Society*, December.

Safilios-Rothschild, C. (1975c), 'New parental responsibilities for the socialization of forthcoming generations', paper presented at 10th International Federation for Parents Education, Menton.

Sainsbury, E. (1970), *Social Diagnosis in Casework*, London, Routledge & Kegan Paul.

Sainsbury, E. (1975), *Social Work with Families*, London, Routledge & Kegan Paul.

Scanzoni, J. (1972), *Sexual Bargaining: Power Politics in the American Marriage*, Englewood Cliffs, Prentice-Hall.

Schaffer, H. R. (1971), *The Growth of Sociability*, Harmondsworth/ Baltimore, Penguin.

Schaffer, H. R. and Emerson, P. E. (1964), 'The development of social attachments in infancy', *Monographs in Social Research and Child Development*, 29, 3, 94.

Schaie, K. W. and Strother, C. R. (1968), 'A cross-sequential study of age changes in cognitive behaviour', *Psychological Bulletin*, 70, 671–80.

Schofield, M. (1973), *The Sexual Behaviour of Young Adults*, London, Allen Lane.

Schorr, A. L. (ed.) (1975), *Children and Decent People*, London, Allen & Unwin.

Schultz, T. W. (1973/74), *Economics of the Family: Marriage, Children and Human Capital*, Chicago, London, University of Chicago Press.

Scott, P. D. (1973), 'Parents who kill their children', *Medicine, Science and the Law*, 13, 2, 120–6.

Scott, P. D. (1975), 'Battering husbands: A complex of causes', *The Times*, 29 August.

Sears, R., Maccoby, E. E. and Levin, H. (1957), *Patterns of Child Rearing*, Evanston, Ill., Row Peterson.

Seear, B. N. (1971), 'Re-entry of women to the labour market after an interruption in employment', Paris, OECD.

Seeley, J. *et al.* (1956), *Crestwood Heights*, New York, Simon & Schuster.

Seeman, M. (1972), 'Alienation and engagement', in Campbell, A. and Coverse, P. E. (eds), *The Human Meaning of Social Change*, New York, Russell Sage.

Seidenberg, R. (1973), *Marriage Between Equals*, New York, Anchor (Doubleday).

Seidenberg, R. (1975), *Corporate Wives–Corporate Casualties*, New York, Anchor (Doubleday).

Senn, M. J. E. and Hartford, C. (eds) (1968), *The Firstborn: Experiences of Eight American Families*, Cambridge, Mass., Harvard University Press.

Sennet, R. (1970), *Families Against the City. Middle Class Homes of Industrial Chicago, 1872-1890*, London, Oxford University Press.

Shanas, E. and Streib, G. (eds) (1965), *Social Structure and the Family: Generational Relations*, Englewood Cliffs, Prentice-Hall.

Shanas, E. *et al.* (1968), *Old People in Three Industrial Societies*, London, Routledge & Kegan Paul.

Shere, M. O. (1956), 'Socio-emotional factors in the family of twins with cerebral palsy', *Exceptional Children*, 22, 196.

Shields, R. (1962), *A Cure of Delinquents*, London, Heinemann.

Shorter, E. (1975), *The Making of the Modern Family*, New York, Basic Books.

Shotter, J. (1973), 'Acquired powers: the transformation of natural into personal powers', *Journal of the Theory of Social Behaviour*, 2, 141-56.

Shukin, A. and Neugarten, B. (1964), 'Personality and social interaction', in Neugarten, B. *et al.* (eds), *Personality in Middle and Late Life*, New York, Atherton.

Siegman, A. W. (1966), 'Father absence during early childhood and anti-social behaviour', *Journal of Abnormal Psychology*, 71, 71-4.

Sillitoe, K. (1969), *Planning for Leisure*, London, HMSO.

Skinner, A. and Castle, R. (1969), *78 Battered Children: A Retrospective Study*, London, NSPCC.

Skolnick, A. (1973), *The Intimate Environment: Exploring Marriage and the Family*, Boston, Little, Brown.

Skolnick, A. and Skolnick, J. H. (1974), *Intimacy, Family and Society*, Boston, Little, Brown.

Slater, E. and Woodside, S. (1951), *Patterns of Marriage: A Study of Marriage Relationships in the Urban Working Classes*, London, Cassell.

Slater, P. E. (1970), *Pursuit of Loneliness*, Boston, Beacon.

Smelser, N. J. (1966), 'The modernization of social relations', in M. Weiner (ed.), *Modernization: the Dynamics of Growth*, New York, Basic.

Smith, C. (1968), *Adolescence*, London, Longmans.

Social Research Inc. (1973), unpublished report, Chicago.

Soddy, K. (1967), *Men in Middle Life*, London, Tavistock.

Somerville, R. (1975), 'Welcome to the menopause: A changing view of the change of life', mimeograph.

Speck, R. V. and Attneave, C. (1973), *Family Networks*, New York, Pantheon/Random House.

Speck, R. V., *et al.* (1972), *The New Families: Youth, Communes and the Politics of Drugs*, New York, Basic Books.

Spinley, E. (1954), *The Deprived and the Privileged*, London, Routledge & Kegan Paul.

Spock, B. (1973) (first published 1946), *Baby and Child Care*, London, New English Library.

Spock, B. (1974), *Bringing Up Children in a Difficult Time*, London, Bodley Head.

Stacey, M. (1960), *Tradition and Change: A Study of Banbury*, London, Oxford University Press.

Stacey, M., Batstone, E., Bell, C. and Murcott, A. (1975), *Power, Persistence and Change*, London, Routledge & Kegan Paul.

Steele, B. F. (1970), 'Parental abuse of infants and small children', in Anthony, E. J. and Benedek, T. (eds), *Parenthood: Its Psychology and Psychopathology*, Boston, Little, Brown.

Steinmetz, S. K. and Strauss, M. K. (1974), *Violence in the Family*, New York, Dodd-Mead.

Stephens, W. N. (1963), *The Family in Cross-cultural Perspective*, New York, Holt.

Stevenson, O. (1974), 'Rapporteur's Observations', in DHSS, *Dimensions of Parenthood*, London, HMSO.

Stiber, C. (1954), 'The psychiatric social worker in the family health maintenance demonstration, pp. 50–74 in *Proceedings* of the Annual Conference, Milbank Memorial Fund, New York.

Stinnet, N., Collins, J. and Montgomery, J. E. (1971), 'Marital need satisfaction of older husbands and wives', *Journal of Marriage and the Family*, 3, 428–34.

Stoller, F. H. (1970), 'The intimate network of families as a new structure', in Otto, H. (ed.), *The Family in Search of a Future*, New York, Appleton-Century-Crofts.

Stolte-Heiskanen, V. (1975), 'Family needs and societal institutions: potential empirical linkage mechanisms', *Journal of Marriage and the Family*, November, 903–16; and Publication no. 101, Department of Sociology, University of Helsinki.

Streib, G. F. (1958), 'Family patterns in retirement', *Journal of Social Issues*, 14, 2, 46–60.

Streib, G. F. (1965), 'Intergenerational relations: perspectives of the two generations on the older parents', *Journal of Marriage and the Family*, 27, 469–76.

Strodtbeck, F. L. (1963), 'Family integration, values and achievement', in Halsey, A. H. *et al.* (eds), *Education, Economy and Society*, New York, Free Press.

Strong, E. K. (1931), *Changes of Interests with Age*, Stanford University Press.

Sugarman, B. N. (1966), 'Social class and values as related to achievement and conduct in school', *Sociological Review*, 14, 3, 287–1.

Sugarman, B. N. (1973), *The School and Moral Development*, London, Croom Helm.

Sussman, M. (1953), 'The help pattern in the middle class family', *American Sociological Review*, 18, 23.

Sussman, M. (1965), 'Relationships of adult children with their parents in the United States', in Shanas, E. and Streib, G. (eds), *Social Structure and the Family*, Englewood Cliffs, Prentice-Hall.

Sussman, M. (1968), 'Adaptive, directive and integrative behaviour of today's family', *Family Process*, 7, 61.

Sussman, M. and Burchinal, L. (1962), 'Kin family network: unheralded structure in current conceptualizations of family functioning', *Marriage and Family Living*, 24, August, 231–40.

Swift, D. F. (1968), 'Social class and educational adaptation', in Butcher, H. J. (ed.), *Educational Research in Britain*, University of London.

Szalai, A. (ed.) (1972), *The Use of Time: Daily Activities of Urban and Suburban Populations of Twelve Countries*, The Hague, Mouton.

Taietz, and Larsen, (1956), 'Social participation and old age', *Rural Sociology*, 21, 229–38.

Talbot, N. (ed.) (1974/76), *Raising Children in Modern America*, Boston and Toronto, Little, Brown.

Talland, G. A. (ed.) (1968), *Human Aging and Behaviour: Recent Advances in Research and Theory*, New York and London, Academic Press.

Talmon, Y. (1968), 'Aging: social aspects', in Sills, D. (ed.), *International Encyclopedia of the Social Sciences*, New York, Macmillan and Free Press.

Tavuchis, N. (1970), 'The analysis of family roles', in Elliott, K. (ed.), *The Family and its Future*, London, Churchill.

Thiessen, V., Rapoport, R. and Rapoport, R. N. (1977), 'Enjoyment careers and the family life cycle', in Cuisenier, J. (ed.), *The Life Cycle in European Societies*, The Hague, Mouton.

Thomas Coram Research Unit (1975), *Progress Report*, September 1973–August 1975.

Thomas, R. and Wetherell, D. (1974), *Looking Forward to Work*, London, HMSO.

Thompson, B. and Finlayson, A. (1963), 'Married women who work in early motherhood', *British Journal of Sociology*, 14, 150–68.

Thompson, H. (1966), *The Successful Stepparent*, London, W. H. Allen.

Tiger, L. and Fox, R. (1972), *The Imperial Animal*, London, Secker & Warburg.

Timms, N. (1962), *Casework in the Childcare Service*, London, Butterworth.

Timms, N. (1967), *A Sociological Approach to Social Problems*, London, Routledge & Kegan Paul.

Titmuss, R. (1962), 'The family', National Council of Social Service Symposium, cited by Fletcher, R. (1962), *Britain in the Sixties: The Family and Marriage*, p. 178, Harmondsworth, Penguin.

Tizard, J. and Grad, J. C. (1961), *The Mentally Handicapped and their Families*, London, Maudsley Monograph No. 7.

Tizard, J., Moss, P. and Perry, J. (1976), *All Our Children*, London, Maurice Temple Smith.

Tizard, J. and Tizard, B. (1971), 'The social development of two-year-old children in residential nurseries', in Schaffer, H. R. (ed.), *The Origins of Human Social Relations*, London, Academic Press.

Toffler, A. (1970), *Future Shock*, London, Pan.

Toman, W. (1969), *Family Constellation*, New York, Springer.

Tönnies, F. (1883/1963), *Community and Society (Gemeinschaft und Gesellschaft)*, translated by Loomis, C. P. for University of Michigan Press, 1957; paperback by Harper and Row, 1963.

Townsend, P. (1957), *The Family Life of Old People*, London, Routledge & Kegan Paul.

Troll, L. E. (1971), 'The family of later life: A decade review', *Journal of Marriage and the Family*, 33, 263–90.

Troll, L. E. (1975), *Early and Middle Adulthood* (part of the Life-Span Human Development Series), Monterey, Calif., Brooks/Cole.

Tropauer, A., Franz, M. N. and Dilgard, V. (1970), 'Psychological aspects of the care of children with cystic fibrosis', *American Journal of Children*, 119, 424–32.

Trost, J. (1975), 'Married and unmarried cohabitation: the case of Sweden with some comparisons', *Journal of Marriage and the Family*, 33, 677–82.

Trost, J. and Norlund, A. (1974), 'Sex roles and lip service: some Swedish data', paper delivered at the 8th World Congress of Sociology, Toronto, August.

Turner, C. (1969), *Family and Kinship in Modern Britain: An Introduction*, London, Routledge & Kegan Paul.

Turner, C. (1971), 'Dual work households and marital dissolution', *Human Relations*, 24, 6, special issue on *Family and Work*, Rapoport, R., Rapoport, R. N. and Willmott, P. (eds).

Turner, R. H. (1964), *The Social Context of Ambition*, San Francisco, Jossey-Bass.

Tyler, M. (1976), 'Advisory and counselling services for young people', unpublished report, London, DHSS.

Ucko, L. E. and Moore, T. (1963), 'Parental roles as seen by young children in doll play', *Vita Humana*, 6, 213–42.

US Census of Population (1970), vol. 1, pt. 1, Table 206, pp. 1–658.

Valentine, C. W. (1962), *The Normal Child*, Harmondsworth, Penguin.

Van der Eyken, W. (1974), *The Pre-school Years*, Harmondsworth, Penguin.

Van Gennep, A. (1909/1960), *The Rites of Passage: the Classic Study of the Ceremonies used by Man to mark the Stages of his Passage through Life*, University of Chicago Press.

Veroff, J. and Feld, S. (1970), *Marriage and Work in America*, New York, Van Nostrand Rheinhold.

Vickers, G. (1965), *The Art of Judgement: A Study of Policy Making*, London, Chapman & Hall.

Vincent, C. (1971), *Unmarried Mothers*, New York, Collier–Macmillan.

Vogel, E. F. and Bell, N. W. (1960), *A Modern Introduction to the Family*, Chicago, Free Press.

Waite, L. J. (1976), 'Working wives: 1940–1960', *American Sociological Review*, 42, 1, 65–79.

Walker, K. and Woods, M. (1976), 'Time use: A measure of household production of family goods and services', Center for the Family of the American Home Economics Association.

Walters, J. and Stinnett, N. (1971), 'Parent-child relationships: a decade review of research', *Journal of Marriage and the Family*, February, 70–111.

Weber, M. (1922/1957), *The Theory of Social and Economic Organization*, (part of *Wirtschaft und Gesellschaft*, Tubingen), translated by Henderson, A. M. and Parsons, T., Chicago, Free Press.

Weissman, M. M. (1974), 'The epidemiology of suicide attempts: 1960–1971', *Archives of General Psychiatry*, 30, June, 737–46.

Weissman, M. M. and Paykel, E. S. (1974), *The Depressed Woman*, Chicago and London, University of Chicago Press.

Weitzman, L. (1974), 'Legal regulation of marriage: tradition and change', *California Law Review*, 62, 4.

Welford, A. T. (1958), *Ageing and Human Skill*, London, Oxford University Press.

West, D. (1967), *The Young Offender*, Harmondsworth, Penguin.

West, J. J. and Farrington, D. P. (1973), *Who Becomes Delinquent?* London, Heinemann.

Weston, T. (1972), *You and Your Baby*, London, British Medical Association.

Whiting, B. (1963), *Mothers in Six Cultures*, New York, Wiley.

Whiting, B. (1972), 'Mothers and their pre-school children in a period of rapid social change', Paper for UNICEF publication on the *Preschool Child*, April.

Whiting, B. and Whiting, J. W. M. (1975), *Children in Six Cultures*, New York, John Wiley.

Whiting, J. W. M. (1958), 'The function of male initiation ceremonies at puberty', in Maccoby, E. E., Newcomb, T. M. and Hartley, E. L. (eds), *Readings in Social Psychology*, New York, Holt.

Whiting, J. W. M. and Child, I. L. (1953), *Child Training and Personality: Cross-cultural Study*, New Haven, Yale University Press.

Wilensky, H. (1968), 'Women's work: economic growth, ideology, structure', *Industrial Relations*, 7, 3, 235–48.

Wilensky, H. and Lebeaux, C. N. (1955), *Industrialization and Social Welfare*, New York, Russell Sage.

Williams, J. and Stith, M. (1974), *Middle Childhood – Behaviour and Development*, New York, Macmillan.

Williams, R. H., Tibbitts, C. and Donahue, W. (eds) (1964), *Processes of Aging: Social and Psychological Perspectives*, vols 1 and 2, New York, Atherton.

Willmott, P. (1963), *Adolescent Boys of East London*, London, Routledge & Kegan Paul.

Willmott, P. (1967), *Consumer's Guide to the British Social Services*, Harmondsworth, Penguin.

Wilson, J., Williams, N. and Sugarman, B. (1967), *Introduction to Moral Education*, Harmondsworth, Penguin.

Wilson, H. (1974), 'Parenting in poverty', *British Journal of Social Work*, 4, 3, 241–54.

Wilson, H. (1975), 'Juvenile delinquency, parental criminality and social handicap', *British Journal of Criminology*, July, 241–50.

Wimperis, V. (1960), *The Unmarried Mother and her Child*, London, Allen & Unwin.

Winch, R. F. (1958), *Mate Selection: A Study of Complementary Needs*, New York, Harper & Row.

Winch, R. F. (1971), *The Modern Family*, 3rd edn, New York, Holt, Rinehart & Winston.

Wing, L. (1969), 'The handicaps of autistic children. A comparative study', *Journal of Child Psychology and Psychiatry*, 10, 1–40.

Winnicott, D. W. (1958), 'Hate in the countertransference', in *Collected Papers*, 194–203, London, Hogarth Press.

Winnicott, D. W. (1964/73), *The Child, the Family and the Outside World*, Harmondsworth, Penguin.

Wiseman, S. (1964), *Education and Environment*, Manchester, University Press.

Wolfenstein, M. (1955), 'Fun morality: an analysis of recent American child-training literature', in Mead, M. and Wolfenstein, M., *Childhood in Contemporary Cultures*, University of Chicago Press.

Wolfenstein, M. (1976), 'Trends in infant care' (first published 1953), reprinted in Brackbill, Y. and Thompson, G. (eds), *Behavior in Infancy and Early Childhood*, Toronto, Collier-Macmillan, 973–88.

Wootton, B. (1959), *Social Science and Social Pathology*, London, Allen & Unwin.

Wortis, R. P. (1974), 'The parental mystique', in *Intimacy, Family and Society*, Skolnick, A. and Skolnick, J. H. (eds), Boston, Little, Brown.

Wright, B. (1975), *Executive Ease and Disease*, London, Gower Press.

Wynn, M. (1964), *Fatherless Children*, London, Michael Joseph.

Wynn, M. (1970), *Family Policy*, London, Michael Joseph.

Yarrow, M. *et al.* (1962), 'Child-rearing in families of working and non-working mothers', *Sociometry*, 25, 122–40.

Youmans, E. G. (1967), 'Leisure behaviour expectations for old age', *Proceedings of 20th Annual Meeting of the Gerontological Society*.

Young, M. (1965), *Innovation and Research in Education*, London, Routledge & Kegan Paul.

Young, M. and McGeeney, P. (1968), *Learning Begins at Home*, London, Routledge & Kegan Paul.

Young, M. and Willmott, P. (1957), *Family and Kinship in East London*, London, Routledge & Kegan Paul.

Young, M. and Willmott, P. (1973), *The Symmetrical Family*, London, Routledge & Kegan Paul; New York, Pantheon.

Younghusband, E. (ed.) (1966), *New Developments in Casework*, London, Allen & Unwin.

Younghusband, E. *et al.* (1970), *Living with Handicap*, London, National Children's Bureau.

Yudkin, S. (1967), *Report on the Care of Pre-school Children*, London, Allen & Unwin.

Yudkin, S. and Holme, A. (1963), *Working Mothers and their Children*, London, Michael Joseph.

Zander, M. (1974), *Social Workers, their Clients and the Law*, London, Sweet & Maxwell.

Zaretzky, E. (1976), *Capitalism, the Family and Personal Life*, London, Pluto.

Zborowski, M. and Eyde, L. (1962), 'Aging and social participation', *Journal of Gerontology*, 17, 4, 424–30.

Zelditch, M. (1955), 'Role differentiation in the nuclear family: a comparative study', in Parsons, T. and Bales, R. F. (eds), *Family, Socialization and Interaction Process*, Chicago, Free Press.

Zuk, G. (1970), 'Religious factors and the role of guilt in parental acceptance of the retarded child', in Noland, R. (ed.), *Counselling Parents of the Mentally Retarded*, Illinois, C. C. Thomas.

Index

Index

421